THE
ORGANISM

BUSARA'S GAMBIT

BY

J.A.B.O.B.B.
&
LEROY J. BARRETT III

JABOBB LLC
10606 Camino Ruiz
8-367
San Diego, CA 92126

www.organismbookseries.com

Ordering Information:
For details, contact orders@organsimbookseries.com

Print ISBN: 978-1-66781-196-3
eBook ISBN: 978-1-66781-197-0

Printed in the United States of America on SFI Certified paper.

First Edition

This series is dedicated to the loving memories

of our friend and brother,

Brian "JUG HEAD" Bates

FOREWORD

This text is a living exercise of how little you truly know about people. Though it's a preposterous notion to believe we could have someone truly 'pegged', we can often engage in the habit of placing parameters of understanding around people. What they 'would' or 'would not' do. Who 'they are' or whom 'they're not'. How they 'could or could not' act. This is not a thing that is broadly done without some degree of thought. No, we go to extreme lengths sometimes to think we know someone only to realize later, in some starkly awakening moment of truth, that we indubitably don't.

Of course, we have our means and mediums to attempt preventing blatant deception. Right? We typically get familiar and cozy with individuals before we assume we've got them down to a 't'. Sometimes we go through dilemmas, even rigorous ordeals, and those times make us certain we've seen these persons at their worst. Or we've, possibly, experienced them at their best. It's highly probable that we've taken some assessment of them during our shared engagements, too. It seems 'they normally do this thing' in particular situations. They might 'do this other thing' in other situations. But, for certain, you pretty much have a handle on their decision range. At least, that's what you think. Everything you believe you know gives credence to your character judgments. You move forward with those supposed understandings as a given because, to a particular point, their consistent actions encourage such thought.

A number of us often find ourselves, sometimes through careful and purposeful positioning, in a comfortable space filled with details of a person. We'll get cool with their parents, know their middle names, birthdays, favorite foods or movies and some massive assortment of both huge and minute details. You might have eaten at their house, or they've slept at yours. Maybe you've shared a host of road trips where you endlessly pontificated about your visions and what life meant to the both of you. These levels of deep yet boundlessly open dialogue engagements and unique experiences create for us a comfort level of certainty about people's character parameters. This is how we, so easily and completely, deceive ourselves.

This is nearly where I found myself with the gentlemen featured in this amazingly powerful but wildly unfortunate adventure. See, I attended college with these guys. I still share a timeless brotherhood with several of them that began in school. Of course, I now share it with all of them. But one of these brothers in particular was truly like my kinfolk on campus. Vastly more so afterwards.

We did things like break in each other's dorm rooms, ate each other's food, had dancing contests together, took out competitors in our craft as a team and met each other's family members. This wasn't an all-rainbows affiliation, though. Shit, we fought together (against other people), shoplifted food and clothes or dine-and-dashed together, too. (You'll soon learn, we were city slickers in a very sweet and naïve town. We took full advantage of that). We did these foolish and mischievous things within our band of brothers and sisters. Our crew connected on multiple planes and we got along famously. Though it is true that our whole crew knew him to be the most mysterious of all people we were collectively connected to, there was a level of expectation from his character within that cryptic demeanor. Part of the expectation was literally that he would do things we didn't see coming. Even with that, though, we perceived, well, I certainly perceived there to be some degree of moral limit.

This brother I'm speaking on was one of the most intellectual of our brother and sister collective. This fact was blithely apparent. However, his enigmatic ways kept him from being literally labeled 'the leader'. It is my assessment that he calculated it as too visible a moniker for his liking, it would have impaired his ability to 'stealthily maneuver'. Still, he was always regarded in the leadership when it was time to make decisions. This was basically maintained without exception. His craftiness allowed him to reap the benefits of leadership without ever officially committing to the responsibility. Like I said, the brother was quite sly.

He maintained a unique practice to ensure he was heard in such moments. Typically, he sat quietly through all deliberations, at least for the open volleys. He would, however, selectively chime in with some weighted angle or option that seemed to champion the moment. What he didn't do was speak a lot in the group setting. This guy thoroughly understood the meaning of 'less is more' and frequently exploited it for impact. He was an intellectual to the point of cleverness and he wielded it well.

I must admit, I'm not the biggest people watcher. Certainly not back then. My personal sense of discernment was more a product of being an empath. I had a heavy reliance on sensing people's auras, it kept me pretty lazy about details. Once the measure of a person's essence told me they were cool or they sucked, I moved accordingly. It was a largely accurate system; I was scarcely surprised.

So, this guy read... all over the meter. The most consistent outlying factor about him early was some degree of loyalty. He was, undoubtedly, a team player. This was immediately made obvious, the largest bulk of his choices steadily reaffirmed it. He made a plethora of self-gain-motivated choices, obviously, but they were basically never the 'betray the team'-type. There are levels of selfishness that are central to having gains in life, he was rarely outside of those bounds of necessity.

He also had an incredibly skilled and seemingly effortless way of leveraging assets around him for gain. Whenever we got in a jam or got hung up on an idea, he would manage to see an exit where it wasn't apparent to anyone else. Then he would present it matter-of-factly; never arrogant or snide. It really appeared that while the rest of us were cleverly playing checkers, he had a game of thermonuclear war going on and kept making bombs on the sly. That's just how adept he was at smartly utilizing apparent elements to which we lent little or no value. He was always impressive like that.

Despite how covert and sly that may seem, his heart was apparent. I don't think I'd ever witnessed him aiming to damage someone. Now, some-thing? Absolutely! When you're talking about an organization or a corporation, psssht, he had little regard for entities. Usually, they were the targets of his best inscrutability. It was his habit to test how drastically dramatic a thing he could pull off against entities. Yeah, he was a fan of seeing how much he could get away with. You could call him a mental daredevil, if you will. Despite this truth, he looked out for people frequently. When he was approached with a need, he typically exhausted himself to help find a resolution for the petitioner. He wasn't a touchy-feely, openly emotional guy but his actions made clear that he cared.

This guy was, and is, like all of us, a veritable collage of both ends and all the middles of the character spectrum. On one hand, his family upbringing was an incredibly spiritual world. He was literally big brother to many, and it shone through in his leadership abilities. On the other hand, he was from my crib and Detroit was not for the faint of heart. Sometimes you had to be equipped with a shady move or two just to make it to see the next day. Home wasn't always like that but you could easily find yourself in a place where life and death decisions were immediate. Knowing he bore this mix as his person, among quite a few more details, I figured I had a lot of reason to believe I knew him well. It should certainly seem like it, right? For a man who didn't clock details of individuals, I could run off an awful long list of things about this guy that I learned from mere observation – that I wasn't attempting to catalogue. My description of detail exhibits the fact that we don't share a shallow connection.

Still, I knew nothing.

He and I spent more than two years together in an extremely close-knit organization. He was a sophomore when I arrived, so he largely showed me the ropes on campus, even. He and his then-roommate were essentially guides for my roommate and me. They were actually our unofficial 'big brothers' on the Yard (campus). Truly, in my erroneous estimation, there was reason to believe I had a grasp on the measure of this guy.

Through the course of that nearly three-year period, he was involved in the Organism operation the entire time. I didn't have an inkling of what he was up to, and he was up to a whole damned lot! Honestly, if you asked me if he was capable of being a cog in such a team, I would have found it easy to believe. He was sorta anti-establishment, he thrived on mischief and relished in testing his mettle. It was already discussed that he was also incredibly intelligent. Yeah, I would have assuredly said he was capable, if I were asked.

But would he? He was a damned mortuary sciences major, man. Dude planned on banking at a morgue somewhere, embalming dead folk. That added a whole different element to his mysteriousness – damned near made him spooky. I guess you could view that with a bit of morbidity, true, but not from the angle that he would supply something that literally killed people. Once you consider his largely anti-active career choice, such a thing certainly seemed out of his range. Truly.

Here's the kicker: I've been writing scripts for 15 years or so. Regarding this specific Organism member as one of the most insightful and creative people I know, he spent the bulk of that time as my sounding board. I had an actual writing partner, we worked together extremely well, but this Organism guy was my personal reference. He'd give honest takes on our work and I'd adjust when necessary or feel better about my directions after well-explaining them. Any position I could defend against his mind qualified to me as solid. His perspective definitely helped me sharpen my skills.

In March of 2020, he approached me with a conversation. He said he and his fellas had done some things when we were all back in school and they had taken over Knoxville. They'd written a book about it and he wanted me to check it out.

My response? "Took over Knoxville? Doing what, break dancing?" I laughed heartily but he was steadfast. After years of supporting me by simply reading my work and providing feedback, the least I could do was the same. It was my honor to help but I still felt... there was just a deep disbelief in his description and its realism. Even though he had never struck me as a liar, I had every reservation of his validity.

How had they taken over Knoxville? Doing what? And when? Was it years after I left the school? Did it include the school? What dudes are we talking about, anyways? I was filled with questions. So much so, that I basically approached the work as a journalist. I's had to be dotted and t's needed crossing. I had serious skepticism about what the folds of their tale would describe.

Then I read it. Candidly, among their group wasn't one writer. My connection to this tale makes that an obvious fact, otherwise they would have told this awe-inspiring tale without me. Fortunately, their absence of literary finesse had no bearing on their history.

And... wow! I easily and rapidly learned that not only was his assessment true but there were verifiable receipts. Loud, indisputable recorded historical facts wholly validated his description! These guys had, indeed, taken command of a market in the small town of Knoxville.

'How' will unravel for you in the pages and the volumes that follow. You will journey through in-depth perspective of their lives, their histories, their vision, and their unlikely alliances. That's not the purpose of this prelude, however. There are a few "why's" that are key to understanding these life stories and this literary offering. Without placing them in the proper context the Organism series would just be another story.

It pronouncedly isn't, though. The very existence of this chronicling is for the purpose of prevention. After discussion and deliberation, we found it essential to exacerbate that this book collection is NOT a tutorial. This work isn't for glamorizing or validating crime. No parts of the Organism collective, nor I, advocate for drug selling or drug dealers or anything that is systemically abusive to our communities. We believe this disclaimer is mandatory due to the first person view of these records and how derogatorily instructional it may seem at times.

Telling these extraordinary happenings provides us the opportunity to vividly illustrate their fates. Our guys were brilliant, incredibly well-planned and disciplined – particularly for teenagers led only by their peers. They maintained and improved a host of attributes that were horribly lacking in their competition. The Organism crew had city-life training that kept them leagues ahead of the local climate altogether. Despite their initial success in their business practices, the drug game still got the better of them. It is the monster we want to dissuade anyone from pursuing.

You will soon learn of their histories, their vastly diverse characters, their variety of strengths, their multitude of triumphs and their tragic heartaches. What is paramount to this message, though, is to learn from their lessons:

Drug dealing has no mercy.

Drug dealing murders communities.

Drug dealers have limited days in the business and, often, in life.

I digress. My collegiate brother had not deceived me. The twist is that he wasn't just the charactered person I had assessed but so much more. He and the gentlemen who took this journey with him are the brotherhood who hired me. This tale is more than 30 years in the telling and they are still unified. It's a testament to all their loyalty, not just his. Their choice to lay bare these experiences to dissuade youth about drugs is about having quality character, not the opposite. So, my read on him was solid, he just lived a path that thoroughly tested his resolve. He didn't always pass the quizzes, but this book is proof of how he and the other brothers have handled the tests.

They could have silently faded into the obscurity of their individual and collective matured lives. It would have been much easier to quietly persist in their post-drug-world successes without exposing the illegal acts of their youth. After all, they paid grave dues and have earned the right to simply move on. They, instead, chose to stand and expose their truths for the benefit of others. That's a powerful degree of selfless maturity and I'm highly honored to share in it. It is, certainly, a 180 turn away from what they did as teenagers. This collection is an evolution from how most of them started, a graphically detailed shift to whom they became and, ultimately, a return to the definitive roots of how their lives began. It's a journey that's come full circle and they're sharing it with you.

These brothers have lived the drug life. They've taken the tests, handled the stresses and faced the perils. Their world was inundated with the success of it and roiled by its pitfalls. Due to their extensive experiences, they made the collective decision to share their knowledgeable conclusion of the drug world.

Drug dealing only has dead ends.

It's not worth it.

CHAPTER 1

THE RECKONING

(1991)

"Hey man! Ain't you one of them St. Louis mutha fuckas?"
Spit out Shan.

"I'm from Milwaukee, man." Said Waukee Talkie, looking for an exit.

"Don't matter. You ain't from here. You in a hurry, player?"
Shan continued to investigate.

So, Waukee Talkie was between gigs. No, I don't mean he didn't have a job, he had just left one and was heading to the next. Waukee was a cool cat, super cool. He was short, about 5'6", fairly handsome and charming enough to get along with everybody. The brother probably had gangs to say because he was quiet all the time. Once he started talking, though, he was like a clever version of Radio: he couldn't iterate his thoughts as rapidly as he was calculating them. Since his speech was kind of erratic and he was from Milwaukee that's how the brother got the obvious nickname. It doesn't have to be logical, it's a fucking nickname, but this time it worked out like that.

Like I said, he had just done a shift in the dope spot and was about to head to an actual clock-punching job. He was the hardest working teenager I had ever seen, and 'hustle' is my life. Hell, I come from a family of movers and shakers and this brother impressed the hell out of me. How? Listen: he had a shift at the dope house, he sold product on the corner to stack his paper, he had a job at one of the express carrier businesses and he was a college student. Sleep? That's a joke. As sharp as he was he still probably couldn't spell 'sleep', he definitely didn't get any. He was all hustle. If you cut him open the wound would just drip coins. Money was in his blood and he was all about his flow staying healthy.

Unfortunately for him, that's exactly what he was facing on the corner of MLK and Cherry Street – getting cut open. As he was waiting for his ride, these local mutha fuckas, with whom we were beefin', rode down on him.

These "mutha fuckas" were led by Shan. Shan was a light-skinned, tall, skinny asshole. He wasn't even from Knoxville: he was specifically brought into town for us by his cousin, Guts. Clearly, both of these names were aliases and I don't know what their actual names were. Nor did I know what the aliases stood for. Except maybe the Shan asshole because he fit MC Shan's descriptions. That was a fitting nickname for him, though, because he was just like a fake ass LL Cool J. I didn't care. They were both on a path to getting handled so their damned names wouldn't matter anyways.

Guts was the local shot caller. I'm overstating that: he was the shot caller for the street soldiers. The real local kingpin, the guy who supplied these fools, was Carl "Skins" Koffy. He was the only source of product for the locals and he kept them on a pretty tight leash. We had a good working relationship with Skins, another weird element of our small town situation. We didn't have any beef with Koffy. Though he should've wanted to eliminate us, he took on a sort of mentoring role and tried to look out for us. We'll get around to all of that, though. It's pretty extensive.

This dude Guts was under no such peaceable terms. He understood the threat we were to his bottom line and intended to threaten us. We, congruently, had no love for that dude at all. He was a sawed-off, troll-bodied... um... troll. The brother's skin was dark like mine, except he was ugly, and his eyes were shifty like a weasel. Really I just say that because we had animosities from the jump and my value for him as a human being was stretched to its limit. Typically, I wouldn't stand in the place where I criticize brothers and sisters for their looks. It's also a self-contradictory position for me to sell that poison to our people which murders our communities, too. But since this 'bridge guardian' brought some dude in town to try to kill my crew while doing the latter... well, y'know, exceptions get made. He was foolish enough to come for me, I was more than prepared to make grave exceptions to my principles. So, insulting that asshole is small peanuts.

They had good reason to be salty, though. My team had come into their town as college students and replaced them in the street drug market. We introduced a product that even the local police couldn't identify when they saw it. With that product and some formulaic plans, we took over everything the locals were doing. We had such clean, mechanical and efficient systems we took to calling ourselves 'The Organism'. The way we consumed the town was exactly like a virus, too. Those cats were losing money like the Detroit Lions lost football games and they wanted to end that. (No disrespect to the Detroit homies, but, yeah). We had a few run-ins that exacerbated the tensions and, for certain, more were coming.

Arriving in town as college students, none of us were in Knoxville to be drug dealers. Obviously. We all had some academic pursuit we wanted to achieve and thought a collegiate education would excel us to the next level of earning potential. Or some brochure-sounding shit like that. But when the opportunity to instantly make drug-mogul-level paper screamed at us... we took it. Then we took over. It happened lightning-quickly, so we were still in 'nice guy' mode for much of the beginnings of our enterprise.

And we were young guys, man. We condemned no one who enjoyed our product. Not only did we forego judging our customers, we often kicked it with them casually in conversation. As college students, we had quite a bit of our collegiate peers who partook in our product. We didn't see them differently, just as partiers. The kind of partiers that we weren't, for sure, but fun-seeking young people just the same. So, when we serviced the locals, we treated them the same as the student body. The situation in the city was friendly and wide open. Capitalizing on that while playing it like Romans was easy for us to do. (You know, when in Rome...). We were cruising our way to success unfettered. We didn't even own guns for the first six months or so of business.

We were the 'Nice Guy Drug Dealers'. Yes, it is every bit of the oxymoron that it sounds like but it was real. If it wasn't a totally stupid, self-indicting idea we might have even made t-shirts. In the ultimate cutthroat business, we were the guys you wanted to be around. Sure, we got away with it for a while because Knoxville is leagues slower than everywhere we come from. But business is business and money is money, metropolitan area or small town, billions of dollars or hundreds. While we were taking the locals' market share, they got hot enough to want to take our lives. So, they were poised to make such attempts.

Fortunately for us, the locals were slow moving as hell. The build-up took long enough that we understood we needed to protect ourselves and had time to arm ourselves appropriately. We assembled a small arsenal but sufficient enough to handle whatever came our way. Our plans still didn't include becoming aggressors, not right away. Getting caught with our pants down just wasn't the way to live. So, we aptly procured some weapons. Our crew knew it was a hot time and we had to protect our necks.

All that said, they had caught Waukee slipping.

"I'm headed to work, man. That's all I do is work." Waukee says to them, trying to make light of a heavy situation. It wasn't working.

"Well, you should've run to work today." Shan pulls out a nickel-plated hand cannon and points it at Waukee's chest. "Now, you gone run them pockets."

"C'mon, man. What the fuck?" Cries Waukee.

"I'm not saying it twice. You can hand everything you got to me or I'll empty it from the pockets of your corpse myself. Your choice." Each of his words were like bullets.

Shit was real.

Shan's eyes said he was looking to empty his gun. Everything about him said he didn't have a problem dumping on fools. There were two more dudes in the ride with Shan. They hadn't exposed any weapons yet but the odds were that they had some. Waukee wasn't going to test it.

Waukee emptied his pockets and pulled out a little more than $1,000. The bulk of it was in five small stacks of $200, each wrapped in a rubber band. He gently tossed the money towards the car. He didn't move quickly or in any way that could be perceived as hostile. Shit like that would've gotten him killed. He left his pockets hanging out because he didn't want to get shot for holding out after he gave everything he had.

That didn't work, either.

"Your pockets empty, huh? That's cute. I don't trust you. Run them shoes." Shan says in a half laugh.

Waukee began to take off his shoes. I don't know what it was about seeing him strip but it, apparently, gave Shan an idea.

5

"You know what? You can just come out of all yo' shit. You gettin' money like this then you don't need it."
Shan's gun was still squarely pointed at Waukee's chest.

Waukee only hesitated in thought. He was pissed and embarrassed but he wanted to live that day. Dude looked like he still might shoot him, even if he did everything that jackass told him to do. Waukee definitely didn't want to give him an excuse. He stripped down to his underwear and gave all of his clothing to one of the guys in the backseat.

It became clear that nothing he would do was going to be enough.

"Obviously y'all got the balls big enough to come to our town and try to muscle us out. I need to see 'em."
Shan said between laughs.
Waukee looked down at his underwear.
"Yeah, them too, college boy. Figure that shit out."
Shan cocked his gun for effect.
"And figure it out quick!"

"Our town"? This mutha fucka wasn't even from Knoxville! Begrudgingly, WT took off his plaid-print boxers and tossed them over to the car. He covered his frank and beans with his hand. Unsurprisingly, this, too, was a problem.

"Hey! I don't trust you mutha fucka! Put your hands up until we leave. You better start massaging them clouds, mutha fucka! Think about putting them down, I'm pluggin' yo' ass! Try me."

Waukee threw his hands up. He hadn't said a word after the initial greeting and he stayed quiet then.

"You gone give your boys a message for me, too. Better yet, you the message..."

POW! POW!

Like twisted movie villains, they screeched their tires and drove away laughing loudly in unison.

Waukee stood shaking until they were around the corner.

His silent approach had worked. Shan had fired in the air then sped off. When Waukee told me the details of this event he never told me if he peed or not when the gun went off. Nobody would have blamed him. He did have easy access.

Waukee's heart was beating like he was one of the M.O.P. dudes, they were the drummers at our school. He definitely could've pulled off a drum roll with his chest that day. After, again, covering his junk with one hand, Waukee trotted rapidly to a pay phone.

His first thought: page Greco! They were mad tight and came up in the game together. Problem is? No change. Dude was naked. He didn't have any quarters to place a call. So, he called collect to the crib where he thought one of us would be. He caught Poppy.

Waukee spent a little more than 20 minutes hiding behind that payphone buck-ass naked. I'm sure it felt like three weeks.

Now, Poppy was from St. Louis. He was part of the reason Shan and his flunkies assumed Waukee was, too. "Poppy" is the nickname of a nick-name. Back in high school he was a winner with the ladies, a favorite of the teachers and an insider with the staff – including the Principal. Everybody around the hallways liked him, he was like the unofficial Vashon High School ambassador. His buddies took to calling him 'Mr. Popular' and it stuck. Now it's just Poppy. He's a heavy set brother about 5'8" with big hands. 'Heavy set' doesn't mean fat, it means you didn't wanna get hit by those hands.

He did some boxing in the 'Lou but that's not saying anything special – everybody did some boxing in the 'Lou. He was a good cat, though. Super cool dude with some integrity. I wasn't playing when I said we were the nice guy drug dealers, it's how we rolled. What was really cool about Poppy is he was an old soul. You could always catch him singing Motown or older cuts. This was in 1990, y'all. It had been a minute since those groups were hitting and that's when our parents were digging them. He would sing their songs in the dorm like they were released the previous week.

We were a super tightknit crew. Poppy, B-Dub, Motown, Greco, Waukee and me. Brothers through and through. Now, Jazzy was down, so was Slick and Double O but they didn't roll like the rest of us. Waukee was really lucky to catch Poppy at the crib, he had just got back in town a couple days prior.

Poppy rolled up around that 20 minute mark. Before the wheels stopped rolling, Waukee ran up to the car and started opening the door. When he hopped in there were designer boxers, a t-shirt and a matching jogging suit, socks and gym shoes on the floor in front of him.

Waukee immediately begins hurriedly dressing himself. His adrenaline still cranking like the entire Tour de France.

"Thanks bruh. This shit is crazy, man! I thought that mutha fucka was gone do me." Waukee rattles off, out of breath.

"That's why he had you strip?" Poppy says with quizzically naivete.

Waukee awkwardly twists his head at him, then gets it.

"Fuck naw! Well, I hope not! That mutha fucka would've just had to shoot me. Shiid!" They both laughed.

"Glad you hurr (here), dawg. We gone handle this shit. This is some bullshit, hurr! These mutha fuckas done lost they damned mind!"

Barely two weeks later, we got a lease and some keys for a new spot. We were out west off the I-40 freeway and North Winston Rd., just opposite of West Town Mall. Things were hot, we needed somewhere new to be off of all the radars. The Organism had a multitude of apartments around town and we'd frequent hotels to get away from it all. Our crew kept it moving constantly, it's just how we handled being hard targets. This apartment was going to be where Poppy and I were going to lay our heads for a while. It wasn't in either of our names, because we didn't move like that, but it was for us.

Normally, only our crew and a select few women knew where we actually slept. This crib was no different. The place was presently empty, literally empty except for the bodies in the building. B-Dub, Jazzy, Greco and Poppy were in the living room with Keisha, LaTonda and Sherry.

Motown and I were in one of the back rooms figuring out our next moves. We were in some deep shit so we had to be smart and careful about how we proceeded. Being smart was way more important to us than being careful. These mutha fuckas were habitual line-steppers, as it were. We had to respond in exponential fashion. The plan was forming.

Out in the living room, Jazzy and Greco were having some words. It wasn't going well. Straight up, shit was foul.

"What *you* do? You were 'dere, mutha fucka, what did you do?" Greco rifled with his New Jersey tint on English. He was damned near hostile.

"What you mean? You wasn't there! How you frontin' on me, dawg?" Jazzy shoots back in reply.

"We know I wasn't 'dere! I woulda did some shit if I was 'dere. That's what the fuck I'm tawkin' 'bout, B. You were 'doe! So, what the fuck did you do?"

About a week after they robbed WT, the same fake mutha fucka that took all his clothes…

Shot my ass.

I'm not turning a phrase here, he literally shot me in the ass. They got the drop on us and started blasting first. It was a full-blown shootout, it resembled something you see on a TV show about L.A. In fact, that's exactly how it was reported on the local news - "SOUTH CENTRAL COMES TO KNOXVILLE" was the headline. It was preposterous that the news was taking their cues from the characterizations they've heard of another city. It wasn't surprising, though. The media always sensation-alizes their stories to appeal to viewers. That's why you can't always believe what you hear from them, they tell stories in particular ways for particular reasons. Those reasons are always money and politics.

Our beef was real, though, that part was true. It spilled out into the Knoxville streets in dramatic fashion. That level of hostility was a shock to the social norms the city was used to. You better believe it was a two-way street, though: they shot at us and we fired back. Hell, we let off everything we had but they still got me. After that, our tensions elevated to the highest level possible:

We were on 'kill-on-sight' watch.

Vigilantly keeping his eyes peeled on that watch list was Greco. We called him 'Greco' because he was into that Greco-Roman world. Being a wrestler from Jersey, he had every edge a brother could have. He had no issues with confrontations and was itching to handle shit that needed handling. His sharp east coast accent was a perfect match and prelude for his no-nonsense approach.

Greco was a sort of dark-skinned brother, about 6'1" and full of energy. You could even call him hyper. He had one of those spirits that just didn't quit. Greco was big on three things: hollering at women and grilling beef were his passions. That brother rarely met a skirt that he didn't want to lift. When we had hostilities with someone he wanted to be the one smoking mutha fuckas.

At the apex of his focus, though, was loyalty. Greco was a devoted brother. Gang members who had to do dangerous shit and still get 'jumped in' to earn their colors didn't have as much loyalty to their set as Greco did with us. He meant that shit from the core of his person. It was, thereby, natural and reasonable for him to expect, hell, demand the same from those in his circle. We were mad thankful he was on the team just so we didn't have to deal with him on somebody else's.

Greco fit into the circle perfectly because loyalty was everything in the Organism. Everything! We treated each other like brothers and we meant it. None of us needed for anything if one of us had it. We flowed like that with everything we did. Greco's loyalty was the reason for his rage in the argument they were having.

Jazzy was a wiry brother from the 'Lou. Other than being a typical brother from St. Louis, Jazzy wasn't particularly confrontational. He was more cerebral and definitely had a focus on making paper. Getting wrapped up into the beef with the locals wasn't his thing. Actually, he didn't want to be in any confrontations. Including the one he was in at that moment.

"Man, I ain't trying to be in the middle of shit!" Jazzy eked out.

"C'mon, G', stall him out. It's done now bruh, just chill." Offered BW.

Boy Wonder. Helluva nickname. It had nothing to do with rocking a utility belt, being a cheesy sidekick or scaling buildings, though. Hell, he could barely jump a fence. He got the name because he never stopped testing his limits with his curiosity. BW had a marvelous mind, it never stopped working. This also made him the most mysterious cat we knew. You would never know what he was up to until he was hooking you up with it or you found out you just got fucked by it. He was relatively diminutive in physical stature, at 5'7" and 'bout 165 pounds soaking wet, but if you thought this dude small you would be making a grave mistake. B-Dub, for short, was a shade darker than brown and I'm surprised he wasn't nicknamed for being furry. He was hairy as shit!

If he was handsome or not didn't matter. B-Dub had that Detroit flavor: his daily ensembles coordinated every piece of garment by color and he rocked that old English 'D' brim all the time. That dude had a 'D' hat in every color, too. If you said he dressed to look like a fashionable crayon you wouldn't be too far off. But I've been to Detroit and it's a thing for the whole city, so I understood it. BW had the confidence of Adonis but he finessed it with humility. You'd never find him talking shit about his game, he just had it. And he was down for the team, super down brother. If the Organism needed it, B-Dub was always dependable.

This moment was a perfect microcosm of that. He was rolling 'J's on the window sill for the whole team while trying to keep the peace. At the same time. You could say he was doing double duty.

In usual fashion, though, Greco was having none of that.

"Naw, Dub! This mutha fucka here wanna talk shit and ain't backed up a damned thing. I need to know what the fuck is up with that. Who he wit'?" Greco barked.

"C'mon, dawg. Chill this shit out. We just getting in this bitch (the apartment). We don't need all that." Poppy chimed in.

Jazzy was standing between the living room and dining room, half pacing. Greco was sitting on the floor near the window where B-Dub was rolling joints.

There was a MAC-10 leaning in the corner of the walls.

We didn't have a true hierarchy. If we did, though, Poppy would be our third. He was like my right-hand man, Motown and I were an even partnership. Despite the fact that he was cooler than the other side of the pillow as a person, he was more authoritative than me. He never beasted anybody because it wasn't necessary, we were grown men with everything we handled. The brothers just tended to listen to him because he was a solid leader.

Once he got in the argument, it seemed like he was going to squash the situation. It didn't work out like that.

KNOCK, KNOCK, KNOCK!

"Who the fuck is this?" Poppy continued.

Poppy walked to the front door and looked out the peephole. He opened it to find his gal, Rita, standing there. In near annoyance, he opened the door.

"What's up, girl? What you doin' hurr?" Poppy questioned.

"I'm here to see you, what you think? And to keep you from being with these other bitches." Complained Rita.

The ladies in the room rolled their eyes at her but kept it cool. They weren't paying her any attention until she spoke on them. The sisters didn't stop staring at her afterwards.

"Girl… how the fuck you even know we here? How you get this address?" said Poppy.

"I don't know the address. I followed you here." Rita defiantly admitted.

"You on some old Nancy Drew-ass detective shit. Man, look hurr…" Poppy turned to the crew on his way out the door. "…I'll be back."

Poppy walked out the door with Rita in tow. With him gone, Greco was right back at it with Jazzy. He was definitely getting angrier.

"Mutha fucka, you need to answer my question, B. Shots were fired! You had a heater, what the fuck did *you* do? Jazzy!?" Greco was on a brink.

"Fuck you, man. I ain't about all that shit, dawg." Jazzy tried to defend himself.

This made Greco stand up. "The fuck you mean you 'ain't about all that shit'? You better be about all the shit, Black! This ain't a game!"

KNOCK! KNOCK! KNOCK!

Motown opened the door to the bedroom and my girl was already talking. See, Keisha was from the heart of New York. She moved like it, had an attitude like it and that dialect was unmistakable. She was sweet with it, though, which made it sometimes difficult to receive in full measure.

Right then her sense of urgency should have been unmistakable, too. It wasn't.

"Busara, y'all nee to cum owt'ere!" She cried.

"We handling something important. We'll be out there in a minute." I threw out phlegmatically.

"Naw! You *neeee* to cum owt'ere right now! Fuh real!" She tried to insist.

I still took her lightly.

"Look, give us a minute. We're coming."

"*Okay!*" She sarcastically spilled out as Motown closed the door on her.

Motown and I were trying to powwow in seclusion. Well, pseudo-seclusion. I was still sore from being shot and not yet fully healed. Believe, we knew the gravity of our situation and we wanted to make sure we came out on top. Again, shit was real.

Motown was my guy. He was another one of those slender brothers from Detroit. Seriously, it seemed like that was how they were produced at the car plant. He had crazy style, another Detroit trait, and he was always nicely dressed rocking a fresh pair of sneakers. Definitely rocked the old English 'D' baseball cap like it was a uniform.

Another part of his daily uniform was a bag of weed. Yeah, that shit was as important as clothing to him. That brother smoked so much weed you'd think it was oxygen. Motown wasn't selfish with it, though: he would make sure he always had plenty to share. You just couldn't smoke a joint with him, not if you ever wanted a hit anyways.

We were Team Mastermind. Motown and I had individually built some clout and clientele then combined our operations to become a power team. Together we built systems to be efficiently productive at what we did. We ran our business like a machine, filled with protocols and contingencies. I was all business, he was all hustle and our Organism had a monopoly on the streets we were connected to. That's why we were in our current state of hostilities.

I'm usually not hard-headed. I knew my girl came to the door for a reason because normally she wouldn't do that. But, to my knowledge, Poppy was out there *with* B-Dub. Both of those brothers were always level-headed and they're leaders. Whatever was going on out there we figured it would be fine because who we had in the front.

Well, that's what we thought.

KNOCK, KNOCK, KNOCK!

It was harder than the first time.

This time I opened the door. Again, Keisha was standing in it. She was much more insistent this time.

I said, "Keisha we…" she fervently interrupts.
"Naw, y'all gotta cum owt 'ere! This shit is serious!"
I'm visibly annoyed saying, "what you talkin'…

RATTA TATTA TATTA!!!!

"What the fuck!" I said as we all started to stand tall again. All three of us had crouched to the floor in reaction.

I looked over to Motown, he already had his pistol in his hand ready to put in work. I nodded to him, and we bailed out of the room.

We darted out into the living room, well I half-limped out. I was still seriously sore. Keisha had understated the truth...

The shit was really real!

There were bullet holes in the ceiling so big that you could see clear through to the apartment above us. Those bullet holes began just over Jazzy's head.

Everybody in the room was standing tall against the wall. They all looked like they couldn't move far enough away from Greco. Everyone was petrified, they looked like they were afraid to breathe.

Especially Jazzy. Jazzy was not a light-skinned brother, but his face was white right then. His eyes looked like teacup saucers because they weren't just big, but he also didn't blink. At all. His chest was rising and falling like a roller coaster ride. I swear his heart was trying to leap out of his chest and run because his legs weren't carrying him out of there. His heart was the smart one. Jazzy was a few hard breaths away from hyper-ventilating, but he was clearly frozen in place. On second thought, had he moved right then it would've definitely been a bad idea.

In front of him stood Greco. He was breathing super erratically, his eyes on fire like red suns. The Mac-10 in his hand was still smoking and he was crying angry. Crying! Tears were basically jumping out of his eyes and marching down his face. Greco was staring at Jazzy, and he was fucking pissed.

I instantly came to grips with one of the largest questions of my life. It punched me in my face like a full-speed Peterbilt truck.

"How the fuck did I get here?"

CHAPTER 2

THAT FIRE

(1981)

THWOOOMM!!!

...what the...?!

THWOOOMM!!!

Immediately, I ducked. I looked up and around, completely frantic.
I was afraid that it was some... random explosion or something. Maybe an
18-wheeler truck had tipped over or a wall had fallen somewhere. I don't
know what I thought it was, but it completely caught me off guard. My eyes
were huge and I'm certain my heart was racing because I dropped the hot
dog in my hand, and I could hear myself... breathing...

I frenetically scanned all the people around me trying to get a clue
from their faces. There were scores of folks in this huge parking lot just like
every year. See, this was the Saint Stephens Episcopal Church Talent Show.
It was on bump every year and this year was typical. There were people
everywhere: folks playing games, eating all kinds of food, waiting in line
for Sno' Cones, smiling and laughing, opening gifts from the church, little
kids complaining because they wanted something their parents wouldn't
get for them... just people. Everywhere. It was a massive event.

The streets were even cordoned off to make room and keep us safe from traffic. So, people hung out wherever they wanted, you couldn't tell where the parking lot ended, and the street began. There was a horde of police cars complete with horses – both policemen on horseback and the wooden horse barriers. Firetrucks were there and an ambulance or two was among the emergency vehicle pool. It's like the whole city came to ensure our entire community participated. And the community responded.

So, I looked from face to face super rapidly, searching for signs of trouble or alert, looking for anyone running: no one was panicking. So, I quietly breathed a sigh of relief. They were, however, all staring in one direction. Every face I analyzed had their eyes trained on the stage. So, I started looking up there, too.

THWOOOMM!!!

(Wow!)

That was my second thought. Well, along with, "they're the ones making that noise?" So, there's these guys, right? It's a bunch of young, energetic brothers – it's a good 12 or 14 of them. They're all wearing the same boots, with similar outfits, and they're jumping around and chanting out loud. They commanded the stage, hell, the whole audience with a sense of unity and authority… I was blown away! I can't even tell you why, but I had to get closer. I had this feeling that this was something I needed to see up close, something I had to get in on. So, I worked my way through the crowd, ducking under people, sliding past folks, constantly excusing myself, "excuse me, pardon me, I'm sorry, excuse me ma'am." I just had to get closer to the stage. So, I kept weaving through the crowd until I could be in the front row of the action.

I made it to the edge of the stage and…

POW!

The guys had just come out of a spin then hopped at the audience like they were bursting out of a box – arms stretched, mouths wide open and yelling. It felt like they were jumping at me! These dudes were GETTING IT! They were lined in formation while they made a bunch of choregraphed moves, then switched positions while doing other hyperactive moves only to form new lines and do even more different moves. All the while, they made music with their bodies. They would slap their hands together then beat on their thighs like… like they were playing Hambone but a LOT cooler. As soon as you got used to one beat, they changed it. Then their moves changed. And the mood around the crowd changed. People screamed out "oohs" and "ahs" and "go 'head, y'all!" It was super intense!

Oh, and it was obvious that they had practiced. A lot! But that's not what I was thinking while watching them. They moved effortlessly. It felt all at once like a spontaneous combustion of soul and power that organically formed in that parking lot – and – a splendidly and carefully choreographed exhibition of a hyper-talented troop of entertainers. Every move they made seemed to have a purpose. Every sound they made seemed to make a statement. Their words were in a language I didn't understand and, still, they bore the weight of great meaning. Somehow, I knew I was beholding something more than my eyes could catalogue.

They did this call and response thing, too: one guy would yell out and the rest would shout right after him. They made the stage literally shake! Just when you thought it was all a brunt display of force or a clinic on testosterone - they started singing. And they were good! But it wasn't like Michael Jackson or Luther or Prince… it was, I don't know, manlier? Yeah, it was manlier. I mean, your ears picked up the sounds, of course, but you felt it in your chest. And everywhere around you. It was as if they had sucked up all the air around us and filled the sky with their voices. I felt it in my bones. Hell, I wanted to shout out with them because it felt like they were talking to me! And, whether they were trying to or not, they were speaking directly to me. It was a spectacle unlike anything I had ever seen. Or felt. Or imagined. I felt like it was all for me.

The crowd stayed in an absolute rage! Everyone in the area had stopped to look. And, trust me, it was extremely difficult to keep the whole crowd's attention at the high energy event. It wasn't for those guys. Girls were screaming their heads off, old people were moving to the rhythms and young guys, like me, were all locked in making sure we didn't miss a move. Or a sound. Or a word. The entire area was electric with energy. It felt like some explosion would go off somewhere at any second: it was completely gripping!

I was frozen in awe just standing there watching, mouth hung all the way open. If flies were trying to migrate, they could've had a new home. I was completely dialed in. I looked around, took it all in and I was certain...

I was hooked.

This is where it all started. "It" being the fire of inspiration in my life. I didn't know it right then, but I had been captivated by something that would have the single largest bearing on my life. In fact, phrasing that in past tense is a misnomer because I'm still proudly committed to that life presently and it continues to have a great impact on my community.

What am I talking about?

Now, I know you're probably thinking, "that sounds like the Ques or the Kappas" or one of the other Black Greek lettered organizations that you find at HBCUs. (That means Historically Black Colleges and Universities for those who may not have known). Certainly, the descriptions fit some of their step routines and the ways they comport themselves in unison.

The group I witnessed had visibly apparent brotherhood. It resembled the same sort borne of clandestine hazing popular with Black Greek organizations and many forms of fraternities. If not an ill-advised process, it often produces a consistent and desired effect of an 'earning it' system. This means of 'paying dues' typically engenders prospective members to intrinsically value the group they join. This invariably creates a sense of pride and esprit de corps where the bonding transcends their differences. This level of camaraderie can be visible to the naked eye, if you know what you're looking at. These guys had that, too. In fact, if you saw them in action, you would probably argue someone into the ground that they belonged to a college somewhere. Probably take it to the point of betting money, even.

Those would be dollars lost. The group I witnessed that day had nothing to do with the Greeks or their organizations. More than not being collegiately connected, the vast majority were high schoolers or younger. I would find out later that what I had seen was more ancient than both Greek college organizations and American colleges altogether. Those dances, the language and the spirit all came directly from the source of life – Mother Africa! Those guys I saw bedazzle the audience in that church parking lot marched with Tabura commands that the great Shaka Zulu used to maneuver his warriors as they conquered villages all over South Africa. Their moves were from the timeless African Gum Boot Dance, still performed in many African countries today. Everything they shared with us on stage that day was rich with tradition and history and purpose.

They sang the songs sung by African workers riding the train home after spending almost a year at the diamond mines. These enfeebled 'train riding' Africans worked incredibly far away from home for eleven months a year, sometimes longer! Their work was grueling, with long hours of digging and hauling underneath a blistering, unyielding sun. The work sites were near the western coast of South Africa, but the workers hailed from the opposite side of the country: places like Soweto, Queenstown, Kroonstad and Johannesburg. They had spent every day of their near annual stay in a comfortless tent community. After persevering the steep price to provide for their families, these brothers would await their home-bound train with the greatest anticipation.

Hot, angry and worn, these Africans would load a train to bare, longing to reunite with their loved ones. They took seats on its rooftops, hung out of the windows, sat on the stairwells – not one of them was will-ing to wait an extra minute before getting back to their village. Like one soul they felt the same sun, the same exhaustion and the same separation from those they held dear. So, they sang about it.

One man would call out, "SHOSALOSA", and everyone would sing:

SHOSALOSA KU LEZONTABA
STIMELA SIPUME' ZIMBABWE

This means, "move fast on those mountains, train from Zimbabwe".

Then one man would shout, "Wen' Uyabaleka" the rest would sing:

WEN UYABALEKA KU LEZONTABA
STIMELA SIPUME' ZIMBABWE

This means, "you are running away on those mountains, train from Zimbabwe."

If you can envision it, imagine the chugga-chugga of the laboring engine taking them home, thick train stack smoke infiltrating their nostrils while wind gusts beat on their faces. This created their accompaniment while they sang these songs with their whole hearts. Every single car would contribute to the rolling symphony with voices ranging from bass to baritone to terrible. As one soul, they beat on their chests and stomped their feet on the down beats.

When I hear it in my head, I imagine them singing it louder every time they round the chorus because with every single note that rang out into the sky they knew they were that much closer to home. I picture them rolling through mountains, across lakes, over pastures and plains, lifting their voices from their lungs and praying the winds would carry their song to their loved ones.

The young brothers I saw rocking the makeshift stage at the Saint Stephens Church that day hit me with all of it at once. They made a version of the 'chugga-chugga' with their mouths and by shuffling their feet. There was a whistle around their necks they used like the train horn. They sang as if the ancestors' voices had come through their mouths. Their feet delivered the 'boom' that shook trains. The 'boom' that shook me!

What I had witnessed was the authentic African article and it was unmistakable in its power. I didn't know all these details when I first heard those guys that day. I didn't know the history, the undertones of the stress and hope or the depth of suffering and pride that went in to making those songs.

But I felt them.

Someone in their group started talking on the mic. I could barely make out what he was saying because it was tough to hear through the roar of the crowd. They told us that the South African Gum Boot Dance is the thing that had captivated my soul. I was already committed for life and didn't even know what it was. I was enamored. Intrigued. Enraptured. I was just… overwhelmed by the sheer strength of its impact. I instantly recognized, though, that there was a host of things I simply didn't know. My mind was awash with questions:

(Who are they? Where did they come from? What is that language they're speaking? Are they African? Yeah, that definitely sounds like an African language, or what I think an African language would sound like. Yeah, they gotta be from Africa. But wait; they can't all be African because I know him, well, I've seen him before… he goes to Clinton with me.)

I was in the 6th grade at Clinton Middle School. One of the guys on stage actually went to school with me. I paused on that thought for a second because it grounded me. For a minute I felt like I had been whisked away, better yet, marched away to some distant land. Totally forgot I was standing not very far from my house. I'm telling you; I was totally in! I continued:

(So, I know they're not all African. Naw, they're not because that brother lives in the Webbe's.)

The Darst-Webbe housing was a group of high rise government projects on the south side of St. Louis, at 14th Street and Chouteau. They were separate housing complexes (Darst and Webbe), each had about eight buildings that were nine stories high or taller. Peabody Elementary School was in the middle of them. In fact, we were on an intersecting corner with the two of them at the church. My apartments, the Peabody Projects, were on the fourth corner of this intersection at 14th and Park.

Now there were two guys in this… this juggernaut group that I knew lived near me, who lived right where I was standing! I was knee-deep in my own neighborhood having an other-worldly experience. It was absolutely serendipitous.

I continued trippin' out as I identified more guys:

(Yep, and that's Wee Jock!)

Wee Jock was a local deejay. He did all the livest parties in the 'hood. Or, at least, that was the word on the street. I wasn't old enough to go to any parties at that point, so I definitely wasn't an eyewitness to anything. Actually, most of the excitement in my life at that time was vicariously experienced. It may have even had some impact on how I was fascinated by the group of guys I watched. I wasn't entirely 'free' to hang out in the 6th grade… but I'll get more into that later.

I recognized more of them:

(And that's Wee Jock's brother, Vick.)

Victor was a light-skinned dude when being light-skinned was in. He pulled all the ladies back then. Other than being Wee Jock's brother all I knew about him was that he had an easy time with the ladies. That gave him an automatic 'cool' card.

I began looking intently:

(…that brother over there goes to Clinton, too!)

I took another look around:

(And he goes to McKinley, plays on the O line. Wait… what's his name? Um… that's Motion!)

His name was actually Charles, but we just called him Motion. I don't know why but nobody asks that. It was just what people called him those days. Dude was a huge, super mean-looking football player who was built low to the ground like an Oompa Loompa. I wasn't going to be the one to ask him to explain his nickname. I wanted to live and, like, go to high school and stuff. Grow old enough to get a kiss from a girl who wasn't my grandmother. Y'know? So… yeah, just 'Motion'. That was good enough for me.

I saw another guy:

(Zip, too?!)

"Zip" actually had the last name Swift. Now, they could have called him 'Zip' because of his last name but I'm not sure. Maybe he got embarrassed talking to a girl with his fly open. Or it could be because he used to wear those gym shoes all the time. You know that commercial where kids slid their feet in straight lines in the dirt then dragged their foot to connect them and make a 'Z'? Yeah, those shoes. I don't know. But he was an older kid and you never asked them why they had nicknames. You just used it, too, hoping you could be cool and fit in with them. You certainly didn't ask the older guy with the nickname, though.

If you thought it was particularly cool or funny, and Zip could've qualified, you might ask someone you thought could've had the info. But you had to make sure it was somebody who wouldn't tell the person who you asked about. That's just not how you do things. I never asked anybody, though, so I still don't know. It's probably a good story, I'm guessing. The nickname is kinda tight. He stood about 6'1" and also had no problems with the ladies. So, Zip also had 'auto-cool' status.

Taking an inventory, this was an all-star lineup of the coolest guys I knew of. They were crazy popular but I had no idea they were in this thing, though, whatever it was. Hell, I still didn't even know what it was! I had never heard of a cool African-type group with a bunch of young brothers who had these moves and dances and stomping and all that... but it was the bomb! That the cool kids were the ones blazing the stage together at the talent show doing the African thing? Man, my mind was blown.

Then I saw a kid I personally knew and, immediately, I got even more excited. Nardy was up on stage with them. 'Nardy' is my guy Nate. He lived in the Peabody's with me and we both went to Clinton. We were tight but... how did he get in it? I was already innately captivated but seeing him sparked a whole new line of questions:

(So, okay, they're definitely from here but... is it an African program? Hold up, what is an African program? I mean, do they have an African teacher? What IS this?)

Seeing Nardy involved made me ask the most pertinent question - how do *I* get in? I went to work on that part immediately.

When the guys finished dazzling the entire audience they left the stage. I was already waiting for my guy, Nardy, when he set foot on the ground.

CHAPTER 3

THE GENE POOL

Nardy came down those few stairs and saw me gazing into his face, my mouth still fully agape.

He said, "dawg, what's your problem?"

I spit out a few flies then said:

> "Man, that was live! When did you start doing this?"
> Nardy said, "I been in this for a minute, dawg. Just doing what I do."
> I said, "I want to do that, too! How can I get in?"

Nardy, 'my guy' Nardy, looked me over real quick. Then he spit fire at me.

> "Man, you can't do what we do! Your Moms' super strict, you can't handle this. We be going to Chi-caaaa-go and stuff, dawg. You can't hang."

Before I had a chance to counter, he shut me completely down.

"Look man, I gotta roll. We got stuff we gotta do."

I was left standing there thinking how did that go so terribly wrong? What stuck with me most was when he said, "…we be going to Chicago and stuff…". He said it like they were performing in European tours or something. "Chi-caaaa-go" – *the most exotic destination this side of Jupiter*. It still rings in my ears. We lived in St. Louis, man. Even I knew Chicago was just a 4½ hour car ride away. Just because they were doing African stuff didn't mean he was hanging out in Egypt or something. Dude was trippin'.

Okay, so clearly it irked me.

But he did have a point. I hadn't even considered what joining their group could possibly mean. And, like I said, I had more than a few challenges with running free when I was ten years old. Straight up? He was telling the truth; my mother was really strict. It was a real test for me to participate in anything.

Now, I want to make it clear, my mother wasn't strict because she was mean. My Ma, rest her soul, was a beautiful and incredible human being. And it definitely wasn't because I was a troublemaker. I didn't live that life and, honestly, I don't think she would have let me live to live that life (if you know what I'm saying). She was simply very… let's say incredibly protective of me. And there were reasons.

I was born Ja… for, uh, "technical reasons", we will not use my government name for the purpose of our conversation today. Let's just call me Busara, it means 'wise' in Kiswahili. Don't misunderstand me, I'm a very humble person made even more so by my journey so far in this life. However, for the dynamic that I contribute to the crux of the story I'm sharing with you, it is befitting. You have to trust me for now. So, I'm Busara. Glad to meet you.

Now, as I was saying, I am the first-born child of my beautiful mother, Gloria. So, in a general sense, she was very protective as first-time mothers can often be …you know what? I had it in mind to say just a few words about my mom but that would be unforgivably disrespectful. And her absolute heroism in my life deserves to be given its proper due.

My mother epitomizes the phrase 'strong Black woman'. And she got it honest, she comes from a line of incredibly strong Black women. I understand people have a tendency to exaggerate the greatness of people they hold dear but this is not that. In fact, let me share a few things with you. I'm going to take you back for a minute…

My Mama, you would call her my grandmother, was born in a little old southern town called Aberdeen.

…real talk, I get goosebumps thinking about her example. Such an amazing woman. Let me continue…

She grew up with a childhood friend, Johnny, who happened to be a little white boy. They played together daily like rural southern children do. They had hours of fun with games of 'Kick the Can', they chased down snakes, made mudpies and pulled critters out of the crick (that's a 'creek' for all you yankees out there). They would spend hours in the woods playing Hide & Seek or sneak into the local pond on those sweltering days that often came in bunches. For the occasional summer evening treat, they would run out into the fields with their glass jars and fill them as high as they could with lightning bugs. (Again, yanks, those are fireflies to you. Please try to keep up). They just shared in simple kid fun. Normal stuff.

Mind you, what they didn't do was go to the store together. Or the Malt Shoppe. And they wouldn't dare walk in diners together. This is the 1920's and -30's in Aberdeen, Mississippi. Yes, *that* Aberdeen. That kind of racial mixing was taking it too far. Even swimming in the pond together was a thing they did without fanfare. Otherwise they both would have most likely taken some licks to their backsides for such 'indecency'. Well, definitely my grandmother because 'young ladies didn't carry themselves in such ways' and 'they had no business consorting with young white fellas like that'. Even wading in the crick for critters together was risky business.

Of course it was just good clean fun. They didn't fathom shenanigans outside of their age range. And, very much unlike our contemporary society, sex wasn't a household conversation that would introduce such ideas to their young minds. Nothing inappropriate was even a thought. But segregation was life back then. The parts that weren't literally written in the law, and there were plenty of those, were assumed and expected. You simply didn't mix or mingle beyond a particular point. It was accepted as general knowledge then that Black and white people were separate and not remotely equal.

This contemptible reality reared its ugly head just a few years later in a life-altering way for my Mama. As they became teenagers, the little boy and his father visited my great-grandfather's house one day. The dad knocked on my great-grandfather's front door and confronted him with an unbelievable notion.

My great-grandfather answered the door. Johnny and his father stood on the porch.

> "God bless you and good evenin'", my great-grandfather said. "How can I help you?"
> "Is your daughter here?" The white man let out in monotones. "Johnathan and I have something we'd like to discuss with the both of you."

33

"Well, she shole is. Give me a minute and I'll fetch her. Would you like to come in for some lemonade? The wife makes a fine brew..." My great-grandfather reasoned.

"Naw. We're fine." Vomited the white man.

"Alright, suit yourself. Give me just a minute."

My great-grandfather turned away, leaving the door open so as to not seem rude. He returned with my grandmother beside him. She bore the look of a disconnected teenager until she spotted her friend. She then bent her lips into a slight smile.

They stepped out on the porch to hold the conversation face to face. Rudeness just wasn't the way of the south and talking through a screen door was just such a thing.

"Now, what can we do for you", offers my great-grandfather.

"Its high time your little girl starts calling my son 'sir'. He's a young man now... she can't keep calling him by his first name no more, neither. I mean," he exclaimed, "he is white after all."

My great-grandfather was a local minister. He was a pastor at several churches, actually. His prestige in that role came with the often cumbersome burden of stabilizing neighborhood peace. He was looked at as much more than a spiritual guide but as a shepherd to corral the Black community and keep any friction from rising. In my estimation it's one of the many ways white America has continued our struggles, subduing us through a belief system.

I digress.

Largely due to his vocation as the neighborhood clergy, my great-grandfather didn't want any parts of civil unrest. But also a serious consideration for his disposition were events of very recent times in Aberdeen. In 1889, Keith Bowen, an African-American man, was lynched by a mob after he "tried to enter a room where three white women were sitting". As the story goes, that's the whole story! He was going in and those women were just... present. My great-grandfather was alive and living in Aberdeen at the time. Not long after that inhumane crime, on January 16, 1901, Hiram Revels, the first African-American Unites States Senator, "died" while attending a church conference. The locals understood better than that headline, they were there and, fortunately, lived through it. Then, just before my grandmother was born, in 1914 Mayho Miller, an 18 year old Black man, was publicly hanged by a mob.(1) No discretion. No hiding it. It was on display for all to see and it was purposeful. And, apparently, well within the bounds of the law in Aberdeen.

Now, do the math: the population of Aberdeen was less than 4,000 people at the time. By any stretch of demographic that's no more than about 3100 adults, probably less. You already know that all the adults weren't white, my great-grandfather had several congregations of Black people. So, subtract Black adults and other minorities from that number then factor in the portion of those remaining adult whites that were males. It stands to reason that many of those event participants were people my great-grandfather conversed with daily. That list of perpetrators probably included the man at his door at that very moment. It's also possible that he knew, beyond any uncertainty, that this man was one such malefactor.

That wasn't exactly the backdrop of a place where taking a racial stand wouldn't have extreme consequences. Conversely, such moral righteousness often came with a mortal price for Black people. Even when it was unintentional, as was the case for the aforementioned Keith Bowen. Thusly, my grandfather had no designs on causing a fuss.

My Mama, on the other hand, was mortified. Instantly, her partial smile had collapsed into a scowl. And she *was* fussing.

> "What?!" She exclaimed. "I've been knowing that boy all my life. And he's my age! What you mean? I'm not calling him 'sir'. I'm just not 'gone do it."

> "I tell you what," the white man offered, "you will give my son the respect a white man is due or there's gone be some trouble 'round here. I can guarantee you I'm gone do that!"

Keep in mind, this was the quintessential small town. The streets were all unlit dirt roads. When you wanted to see at night you carried a candle or some form of lantern. It was a life filled with 'the daily grind' and 'work as usual'. If anyone knew your business in the community then everyone knew it because there were few things to converse about in general. Should any type of commotion arise it instantly became the focus of the town. And there was no such thing as privacy. If you had a public situation the public would stop and watch it. Accordingly, all the passersby in the neighborhood had stopped to watch their exchange at this point.

With the audience of onlookers honed in, Mama looked at her father with defiance. She wasn't rebelling against him but thought he would share in her rejection of this asinine idea. She bore the disdain on her face hoping to find comfort in his reply.

Sadly, it wasn't to be so.

At the insistence of the white man before him, and a generous portion of the community watching, my great-grandfather decided to stand firm in compliance.

"Now, you mind me and you make sure you stop calling him by his name. No more of that, y'here? He's a mister now and that's what I want you to call him. Okay?"

My grandmother was, again, beside herself. She couldn't believe her father hadn't sent this man packing with a few choice words. Much less could she have previously conceived that her dad, my great-grandfather, would go along with this madness. Despite her incredulousness in the moment, she was not remotely willing to waiver.

"Daddy, I respect you. You know I do. And I respect him just like I do everybody else. But daddy I'm not willing to call Johnny 'sir'. It just don't make no sense, is all. I've known him my whole life. It ain't right." Mama made her argument as soundly as she could.

"It's clear to me now what the problem is, preacher man," said the white guy. "You got you an unruly daughter. Hell, I'm more convinced now than I was coming here that she needs to give Johnny his due. It's her maturity level. She needs to learn a nigger girl's place." He paused for effect. "It'd be a damned shame if somebody had to show it to her."

My great-grandfather knew what was in the offing. He was vividly aware of the implications and how they could gravely affect his family. For starters, and immediately, how it might impact my grandmother's life. As already illustrated, their town was known to hang Black people for much less. But he also knew that it, likely, wouldn't stop there.

I'm certain my great-grandfather was tested in his compromised position. I don't envy him and I'm glad I'll never face a choice like his. But he was facing the option of ridiculously humbling his daughter or risking her life, and possibly his whole family.

He did what he thought they could live with. "Live with" has several connotations.

"Now, I don't want no more sass out of you, hear?" My great-grandfather said. "You mind me, now, and you call this gentleman sir from now on. Y'hear me?"

My Mama stiffened her back. I believe she spoke her next words with the solemn strength of our ancestors.

"I'm not gone be able to do that, Daddy."

"Listen here, now," my great-grandfather pleaded. "Baby, I need you to do what I tell you. You're gonna call him sir from now on and I don't want to hear another word about it. Okay?"

My every thought tells me he was trying to make it through the situation with as little harm as possible. He didn't want to further compromise himself or my grandmother. Most importantly, he certainly didn't want it to escalate in any regard and he needed my grandmother's cooperation for that to happen. He was desperate for it. He simply felt this course of action was what he needed to do.

My grandmother also did what she felt she needed to do.

"I won't lie to you, Daddy. I never do. I'm just not gone be able to do what you asking me." She explains, "that's Johnny. He been Johnny and he gone be Johnny. So I'm gone call him Johnny."

I want to take a second to adequately underscore my grandmother's bravery. This is in the 1930's: you don't tell your parents 'no'! Moreover, this is the heavily racist and racially suppressive south where Black people had been publicly murdered all over the region on a regular basis. Even recently in their town! My Mama is no fool. I'm sure she knew she was in jeopardy of losing her life, too. But, like I said, 'what you can live with' has multiple connotations. She couldn't live with subjecting herself to becoming some form of underling. Everything in her wouldn't let her do it.

Powerful! She's a warrior as far as I'm concerned. Nothing short of a queen who knew her royal stature shouldn't be compromised by the whims of the foolish.

My great-grandfather began to slowly turn his head from my grandmother to the white man with but a modicum of hope. He hoped that when he sees the man's face he would have shifted his stance somehow, that his countenance might have loosened. Maybe in seeing the girl's determination he might believe it wasn't that big a deal. Maybe Johnny's dad didn't want to continue pressing the issue. Possibly reason would have set in with him. Maybe Johnny had looked at his dad and frowned in disapproval, lessening the importance of it. He silently prayed that decency would tell the white man this was nonsense and a waste of time. Prayed that God would intervene as the voice of peace. Of compassion. Mercy, even. Or maybe the white man would have just a little respect for...

"What you gone do, boy? This here can't stand." The white man barked with the compassion of an axe.

All that hope was instantly dead, murdered by this white man's words. Reality was staring my great-grandfather in both his eyes and daring him to make a wrong move.

Unfortunately for my grandmother, he did. Turning his head from the white man and his son to my grandmother and back, he felt he had but one viable option.

He removed his belt and gave my grandmother a whipping on their front porch.

Right in front of Johnny and his dad. And their entire community.

Damn.

When my Mama told me this story she said she was shielded in principle as she took her beating. She was heartbroken and flabbergasted but steadfast.

> She thought, "Daddy, you gone whip me? For this?! It ain't right! It ain't right, Daddy. You gone whip me because he said I should call him 'sir'? I've been knowing him all my life. This just ain't right, Daddy. It ain't right."

She refused to cave. Whenever it became an issue she always took the beating. She was not going to be broken because she knew she was right. Calling him sir, shrinking her value, was wrong. She wouldn't do it. And she didn't.

As she told me this story, I felt sinking anguish and blistering rage at the exact same time. I could see that it pained her greatly. I don't believe it had much to do with the beating itself. I mean, corporal punishment is a terrible thing and no sane person would volunteer for it. But it can often be the most short-lived portion of trauma. No, she was undone by the indecency. The embarrassment. But, most of all, she was stung by the betrayal. Her father didn't stand up for her when she was in the right. The wrong thing was that this white boy received more regard than she did as a human being. Her father let the wrong thing prevail. For her those were unforgivable transgressions.

My Mama made sure I understood that there is no man alive more valuable to my world than me. That there is no group of people more worthy of homage than my family. And she made it vividly clear that as a Black man I'm one of the first people of the Earth. Always love myself and let no one lessen my fervor for being me. This reality became a pillar of my life-guiding principles.

Not many years later she moved out of his house. No, she didn't have a fortune or a bunch of friends to lean on. Again, we're talking the 1930's and -40's. People didn't live off of friends like that. They didn't leave the comfort of home like that. Particularly women. You stayed where it was safe, with your parents, until you could comfortably move forward to your next phase. Often for women that was by marrying someone.

"Safe" wasn't necessary for my Mama. Her sense of dignity told her she needed to move on. That's precisely what she did.

So, she found a plot of land and built a log cabin.

Herself.

Yes, my grandmother built a log cabin by herself. You read that correctly. And she lived there for some years until she decided she had enough of Mississippi living. She left the house she built and headed for St. Louis. Again, there wasn't an abundance of family members or friends in the 'Lou. She didn't have folks she could lean on. What she did have was her sense of purpose and self-sufficient work ethic. She was certain it was all she needed and my birth in the 'Lou, an entire generation later, is a testament of that. So, to my point, my mother comes from an extraordinary cut of woman.

And I have goosebumps right now.

CHAPTER 4

MORE "GENES"

My grandmother was more than a phenomenal woman, she was an exceptional human being. And she never slowed down. When she relocated to St. Louis she met and married my grandfather. Together they had the gift that is my mother. She was the fourth of their twelve children. Twelve! Yeah, that's a lot. I don't know about you but if I had a dozen kids I'd seriously consider farming. Or a vasectomy. Those times were not these times, obviously, and big families were much more common. They definitely had their house full and she handled it like everything else in her life – with aplomb.

Well, my mother met my father when she was twenty years old. She got pregnant and my father got scarce. I misunderstood what that was all about for nearly all of my childhood. Fortunately, I lived long enough, and my father lived long enough, for me to get some understanding and some closure. More on that later.

My grandfather, erstwhile, was a coarse man. He was not at all pleased that my Ma had become with child while living in his house. Moreover, it was his firm belief that children should only be born in wedlock. He was terribly miffed that she wasn't married. Even worse, he was upset that my father was absent for my impending arrival. He took that out on my mother. My grandfather spent so much focus and energy on pressuring her that, before I was born, he forced her out of the house.

Well, technically, he forced *us* out of the house. So, pregnant without much of a support system, my mother struck out on her own into the 'Lou.

Now, my grandfather was a mean cuss. It's true that I may be a bit jaded because he put my mother and I out before I even arrived on the set. I willingly admit I'm likely a bit salty about it. However, it was also the consensus of my elders who actually knew him. I have no recollection of the man because he passed when I was one and, sadly but honestly, he hasn't been missed.

My grandmother went to work picking up the slack. She maintained that sense of self-sufficiency from Mississippi in everything she did. She was an absolute professional at 'making her own way' with whatever she had. Her early life showed her that nothing in life was just there for her, if it was going to be gotten she had to go get it. Mama's work ethic and toughness, her self-reliance just moved her to do and handle things. It's how her experiences taught her to operate.

At the time, my mother was busy erecting a structure for our lives. She joined the Independent Ladies' Garment Workers Union and put in the elbow grease to get us settled. In the meantime, we were staying with a friend of hers from high school and that she knew from the Pruitt-Igoe projects. She was committed, though, to making a home for us.

My grandmother had a lovely home in Walnut Park. She helped us by taking me in to help save money. She refused to let strangers charge my mother to babysit me when I could be with family who was more than willing. Because my Ma worked long and often awkward shifts, they decided I should move in with Mama.

It was a huge sacrifice for my mother: I'm her first child. She wanted to spend every waking moment with me, guiding me by her hand to develop and groom me as she saw to lead me. It took a lot for her to allow my grandmother to keep me but she knew it was the better choice in the situation. And, of course, she trusted my grandmother implicitly. So, I lived with Mama for a precious few of my formative years.

I was with her at such a young age that the family took to calling me 'Thirteen'. In every functional way, I became her thirteenth child. It's also why I call her Mama, we were that kind of close. She doted on me, for sure, still she led with a stern but fair hand. It was this close tutelage where my grandmother made indelible impacts on fashioning my life perspective. The way she handled life gave me a sense of value for both my mother and my grandmother. Her brand of respect and honor instilled in me my reverence for the Black woman and the Black family. It continues to be a constant motivating factor to have been mentored by someone whose character I aptly regard with astronomical esteem. I could write a whole book about my respect, appreciation and love for my grandmother. This isn't that book.

Before long, Ma got a place for us in the Peabody Projects. Still, I stayed with Mama until I got old enough to be responsible for myself. Avoiding the necessity for some type of daycare was the plan. When I turned six they thought I was responsible enough and my mother had a routine for her career so it was time. Living with my grandmother was incredibly enriching but I was excited to have a new home with Ma. When we settled in it was just her and me. It was beautiful except for the parts that weren't. See, Ma was born in the 'Lou. She knew it could be rough and that kids easily fell into bad circles. Without my father around she was my only protector and she took that job *extremely* seriously!

Now, knowing my grandmother's history you already know my family stock is about tough women. Well, that toughness in my mother translated into an incredibly stringent approach to protecting me. As I matured, I was restricted from all sorts of things. And, she was just as serious about me being responsible for myself as she was about protecting me.

So, she kept me in chores. I had chores, plural, before all of my fellas had any. They tripped on me about that. Before I could go out and play my chores had to be done. And my homework. Ma did not waiver on my academic discipline. That absolutely had to be handled before I could do anything else. I got called a bookworm or a nerd, and such, but my grades were always tight.

Wanna know the toughest thing about hanging out as a kid? I was the last one to join everybody to play and the first to leave. I had to always go in the house for dinner and whenever the street lights came on. That dinner thing was the kicker. It wasn't just that I had to leave for it but it was a big production every day. It was a like a scene out of some over-the-top movie.

Ma would hang half her body out of the window and yell my whole name in a strong vibrato for the entire neighborhood to hear.

"BUSARA ANDRE DIZZY", she belled at the top of her lungs. "It's time to eat!"

My homies would clown me. Everybody had to go in around the time it got dark, so that wasn't a big deal. However, I was the only one who had to go in for dinner. That was around 6:00! We would always be in some type of game on the street, too. Tossing a football around or shooting some hoops, some kind of group fun where everybody was participating. In the middle of it, just when it was getting good, I would get the call.

"BUSARA ANDRE!"

"Man, yo' momma strict," one of my friends would say.
"Dude, you can't do nothing", says another. I might mumble something like, "Man, I don't wanna go home. I wanna kick

it a little longer." And someone would say, "you betta get home like yo' momma said or she 'gone kick yo' butt a little longer."

Everybody would split a rib while I trotted away, trying to make sure my Ma didn't actually 'kick my butt a little longer'. So, not only was I frequently called out about my Ma being strict but I got laughed at about it. A lot. I tell you what, though: they could cackle all they wanted. I wasn't about to try to play tough or brave and compromise myself with my Ma. No sir!

Ma was not a small woman. She had a voice that commanded attention, it was booming and authoritative. Her intense facial expressions read like a dramatic novel. When she spoke everyone either agreed or turned into crickets. Nobody interrupted her, though. I swear a few times even passing buses stopped moving because she was talking. They probably made those E.F. Hutton commercials because they had seen my Ma in action! Challenging that woman wasn't a thing you did. It just didn't happen. You could say she just had the aura of respect about her, and that's certainly true. But I'm gonna have to include an element of scariness in that mix, too.

In fact, she publicly announced (more than a few times) that I was going get my butt whipped when I got home. Normally, that's a thing your fellas would tease you about. But, naw. Her proclamation was enough to spark silent crocodile-sized tears to leak from my eyes. They escaped silently because if I started whining or making any noise at all she probably wouldn't wait until I got home. Don't act like y'all don't know what I'm talkin' 'bout! The proverbial 'don't start all that crying or I'll give you something to cry about' was a neighborhood momma credo. I wasn't about to volunteer for that '...something to cry about'. Only the insane volunteer for corporal punishment, remember? I was already terrified enough for the impending wrath. My fear would make onlookers turn immediately sympathetic.

You could see the empathy on their faces,

"po' baby. She 'bout to tear that ass up."

It was bad enough to turn my homies into concerned grandparents. You know that's crazy.

But her protection efforts were more than just stringent scheduling. She wouldn't let me play little league football at Herbert Hoover, either. That was a Boys and Girls Club in our neighborhood on Grand and Greer. They hosted sports and activities for kids that I could only hear about because I couldn't do them. In fact, the St. Louis Cardinals played their home games there for years before they built Busch Stadium. Knowing I could've played sports where the Cardinals played but wasn't allowed to was tough to deal with. She didn't want me to get hurt or to be with the wrong sort of kids. Her version of 'better safe than sorry' kept me both safe and sorry at times.

Ma also kept me in church. I was 'gone worship if I didn't do nothin' else. We were in church on every Wednesday and Sunday. She even took me to choir rehearsal with her on Thursdays sometimes. I don't know if she thought the kids at church were a bastion of angels (they weren't) but that was a risk she was willing to take. Ma did all she could to shelter me from everything that she knew were present bad elements in our rough and rugged environment. She intimately knew those temptations and tests.

See, before me, Gloria partied. That's how it is in the 'Lou – you party! It's a community of life-celebrating people. At least the Black community definitely is. The 'is' is still accurate, book a trip to the 'Lou if you want to have a good time. You will not be disappointed. Gloria was enmeshed in that life. She partied hard: hit the clubs, drank at bars, just lived the life. She knew everything and everybody that was out there and knew what it could lead to.

Then she became my Ma. She turned her life around on a dime. She stopped drinking, she didn't smoke anything, she became a seamstress in the union and hyper-developed her spiritual relationship and connection to the church. She rerouted her whole life.

For me.

I have homies whose mothers continued to party until they left the planet. This is the 'Lou, there are lots of places where you can 'cut a rug' well beyond retirement. I told y'all, we party! But my Ma ended that for her life. She separated from all her childhood buddies because many of them were still in the streets. She sacrificed a lot of bonds she had made over the years, stopped them cold and disconnected. Then began anew with me. For my life. Protecting me from those things, well, that became her world.

That's the toughness of my matriarchal lineage that moves me so. My grandmother, rest her soul, was just the epitome of humanity. She was power incarnate and made strong impacts everywhere she went and in everything she did. In fact, it's the way she ended her days. Again, this is not a jaded admiration. I have more receipts.

Sadly, Mama developed diabetes in her later years. It progressed to the point that she had to get her right leg amputated. So, she got a prosthetic leg and kept pushing. It was nothing to find her atop a ladder painting her house. Or tending to the garden in her yard; weeding, tilling and harvesting. All with her prosthetic leg. She refused to let anything hold her back. She did everything she wanted to do with that limb until she couldn't 'do' any more. My grandmother was just a stellar example of life. Damn, goosebumps.

Ma was also her own brand of amazing, too. The ability to see the error in your ways is a toughness in itself, but changing your entire life for the true benefit of someone else? The necessary level of introspection and honesty coupled with the discipline and selflessness to make such a sacrifice? Those are amazing traits for any one person to have. But exercising them solely for the benefit of your children? There is no greater love. She fought through the life she had lived and the environment we lived in to deliver us the best lessons she could provide. All while protecting me but still fostering a way for me to grow to be a man. This is what my mother did for me. Superhero status, for sure.

Now, one of the other motivating factors in her strictness had everything to do with the other half of my parentage. My father.

Bubba was a man, an incredibly resourceful and mechanically inclined man. He was exceptionally skilled with his hands. He built houses and could work any portion of it by himself. My paternal family, particularly my uncle Ronald, owned a chain of funeral homes. Bubba was a godsend for them because he would fix everything for cut rates. He just demanded cash (more on that later). Plumbing, carpentry, electricity – any part of putting a structure together or repairing it, he could handle it all.

If I had to guess, I would say he was a big fan of plumbing. Bubba would work everything in a house, including the lady living there. My dad had a way with ladies that was seemingly effortless. You can't quote me on the ease of his female partner acquisitions but you can believe, whatever his methods, he was effective. He was regularly effective. I mean the kind of regular that your doctor wants you to be when they prescribe you some fiber. I don't think he was ever in the '80's rap group 'Whodini' but he was definitely a hoe. "He's a hoe, you know he's a hoe…". He was always entangled with women all over the country. Some of everywhere.

Let me quantify the 'everywhere'. See, Bubba did some truck driving. He did it for a long time, almost 25 years, and he did really well for himself with it. This took him all over the region so he made his rounds through parts of the United States. When I say he made his rounds I really mean it. He connected with women all over the country. If he had a stop in a city somewhere, he had a rendezvous partner there. Or two. How do I know this? Well, let me tell you another story.

So, once I got older, Bubba and I formed a solid relationship. He had a thing for a while where he would bring cars around to the house and let me drive them, even. I thought he was being kind or thoughtful. "Maybe he's thinking about buying me a car," I would say to myself. Naw, that wasn't it at all but that's a story for another day. My point is we were really good on each other, things were working out.

Once I got my own rides he introduced me to a really good friend of his named Gene. Gene was a spectacular car mechanic. Whatever was wrong with your car he would put his mojo on it and it ran like a dream. Well, the first time I had some car trouble I told Bubba about it. I described to him what was happening and how it wasn't working right.

> Bubba said, "you need a fuel pump. Call Gene, that's my best friend, awesome guy. He'll get you straightened out."
> "Okay." I said. He gives me the number and I call Gene.
> "Hey Gene, I'm Busara – Bubba's son. I gotta get a fuel pump on my truck. Bubba told me to call you."
> Gene says, "alright! I'll be right over."

Gene dropped everything and came over right away. Bubba met us at the house and we were all there while Gene worked on the car. So, while Gene is outside dinking and doinking around, we're bullshitting in conversation for hours. The repair takes four, five or six hours but all of us (Bubba, Gene and I) are standing around like we don't have a care in the world. I'm sure I was the only one thinking, "are we 'gone fix this damned truck or we 'gone stand around telling stories all day? What the hell is going on?"

Finally, Gene wraps up. I'm ready to pay the man for his time and expertise.

"Hey, Gene, thanks brother. What I gotta… what do I owe you?" I questioned.

"Aw man, don't worry about it." Gene responded. "Your daddy told me to come over here and…" yada, yada, yada.

Long story short, when he left that day Gene didn't accept any money from me. Over the years this was a regular occurrence. When I had car trouble I'd call Bubba's friend Gene and he'd come over right away. Bubba would usually meet with us and hours would tick off. Gene would never take my money.

A few years later, unfortunately, Bubba passed. Not long afterwards, I was driving in the rain one day and caught a flat and I didn't have a tire iron to change it. Who could I call? Bubba was gone but I still had Gene's number. I gave him a call to see if he could help.

"Hey Gene…"

Gene dropped everything and sped to my location, got out and began working on the car in the rain. Now, I knew the modus operandi and I wasn't allowing it again. I wasn't out in the rain working on my *own* car but he was doing it for me with a smile on his face. That man needed to be compensated. The way I was feeling it, he needed to be paid well.

I had money in my hand when he finished.

He gets up when he's done and sees my money waiting for him, "…aww, y'know you don't have to…"

I interrupt him abruptly, "naw Gene, I ain't taking that, man. I owe you money, brother. You changed my tire in the rain and it's not decent for me to let you go without…"

He interrupts me. "Listen here, young brother, let me tell you a story…"

I was a little reluctant to let him tell it to me because I knew it's his way to, again, refuse my money. But I figured if the man is worth paying for the work he did he's certainly earned my ear. So I sat quietly.

"Busara, there was this man who drove a truck. He rolled into my town where he met a really nice lady."

"They had relations, like men and women do." He chuckled a bit and shrugged his shoulders.

"Anyways, because the routes he ran took him through the town on a normal basis, he visited this lady frequently."

He continues, "this lady had kids and this truck driver was really good to them. So good, in fact, that they ended up having a child together."

He said the next part patiently, "my mother is really glad she met Bubba."

Then he stood silent, looking me directly in my eyes, waiting for me to figure it out.

His mother was regularly visited by *OUR* father! The whole time I thought he was Bubba's friend but…

Gene is my older brother!

If you're blown away by this then that makes two of us. It hit me like a twist in a novel, I really didn't see that coming. All that time I spent with him I thought this older guy was just someone Bubba knew but it was my big brother who was doing me a solid. All those years! Mind-blowing.

When I found this out, Bubba was in the ground already. I couldn't question him about it, give him shit, find out more information – nothing. Right then I just had to make peace with the facts and be glad that I had a brother that I didn't know about. A big brother, at that! Fortunately, Gene is a really good man and I like him a lot. But I didn't get a sibling vibe of any sort until after I learned the information.

So. Yeah, Bubba got around quite a bit but I wouldn't classify him by it. That story was only a small fraction of whom he was. I'm thankful for all of the family I have and that wouldn't be possible without him. He was easy to get along with but he was a complex person. He spanned the whole dichotomy of a man, sometimes awful but at other times absolutely beautiful. As I told you, I thought in my earlier years that I was abandoned by my father. Turns out his affinity for women had a hand in that. But so did drinking.

He struggled with alcoholism. I am loathe to say he was an alcoholic because he functionally ended all drinking in his life long before he died. But he was an alcoholic because Bubba was addicted to alcohol. It was its worst when I was very young. I didn't see any episodes that I can remember, though, and it's possible that he was trying to spare me that.

But, once he started to come around we couldn't keep him away. When that began, I had a few situations where I would just declare, "I'm hanging out with my daddy". Well, he would pick me up and I would end up in the lounge portion of a bar somewhere. Eating a burger and talking to the female bartender. Maybe I'd shoot a few pool balls around the pool table.

In the bar.

The 1970's and '80's were a wild time. These days a parent would be part of the cement they used for the foundation of a jail if they hung out at a bar with their child. But back then I was hanging out with the lady bartenders eating beer nuts and nobody blinked. Different times.

Bubba visiting me often made me feel like he would drop anything and come check on me. Except for work. Bubba worked constantly. And it wasn't the 'walk in to work and punch a clock' kind of work. He hustled with all his soul. He was always working. As with most things, there's some backstory to this, too.

Apparently, hoeing has a price. That price is regulated by the Friend of the Court. The Friend of the Court set a few prices for Bubba, so, Bubba had child support issues. And I do mean Is-Sues! I gave you a prelude to his philandering nature and that was but a microcosm. His extreme, uh shall we say, 'habit' racked up pretty high prices. Bubba did drive a truck for a long time and, like I've said, he did pretty well. Problem is, those child support bills were so high that he had to do odd jobs to keep money in his pockets.

This is why Bubba did his handyman work under the table. Those were always 'cash now' situations. His appetite for women was causing him problems with literally trying to eat. He never begrudged taking care of his kids, though. He had a lot of children, and that was a test for him, but he compounded that issue with good character. Let me explain.

During the last 11 or 12 years of his life, I lived with Bubba. I got to know him very well as an adult man. It helped me understand more about myself and to understand him in better detail. In retrospect, I was able to actually gain insight on who I am because I got to know him better.

For some reason that I can't recall, he decided to use his charms to set me up with a young lady named Evelyn. She was nice and we got along well so we kicked it for a while. Every blue moon she would come through by herself, other times she would bring her kids along.

One day she came by and knocked on the door. This particular afternoon, her younger son was with her. I was in my room upstairs when Bubba answered the door. He politely invited her in then ascended the stairs to get me.

"Your family downstairs." He randomly says to me.

"Who?" I thought that was weird and I was a bit lost. "What you mean?" I asked.

"Your family. They downstairs."

I looked at him as quizzically as my face could communicate.

"Evelyn." He said in a sober and even tone. Then he said again, patiently, "Your family downstairs."

"Bubba. Them kids ain't mine, man. That ain't my family. I mean, me and old girl we…"

"Naw, son." He stopped me. "If you with her… that's your family. It can't be different than that."

And he meant it. That's how he handled every situation he dealt with when women had children before he met them. If he's there, those are his kids. His decency and sense of honor made him a much larger father than his loins ever could. When I learned that truth it changed how I saw him. Not because he was perfect but because the tests of his life made him one of the best men I've ever known. If I turn out to be half the man he was I'll be alright.

It wasn't all gravy, though. Actually, he ran afoul of one of the largest heroes in my life – my grandmother.

So, my grandmother wanted some work done on her porch one year. Bubba was the consummate repair guy/handyman and he always needed money on the low. You know, 'prices' and all that. My grandmother contracted him to do the repair for her and gave him $900 to get started.

Bubba took the money and said he would be back with supplies and get to work.

He didn't return to do the work. Ever.

I believe it was during the course of him struggling with his alcohol addiction because I've since learned that nothing about this incident was his way. It's simply not how he conducted himself or business. Be that as it may, he did stiff my grandmother for that money and the porch went undone by him.

When my grandmother told me about what he did I was livid. I was really young, I don't think I was a teenager yet. That didn't stop me from wanting to kick his ass. It was wrong. He was wrong. And he did that to my Mama. In the course of my reconciliation with Bubba, we had to walk that mile so I could understand what happened. He also needed to know that I didn't approve. We handled it like men and put it behind us because, literally, it was behind us. Fortunately, I did learn that it was an anomaly. He was a much better man than that, rest his soul.

Still, there was a situation he put me through that closely resembled what he did to Mama. This is another of those episodes that I thought were heavily influenced by alcoholism.

St. Stephens Church had a great community outreach program. This was the same place where the African-type group who captivated my soul had performed – that event was part of their outreach program. During the Christmas season, they would give gifts out to all the neighborhood kids. I don't know who their benefactor was but they laid it out every year. The way it worked was they had a list where you could sign up at the beginning of December. We knew it wasn't necessary to sign up but it was fun to do. In years past, they gave away troves of gifts to whomever arrived. So, maybe you put your name on the list or maybe you didn't but they always had more than ample gifts on Christmas for all the kids that came to the event.

On Christmas Day this particular year, kids in my neighborhood were walking past me from St. Stephens with trash bags full of toys. Their arms were loaded with all they could carry. Even their smiles looked too heavy for their faces. It was like Toys R' Us was emptying their shelves in my buddies' hands. They all passed by laughing and playing and having a good ole time.

I wasn't going down there.

Bubba had called Ma and made the promise that he was on his way with Christmas gifts. She told me he was coming and I was beyond excited! My dad was going to come through with everything I wanted because anything he brought me would be great. I can literally remember thinking my face was probably glowing because I was smiling so hard.

So, I was sitting in the window with the screen out, waiting for him to show up. I was hanging out of that bad boy looking up and down the street for his car. I wanted to see it on approach. I was like, "is his car coming? Is that him?" I did this for hours. Even after nightfall I still thought he was coming.

Kids kept walking by with the booty they claimed for the day. Every last one of them was excited and hyper. They were looking at each other's bags, comparing gift sizes and joyfully arguing about whose was the best. They were downright floating down the street in happiness.

Every time they passed me, they let me know they wanted me to get in on the goods.

"Busara, Busara! Man, you better head down to St. Stephens, dawg. They giving out mad gifts!"

"Get you some, man! You better go down there... man, I'm finna go back down there and get me another bag!"

With my enthusiasm lessening by the second I said, "naw, I'm good. My old dude on his way."

Bubba never showed.

My mother came and picked me up out of the window. When she pulled me in I was crying and shit... I was about eleven. I had the presence of mind to commit to logging that incident permanently: I would never, ever - NEVER forget that moment. You don't make a promise like that to kids and leave them hanging. They are on edge and filled with anxiety. I certainly was. It was a lesson that maturity within me beyond my years totally understood. Don't ever compromise your children with an empty promise. I decided I would never allow me to be that parent. That's the oath I made because of his empty promise. From then I had it hardwired within me what it meant to keep my word. All of my honor will be bound to my word until I leave planet Earth.

All that said, Bubba and I were very close by the time he passed. It is a powerful thing that all of that bad history was able to be cleared up. I could tell you more about how he would sacrifice for others regularly but I'll just some it up by saying: I am proud that he was my father. And I'm truly thankful I got to know him and see him in the light of high regard.

I don't want to mislead you, my mother and father got along famously. They were good friends until the end. Some of their fondness for one another helped me understand that my thoughts about 'father abandonment' was largely a misunderstanding. Ultimately that panned out to where I could see it more clearly and I'm glad about it. But as a kid, I just didn't have my dad around. And my Ma was doing her work to keep me protected from the kind of influences that would make me the same guy.

So, yes, my Ma was strict... with reasons. Plural, right? I was terrified she might literally kill me if I stepped out of line, for sure. That was my daily stature - afraid that Ma might 'kick my butt a little longer'. She loved me dearly. She made me as certain of that as I am sure of my name. Her way to best show that was to protect me from some of the things that had befallen her and my dad. Largely, though, Ma's methods kept me pretty scared.

This is what I faced while my guy, Nardy, was walking away. From everything I knew and could guess, this African-group-thing was going to demand time and effort and I didn't think there was any way she would approve. I knew what I was up against and that it likely wouldn't work in my favor. But the way everything about that performance had gripped me that day... I was committed. Period! So, I decided I would take a shot at it. I had to! Maybe it was the 'get it done' commitment from my grandmother that put a fire to my butt. Or the 'do what you gotta do' drive that Bubba had. Maybe it was the 'put first things first' discipline that Ma lived for my little sister and me. I don't know. But I was going to make it happen. How was I gonna pull it off?

Watch me.

CHAPTER 5

CLEVERISH

Straight up? 'My guy' Nardy was trippin'. How he 'gone not give me the information I needed to be down with that awesome crew? I thought we were cool… let me slow down. To be totally honest, it's not like we were on "best friend" level or anything. I don't think it's entirely accurate to have even classified us as 'tight' at that time. We had homeroom together, though, so we were incredibly familiar: Nardy and I saw each other twice a day every school day. So, I thought he knew me a little. Clearly, he didn't… but that also makes sense. Hell, I didn't know myself! Basically, I was trippin' all the way around. So, never mind the Nardy bit.

This test was defining me: I had never felt this level of commitment to anything before. It was definitely teaching me about my character. Weirdest thing? I still didn't even know what it was that I was committed to! I didn't care. I felt it, was compelled by it and, somehow, I had connected to it. It had become my mission: I was getting in and nobody was going to stop me. The least of the hurdles was Nardy. But there were, indeed, Olympics-level obstacles that would need to be negotiated. I went into it partially expecting that so I was already mentally prepared to get my decathlon skills up. It will prove to be incredibly ironic that I chose this analogy.

I woke up that Monday dead set on seeing Nardy. Why did I wait until Monday? There were more than a few mitigating circumstances that delayed my inquiry. First, I didn't know that Nardy and I lived in the same projects. We did. If I had known where he lived, I would've hit him up the next day on Sunday. Might've even gotten in trouble trying to catch him late that Saturday night. For real y'all, I had to have it. Crazily, he actually lived on the other side of the Peabody's. But, as I said, we weren't the best of homies and I never even saw him walk to school. Second, I also wasn't exactly an adventuring kid. Ma wasn't for all of that. There was a super slim chance I would've happened across his crib or his block, even. So, it's not surprising that I didn't know we were relative neighbors. If I knew, I actually could've hit him up about everything the next day. I definitely would have! Be that as it may, I had to wait.

...but I'm overselling the Sunday thing. Because, lastly and most importantly, they were incredibly busy days for me. Crazy busy! We had church in the morning, the choir sang in the afternoon and Ma always cooked a big Sunday dinner. We already dealt with the dinner situation, right? Right, let's just move on. We can... freely assess that I didn't have a lot of exploration time on Sundays, okay? So, I couldn't really leave my area to go see him even if I knew where he lived. Hence, Monday.

This was also 1981 and I was 11. We didn't do phones like that. Especially with fellas. For the girls, when we were into them and lucky enough to have their number, we would try to have phone conversations. 'Try' is super operative. Usually it wound up as a breathing contest with no clear winner. There was ridiculously little to converse about at 11 years old.

You know how those convos went...

"Hi", fellas would pensively say.
"Hi", girls would nervously respond.
...
...

62

...

"What you doing?", fellas would offer.

"Nothing really," girls would admit.

...

...

...

"What you doing?", girls would sweetly ask.

"Nothing," fellas would sheepishly throw out.

...

...

...

If you've ever been eleven years old with a phone at your house and talked to the opposite sex then you know each one of those ellipses represents about 7 minutes. We would watch whole television shows together without a word spoken.

Just... sitting there. Holding the phone.

Somehow we were stuck in the 'What-the-hell-do-I-say-next' Zone. Yes, that's an actual place. And, yeah, I know there are some guys who were smooth right out of the gate, hit it off with the ladies immediately at a young age. Those guys never had a hitch talking to the ladies and were super comfortable rapping to them. They just had that knack, y'know? My circle wasn't those guys.

Hell, I didn't even *try* to call girls at that age. I just know how it went. Still, we were more than geeked to get a girl's phone number. It was a huge deal in the social circle. We acted as if it meant something more than the equivalent of a prank caller panting through the receiver. It didn't.

Calling the fellas though? Nobody had time to be on a phone! I don't even remember having my dudes' phone numbers in middle school. For what? Talking about Thundarr the Barbarian, the Batman show being in Technicolor for the first time or Spidey and His Amazing Friends was a hundred times better in person. Nobody wanted to be on the phone to talk about 'Lost In Space' or 'Leave It To Beaver'. We were outside imitating the 'Six Million Dollar Man' while moving in slow motion talking about, "ni-ni-ni-ni-ni-ni" – between every painstaking off-balanced step.

Here's the score: Nardy wouldn't let me rap to him Saturday, I was beyond detained on Sunday and calling him was against the young bro code. So, Monday.

That morning I woke up, took a shower and was half-dressed before Ma came to wake me up. Most days she got up long before I needed to because she worked really tough shifts. Ma would get up, get dressed and prepare breakfast long before she woke me up. At the time I hated it: what kid wants to wake up early if it's not for the Saturday cartoons, right? I didn't complain, though, because, succinctly, she wasn't having that. And I had real breakfast every day. She didn't leave boxes of cereal out or make me choose some dry toaster pastries. Ma cooked for us daily. At 4:00 and 5:00 in the morning, she was cooking for her children. That's love, man.

This particular day, though, she was off work. So I could have, get this, *slept in*! Every other morning I would be all over some extra z's. But naw, when she came in my room I was fully dressed and damned near singing. I woke up at the normal time and started putting myself together. That's the day I was determined to get the drop on that banging group.

Ma was smiling when she walked in.

"Hey, Man! Wow, well aren't you all ready to go? You got a hot date?" She said.

"Huh? What you mean?" I replied.

"You all up and ready and happy; it looks like you're about to start whistling. What's her name?" She said with a knavish grin across her face.

"What?! Who... wait, what?" It felt like I got caught for something that I didn't even do.

"Naw, Ma. There's no girl. Naw."

She laughed quietly to herself, the kinda chuckle that made her shoulders shake.

"Well, what's going on, Man?" She said, still partly trying to contain herself.

"Nothing special," I claimed. "Just feels like I'm gonna have a good day."

"Well, that's good," she said. "I'm glad I cooked breakfast already so you can kick it off with something on your stomach."

"Thanks Ma."

I'm gonna tell y'all the truth: I thought she was going to bust me for the operation before I even got started. With our extensive history of her disallowing me to join things, my plan was to keep her out of this one. Don't ask me how I made that plan (I didn't actually have one) but it was my plan. And it was time to get it going. I left the house, virtually skipping out the door. I was in a half run through the projects until I reached the Ledge.

The Ledge was a 3' white stone wall around the back of the 'jects. That's how you know if someone is from the Peabody's or not – if they know about the Ledge. First thing in the morning, like when I went to school, there was virtually no one there. By the time I got home, though,

65

it was a mecca of convivial happenings. People would be there in droves talking in groups, shooting dice, drinking, singing Motown cuts or the latest jams, smoking (cigarettes and weed) and the whole 'hood would be there. Just chilling. Maybe the occasional dice game went south or something but it wasn't a typical spot for static. It was like the neighborhood version of Canada: despite being really active, it was a very peaceable spot. The cool guys all hung out there and that made it the cool thing to do. Everybody else seemed like they were there to graduate to cool status. It was the neighborhood social pit stop and it basically marked the halfway point to my school.

Disclaimer: if you're from a younger generation you probably don't know the Ledge like I do. Because, as usual, when it became clear it was a Black hang out, the cops started coming to fuck with us. They began brutalizing people, taking their beer or liquor bottles (usually breaking them, creating pollution in our neighborhood) and started arresting people. Rest assured, if Black people gather in harmony the government will find a way to wreck it. Of course, the press reported it as "hoodlums, violence and lawlessness" that the police were "cracking down on". That's the most insulting point: they sold that infiltration and disrespectful disruption of our community as if the cops were doing us a favor. They weren't.

Factually, the press has been responsible for continuing the oppression of Black people. Their disparaging and, terribly often, woefully untrue narratives about us as a people has branded us with contemptuous stereotypes. In fact, the press has been as destructive to our people as the police. They've painted a monolithic derogatory picture of us to millions of Americans, and global citizens, who have very little other exposure. That continues to be our test.

Like most of America that I know about, Black life in the 'Lou included a foul relationship with cops. The police were created that way. They were Slave Catchers (2), the 'Overseers', at their inception and not much has changed except their militarization. That means they're better suited to kill us now. Watching this dynamic and personally experiencing it is one of the many reasons I have always harbored disdain for the police. It's a standard distrust within the Black community: their efforts always seem in opposition to our well-being. I never got to hang out at the Ledge like that, I was too young, but I saw how it died and I felt it. I know who's responsible.

After hustling past the Ledge, I got to school super early. Normally that was an absolute no-no. There was a reason.

So, this was my first year in public school. I had attended parochial schools until that 6th grade year. My mother was committed to getting me the best education she could afford. I genuinely appreciated that at a really young age. So much so that I was double-promoted in the third grade. Real talk, I was pretty adept scholastically and worked really hard to stay that way. This particular year, 1981, was fiscally tough for us, though. So, I had to go to Clinton Middle public school for a year. It was cool with me. Going to junior high a year early came with a whole bunch of clout and it gave me a major boost in confidence. I felt like I could handle everything that school would throw at me.

Except Bubba Johnson. That wasn't his real name but it was fitting as hell for this huge, half-brained behemoth in my class. I was double-promoted but he had failed a grade. Our physical development magnified that two year gap. By a lot! Whenever I came in to class early I would have to deal with that ole porno-mustache-having, musty-in-the-first-class-of-the-day-ass, grown ass man. Yep, I said 'ass' twice! It's for some reasons. And I'm saying... dawg! How the hell do you *walk in* to school stankin'? You can't even *start* the day with deodorant? I swear he had kids somewhere already and, like, three tattoos. He probably drove to school. In the sixth grade!

First day, my personal inaugural day in a public school, I arrived a little early. I sat up front near the teacher because it was my habit. I thought I grasped lessons better the closer I was to the messenger, it was just my thing. You could call me a 'square' or a 'nerd', and I could roll with either, but it worked. I definitely handled those grades. While I was sitting there waiting for class to start, 'Boris' came in and sat behind me. I didn't see him come in or sit down. I just felt a sudden and crazily uncomfortable pressure on my pants pockets. I looked to the side of me and down and saw a pair of massive boats docked at the back of my seat.

(Man, no this mutha fucka didn't put his feet...)

The first time I turned around to tell him to fix himself was the last time I did it.

"Hey man, your feet are in my... seat," I said in protest as I was twisting to look at him.

(Aw shit.)

Then I saw his huge ass. His torso was so damned big he looked like he was still standing up. His facial hair was so prominent he could have done Gillette commercials.

(Is this somebody's daddy? Should I call him 'sir'...?)

He sat there and stared at me for a minute. For some reason he just looked, um... hungry. That DID NOT make him look friendly. After letting his disrespectful stare set in for the right amount of seconds... he belched.

Dawg, he burped at me. Pure disrespect. I took another shot at it.

"Hey man, your feet are in my seat." I eked out. "I can't sit
back with them there."
"Leave 'em there." He belched that out, too. It wasn't a literal
belching but that didn't stop it from stinking.

That breath came out angrier than a mutha fucka. Instead of saying
his breath stank I'm just gonna say the room was, uh, 'warmer' whenever
he spoke. At the exact moment that breath hit me so did his body odor.
It was like... like apple vinegar, mustard and wild moss. Dude was saucy.
Y'all ever smell something closely related to, like, skunk spray but was
looking in the face of the source and tried to control your reaction? Or is
that just me? Well, while I was trying to hold all of that in, another really
bad whiff assailed my nostrils.

In my half-turned around state, my nose was directly over his shoes.
The Trax sneakers he was wearing weren't built strongly enough to contain
that odoriferous emanation, either. Everything about this guy's hygiene
profile made me reconsider my desire for manhood. Mind you, he was
only supposed to be a seventh grader.

Meanwhile, this mutha fucka was still sitting low in his chair with
his stankin' ass size 13 feet on the back of my seat. His filthy, funk-emitting
shoes were half in my butt. Actually, they were only touching the back of
my jeans but I felt violated just the same. Just because I was significantly
smaller than him didn't mean I wanted to take that. Sadly, not much of
'what you want' happens in middle school.

"Hey man, I can't sit like this. If you don't move I'll have to
tell the teacher and you'll be in trouble with the Principal."

I tried to say it 'toughly'. It failed worse than that word I just made up. He sat up and asked me one of the scariest questions anyone had ever posed to me as a middle schooler.

"Do you want me to be in trouble with the Principal or do you want to be in trouble with me?"

This was a uniquely frightening question due to the sheer idiocy of it. What he proposed as competing ideas were the same thing. If I got him in trouble with the Principal then that's how I got in trouble with him. His 'either/or' presentation of the same idea made him inherently dangerous to me. That level of stupid couldn't be safe. That was the 1981 version of "is we finish or is we done?" Rank vacuity.

I passed on reporting the Smelly Jean Giant and changed my seat for the semester the next morning. I assuredly wasn't trying to get to class early to socialize with him. Particularly because I didn't own a gas mask.

I uniquely disapproved of that situation, though. I didn't like the fact that a dude could be a bane for me. No one should have that kind of effect on your life. I didn't approve of how I acted, either. I didn't wield the power in that situation and I couldn't allow that to be a trend. I attributed my failure to my momentary responses. Clearly I was smarter than that guy, I could certainly best him at logic. Since I trusted my ability to calculate, I decided to be a planned person. From then on I would take the requisite time to diagram a way to succeed no matter what I faced. My routes to success would include plans. Yep, I was sold. Planning would be my thing.

Arriving early the Monday after seeing those African dancing guys was awesome for me, though. My homeroom teacher was fine! She was so hot that I'm surprised I didn't try to be early every day – despite 'Bully Le Pew'. I walked in the room and there she was, smiling like she was in a toothpaste commercial. Her scent was like baked sugar and prettiness. Yeah, she smelled like prettiness - I said what I said. Her name was LaGina Wells, but I rarely said her last name because I would always use mine in my head. When I responded to her I just said 'yes, ma'am' a lot. She had this delicious mocha-colored skin, a fantastically thick shape and a smile that could steam the wrinkles out of linen. Oh, hell yeah, I had a mad crush on her. To me, it felt like Jane Kennedy was teaching me math. I'm telling y'all, there were worse ways to start a day than to see a Black goddess smile at you.

Catholic school was decidedly NOT filled with honeys. Sister Margaret, Sister Joan and Sister Mary Elizabeth did not a young man's loins arouse. And, seriously, they shouldn't have. Not only was I an adolescent/pre-pubescent kid but what kind of freak fantasizes about nuns? You know what, never mind that question – I didn't.

And, as if this needs to be said, they weren't all sisters! Maybe evolution just hadn't caught up with them yet but back in the 70's white women weren't normally shapely like Black women. All the curves just weren't similar or, rather, they just didn't seem to have as many. At least that's how I looked at it. Nah, it's not just how I looked at it - it's because that was the TV programming back then. They always stuck some surfboard-bodied white girl on the screen and told us she was the image of beauty. Man, no matter how many 'Gingers' or 'Samanthas' they ran across my face, you needed to have a booty for me to call you a cutey. That's just the thing, though: they weren't marketing for us. They were trying to program us to be assimilated. Culturally reappropriated. Mentally colonized.

Nah.

I learned early that I liked curves on a woman. And I wasn't into the lifeless-hair thing, either. Something about the thick, sun-enriched locks of a Black woman… it just does it for me. Adorn the timeless gorgeousness of a queen with her full natural crown of endlessly curly hair to top off those beautifully crafted contours and we got the stuff of my dreams. I loved that about sisters before I even started getting erections. No, I won't be commenting further on that.

Of course things are largely different these days. The physical esthetic playing field is a lot more balanced. Other than the popularity of enhancements and plastic surgery, I personally blame McDonald's. McDonald's is the devil, man. The entire fast-food industry has our kids blowing up because of steroid-filled and otherwise genetically modified food. It's crazy. So, the curvaceousness has now permeated across the racial spectrum in America and women's proportions are consistently more voluptuous it seems. That's not entirely a complaint. There's a pressure now on ladies who are not naturally adorned with sexy lumps to 'step up their games', through plastic surgeries or strenuous workout regiments, to level the playing field. That's not necessarily fair but it's how it is. Personally, I'll never be a fan of the fake stuff but athletic women are mad attractive.

Still, I'm an 'au naturale' kind of guy. The sisters have always been the blessings of nature. And don't get me wrong: there were more Black people at my school than white ones. Almost all of the student body was Black and we had several Black teachers. Most of the female teachers in elementary school weren't curvy, though. None of the Beckies at Catholic school were at all. Maybe that's why I didn't really pay attention like that until I left. But then again, we are still talking about teachers here and I wasn't some 9-year-old pervert, anyways! I just wasn't into women yet. So, I couldn't wait to escape my elementary school classes every day. But sixth grade? I only heard half of what 'Mrs. Dizzy' said most of the time because I would get caught thinking about her hugging me. Yeah, hugging me…

Once I awoke from my daily daydream, I realized Nardy had shown up. When he looked at me he had this shit-eating grin on his face. I knew that meant he was going to give me a hard time. Just felt it in my spirit. I decided not to play it straight up, I needed what I needed. I was going to have to work it out of him. Here was the first test of my new commitment:

(What's my plan? How do I get what I need from this guy?)

Everything about him looked like he wasn't going to help me. Shit, he had already rejected me directly. He was most definitely going to front on me again. What could I do? What would work? ...I had to feign weakness and let him have the upper hand. Leverage his pride of holding all the cards and get him to talk. Goad him into telling me what I needed to know. I didn't know him to exactly be a rocket scientist, he'd spill it and smile spitefully as if he didn't.

I took another look at him and that smug ass smile.

(Yep. Let's go.)

"What's up Nardy? That dance y'all were doing was live, man!"

"It was fresh, huh?" He said.

"For real! I'm trying to get in, man. Hook me up?" I pressed.

"I told you, dawg, you can't ride with us. Your momma too strict."

"Yeah, maybe you right, man. You might be right. I mean, there's a lot of time tied into it, right? Y'all have practice and everything, huh?" I said, feigning defeat.

He made that sarcastic stank-face. You know the one where it looks like a person simultaneously smells something terrible and it looks like their breath stanks, too. ("Stanks" not stinks, they're different levels of putrescence).

"Of course, we do, man. What you thought?"

"Well, you a school kid and the rest of those dudes are in school, too. It can't be too late, right?" I said baiting him.

"For you it would be," he coldly spit out.

I thought (be ridiculous, make him defend it). So I said,

"Is it like real crazy hours and stuff? Do y'all start at, like, ten o'clock or something?"

"Hell, naw. My momma would kick *my* ass for that."

Another stank face.

"We're there at 7:30 sharp or you gotta do push-ups - three for every minute you late. Can you handle that?"

(Okay, keep going)

I said, "I wouldn't have to, I just wouldn't be late."

"Yeah, whatever." He said. About to turn away.

"But y'all do that on Saturdays, right? I mean you still gotta go to school. Y'all can't do that on school nights, right?" I'm trying to get all the info. He was unctuously spilling it.

"Nope. We *perform* on Saturdays, sometimes it's the whooooole (whole) weekend." He teasingly said.

"We *meet* on Tuesdays and Thursdays, though. *Week-days!*"

He was trying to murder my dreams. I let him think he was.

"Wow. Okay. That's why you said my mom wouldn't let me go. I get it now. How do you get there? They pick y'all up or something?" One more detail man. Don't let me down.
"Hell naw!"

More stank face, sorta funkier.

"Ain't nobody gotta pick me up. Saint Stephens is just around the block. I walk there, dawg. They'll take us home sometimes, yeah, but that's 'cause it can be kinda late."

(Oh shit.)

"How late?" I was pensively sweating this answer.
"We're there about two hours. Sometimes it may last to like 10:00, though. You never know." He casually throws out.
"Wow, that is late for a school night." I said, doing the math.
"Yeah, good thing you don't have to worry about it 'cause you can't do it no way." He laughed in my face then walked off.

I had one thought:

(Got 'im!)

Tuesdays and Thursdays from 7:30 to 10:00 at Saint Stephens Church. Yes, he said two hours, to 9:30, but it was better to account for the longer meetings to put my strategy together. It's a good thing I was going to do this on the down low from the jump because this operation would NOT have been sanctioned. Ma would have probably saved me from all my future troubles by killing me for asking to be out past 10:00 on a school night. Naw, she wasn't going to get behind this one, not a chance. Snowballs had a better chance at surviving a spirited bonfire in hell. Hands down, this had to stay a clandestine mission.

Quietly though, I was really proud of myself for being able to extrapolate every bit of the information I needed with ease. Plans work! It went so smoothly that it made me feel like fate had spoken again. I was supposed to do this thing! Once I understood the logistics I was better able to formulate my stratagem. Time for the next planning phase.

I was screwed! Getting to those meetings was going to be a lot tougher than I thought and my first thoughts were that it would be impossible. It couldn't just be on a casual Saturday afternoon or something, that would be too perfect. No, I had to make a plan to be away from the house for almost 3 hours, on a school night and not get caught by mom or the neighbors! It seemed worse than impossible. How the hell could I do that?

Well, instead of blithely surrendering I decided to break it down one day at a time. I figured if I walked through the situation slowly I might be able to sort it out. Do some math. Work some magic.

So, on Tuesdays… Ma would be home relatively early, maybe 5:00 for the night.

That's done. Tuesdays are out.

Thursday was also… wait a minute: on Thursdays Ma went to choir rehearsals at the church. She took my baby sister, Lori, with her so I'd be at the house…

By. My. Self.

Boom!

The rehearsals were from 7 to 9 and she had to drive about 20 minutes to get there. I thought, 'this could work!'

My little sister was born when I was ten. I was really happy when she showed up, she made me a big brother. I always thought that would be cool. If you take the 'G' and the 'A' off Ma's name then you get my sister, Lori. That's a dope way to name a daughter after her mother, right? Yeah, I think so too. I'm sure Gloria (my mom) was feeling herself for that one.

While it was clear that I may have had an opening, there were still huge kinks in the scheme. She would definitely be gone before 7 so I could be on-time every Thursday and that was awesome. I wasn't looking forward to those push-ups so I was good there. They also really got into their choir rehearsals, I've been there more than a time or two. They took that shit seriously!

And, yo', I know I mentioned that the choir recorded in the studio but there was a reason: my moms could sang! If you're not Black but you have a Black friend ask them about "sangin'", it's just not the same as 'singing'. My mom was such a powerful singer that the choir was converting Gladys Knight songs into gospel tunes because Ma could deliver. Yes, she sang like that! Ma sang lead frequently but she was a microcosmic sample of the entire choir. They were some sangin' people. That was a typical thing to expect in the 'Lou, Black people flexing their extraordinary talents. We were used to having bombastically entertaining shows for little reason at all. It was just a city full of gifted people. My mom and that choir exemplified that.

Here's where the math got extremely hairy for my plans. They got out near 9:00. They 'said' 9:00 but it never started starkly at 7:00 so it never ended on the mark. This was also Ma's social circle so, like all church women I've ever known, she couldn't leave without socializing. She was going to spend a good 20 minutes hacking it up about nothing. Some nights it was longer. Factor in 5 minutes overtime, 20 minutes chatting and 20 minutes driving home and you have 45 minutes. So, she would get home at 9:45-ish. That I could recall, she would arrive more near 10:00. Later is terrific, so if she spent more time in any segment it's gravy. But, if it ever took less time then it would definitely cost me my ass. I had to make sure I stayed in that very slim safe zone. We're talking high level tight rope walking stuff, people.

The dancing group was finished at 9:30 but Nardy said it could take longer. If it ran long I would be in serious trouble so I would just leave early. That's what I thought, anyways. It is just practice, after all. People leave practices early, right? Hell, it was just down the block at Saint Stephens, about a 7 minute run away. I thought if I ran like Sonic the Hedgehog I could beat her home. That might seem farfetched as a thought, because it is. But I knew I would be running as if I were in a jailbreak so it's not too far off of a comparison. With all that risk I still thought I could manage it. Spectacularly, the challenges weren't even exhausted yet.

Our neighborhood was a village. Everybody knew everybody. One mom was all moms and all moms were your mom... and they were all nosey! If you did something wrong and any mom caught you, that mom would kick your butt then send you to your mom for you to get your butt kicked again. Then, at some point, all the moms would talk about what you did and be on the lookout for you doing it again. That's the 'Neighborhood Network', man.

All the moms knew that Ma sang at choir on Thursdays. When you sang like her people knew about it. Ma had also asked a few of them to look out for me because I would be at home alone. So I had a whole tribe of eyes keeping watch on me while she was gone. That sucked. Well, it sucked for me trying to pull off this caper. It was actually cool to belong to a village like that. But that's my more mature perspective, of course. As a kid? Yeah, it just sucked. I knew if I left the house after 7:00, or ran up to the house just before Ma showed up, you 'best believe' they were gonna tell her. Particularly if they saw me running like Jesse Owens, in a flat out panic, to get to the door. That was NOT going to work.

So, I had to leave the house after my mom, sneak to the practice, get out of it in time to beat my mother home AND not let the neighborhood moms see me streaking to and fro like a madman. Yeah, that's a serious collection of challenges. Don't forget that, in my mind, failure of this operation meant death! I always thought Ma was one bad grade away from ending it all for me. She had instilled the 'fear of God' in me, for sure. The James Bond mission I was plotting to undergo would have definitely sent her into a homicidal fury if she caught me. As the great Hip Hop group De La Soul would say, "stakes was high". My room for error was skin-tight.

This situation taught me that if you focus on problems you'll just have problems but if you focus on solutions you create possibilities. I refused to be defeated so I looked for solutions. Fortunately, everything wasn't a negative.

Saint Stephens was, again, just behind my house about five blocks. The alley behind my house could take me directly to it. I figured I would exit from the back of our place and travel through the alley to keep a low profile. That's the only way it could work. The moms in our 'hood would normally sit on their porches and watch the neighborhood breathe but nobody was watching alleys like that. It would also keep me from getting caught on the way back should my mother show up in front while I'm racing to get home. It would be the absolute worst if I was walking up to the door and got caught. Leaving out of the back would also be unexpected because we lived one floor above ground and there was no backdoor. I was certain that could work so it became the plan.

There was one more sizable challenge in that plan: we lived on the second floor of the Peabody's!!! My only option was for me to climb out of and jumped down from the kitchen window. Yeah, it was definitely some Brown Hornet-type shit. I was young, man, the thrill and daring might've been why I was actually willing to pull the trigger. The adventure felt like some comic book shit and I was there for it. I was thinking, "man, I can jump to the street from a window. It's not that big of a deal." Being young is fucking crazy.

Speaking of which, I was still in class pondering my 'Friendly Neighborhood Arachnid' moves and realized I needed visual reconnaissance. I couldn't recollect what the back of our apartment actually looked like. It's not like I hung out back there or something – it's a frickin' alley. Since I had never pondered climbing out of our window before I didn't know if it was possible at all. This was pivotal information!

If there was no way to climb down then I was cooked. That became my self-pact: if there's a way to travel through the back then it had to be done. Once that ultimatum ran through my head I thought, "yeah, that's it! This is pure genius!" The pact was sealed. I almost gave myself a handshake to make it official but that was too damned awkward. I was still in class, after all. Somebody would definitely catch me and start some craziness about me doing weird shit with my imaginary friend or something. Kids' social lives suffered tragic and gruesome ends for much less. That was not about to be me.

At the time of the architecture-epiphany/pact, I had maybe an hour of school left. I was damned near trembling with excitement to see if my self-described 'ingenious' scheme could work. So, of course, it felt like seven hours passed before school was over.

When I arrived at home it was Wednesday evening. Naw, I'm kidding. It was probably less than two hours later but it felt like weeks. I was so amped for the caper! When I got there I walked straight past the front of our building into the back to do my recon.

Directly below our kitchen window was an industrial locker. In retrospect, it looked like a massive circuit breaker box. It was basically the size of a house door, the frame was all brick and it was about 8-10 inches deep. The front of it was a metal door with a huge lock on it.

At the time I wasn't sure what it was I just knew it was sizeable. Also that it was random because it didn't lead to anything: the 'door to nowhere' bricks were different than the rest of the building. That made it really weird. From what I could see, though, it looked like the top of this awkward outdoor closet was just my body length below our kitchen window. What did that mean?

It was on!

CHAPTER 6
LOGISTICS

Thursday came and I was sweating bullets.

Ma had left the house at around 6:45, as usual. I waited in my room so she could tell me bye from the stairwell, as usual. I walked her to the door and she kissed me on the forehead, that was also our usual thing. Then, after closing the door, I stood there with my heart pumping like a locomotive engine at full throttle. That was decidedly not usual.

I may have sounded tough and confident while making my assessments but speculation time was over. The moment had come to put the work in. To defy my mom, my disciplinarian mom, and leave the house late without permission. To slink out of a window and scale a wall in order to hide from 'Woman Watch'. All to go to a function of an organization I didn't know, that I couldn't name and that I wasn't invited to. It was time to put my (lack of) money where my mouth was. I had no idea what I was getting into and all I had seen were some dancers move with African flavor. I didn't even fully understand what I was looking at when I saw them. Was I really about to defy my momma and become a superspy to do it?

You damned right!

After stewing in fear about it, at around 7:10 I said 'fuck it'. I ran to my room and got dressed. My main knowledge of the group is that all the kids performing were the cool guys in school. To my mind that made it a social gathering. Since I didn't want to stand out as a nerd, I rocked the freshest gear I had, which wasn't a lot. That just wasn't my life. Clothing wasn't my focus, being fresh wasn't my focus because women weren't yet my focus. Without being into the ladies there was no purpose for it.

Besides, most of my wardrobe consisted of blue khakis and white button down shirts (Catholic school uniforms) or hand-me-downs from a friend of my mother. She had gone to high school with Ma and was in the church choir. The lady worked at the post office and her son was two years older than me. Everything he outgrew became my new clothes. It was nice stuff and I was happy to get it. But, basically, I was used to getting dressed to play outside, end of story.

So, I wore every item I thought had some appeal. I was wearing about four name brands all told. The fact that I wasn't in matching designers was a 'Black fashion' faux-pas in itself but never mind that. Straight up? I'm not even sure the things I had on were matching at all! My money would be on me having left the house with a half-rainbow outfit, quietly. I'm just gonna keep it real with you. What I do know is I was wearing the best looking pieces I owned. The last thing I could afford was to embarrass myself when I got there. So, my best outfit became my repelling uniform. Nothing like being fresh dressed while doing some stupid shit, right?

I then hustled into the kitchen and went to work. I was definitely in hurry mode. It's amazing how you could be focused on a timed situation with plenty of time to spare and still manage to wait to get going until you make yourself late. Then, of course, you regret it and start bitching at yourself knowing you could have left twenty minutes earlier and you would've easily been punctual. I was mere seconds from that exact status. Perfect. I was mentally preparing for pushups.

Ma kept our house immaculate. More than that, she was meticu-
lous. She believed everything had a place and it should always rest there.
This had been drilled in my head for as long as I can remember. "If you
move something put it back where you found it." That was the household
mantra. Though it was said to me more like, "boy, if you move something
you better put it back where you found it or I'mma put you somewhere
you can't be found." Yeah, it was more like that.

The kitchen, where the food is, was a specific and heightened focus of
this principle. She was unco particular about cleanliness and food. I won't
go into how things were merchandised on the shelves where you could
read every label as if you were in the grocery store but… yeah. She knew
where everything was and could pinpoint any item in the kitchen from any
other room in the house. She had a hatred for hunting for her own stuff.

Let me not tell y'all a lie: my mother never hated anything so she
definitely wouldn't say it. Her heart was too beautiful for hatred, that was
violent to her. She treated the word like a curse word, even. In retrospect, it
may have been her sweet tender heart that made her such a disciplinarian.
It was a way to keep her from being too vulnerable. Ma probably created
her outer shell to keep herself from being compromised. As a child, I
never felt or thought she was vulnerable but I'm sure that was part of the
successful design in how she handled it.

So, no, she wouldn't have said she hated searching for her own stuff
but she loathed it with a passion. She said it was the biggest waste of time
anyone could ever undergo – searching for their own stuff. She made it a
thing to always assign a location for her items.

Ma also had green fingers. She didn't try to plant enough to be
classified as having a 'green thumb' but she nursed a few plants in the
house. If I remember correctly, it was a total of four and they were all
edibles. She was strategic with it: all the plants were herbs that she kept in
the kitchen window. This way they were located where she used them, got

plenty sunlight and helped obscure the view of anyone trying to catch a peek. My mom was serious about systems that made her life easy. I knew and understood those systems because I wanted *my* life to continue.

For that moment, her systems were complicating my life. In order for me to get out of the window I had to clear out the dishwashing liquid, the hand soap, the tray with the scouring pads, the two plants on the sill below the window and the compost juice. I don't know if that's the official name but she would soak eggshells in a jar of water then water the plants with it. I'm gonna call that compost juice. The trick was I had to remember where every one of those things were because you can bet your ass she would remember. There was no way I could rearrange them and not get caught.

So, I carefully placed those items on their respective sides of the sink to put them back when I returned. Since I had to put my feet out the window first to land correctly, I tried to not touch the sink with them at all – that's our sink, man. I checked to ensure that my gym shoes weren't packed with dirt before climbing out but I made a mental note to thoroughly clean the area when I returned. That was super important because 1), again, shoes are nasty and that's where our food goes and 2) she would immediately notice any wonton dirt. The operation was about doing what I wanted to do while not dying, huge emphasis on 'not dying'. I reached behind the two hanging plants in the window to pull the screen out and all that was left was for me to repel to freedom.

(Shit! I'm late as hell and I still gotta run to Saint Stephens. I'm definitely doing pushups, man. Damn it.)

I set the window screen down next to the sink and climbed feet first, between the hanging plants, out the window. With my feet squarely on the 'tomb box' outside, I reached back in the house and grabbed the screen, replaced it, then climbed down. Yeah, that screen had to be in, y'all. In case you don't know, the Midwest is an official sponsor of insects. If there was nothing in our window to protect us, I would've returned home to a whole hive of winged critters having a siesta on the living room ceiling. That would have also meant a funeral for me. I'm sure you've noticed, all bad things lead to my burial. I was focused on keeping that from happening.

Let me reiterate something for the record: my mother loved me. Unequivocally. Despite being deathly afraid of her I never questioned her love. She changed her life for me and valued nothing more highly than me, my little sister and God. She had a fervent faith and a strong relationship with the Lord. But Ma was old school. She didn't take any shit and would dish out plenty when necessary.

I would imagine that dealing with a son alone for my first ten years of life was also part of why she took such a disciplinarian angle. It wasn't anomalous among single moms. No woman wants to be overrun by their sons. She probably thought it was better to keep me in line than to let me cut up then try to get me back into line, y'know?

I've painted a pretty tough picture of Ma so far but I absolutely adored my momma. That's my girl! I attribute my life survival skills in no small portion to her character, leadership and sacrifices. Her strictness played its role, too. She is the foundation I was thankful and proud to have. Me being terrified definitely kept me away from and out of a lot of detrimental things to my life. My fear of her gravely impacted me but she never would have damaged me beyond a spanking. My mother cherished me and I knew that.

But I was a budding man. I innately felt this was my rites of passage test. I couldn't have explained it to you like that then but it's what I felt. And, yeah, I already hear all you know-it-all-ass people talking about, "you ain't about to be no man at 11". I'm going to let you in on a little something… you wrong as hell! The correct way to say that is 'you're wrong as hell' but I said what I said. You wrong as hell. And if you've never been a little man (that's you, ladies) then you can't know what that's like and it's a great time to listen.

Manhood comes for the little man who's ready. Period. That varies from person to person, like all things. If you have a son who's going through things sometime after turning ten, and maybe he seems like he's trying to step outside of his boundaries of childhood, then it's likely because manhood is calling him. It would be good for him, and your relationship with him, if you keep that in mind and dealt with it accordingly. It can be a pivotal time and not only do you want to make sure he traverses it healthily but you don't want to miss it. You certainly don't want to be in the way. He won't return to that child again, provided it goes well and you want it to go well.

As for me, I was ready at eleven and it was time for a test of that readiness. To pass, I had to face my fears.

Facing fears, I jumped from the 'crypt keeper's gate' and hit the ground running like I was in a 40 yard dash – against horses. I was stroking it through the alley. If anybody saw me they would've started running too, I was that panicked. It was going to be my first time at practice, being late sucked. Not to mention I could've been early if I would've... never mind that. I had already mentally beat myself up about it two or three times. At that moment, I was just in a flat out run trying to get there.

Until I started listening. Let me tell you something about St. Louis: it's kinda like a superhero with an alter ego. Naw, to be accurate (and to keep it totally real), I would call it a super villain with a mild side. During the day it appeared, to me, to be a relatively ideal family-raising environment. We were a village: we all knew each other. People were kind, decent and had a visible and seemingly omnipresent moral fabric. Everybody was courteous and would help you however they could. It felt like people just tried to do the right thing, y'know? All the good things of the city were prevalent while the sun was out. I was certain we had a great city to live in and I was proud to be from the 'Lou.

Don't let me wax too poetically, we did have daytime strife. It could get more than a little bit rough sometimes. It was the projects after all. There were some fights, shootings and police activity in the day but they weren't constant. We did have some relatively fluid low-level drama, too. I mean, there are no human habitats where everyone gets along perfectly. That would be utopian.

The Peabody was divided by lanes. Rutgers, Hickory Lane, Webbey, Dawes, etc., and each of them had a football team. This generated a team spirit/fandom/competitive edge milieu that sometimes created hostilities in the neighborhood. So, skirmishes and whatnot did happen. Of course, that wasn't cool.

But what was cool was Ms. Carol Ann might give you $1 to sweep her steps. Ms. Larry or Ms. Belinda would greet you with a smile every time they saw you. Probably ask about your momma. It was definitely cool when Mr. and Mrs. Stewart would hook us up with popsicles on hot summer days. Loved those.

In the exact same breath, though, Ms. Thurman's mean ass could be yelling at you through her screen door, "y'all get off my got damned grass!" She had some kind of health condition that caused her to wear a ventilator that covered her nose. It made her sorta sound like Froggy from the Little Rascals, especially because she was mean as hell. Talking 'bout some, "get off my damned flowers. I hope y'all get stung." She was a mean old hag. "Don't put that ball on my lawn," old raspy chronic smoker with bronchitis sounding... she used to piss us off.

Why? Because she didn't have a damned lawn! Nobody did! She was on the end unit of a building so there was a miniscule patch of grass near her door. It wasn't *her* grass. She didn't take care of it. She was just standing in her screen window sounding creepy like that dragon lady behind the sheer curtains in Golden Child.

Even with that, Ms. Thurman made the neighborhood a neighborhood. It wasn't all gravy but incredibly few things are in real life. I was young so I was inclined to see the good more so than even the visible bad because of my youthfully optimistic perspective. The sometimes apparent stressors weren't on my responsibility level so they didn't register as vividly. Even though the neighborhood had its tests, I loved being there. I had some scares but overall the daytime life was super cool.

When night fell? The veneer of 'all good things' slid down the utility pole and transformed into° some kind of creature with horns. And a vengeance. Gunshots were a nightly occurrence. You could damned near set your clock by them. Sirens often followed or preceded the violent sounds accompanied by screams, shouts and seemingly random collections of expletives. Every blue moon, if I went to the bathroom late, I could hear feet running through the alley behind us or people in muffled conversation. The night life was a completely different persona than the day.

Since I wasn't allowed outside during such hours I would hear the sounds of the city from the muted comfort of my bedroom. Sirens, the random gunshot(s) and street conversations barely dented the backdrop of my home life. Sure, they were there but they were faded and distant. They didn't even register to me as dangers – it was just what happened. The sounds of the city, as it were. I never thought much of it, really.

Until I was out there in it. I quickly found out why I wasn't allowed out during those hours. Suddenly those sounds were MUCH closer. That life was much closer. The danger was breathing-down-my-neck closer. Red-eyed corner boys were scrutinizingly watching me run through the alley. The 'running feet' and 'muffled conversations' from under my window had transformed into pop-eyed dope fiends and gun-toting hustlers brandishing their pistols. The shooting had to come from somewhere, right? It seemed like I could literally feel the concussive bursts from the gunshots that were no longer so distant.

Because I was running, it also felt like the multitude of sirens were coming after me. Hell, I was guilty of an illegitimate escape, my conscience reminded me of it steadily. So my self-incrimination kind of connected me to the police chases, too. I could both hear and feel them and it registered personally. While I was out there it seemed like somebody was always yelling somewhere for something. Worst of all, no matter what I focused on it seemed like someone was always watching me, even when I didn't see anyone.

The villainous city vibe was foreign to me. Some of the people I knew from the daytime would still be outside, sure, but that didn't provide any reprieve from the unknown and unfamiliar elements that slinked through the dark. Being on the block at night was undoubtedly much scarier than hearing the audio of the city from my room. I was out there living it! During this revelation I surprised myself with another gear. I put my head down and pounded the concrete with all the speed I could muster.

I arrived at the lighted grounds of Saint Stephens panting like a thirsty dog. It felt great to be somewhere I recognized as a safe space. I looked around and…

Nothing.

No one was outside. No one was walking around the building or heading in. I didn't hear any sounds from the building. The doors were closed, not flung open like they are on Sundays.

Nothing.

Running up the stairs of the church I was nervous about opening the door. Now, when I say, "running up the stairs," it may sound like it was an illustrious cascading staircase but, dawg, it was like 3 steps. Straight up. My mind was moving so fast, though, it felt like it took ten minutes. In mid-step I thought,

(Fuck it. I'm here now. And I'm definitely not trying to stand outside! Let's go.)

You're probably thinking, "wow, he sure had a lot of 'fuck it' moments". That's because courage can only exist when you're afraid and I was quaking in my shoes. A wise man once told me that all stories of the brave occur on the other side of fear. I was literally embodying that in the moment because I was experiencing multiple levels of fear simultaneously.

Fuck it.

Taking in the scene, it did cross my mind that maybe they didn't have practice today. I mean, there still was no music or anything. I hadn't heard people making noise and stuff, no shouting like I heard at the show. There were still no traces of anybody anywhere around the building. AND... who learns a dance routine in a church? Maybe they weren't there at all. Maybe Nardy lied all the way around. If he did we were going to go from not-quite-tight status to 'beefin'. That would be some bullshit. And I would still find out where they had their rehearsal! I had just broken all kinds of rules, codes and barriers – hell, I overcame major fears: the shit was on another level.

As I reached for the doorknob another kid rounded the corner in a hurry. He was kind of portly so he lumbered towards me and he was winded something terrible. Every step he took looked like he might fall. I smiled at him then grabbed the knob thinking, "I'm late but I'm not alone. At least someone has to do pushups with me". I tried to pull the door open, completely intending to let him go in first. I didn't know where I was going, maybe he did. I would just follow him in.

That didn't work out, either. Turns out that kid was new, too. Otherwise neither of us would have been trying to get in through that door – it was locked and not budging. Ultimately we realized it wasn't in the sanctuary but the community center annex. Duh. We walked to that door and it opened right up.

Saint Stephen's was not the most welcoming church in the world. Actually, it was very dark and foreboding, not because of the lighting but the aura in the place. It felt more like a place people went to die than one that addressed eternal life. There were a lot of ritualistic symbols on the walls, graphic paintings and statues that you swear were rocking Scooby Doo eyes when you walked by. The creepy factor was close to ten, straight up. It gave you the sense that maybe they dealt with eternal life because they were trying to send you there. One stop shop and all, y'know? That would be the most morbid version of 'you don't have to go home but you can't stay here'. Right? Okay, so I may be laying it on thick but this was received through the eyes of an eleven year old. St. Stephens was normally kinda spooky.

But not this trip. I had been to the church a number of times before because of their community events. This time it felt like a safe haven and I was remarkably glad to be in the building. I physically felt my shoulders drop in relief. The other late kid, Drelon, and I had entered into a collection of offices in the building. We walked into a sort of office foyer that wasn't lit at all. Talk about creepy. But once we got through that area it was incredibly well lit. The group area was a vastly different vibe than the rest of the church. I could immediately sense a change. I don't know if it was because there were less pictures of white Jesus or missing ritual symbols or cooler furniture... something felt different. Lighter. Better.

So, Drelon and I rolled into the meeting and it was as if we were wayward out of towners in an old western: the piano stopped playing and everyone stared at us. Except there wasn't any music. Just staring.

Aw shit.

CHAPTER 7

WORTH THE SQUEEZE

There was so much going on in the meeting room and in my head…
I'll try to share my inner thoughts as we move through things.

The room was filled with teenage young men and four adult leaders,
two men and two women. The kids ranged from fourth, maybe fifth graders to high school seniors. They appeared to be in formations of separate
age groups. The most senior formation was closest to us, which happened
to be nearest to the door. All the young guys were standing at what looked
like some form of military attention. The man in front of everyone gestured
for us to stay where we were.

(Aw man, don't tell me we're in trouble already. Why I have to be
late, man…)

There was a tension in the air: it was sharp and attentive, I would
describe it as discipline but it was more than that. This presence gripped
me as a focus and a unity – like everyone there would move together for
any purpose. Like they were tied together by an invisible string. It was
as if they were, simply, one. I felt empowered by it, drawn into it and

94

immediately liked it. It hit me the same way that seeing them on stage did. It felt... bigger than me. And I wanted that.

Mind you, 'everyone staring at us' just meant the adults. The young guys in formation never flinched. I watched for a minute, even, and they seemed downright statuesque. It was simultaneously intimidating and cool. It hit me like a group version of 'I wish a mutha fucka would'.

(Dang. What in the hell is that all about? Do they even blink? How long do they stand like...)

"Kuligea!" The man standing in the front of the room shouted.

I visibly shook. Hell, it caught me off-guard. I promise you would've done the same thing in the same spot.

(What the...?! Scared the crap outta... hey, I remember him. He was at the talent show!)

All of the kids relaxed from their positions of attention. They didn't make any noise or anything they just stopped standing so rigidly and intensely. I'm sure it was a command of some sort. The man who shouted the command nodded to the man standing in the very rear of the room. That man was incredibly mysterious as he stood against the back wall. It felt like he was either watching us or watching over us, I wasn't sure which one. His arms were folded and he looked really grim. It would have been easy to misread him and say he was angry but I'm sure it wasn't that. He was serious. Locked in. It definitely made him a loadstone. It was easy to surmise, though, that the two men were the leaders.

(Are they the Africans? I mean, whatever he said was something I didn't understand... gotta be African.)

They looked at each other with a smirk and I was certain the worst was coming:

(Dang. Pushup time.)

The guy in front of us then looked directly at us and began with a booming voice.

> "Good evening, young brothers. My name is Mwalimu. These ladies are Mama Amina and Mama Mlinzi. Behind you is Brother Omni."

FULL DISCLOSURE: I have created an alias for the gentleman whom we are going to call 'Omni', which is my slang for ominous. It's safer for me this way, real talk. End of note.

> Mwalimu continues, "welcome to the Kowrie Group. We're glad to see you here."

(See? African! Wait, what did he say this was? Welcome to what...?)

> "This organization exists as a rites of passage for young brothers such as yourselves to become men." He continued, "only you can decide if this test is for you. I promise you, though, that there will be tests. And if you pass our tests you'll be certain of your manhood."

I'm sure my face screamed bewilderment. I ain't know where he was coming from. I was here for the dancing and stuff. What Mwalimu was saying seemed, frankly, much deeper than that. I snuck a peek to the side at Drelon but he seemed incredibly comfortable. Maybe it was just that he was much more comfortable than me.

"Talk to us brothers. Tell us why you're here."

(Oh shoot! I wasn't prepared to do any talking. What do I say...?)

Neither of us said a word. He likely saw cluelessness on our faces, it was surely on mine. So, he tried to help us out a bit.

"Why don't we start with your names. What's your name, young brother?" Mwalimu said.

He looked me directly in the eye. His stare was unwavering.

(Why I gotta be first?)

"Um, I'm Busara Dizzy, sir," I said as if I weren't sure it was my name.
"The respect is noted and appreciated. Why are you here?"

(What kind of stuff is that to ask me? I'm here to do that dope ass dancing stuff y'all did at the... well, I can't say nothing dumb. 'Rites of passage' sounds serious so...)

"I'm here to find myself." I leaked out.

But I delivered it like it was profound and as if I was… confident. It likely just came off wooden or contrived. It was both.

Mwalimu and Omni caught each other's eyes and had a nice laugh. They enjoyed it so much that the whole room was lighter for a moment. It shifted the energy a little bit.

"What you mean?" Mwalimu said, trying to gather himself. "I found you, you're right there."

They chuckled for a minute while I stood in silence, looking for words.

"There's… something about my people… that I wanna know. I feel like… like, I don't know, maybe y'all can help me with that."

Omni stopped laughing immediately. He cocked his head as if to say, "I'll be damned." Mwalimu abruptly ended his laughter, too. Then he sorta hummed to himself a quick, "hm".

"Alright, young brother Busara. I can tell you now, though, all your answers are inside you. We *can* help you with a library of information and true history you don't yet know. How you interpret that is about what you're made of."

He took a brief pause looking at me then said,

"…but we can help you build your sense of discernment through an empowered strong Black lens, too. It's why we're here." He cupped his chin with one hand briefly then used that same hand to point at me and said, "I think you're in the right place."

He nodded to me. I smiled then caught Nardy looking. I gave him the quick 'up-nod', as if to say, "see, mutha fucka?"

Mwalimu turned his attention to Drelon.

"How about you, young sir? What's your name?" He was smiling as he asked.

"Oh, I'm Drelon Buck... um, sir. I'm glad to be here." Drelon tried to say confidently.

"We're also glad that you're here, Drelon Buck. Why are you here, what brings you to us?" Mwalimu said.

"I'm, uh... I'm here... here to find myself." Drelon stammered as he said it.

Mwalimu and Omni cracked up laughing. This time was much more loudly than when I said it. A few of the other guys in the room chuckled, too.

(He said the same thing I said. That is kinda funny but I ain't laughing. I'll probably get in some kind of trouble.)

"It appears they really need to teach land navigation in school these days," he squeezed out between snickers. "Lot of kids getting lost when they shouldn't be." Mwalimu said.

My guess is that both of us felt a bit sheepish, I know I did. But it wasn't because they were making fun of us – it didn't feel like that. It just happened to be one of those icebreaking moments that wasn't exactly smooth. That said, I actually felt encouraged. I could tell that, in a sense, he regarded me exactly the way I felt in going to that meeting – like I belonged there. It was a confirmation for me that I took a good risk. Rather, I took several extreme risks that were worth it.

"We don't wear hats indoors, young brother. Make sure you remove that." He said firmly.
"Oh, uh, yes sir."

(Here ten minutes and I'm in trouble already. Shoot. Awesome, Busara. Minutes... what time is it?)

I quickly ripped the hat off my head and held it in my hand as I put my arm down. He smiled to make the welcome official. I was thinking about Ma catching me.

"However you young brothers landed here with us, it's a good thing. We are truly glad to have you."
His smile converts to a grimace.
"There are more than a few things for you to learn and it's our responsibility to get you up to speed. For a man, responsibility can *only* be taken seriously. First, you will be punctual. A man honors himself by being punctual. He disrespects everyone when he isn't. That's your responsibility. It is not an option."

(Aw shoot. Here we go.)

"We begin the second the clock strikes 7:30 and not one second sooner or later. Should you arrive late you will have 3 pushups for every minute past 7:30. Any increment of seconds beyond the minute counts as a new minute."

(Okay. See? If I woulda left *the minute* she walked out the door…)

He continues, "we won't hit you with that today. We can't expect you to have known that rule so we can't hold you responsible for it. Now you know. This is your only pass."

(Whew! So I'm not in trouble…)

"Second, we *only* support our people and the African diaspora. No other brands are welcome here."

(Wait, what?…)

"You will remove any white corporate insignias before coming here or turn them inside out. Any logo that is still visible will cost you pushups or you'll attend the rest of the meeting shirtless – your choice. That includes your jeans. If your Levi's or Vidal Sassoon's show their brands then untuck your shirt and cover it. We don't accept or promote European propaganda or programming here." He said with disdain. "None. That's a rule we won't wave, not even on your first visit. The salvation of our people lies in how we support ourselves."

(Aw man, I wore the wrong damn shirt… I put on my freshest stuff for nothin'. I bet I'll get it dirty getting back in the window, too. Damn it!)

(I really hope Ma doesn't catch me when I... what time is it? Oh, 7:47. I'm okay.)

"Young brother?" He said staring at me. I snapped out of thought.
"Huh?" I said once I awoke.
"Fix yourself." His words grabbed me with finality.
"Oh. Okay."
"We'll wait." He said with great patience and sarcasm at the same time.

(I better hurry up. I'm not getting in trouble my first day. Nope. No, I'm not.)

Literally, the whole room did nothing until we, Drelon and I, finished. I peeked around a bit while I adjusted and there were no eyes on me. They didn't stare at me, I didn't get ridiculed, no dirty looks, none of that. No one did anything extra. They all patiently waited until I tightened up my look. I was actually wearing a Cardinals hat: I don't even like hats! It was the only one I owned. But it was the 'Lou, I was trying to be fresh and everybody wore 'Lou hats. I sat the hat in my chair, flipped my shirt inside out and I was good.

Next to me, Drelon had just turned his Nike shirt inside out. Unfortunately for him it didn't make a difference. It was embroidered so the logo was plainly visible. Since he was a bit sizable I guess he didn't want to walk around shirtless. So he survived 15 pushups but it was a close call. By the time he was done I thought we might need the paramedics. He probably needed to eat one less burger per meal or something. Dude was trippin'.

"ANGULIA!" Shouted Mwalimu.

Everyone snapped back to attention. I imitated the guys as best I could.

(Hope I don't look too crazy. When do we start dancing?)

"We have an event this weekend. We want to make the best possible impact we can, of course."

(Aw this is dope! I'll be with them for a performance this weekend. Get right in and get busy. This is perfect!!!)

Mwalimu continues, "Brother Omni is going to go over the weekend assignments."

(Assignments? For dancing?)

Omni moved out of his perch from the back and started walking forward.

(Dawg, he look like the grim reaper walking up to tell us how many of us won't make it through the night. Dude is scary.)

As Omni arrived at the front, Mwalimu stepped to the side and Omni moved to the center. This brother looked like the muscles in his face were completely incapable of, and entirely disinterested in, forming a smile. Ever. His head stayed on a swivel and his eyes were never still: he scanned the room constantly. There was an intensity about this man that just seemed… dangerous. An aura of seriousness hovered around Omni, you could just sense he was not to be trifled with.

(This dude seems like the real dea…)

"We have a Progressive Emporium booth this Saturday at the African Arts Festival located at the Forest Park Community Center in the Multipurpose Room. Our presence is requested at 1000 hours so we will be there at 0930 hours." He was all business.

"Victor and Charles, you have been selected for the security overview. Victor, you are the lead. All assessments will be made and reported by 0900 Saturday. Wee Jock, you have been selected to lead Nate and Winston in the sweep."

(…uh, what kind of dancing… this don't sound like…)

"Hapa!" Victor yells out.

(What?! What the hell was that? Did he just call that dude his fath…)

"Yebo!" Omni aggressively shouted back.

(Uh oh…)

Straight up? That shocked the shit out of me. Again. I had no idea what was happening. Both comments were loud and aggressive, I thought they were beefin' or something. And, it was completely random to me so it made no sense at all. I was lost. I'm sure my eyes told all my business.

Victor was standing straight up, arms folded in a particular way and his feet at a 45 degree angle just before he spoke. All of the kids stood this way. He had stepped forward and put his right arm at a right angle with his fist up to the sky. His left arm was parallel to the ground with his fist at his right elbow. It sorta looked like the Ultraman move where he shot the beam out of his hand except Ultraman's hand was open, Vick's was in a tight fist. I only noticed all of this once he spoke again.

> "Appreciating what's been said, if I understand everything correctly, I am leading Charles in the security assessment for the Multipurpose Room in the Forest Park Community Center at 0830 hours for a 0900 hours report this Saturday." Vick looked as serious as AIDS while he said it.

Omni responded with a slight nod,

> "Yebo. That is precisely correct."

(So "yaydo" means... yes?)

> "Hapa!" Wee Jock then randomly shouts.

Wee Jock was closer to me so it shocked me even more. I almost jumped up and said something. So glad I didn't.

(Man, these bastards gone give me a heart attack!)

> "Yebo!" Omni responds again.

(Oh! He's saying yay-bo! Okay, I got it. That's definitely yes. Or something like that. I can learn this.)

"Appreciating what's been said, if I understand everything correctly, I'm leading Nardy and Winston in the sweep after the African Arts Festival booth event this Saturday."

(He's gonna say…)

"Yebo." Says Omni. "Your responsibilities are clear."

(Man, I'm all over this! I could do this forev… what time is it… 7:58. Another hour or so before she's done).

"I'm gonna hand y'all back to kadamu Mwalimu."

Omni, without ever smiling or loosening, heads directly back to the rear of the room. His eyes busy as ever, carefully scrutinizing everything that meets his vision.

Mwalimu returns to the front.

"One more item: D Smooth, you will lead the Kobe class today. Make sure our new young brothers learn the process."

"Hapa!" D Smooth shouts out.

(Man, that dude was loud. I sorta expected it and I was still a little thrown. They 'gone make my nerves bad… now I sound like my momma.)

"Yebo!" Mwalimu responds.

"Appreciating what's been said, if I understand everything correctly I'm leading the Kobe group in the lesson today." D Smooth firmly states.

"Yebo. It's time for you to take this next step. Make sure they know what they need to know."

(This is intense but we gotta get this practice in. I'm runnin' out of...)

"Let's get prepared for our lesson today." Mwalimu continued to everyone.

(Right on time. Yeah boy! Let's do this!)

"Kuligea", Mwalimu shouts.

(Oh shit! What are they doin'? What do I do?!)

I began looking around in a quiet panic.

(...and what did he say that time? I didn't catch it.)

All of the guys around me spread their feet about shoulder width apart and relaxed. They may have shifted in their stance a bit but they all stayed in formation. No one spoke but they appeared to loosen their tension a bit. They looked around, some bent their knees a little and it felt like a collective exhale.

I took this quick minute to look for Nardy. When I found his eyes he was already staring at me like, "what you doing here?" I gave him that quick measuring look (you know, when you look down at someone's legs then quickly scroll up to their eyes then cock your head ever-so-slightly to the side), "whatever I want, mutha fucka!" And he bet'not (as in, 'better not') come at me with some bullshit. Not having it.

(What time is it? 8:09... she'll be home in less than two hours.)

I was not mentally prepared for what happened next. Mwalimu had us sit in a circle of chairs to do a breathing exercise. He gave us some instructions before doing it but I didn't get them. I will still spacing out, trying to take it all in. So, I was sitting there... breathing.

(...this is deep. Like, who concentrates like this to dance? I know he said something about try not to think what you're about to do next but... I don't exactly know what we're going to do next! So how do you do that? And what am I supposed to be thinking about instead... pink elephants? Yeah, it's just like that, like somebody telling you not to think of pink elephants. That's crazy. I mean, why *would* you think of pink elephants anyways? Elephants ain't pink! And why would you try not to think of them? My first thought is: who the hell made the elephants pink? They don't come in no damned pink, they're not born... man, I'm trippin'. Damn some pink elephants. That's funny, though. I bet they would look wrong as hell... how long are we gonna do this? I don't have all night and I need to get to these moves and...)

"Angulia!" Mwalimu shouts.

Everybody jumps up and quickly, crisply returns to the open space to form the ranks again. Drelon and I are both look at each other like, 'I don't know what the fuck I'm doing.' We didn't.

"Alright, it's time to go into group and execute the plan for today. KWISHI!"

STOMP!

The fully carpeted room couldn't mute the forceful thump the group made in unison. The young guys all stomped their feet once then raised their folded arms like a martial arts block. They did a 180 spin and walked out of their formations. All the groups then proceeded to separate offices.

(We going to another room to do stuff? It's cool, this didn't look like it had enough room for dancing anyways. What time is... oh, 8:11. I thought it was a lot later. Cool. Cool.)

For some reason I kept my eye on D Smooth. When he was given his 'assignment' he looked over to us so I thought we were going to roll with him. My instincts were on the money. He left what I would call the senior formation and went to the group furthest from us. It was about six kids near my age. Even though I hadn't asked him, I assumed Drelon was around my age, too. D Smooth had all of the junior kids follow him as he walked over to us.

"What's up, y'all? I'm D Smooth." He said.
We both replied, "'sup?"
"Hey man, that was a cool answer. Deep. It was definitely better than mine." He said to me.

"Thanks, man." I was just hoping he didn't ask me any questions about it. "Listen, I have to be home before 10:00, so, I may have to leave early to make sure I make it."
He laughed.
"There's a ceremony we have to do to be released. We get out of here officially at 9:30. You should be fine."

He continued with a light laugh. He wasn't laughing at me but he was tickled by my boldness, I think. I liked him straight out.

"I got a lot to show y'all, so let's go." D Smooth said.

Our crew of about ten rolled to a room not far down the hallway. We cut the lights on upon walking in and he started directing us on what to do.

He showed us the ritual of how to start a meeting. It was a lot to learn. There were terms that we had to know, positions to take, how to fall in and out of formation, and, how to ask for permission from the elders to speak. I thought that was super radical: we had to ask to speak! That's what they were doing at the beginning, I just didn't get it.

All of the processes were steeped in African tradition, culture and languages. Which meant, that in order to have full participation with the group I would have to learn African languages. I was gobsmacked! Before the Kobe session it just hadn't occurred to me that I was going to be learning a new language. I had heard some things they had said and I was trying to figure it out. But up until that moment it just hadn't really sunk in that learning them would be part of the program. The bulk of the exercises, facing movements and communications were in either Kiswahili or Zulu. Wow! I got really excited about being bi-lingual. Actually, learning the both of them would make me multilingual. Even cooler.

The more he talked to us and educated us on the basics, the more I understood what I didn't understand. This was a group built on honor, dignity and self-respect. It was militant in nature and, thusly, paranoid in its processes. It scrutinized everything and everyone until things were verified as safe and secure. He didn't explain all of the reasons for it but it was all connected to our plight in America as Black people, Black men in particular. And, even bigger than that, our standing as African descendants around the world. This organization was about standing up for our people and steering our plight to a greater future through empowering our youth.

I was more convinced about my risky choices by the way this new information made me feel. It charged me in a way I hadn't previously fathomed. Something was calling me to join, maybe it was our ancestors. My ancestors. I still wasn't entirely sure of what pulled me in but I was glad as hell that I had listened.

(This is dope, man! I never heard of this stuff and its fresh. We haven't even started dancing and I'm already... what time is it?!)

KNOCK! KNOCK! KNOCK!

(long pause)

KNOCK! KNOCK!

Someone beat out the coded knock at the door then kept walking. D Smooth immediately responded.

"Alright, that's it for us tonight," D Smooth said.
"It's time to get back to the kadamu so we can close out."

"Can I just bounce?" I threw out. "I really gotta get home. I can't leave here late".

D Smooth laughed to himself, respectfully.

"It's good, little brother. The kadamu is big on being punctual, we leave on time every night."

"I really can't be late," I insisted.

He paused in thought then said, "Listen, they normally call everybody back after the first group returns."

"That's what that knock was, right?" I asked.

"That's right." D Smooth answered. "So, whenever I lead a group I'll leave a bit early so they call everybody back. Once we do the closeout ritual you'll be good. How about that, little brother?"

That struck every right chord with me. On the low, I always wanted a bigger brother. I was an only kid for ten years, having an older brother was like a wish list item for me. And there he was, committing to look out for me 'just because'. He didn't even know I would get murdered if I got caught. I only told him I was pressed and he tried to handle it for me. That's dope.

(That's one cool dude, right there. If we got tight that would be awesome.)

"That's cool, man. Thanks bruh." I said.

"It's good, I got you." He said with a smile.

We started walking out of the room to head down the hallway. I was walking next to him.

"Hey, what was your name again?" I asked.

"D Smooth. And you're Busara, right?"

"Right!" I was trippin' that he remembered my name. I continued, "so, what does "kuhdoomu" mean? I heard the scary dude say it about the leader guy. What does that mean?"

He laughed out loud.

"Omni is kinda scary, for real." He was still laughing, "but 'kadamu' means leader or leadership. So that's a great catch. I didn't get any of that for the first bunch of meetings. I was swimming in the language. But you're all over it."

I started smiling, proud than a mug (prouder than a mother fucker – without the cursing).

"I was made for this, man."

We both laughed.

He said, "you know that's corny, right?"

We got into formation like D Smooth showed us. Then the kadamu, Mwalimu, handed Drelon and I some papers. He told us to take them home, have our parents fill them out and return with them next week. We all know that wasn't going to happen. So, I took the paper and simply said, 'yes, sir'. Fortunately, he accepted that and he moved on.

Mwalimu then chose one of the young guys from the senior group to lead us out. D Smooth basically showed us how to begin and end meetings so we wouldn't be lost. Being in formation felt like a privilege. I was fired up, it felt like I had arrived or something. The formation represented, like, a world-changing unified movement and I was in it. I was a part of something. Hell yeah!

The closing was a powerful call and response that made me feel like a superhero for participating in it. I yelled my confident parts at the top of my lungs. Craziest part? It didn't even make me a standout. Everybody was using their 'big man voices' so I fit right in. I don't think I had ever been anywhere where cutting loose like that was even allowed. It was encouraged in the 'Group meetings! I'm telling y'all, I knew right away, I could live like this!

But I couldn't live long if I didn't get the hell out of there. The moment Mwalimu said "Kwishi" again I made a brisk walk for the exit. As I was walking away D Smooth yelled out for me.

"See you next week, Busara." He said.

I threw my hand up, made a beeline for the door, grabbed my StL hat off the bench and headed out.

The clock read 9:31.

CHAPTER 8

THE RETURN

"huh… huh… huh… huh… huh… huh… huh…huh… huh…"

(She's gonna kill me, I'm gonna die, she's gonna kill me, I'm gonna die, she's gonna kill me, I'm gonna die…)

Man, I was all 'ass and elbows', expending everything I had in the tank to get to the house as fast as possible. Now, it might seem as if I were unduly terrorizing myself with that steady drubbing of morbid extremes running through my head. I assure you I wasn't. These fears playing on repeat in my head weren't exactly as redundant as they sounded, either. I was caught in a dual-dilemma, both of which were dire. Yes, if I got home after Ma got there she was going to kill me and I would, of course, die. But when all the terror in my body was screaming 'I'm gonna die' it wasn't referring to her: that was about not making it home at all.

(tick-tick, tick-tick, tick-tick…)

It was rapidly approaching 10:00 at night! I wasn't wearing a watch but the pressure felt like the minutes were counting off in pairs. Meanwhile, I couldn't escape the bone chilling fear of being a dead man running because the streets were downright apocalyptic! Drug zombies, corner boys, stick up kids and the homeless were crawling all over the streets. Sirens went off constantly just like the gunshots, so ambulances were blaring through the night right along with the cops. It felt like everything was focused on me because I didn't belong there. I was breaking all the rules by being on the streets that late and I could feel it. That reality was a true motivating factor for my insanely harried pace.

The streets were bustling with activity, it felt like it was… crowded. It wasn't but I felt like it. Paranoia had set in and it seemed like I didn't have enough room to run in the empty alley. So, I ran dead in the middle of it to make sure I'd have an extra second of response time if something or someone creepy jumped out from the walls. I'm telling you, I was running for my life. Literally!

Because the alley was relatively empty, my own steps were scaring the hell out of me! Every time my footsteps hit the ground they echoed off the concrete then that sound bounced off the walls. Of course, those echoes rang out seconds after my actual steps so they sounded like someone else's. The faster my steps the more the echoes ran together. Add my half-hyperventilating breaths to the reverberation and you damned near have a gang chase going on. It sounded like a whole crew was running me down, determined to catch me. I promise you, I turned around about 18 times with my fist in the air like I was going to punch somebody. I wasn't going out without a fight! Gladly, there was no fight to be had. It was just me, trippin'. Scared as hell.

What made it declaratively worse is that I was clearly cognizant that my maximum effort had an immutable diminishing return: every step I took I would still arrive later than the last step. And with each gadarene move the streets seemed fuller, louder, busier and scarier.

Deadlier.

AND, don't forget, I was running out of the frying pan into the fire! If my mom was at the house when I arrived it was curtains for me. Yeah,

I was so terrorized that I've resorted to white people slang to describe my death. Fucking curtains, man! I didn't know how gruesome her vengeance for my sneaking out would be but… gruesome, for sure. I mean, she didn't whip me often but, believe me, the frequency was irrelevant. Every one of those corporal punishment experiences was a definitive dissuader for the next. I just wasn't trying to be in that space ever again. And this offense? This would easily be the worst violation I had ever committed. The stark fright I had of her fury defined the level of bravery for my defiant excursion of the evening but was now hitting home with grave seriousness.

Grave. Seriousness.

Despite all my fearful anxiety, and my impending probable doom with my mother, I couldn't get the meeting out of my head.

(What was that? Man, it was so dope! What language was I learning? I got a few of the words, though - "yay-bo", "kuhdamoo"… I think I just adopted a big brother. That's crazy! I always wanted a big brother. Drelon was straight, that scary guy was… scary but even that was dope. I connected with the lead dude, too. "Wahleemoo"…? I think that was it. Yeah, the Wally-moo guy. He knew I belonged there.)

(I'm made for that.)

A satisfying smile flashed across my face. Then it was again stretched with extreme trepidation as I heard a bottle shatter on the ground nearby. I about broke my hip trying to hit another gear and hightail it out of there to get home. Our house was five blocks from St. Stephens. It felt like I had taken a trip to Calgary and was doing an Olympic long distance trial route to my house. No matter how fast I ran I didn't feel like the house was getting any closer.

(...tick-tick, tick-tick, tick-tick...)

At least, not until my eyes were filled with our apartment complex. I locked in on the 'Door of Doom' then looked just above it and saw the light on in our kitchen. I lost my breath mid-step and stopped running. I stopped so abruptly that if you were around you would've sworn my shoes made an audible noise like tires screeching on concrete.

I stood staring at the window.

(Mutha fucka! I *AM* gonna die! I don't even get to kick it with the Organization again before I get murdered. What the hell made me think I could get away with it? Man, I'm dead. Just dead. That last whipping... man... naw. Hell naw, I'm not taking no more beatings, man. Nope. I'm tired of that. I'm just not doing it... nope. I ain't going home. That's it. I'm running away. I'm leavin'. I'm just gone leave right no...)

As I turned to run away it hit me...

(Dumb ass! You never cut the light off. How could you... from outside?! Get yo' ass...)

Then I was off. I darted the last dozen of yards or so until I got to 'Hell's Gate' (I've called that box something different every time. It was probably an industrial fuse box or something but who cares, right?) That's when it was, again, clear that I was fucked. The glaring hole in my plan became evident.

I couldn't reach the top of the 'Door to Nowhere'. I wasn't exactly the tallest 11 year old in the neighborhood. That was also when I realized it was a shard higher than a normal door. It was just tall enough to be out of my reach. I tried to kind of scale the sides, hell, I tried to use the knob to get up but neither worked. I jumped to grab the ledge – and I grabbed it! Sorta. It was a fingertip hold without any leverage to help me up, so that was a fail, too. None of that worked. It's surprising my ankles made it through all of that in one piece. Probably should have twisted or sprained one of them a couple times.

(tick-tick, tick-tick, tick-tick…)

In my original reconnaissance mission, I only concentrated on getting out of the house. I didn't calculate how to get back in. Seriously, who thinks about how to *break in* to a jail? My home wasn't a jail but you know what I'm saying. I only focused on leaving it. My logic was that if I could get down then getting back up should be relatively the same test. Obviously, I hadn't thought that through too well. I needed help.

(If somebody could give me a boost… man, I can't ask any of these people out here, though. Nope. That's out. And crazy… shit!)

(Hmm…)

(I don't have a ladder, there's… none… laying around.)

I looked around half hoping for a miracle. Naw, I was totally searching for the impossible. I will easily admit, it wasn't the cleanest neighborhood, no doubt, but no big ass ladders were going to just randomly be 'found' outside, either. It was never that level of nasty. And ladders are useful: the dope fiends would've sold them to someone for a few bucks so that they could score. There was no chance of finding something valuable like that just lying around. Damn it.

(Rope? No. Trampoline? No. Jetpack? No. Hell no! I'm tripping hard... I gotta get up there and now! Can I stack some bric... YES! That'll work.)

I looked around for a few bricks and ran into a milk crate in some high grass. As I reached down to grab it I saw another one not far away. Our alley wasn't junky enough for a ladder but some useful junk could be found.

(Oh yeah, I'm in business. Let's go!)

I stacked the two crates next to the 'Unknown Portal', made a few moves, climbed up to the window, crawled through and...

(OH SHIT! Somebody is in the living room! I see... that... its... aw man, that's just the curtain moving. Why would the curtain... because I just came in the window. Probably the wind from... yeah, it's me. WHOO! Let me check...)

I did a panicked sweep of the house and found it empty. Peeking out the front window, there was no sign of her car. It wasn't parked outside so she hadn't made it back.

(I'M IN THE CLEAR!!!)

But I knew I wouldn't have much longer. So, I rushed back in the kitchen and carefully set everything back in the spaces they belonged. As I started wiping off the counter I heard a car out front. I figured it was Ma but I was almost done so it was cool. I was doing last checks.

(Soap dish, dishwashing liquid, scouring pad tray and compost juice. All good. The plants are all there. One last wipe of the counter. Bam!)

(Whew!)

Real talk, from the acceleration of my heartbeat alone, I had probably done enough cardio, in just that one night, to last me until I was 45. I wrapped up real fast and turned to leave the kitchen.

Ma walked through the door with my baby sister in her arms. I met them in the living room.

> "Hey, Man!" She seemed sorta surprised to see me.
> "Hey Ma." I did everything I could to seem calm. I had just noticed that I was still breathing heavy and tried to calm it before she...
> "Why you breathing so heavy, Busara? You alright?"
> Had to be quick. Shit.
> "And why are you still up and bumpin' about?" She added.
> "I was excited about a show and... uh... ran down there, I mean down here... to the kitchen... to... get some water."

I turned to show her the sink as if she didn't know where the water would come from. She started walking towards the kitchen.

> "Did you leave dishes in my sink?" She said in a scolding tone.
> "No ma'am. I took care of it."
> She arrived at the sink.

"Well, that explains why you all wet. You look like you're sweating. And you didn't take care of my counter, either. The whole thing is wet. Were you and the entire counter thirsty?"

Told y'all, she doesn't miss a note.

"Um, no ma'am. I, um, turned the water up high and spilled a little. So I just decided to wipe everything off because I was there."

(That was easy. AND I accounted for the sweat. Didn't even plan that one. Nice.)

"You spilled how much water, Busara?" Ma asked expectantly.
"Nah, it wasn't a lot. 'Spilled' is over stating it. It splashed and instead of wiping up my drops I wiped it all. Like you do. I... I just didn't wanna leave a mess."
She analyzed me a second before speaking.
"Well thank you, baby. That's my son."
She gave me a kiss on my forehead.
"Yes, I am."
I turned to leave.
"Busara?" she said.

(Aw man, what did I miss?)

"Yes ma'am?" I responded.
"Baby, why is your shirt inside out?"

(Details, man. Details. I better have a reason... use the truth!)

"Oh, I watched something that got me thinking. I'm not supporting anything or anybody that's not my people." I pitched my gamble.

"That's not what you were wearing when I left, why did you change?"

Misses nothing. Not a note.

"Um, that was the program. They, uh, had us put it on to see... if it felt different than regular stuff. It doesn't. And I don't need it."

(That boy good!)

"Well... that's good baby. That helps me save my money. Just don't be running around here in your good clothes for nothing." She paused a moment.

"You smell like outside in them right now. Make sure you putting deodorant on in the mornings, Man."

"I do, Ma." I felt confident, "that's just manhood talking."

"Well, I need your manhood to be more quiet."

(I think I may survive this without a scratch! Crazy! Be cool, Busara. Be cool, be cool...)

"Right now you better get your 'manhood' butt upstairs and 'watch' your eyelids. You need to be in bed, Busara. It's late, Thirteen."

"Yes, ma'am."

(Always using my words against me. The double-dip this time, too. She be trippin'.)

It appears she was in a really good mood. She rarely called me the family nickname. Whatever it was it meant I could live another day.

"Uh, Busara?" She did not sound happy.

(What now?)

"Yes, ma'am?" I said innocently.
"Um, what is that in your back pocket?"

(Back pocket? What IS in my back pocket?")

I reached back and pulled out a folded sheet of paper. I unfolded it and saw it was the application from the organization. Forgot all about it.

(Um…)

"It's an application for a, uh, club. At school." I offered.
"Oh, you ain't joining no darned clubs, Busara. I don't have the money for all that." She turned to walk away as she said it.
"It's not about money, Ma." I bargained. "they're about Black awareness, unity and empowerment. It even has roots in Africa and African traditions. It's a really good program, Ma."

(I wanted to test the waters. We were there anyways, might as well. Right? I mean, what could it hurt?)

"It's always about money, baby. The world runs on it. If you trying to do something with a bunch of people it's going to always need money. And I don't have it." She continued her rapid fire, "and you don't need some group to tell you you're Black. I got a lot of mirrors in this house. Look in one, you'll be aware that your Black. Looking at you from here, I can tell you that." She moved closer and touched my face.
"You're Black, Man. Now you're aware."

I knew that was coming and I wasn't sweating it. But I knew if I didn't fight for the idea it would probably come off as suspicious and my mom could smell suspicious. So I figured it was best to be normal. So, the next things I did were normal for me, too.

"I thought that's what you might say. That's why I forgot it was even in my pocket." I said this next piece carefully, it had to be delivered right.
"I do wanna do things sometimes though, Ma."
"Well, the thing you can do right now is what I told you. Go'on to bed now, Busara." She said almost coldly. Then she regrouped.
"Maybe we'll talk about it tomorrow. Okay?"

(What?)

"Yes ma'am." I said with less hope than that response warranted. "I love you, Ma."

125

"I love you too, baby." She said as she kissed me good night.

"Good night, Man."

"Good night, Ma."

Saying she shocked me is a gross understatement. My guess is something unpredictably fortunate had happened at rehearsal. Nothing can lift your spirits like positive surprises, right? I don't know what it was but she was in an extremely good mood if she was even pondering permission to let me join something. Organizations, clubs, teams, functions... they got "no's". Period. That she sounded like she would waiver at all was a huge deal.

My guess was that the mood would pass. That was my hope because I had lied: it was not a school group. My response was off the cuff, I wasn't planned for a follow up. If she asked any more questions at all then I would've been in bad shape. That was one time I wasn't worried, though. I knew if I didn't bring it up again she wouldn't either. I was counting on it.

When I made it to my room, I took inventory while sitting in disbelief. Checked my arms, legs, hands and my neck; they were all still intact. No bruises on my ass, no aches from my ego... I made it! I was good. I did that shit! I braved all the things that made me feel caged, defied them and joined an amazing group. So amazing, in fact, that I didn't have any qualms with not learning any dance moves. That's funny: nobody mentioned the dancing at all.

I pondered that for a minute. It was a little surprising that I wasn't at all disappointed about the dancing, but I wasn't. Not at all. While it was the thing that drew my attention, I was awed by the entire organization. It was their visible connection, the confidence in their movements and the... the "us"-ness, the Africanism that pulled me in. That's what got me hooked.

The meeting confirmed what my instincts had surmised in the first few minutes of seeing them on stage that day: something was there for me. Incredibly important things were happening with those brothers. I could tell, I had a sense - this was something big. I couldn't explain it because I didn't understand it all but that's okay. It was going to become clear in due time, that was my thought. As long as I kept going then more would be revealed to me. I was confident in that.

Sitting there in my bed, I reveled in a plan mostly well made. I mean, there were a few missed details, sure. My tardiness greatly frustrated me but it was easily remedied moving forward. That wouldn't happen twice. Fear was an astronomically larger factor than I thought possible and getting back in the house was a total oversight.

But I experienced what the streets moved like at night. I knew what to look forward to after facing it once. The milk crates were a fortuitous find and they delivered for me in the clutch. They were stashed where they could be used repeatedly. So, getting back into the crib would no longer be a challenge. Passing those tests gave me every confidence that I could keep going to the meetings because I had conquered my odds.

The streets definitely scared me but fear is not a directive – it's a warning system. It tells you that shit is serious: focus and think critically as you proceed. Didn't think I'd be afraid like that in my neighborhood. Shit, I didn't know it was that scary. One night of experience taught me plenty. And, all-in-all, my operation was successful! *I* was successful and I knew I could do it again. I started laughing out loud in delight. It was a collection of wildly empowering revelations.

"Busara," Ma called through the bedroom door.

"Yes, ma'am?"

"I hear you in there laughing, are you watching TV? You supposed to be sleeping. You know you have to wake up for school in the morning. I'll be in there to get you, same time as always. I don't wanna hear no mess out of you, either. Go to sleep, now."

"Yes ma'am."

Like I said, she missed nothing.

That was the crux of my pre-teen challenge. I thought my mother was suffocating my freedom and I felt constricted by the circumscriptions of her parenting style. My hunger for life and her constant, omnipresent pressure continued to drive my ambition. It fueled my desire to graduate from my stature of 'child' and manifested my craving for independence. At eleven, I felt the vestiges of manhood that were swelling within me were being snuffed out. Often it felt like I just couldn't breathe. I was starving for some space to grow. I needed breathing room. I had to have a universe to operate in. My own universe.

That's a pretty big vision for an eleven year old little man but I had it. And I wanted that vision to come to fruition. Let me tell you: don't underestimate kids. You don't know what they have in them unless you ask and listen or if they're the kind of unicorn that makes it happen while they're still young. Those occurrences are rare and, unfortunately, it wasn't my story.

My point is, greatness resides in children. Encouraging it can help establish it and there is every reason to do so. The best dreams and unlimited ideas come from the boundless minds of kids. I wanted to do huge things in the world and I knew that as an eleven year old. The Organization had tapped into that yearning, that need. When I was there, it felt like I could explore that realm. That's precisely why I knew what was happening that next Thursday.

I was going back.

CHAPTER 9

FOUNDATION

The following Thursday went much more smoothly. As soon as I watched Ma pull off with my little sister, I closed the curtains in my room and darted for the back window. I was NOT going to leave before seeing that car drive away, in the off chance she forgot something and came back in. I've seen way too many TV shows for me to fall for the okie doke. Besides, there was no room for me to get sloppy because I was still terrified. So, with the coast clear, I ran into the kitchen, placed all of the sink items carefully on the sides and caromed out of the window. By the time I hit the ground it was barely 7:00.

I landed on the crates then started to leave. After a few steps, I looked back at the crates and they hit me wrong. I thought that it was probably a bad idea to leave them sitting there. It was like suggesting that someone should use them. It was the Peabody's after all, it's not like someone would pass up the opportunity to loot a place. Talk about being killed by Ma...

I shot back to the crates, tossed them in opposite directions then took off again. Feeling a bit better, I switched my focus to running my ass off. I was determined to be at the meeting before everybody else.

Why? More than a few reasons. I was geeked to go! Period. On a scale of one to ten, my excitement level was on 14. I still felt bad for being late the first time, more than a bit frustrated that I blew it. So, the second meeting was going to be a personal redemption for me. Also, meeting guys without rushing would be cool. Whenever the sessions were over I would always have to immediately bail but I would have time to rap to them and kick it before things started. That way I would get to know some dudes. I wanted to see what it looked like early, too. How did they get along when people first arrived? Were they just regular cats or did they show up locked in?

Lastly, I had to see this 'begin on the second'-thing with my own eyes. I mean, it's not like I hadn't been somewhere on time or seen people be on time but, like, 7:30:00:00 to start a meeting? That's extra as hell. Conversely, I've dealt with a lot of situations in life that were on CP time. (That's 'Colored People Time' and refers to Black people being casual with punctuality. Don't run around saying it if you're not Black, though – that's a party foul). So, I just wanted to see if they were that particular. And I was curious to see how everyone responded to it. How many guys that knew about it (as in 'not new') would be late? I had to see it for myself.

Mostly, though, I just didn't want to be in trouble. Hated it. The pushups never scared me for real. I could do some damned pushups, man. I just didn't want to be punished for being in trouble. I committed to being early, by a lot, just to make sure that wouldn't be a concern for me.

When I walked into the room it seemed like there was a memo I didn't get. The place was packed! It almost felt the same way it did when we left the meeting the week before, everybody was there. Shoot, I started thinking maybe my clock at home was actually wrong. Before I let panic set in, I took a sharp look at the clock – 7:12. Wow! At first I thought they were all like me and they just didn't want to get in trouble. I stood observing for a minute and, sure, maybe that had something to do with it but there was more. Some of them were here incredibly early just to kick it.

Another note I missed: everybody was wearing black. Everybody. It wasn't an official uniform but it was an apparent social agreement. Thinking about it, I realized it was the same as last week. I was so wrapped up in the idea of not doing push-ups for being late and flipping my clothes to hide logos that the group 'look' didn't register with me. I'm usually pretty good with details but, damn it, I was eleven. Some shit falls through the cracks, man. So, again, my wardrobe was not the business. Even the homie Drelon had come back and was rocking all black. How the hell did he catch it? Maybe he was here Tuesday and figured it out or someone had put him up on game. Nonetheless, he fit right in with the program. Me? I was wearing an all green shirt and blue jeans, 'sore thumb'-ing the hell out of it.

Watching everyone carelessly enjoying conversation, I decided to keep my eye on the clock. I was dead set on seeing this exact time thing. After being there a minute, Nardy and I locked eyes then he walked over to me. I'm not exactly certain of which version of stank eye I was giving him but he definitely got one. I probably had several variations of stank eye going on at once.

> "What's up, dawg?" He said with his face lit up. "After you missed Tuesday I didn't think you'd be back. It's good to see you come through."

He reached out to give me dap. I gave it to him the way I felt about him. Then I told him.

> "Whatever man. It didn't look like it. You wasn't trying to help me when I asked you about it. You was too busy fronting on me." I shot at him.
>
> "You right. I was tripping, dawg. But we here now and we brothers, man. Stop bringing up old stuff." He said with another smile.

We chuckled a bit.

"Let me introduce you to my boys." He said.
"Cool." I replied.

As we talked to the other young brothers, all I thought about was asking them what is was like being here. You know, what did they think about being in a group like this one? But that's not how it went. We rapped about everything; TV, sports, kinds of bicycles, girls, everything. I even asked them about the 'all black' look. In the middle of laughing really hard at a joke a thought flashed in my mind.

(What time is...)

"NDANI!"

My head automatically snapped to find the source of the sound. These guys really understand the 'book-dropping-in-the-middle-of-a-quiet-class' effect. Instantly, the whole chilled conversation vibe turned into a living ball of energy. Everybody stopped mid-sentence, shifting all of their focus to purposely moving about. Though every single person was hustling to a spot somewhere in the room, not a sound was made except the shuffling of feet on carpet. It was the fastest I had ever seen a hush fall over a room while simultaneously activating it to action. I looked around and saw all these young guys hustling and realized it was significant. You know that getting in trouble wasn't my thing, so I was hustling to my spot, too. Then it was like something out of a cartoon: one second there was total pandemonium and the next...

Perfect order.

(Damn it!)

Busy hurrying like everyone else, I totally forgot to check the time. We had been resetting for about ten seconds when I looked up at the clock. Sure enough, the seconds hand was rounding it's way to the three. My guess? 7:30:00:00 was a real thing. When the seconds hand got to the five, Mwalimu was already talking. It was still 7:30. These dudes are all business.

Mwalimu was back out front. He greeted everybody and ran down a few items of business. Again, I got to watch the dynamics take place in front of me. Young guys asking for permission to speak and handling their business with confidence and authority. I was feeling every bit of that.

After handling what seemed to be rudimentary items, he turned to me.

"Welcome back, young brother Busara. We missed you Tuesday, glad to have you back." Mwalimu said.

I raised my hand to respond. More than a few people laughed. Mwalimu was among the laughing.

"I appreciate the respect but that's not how men ask to be recognized. We'll show you how, though." He chuckled, "I talked to you directly anyways so you're good. What you got?" He asked patiently.

"Yes, sir. Yeah, um, I can't make Tuesdays. I have stuff with my mother." I said.

"Well, we won't ever come before moms. I totally understand that." He still said with a smile.

"Did you bring the permission slip?"

"No sir. I forgot it."

(I did actually forget about it, that's the truth. While it's also true that I can't ever bring one, what I said was the truth.)

Yeah, we know I was lying, though. We'll keep that between us.

"Alright. We'll get you another one. We need you to take care of that." He said sternly.
I simply said, "yes, sir." It's all I had.

Next to me, Drelon had leaned over to D Smooth and whispered something. D Smooth whispered back then Drelon took a step forward.
Drelon formed his arms in the specific perpendicular ways I saw last week. Obviously he had learned a lot on Tuesday. He was preparing to speak.

"HABA!" Drelon belled with confidence.
"Yebo!" Mwalimu responds with a chuckle.
"I appreciate what's been said. I have my parental slip. But I'm having a hard time trying to learn the words you're saying. I need help, sir." Drelon said.
"I appreciate you being brave enough to stand out and speak your piece. The word is 'hapa' but we'll work on that. Let me ask you a question, young brother Drelon: have you seen the movie Conan the Barbarian?" Mwalimu asked.
"Not yet, sir." Drelon answered, "but I want to."

There was a spattering of laughs. Including Mwalimu.

"That's because the white man is good at what he does and he's always trying to get you to praise him. To think he's superior somehow. Always know that you are the first man, Drelon. All things that ever exist from humanity come from your people. You should always be weary of anything and everything they want you to do. It will never be a thing that's best for you. Remember that." He paused a second for effect. Then spoke again,

"Let me ask you another question, young brother Drelon: do you know the actor's name who plays Conan?"

"Yes, sir." Drelon responded with some sense of pride. "His name is Arnold Schwarzenegger." Drelon beamed.

"That's right. He's from Austria and his name is Austrian. We speak Kiswahili and Zulu here. If you can say that white boy's name you can speak everything we speak here. Know that you can and you will. It's that simple."

Again, he paused for effect.

"Make sure you turn in that permission slip when you fall out of formation."

"Yes, sir". Drelon replied.

It was super cool that he tried to speak in formation so early. I wasn't exactly afraid but I would have waited. Something about him doing it made me think I should stand up whenever I had an issue or a question or something, and voice my position. Seeing him do it made me more confident about it. I was really glad he did it.

After that we did the meditation thing again. I supposed they were going to do this every time. It's a preparation for the lesson we were going to receive. That also meant we were going to learn lessons every time we met. That's when it struck me:

(This ain't a dance group at all! How is that...)

Now I had to start asking questions.

(What actually is this group? What are we doing? Where is all of this heading? Why did I see those guys doing those dance moves and stuff? I mean, I heard what he said last week but what does that mean?)

I had questions. Even though I had just watched Drelon stand up and be heard I wasn't about to ask my questions in open forum. What I wanted to know seemed like it was more personal somehow. It just didn't seem right to ask Mwalimu and hold up the process for everybody.

It was also somewhat embarrassing. There I was, risking my neck to attend this thing that I couldn't define. I told those guys I was there to 'find myself' without taking the time to find out what I was involved in. It only made sense to me that everybody else knew what was going on. Openly asking in front of everyone would've looked foolish to me. That would certainly be a bad look. Nah, I was going to wait until we separated.

Besides, D Smooth was like my new big bro. He's been here a while, at least that's what it seemed like. He should be able to answer my questions. He could tell me how long he's been here, too. D Smooth probably had all kinds of things he could put me up on. So, I couldn't wait until we went into the group session. I was going to get to the bottom of this and get to the next level. My mind was made.

I opened my eyes just before Mwalimu called attention or 'angulia'. We all hopped up and things proceeded as they did before. Mwalimu handed assignments out to guys, they responded to confirm. It was all flowing along until his last assignment.

"Victor, we need you to take the Kobe class today. Help reinforce their understanding of how we open and close by telling
them where it comes from."

(Aw man...)

"HAPA!" Victor vociferated. It was so thunderous it likely
startled a few dudes.

(Damn! That dude is super loud.)

"Yebo." Mwalimu responded.
"Appreciating what's been said, if I understand everything
correctly, I'm leading the Kobe group in the lesson today. I
will teach them why we open and close the way we do and
where it comes from." Victor confirmed.

(Well, there went that plan. Now what?)

"Yebo." Mwalimu said. "Be thorough, Victor. Which also
means be patient."
"Yes, sir," Victor replied.

"KWISHI!"

Mwalimu gave the order and we performed the moves to fall out
of formation. Then split into groups and left to our individual rooms.
We walked to the room as a group. I was a bit frustrated.

(What the hell, man? I thought D Smooth was going to be teaching us. This dude is one of the cool cats but I don't know him. If I ask him, he might just trip on me and stuff. I'll just wait and ask D Smooth. Maybe I can catch him early next week. Yeah, that should work.)

(What time is it?)

When we got to the room it went just as the instructions that were given. We started with the meeting opening ceremony and learned all of the commands and what those words meant. He shared with us that all the movements came from Shaka Zulu, the iconic South African Zulu leader himself. We were doing troop movements of Zulu warriors and all of the commands he used to move them. That hit me hard: in real life, y'all, at eleven years old, I was doing Zulu warrior stuff and speaking the same language they did. That's fricking cool! My chest instantly swelled with pride just for being there. I committed to hitting the library hard to learn as much about the Zulu as I could.

He then talked to us about how to be recognized to speak. Both Drelon and I had fouled it up that week so we paid great attention to what he showed us. Then he explained it. He taught us that, despite popular opinion, respect was a one-way street – it emanates from you. If you respect yourself and carry yourself with respect you will demand it from all you encounter by how you comport yourself.

However, this level of respect is taught by demonstration. Learning what respect actually is often requires the exercise of giving it. It is also a standard of our ancestors' culture to honor our elders. Their wisdom should always be highly revered, appreciated and adhered. So, in learning to honor them we achieve a grasp of what respect means and, eventually, internalize a level of dignity that becomes our character.

That's deep, right? Once it was broken down like that they had me. It was a dope approach to building character. So, when we started working on how to dismiss, I was laser focused. It became a top priority for me to get it down pat so we could move forward. There was more to learn and I was fired up about getting to it.

We returned to the formation shortly after that. When we dismissed, I felt confident in what we were doing. Pride, again, swelled in my chest during every bit of the process. It felt like I was officially part of the group. I'm not sure if it's just because I was doing what everyone else was or if it's because the reasoning behind all of it resonated with me. Maybe it was both. My chest felt like it was physically puffed out a little further when we were done, though. I was straight up geeked to be connected to the organization.

The moment we did that 180 spin to dismiss, I was stepping spryly towards the door for two reasons: I didn't want to get another permission slip and, of course, I wanted to live. That permission thing had to be strung out as long as possible. So, I wasn't trying to face getting handed another copy. Fortunately for me, I slipped through the cracks that night. Most importantly, getting home before Ma was mandatory.

The clock on the wall read 9:31.

Just before I reached the door I saw my dude D Smooth. I raised a fist at him on the way out. Other than a universally understood sign of Black unity, I have no idea where that came from. It's highly likely I was just trying not to draw attention to myself so I didn't want to yell out anything. The fist is always a solid communique, though, so he shot me one back as I bailed.

On the return home, I was a bit more confident. Yeah, the sirens were still wailing, the dope fiends and corner boys were entrenched in their melodrama and gunshots still completed the opera. And I was still scared as hell. So, maybe it wasn't a matter of confidence, I could've just been wrapped in thought.

I was thinking about how many answers they gave me at the meeting. The Organization began making sense to me, just learning what it was all about and how to carry myself in the proceedings. I was going to practice everything they taught me until the next week and return much sharper. I was kind of glad that Victor led our group. He was cool and it helped me meet another one of the brothers. That Kowrie-thing was alright, man. I kept running hard as hell while thinking about the choice I had made. It was a good one.

Before I realized it, the house was right in front of my face. Everything was where I left it, which means I easily found the milk crates. I set them up, climbed up to the window, caterpillared (yeah, I made a word) inside the house and everything was good to go. While I reset the kitchen the milk crates crossed my mind again. I decided to scatter them in the morning because leaving them as 'suggestions' all day while everyone is gone couldn't be the best idea.

This time I hustled to clean and have everything set in time to make it to my room. I didn't want to be downstairs in clothes when Ma arrived. She was too smart to fall for that weekly. And I definitely wasn't going to bet on her being in another terrific mood. That would've been asking too much.

I squared everything away, got my clothes off, got in the bed and cut the lights off before the car pulled in front of the house. A few minutes after she came in the house, she opened my door and checked on me. She even kissed me on the forehead and said goodnight.

"Ooh, Busara. You're running a little warm, Man. Let me open this window for my baby." she whispered.

You couldn't tell me shit! I was proud as hell that I was successfully in a club that was focused on my manhood. And my mama didn't even know about it.

(I got this shit!)

CHAPTER 10
THE SQUEEZE

The program was on lock! When Thursday rolled around again, I knew my routine was a winner. I made sure that I was, again, in my room so Ma could call me out. Just to put some stank on it, I told her I was kind of tired so I didn't go downstairs. She came to the room and kissed me goodbye. As she walked my sister out to the car, I was changing into my all black outfit. Then I gleefully watched the car roll off from my bedroom window.

I did the clear-the-kitchen-counter-thing, the sliding-out-the-window-thing and the scaling-down-the-wall-thing. I jetted down the alley like I had stolen something.

Clockwork.

It was only 7:09 when I walked into the meeting room. Again, the house was full. After giving Nardy some dap and talking to him for a second, I saw D Smooth walk into the door. I still had questions after learning a few things the previous week. D Smooth would definitely put me up on game and not embarrass me.

I rolled up on D Smooth when he started talking to a couple guys.

"Hey, y'all." I said. "What's up D Smooth?"

"Hey, little brother!" He was a bit surprised, D Smooth hadn't seen me approaching.

"What's up?"

(Yep, he's a cool dude. We can rap.)

"I wanted to holler at you about something."
He shifted the smile on his face to a channeled focus.
"Aight. What's up?"

He took a step away from the crew he was standing next to. He could sense I didn't want a public conversation, so he tried to give us some space. Cool stuff.

"I was just wondering, man, uh, why did you join the group?"
"What, Kowrie?" He asked.
I nodded yes.
"Oh man, that's easy. I wasn't doing nothing else. A couple dudes I knew were in it and I wasn't up to much. Once I got in and saw what they did, how I felt doing it, I just stayed around."
He said it all very matter-of-factly.
"Oh." I followed up, "did you know what it was first or did you learn as you went along?"
"Nah. I just wanted to do something. This was cool. I only got understanding later while doing it." He paused.
"Hell, I told you, when they asked me why I was here I didn't have an answer as cool as yours. I said I was bored and wanted to do something. I meant it."
We both laughed.

"What's up, though? You alright?" He continued with concern.

"Yeah! For sure. I just… I don't exactly know how to describe it." I said.

A light came on in his face.

"Oh, I get it. You wanna be able to explain it to somebody."

I nodded my head off. "Yeah!"

"I got you. The Kowrie Group is exactly what Mwalimu called it – a rites of passage group for young Black men. I probably can't give you the textbook description but that means it leads young dudes to become men. It teaches discipline, unity and a sense of community through… channeling our ancestors. Mostly, though, it just helps you build you to the man you want to become."

I paused in thought. He had an epiphany.

"Shit, that might be the textbook answer. Maybe I was made for this, too."

We laughed at the comeback.

I regrouped.

"So, it's not about Black Power?" I asked.

"Well, let me ask you this: are you Black?"

"Yeah!" I said with pride.

"If the 'Group helps *you* understand your power then Black power is everything it's about."

"NDANI!" Someone shouted.

As we ran into our place in formation everything that D Smooth said stuck with me. It was something about understanding my own strength that just wouldn't leave my mind. Manhood, community and Black power; it was a lot to absorb. It was mad heavy but I liked it.

Once we went through the opening ceremonies we got back into the circle. This time I participated differently. After we did the meditation, well, it wasn't actually called meditation. Because the Kowrie Group dealt with kids it had to respect their parents. There were people who had real problems with the word 'meditation' because of their religious beliefs. So, it was called 'Breathing Exercises' to ward off those concerns. It's amazing that the only thing that changed was the verbiage and they didn't have any issues with parents about it because of that. People.

I sort of glossed over a massive amount of details in the earlier meetings because I was more than a little freaked out. It's also why I kept re-evaluating whether it was worth it or if going to the meetings was a good choice.

Or if I belonged.

As much as I wanted to learn, I was hampered by my fear of being caught by my mother. "Am I gonna get caught? What time is it? Did she leave church already? I hope she's not home yet?" These were my steady stream of thoughts, I was completely preoccupied. I had to constantly reinforce my way through the process. I used every small flash of positivity as a huge sign to push through, to stay the course. Even the smallest of affirmations became self-confidence builders, they helped me to keep going. A lot of the meeting beginnings were a blur. I only heard half of what was being said and consciously engaged just enough not to get in trouble, another of my constant concerns. By the third meeting, I settled in a little more and that allowed me to let things sink in.

The breathing exercises were one of those things I took more seriously the more comfortable I got. They were highly specific in their detail and, initially, I was doing it all wrong. Mwalimu would give specific instruction of how to proceed with them to get the best results out of the segment. Like all things with the 'Group, there was not only a method but a reason, a history and a goal.

Let me be forthcoming: the details of those methods are things I cannot share but you should know that they were elaborate. Many of the Kowrie processes are on the level of sacred so it's unacceptable to reveal everything. Unveiling them for or as general knowledge would be a violation on several levels. Much of what I've already shared will require forgiveness so I *will not* go into the minutia of what the breathing exercises entailed. I can tell you, though, that the segment was vastly more intense when I listened and proceeded as instructed. When it was over, opening your eyes was an arrival. For me, it was an effective preparation for the learning segments that always followed.

Another powerful thing about the systems were the report segments. Right after the breathing exercises, Mwalimu would point out one of the guys and he would give a news report. The report came from a news article or telecast that we had to learn about between meetings. You were required to have the five W's (who, what, when, where, and why) and the how about any topic you chose. We would go around the entire circle and everyone would get to tell their report. If you didn't – pushups. They were building warriors, y'all. Everything was aimed at getting us stronger, in every arena and for every reason.

I didn't initially like the reports. Drelon and I got a pass on the first one but we knew we would have to speak from then on. I didn't want to do that. Remember, I was looking to do a dance – this was decidedly NOT dancing. I was frustrated due to my expectation and distracted by fear.

However, as the meetings continued I felt growth happening. Receiving all of that information was cool, too. It was like we had watched a huge newscast by the time everyone got done. And many of the topics were interesting or wildly unexpected. They made me feel like I knew what was going on in the world. It was a segment that got better for me the more times we did it.

We broke into groups after the reports. The group segment was dope. We did more drilling, learned more terms and got more comfortable with what we were doing. D Smooth got to lead us again and that was cool. I would have more questions and he would have more answers. It was really cool having a dude that was like my big brother. I would soon learn that most of the older guys in the organization looked out like that. It made perfect sense, brotherhood was the lifeblood of Kowrie. Every meeting was filled with lessons and revelations. That wasn't unique, it was the same every time I went: I learned more, I grew more and I wanted to come back even more.

Getting back to the session, we finished the group segment and went back into formation. Then Mwalimu had another note of news for the calendar.

> "Gentlemen, camp is three weeks away. As usual, we cover the transportation, the food for the weekend and all the activities. All you have to do is bring your $7 by next week so we know how to complete our reservations. If you have it today make sure you turn it in to Mama Mlinzi before you leave.

> (Aw man! Ma will never give me money for a thing she doesn't know about. And a whole weekend! She not about to let me... how am I gonna... man, damn it.)

> Then, because when it rains everything gets wet, Mwalimu reminded me I had obligations.

"Young brother, Busara. You have something for me?"
Mwalimu said.

"Um, no sir." I said quizzically.

"Are you sure? We still don't have a permission slip from you,
young brother. We need your parents to sign it and for you
to bring it back."

(Double damn it.)

"Oh. Um, yes sir. I just forgot it." I tried to feign innocent. I'm
sure he wasn't buying it.

"No problem. We'll make sure we get you a fresh one so you
can take care of it. We need you to take care of that, young
Busara." Mwalimu said with compassionate authority.

"One of the Mamas will hook you right up. Make sure you
grab it before you leave."

"yes, sir."

(Triple damn it!)

He called kwishi shortly after. I moved lively to retrieve the permission slip from Mama Amina, and I was out the door. It was 9:32 and I was
in a half-panic.

In a flat-out sprint for home, I realized my life was a collection of
closely averted catastrophes. The first is that I was walking a super thin
line by going to Kowrie meetings at all. Actually, that's the first two – you
might even call it three. I had to move without my mom knowing, without
'Momma Watch' catching me, and I had to make it to and from the meetings without being abducted or killed by stray bullets. Or intentional ones.
I could have also been mugged just because I was out there. Of course, I

had nothing to be taken but muggers don't know that until they try to take something, y'know? I was dealing with my mom, everyone's mom and the mother of all scariness in the streets all at the same time. So, yeah, that was definitely the terror trifecta.

Second, I was fully participating in an organization that required parental consent – a thing I *would never* get. So, week-to-week I was just surviving until the next week. Every meeting, so far, they were asking for the consent that wasn't remotely gonna happen. And I was pretty sure that, sooner or later, they would say something about how I got ghost at the end of meetings.

Then I got hit with a double-whammy: I had to get money to spend a weekend with the 'Group. Money AND a whole weekend! Where was I going to get the money from? Much more importantly, how was I going to spend an entire weekend away from the house? From what Nardy had told me, it was certain that something like this was coming. That still didn't prepare me for it.

Sounded like an ideal situation for a plan.

The one option that would make it easier for me was just not planning to go on the camp weekend. I could say my mother wouldn't let me or something like that. That would certainly be true, more than I would care to divulge, even. But, man, hell naw! I joined the Kowrie Group because they blew my mind. I was inspired to keep going because of the brotherhood. This was precisely the kind of thing I was looking forward to. Nope, I had gotten to the level of taking trips and I was going to camp with my brothers. Period. I had figured out everything to that point so I would figure out how to go to camp, too.

Again, fuck it.

I got to the house and everything was everything. Stacked the crates, negotiated the window, set the house in order and got in bed. Mom arrived to a dark, quiet house. Another week in the books.

Speaking of books, school continued to happen, of course, but that's just school. Nothing special happened in middle school. Not one damned thing was noteworthy enough to mention in the same breath as my Kowrie experience. I kept my books square, for sure, Ma would have absolutely murdered me otherwise. But I studied or worked on as many Kowrie Group topics as I did schoolwork. It was a big deal for me to be prepared for the report segment so I watched the news as often as possible, looking for an interesting story. I was going to be ready when the following Thursday arrived.

Meanwhile, I was sweating the hell out of that $7! There was no way I was going to be short. I had to have it so the hustle was real. I put a plan into full effect! Throughout the week I hustled to do little errands or yard work for the neighbors. Some of them worked out and the money began adding up. A few dollars in hand made me even more determined.

The last dollar came from Ma. Normally I never asked her for money because she does so much and I knew things were tight. That Tuesday, though, I got up the nerve to ask her to get some candy from the store. I thought she might have said no and given me one of those 'mom speeches' but it didn't happen. She looked at me, cracked a sweet smile and said, "hand me my coin purse, baby." Blew me away.

I ran to St. Stephens that Thursday with a purpose. I walked in the door at 7:07, set to chop it up with the fellas. Everybody was there and already kicking it. There was no wonder why everyone was punctual. The socializing before the meeting is how we shared in our brotherhood. There was an understanding about the Organization, we knew we were in exceptional space. Space that we, basically, only shared with the people in it. We were all business for the disciplines, the drill and all the segments but just chilling with guys seemed like some sort of elite social club. I was definitely down with that.

This particular week, my story for the report segment was the bomb so I couldn't wait to get to it. And, despite the odds, I had the money I needed for camp. Working out how to go was just the next challenge. I hadn't figured it out by then but I thought that was a matter of time. My confidence was at an all-time high. I was sort of intoxicated by empowerment.

After we made it through the opening ceremony and the breathing exercises I could barely contain myself. Mwalimu saw me chomping at the bit and I think it made him curious.

> "Young brother Busara you look like you either drank too much soda or you really have something to say." Mwalimu apparently tickled himself with the light humor. "I think we'll start with you tonight."
> "Yebo, kadamu," I spit out with great confidence.
> "That's not exactly how you use yebo but I'm really glad you're working on it." Again, he smiled.
> "Please proceed, young brother." He said gave me the floor.
> "Well, Egypt is in Africa," I said.

I don't exactly know why I paused afterwards but I did. I scanned everyone's faces for a minute, watching their reactions. It could have been that saying it out loud defied much of what we'd been programmed. Maybe that jolted me a bit. Every film we had ever seen about Egypt had a bunch of white people in it. And this is ancient Egyptian stuff, history that we're talking about. There was no way we would equate Egypt with Africa when it's a bunch of white boys running around as pharaohs. When I said it out loud that may have hit me.

It definitely could have been that I simply lost my place, too. Speaking in groups wasn't my thing, I could have just temporarily stalled out. Whatever it was that caused me to clam up, I had, apparently, sat there silent long enough that Mwalimu thought I needed a push.

"Yes, young brother. Egypt is one of the 54 countries in Africa. Do you have more for us?" Mwalimu said.

I snapped out of it.

"Yes, sir. Uh, last week, Muhammed Anwar el-Sadat was assassinated in Egypt. Mm-hm, he was killed by, um, the Fundamentalist Army on October 6. He was the third President of Egypt." (3)

I took a long pause again.

"That's a stellar report, young Busara. Is that it?"
"Thank you, um, kadamu. No, sir." I said.
"Alright. Then please continue." Mwalimu beamed with either delight or pride. Maybe a combination of the two. Not sure.
"Okay. Yes, sir." I continued, "Mr. el-Sadat was a two-time Vice President and he won the Nobel Peace Prize for a peace treaty he made with our President, Jimmy Carter."

I took one more not-as-lengthy pause.

"That's it." I said.
"Wow," Mwalimu exclaimed. "That's a real report, young Busara. It's really impressive. Just be careful calling those white boys 'our President'. They're not in office for us, they're not working for us, they don't represent us. Don't fall for the

patriotism propaganda they try to sell you. Be careful with that. That's an amazing report, though. Great job. Great job."

"Thank you, sir." I replied. It took everything I had not to smile in pride.

"Looks like you're next, Drelon." Mwalimu said.

Man, I was flat out soaring after that. I mean, it didn't make me think that being a public speaker would become my thing or anything. That would have been ridiculous. But I was super confident after that. It was the first time I had ever given a public presentation and it went pretty well. It felt great! My commitment to top it the next week was automatic. I was going to try to have the best report every week.

We split into groups and our crew rolled with Wee Jock. He taught us a vast degree of detail about drilling. Not just the moves but, like usual, the history of it was shared with us. He explained to us that it is properly named 'Tabura'.

The Tabura is a secret, sacred drill. It is an extensive system that incorporates a fighting style and dance movements. He reiterated that it was the basic military formation used by Shaka Zulu and the Zulu nation. It's what they utilized to defeat the British and the Dutch.

The Gumboot Dance, or the South African Gumboot Dance, came directly from the Tabura. A multitude of Gumboot dance steps are utilized in the Tabura so they go hand-in-hand. He made it clear that the Tabura was not for public use. It's a private secret style of movement used only by the 'Group. It was not for us to share with friends or anyone else who wasn't Kowrie.

The Tabura served multiple purposes for the Kowrie Group. We not only utilized it to stay physically fit but it helped build the culture of the organization. It increased mental sharpness, taught Kiswahili and promoted teamwork by operating in unity. The Tabura was made to organize the Zulu warrior in order to mobilize for action. It's the exact application that became the backbone for the Kowrie Group.

To say I was astonished is putting it mildly. Learning about how much of the Zulu traditions that the 'Group observed and preserved was breathtaking! I hustled back to the formation with warrior pride in my chest. This shit was fucking awesome! The Kowrie Group, itself, was totally awesome and I was one of them.

It appears there was a reason he taught us so much about the Tabura. I was about to get a real life lesson in it.

Mwalimu began to wrap up the meeting as he always does, with a visionary word.

> "Next week, both Tuesday and Thursday, we'll work on the South African Gum Boot Dance. Of course, all of you won't get a chance to participate because it is a privilege you earn not a right to do. We do want you to be up close and personal with it, though, because it embodies who we are. It moves in togetherness and unity, it is strong and impactful and it is the very essence of our elders. Because of that, you're a part of it even when you don't participate. We need you to see what that looks like. So, we're going to run it next week." Mwalimu said.
>
> "If you have your dues for camp make sure you get them to Mama Amina."

(Oh, HELL YEAH!)

After a brief pause he looked directly at me.

"Young brother Busara, before you dart out tonight make sure you get a new permission slip." He then leans towards me.

(Oh no.)

"Yes, we know you run home. It's cool, get the permission slip first."
"Yes, sir." I said with feigned confidence.

(Damn it.)

"I have the money for camp!" I was proud to say.
"Fantastic. You can leave that with Mama Mlinzi, too."
"Yes, sir." I replied.

He dismissed us from there.

Right after our 180 degree turn in dismissal, I went to Mama Mlinzi who had the permission slips. I thanked her and made a beeline for the door. Shot the fist to my guy D Smooth, checked the clock on the way out and it read 9:32. I'm good. Time to fly.

The second I walked out the door, I took off running and absolutely lost it out loud.

"YEAH! Let's go!"

(We about to make this happen! I'm gonna learn all those moves and make the stage shake... like they did. BOOM! But it'll be me this time. Yeah, boy. This is exactly what I'm talking about. Helllllll yeaaaaaaaah! Let's go!)

I was beyond geeked about getting to experience the Gum Boot Dance up close. My whole run home was spent envisioning myself learning every move while they practiced it. It was already a done deal for me.

(I got some understanding today, I know what's going on, feel better with what I'm doing – I get it - and it's as awesome as I knew it would be. Learning another language... two languages... now I'm about to learn the Gum Boot Dance? Shiiiiid!)

My energies were so high that the sights and sounds of the "Night 'Lou" weren't even background noises. I was living in my own universe, running through stars and bouncing off asteroids. I was high as hell knowing the next level was coming. You couldn't tell me shit. My mind told me that I was running fast as hell but it's just as likely that I was skipping. The hustle was happening, for sure, shit, I was running my ass off. But, I don't know... I was just in another place. Everything was panning out for me and I was ecstatic about it.

I bent the alley corner to the house and spotted the milk crates exactly where I left them. I grabbed them, stacked them at the 'mystery door' and began scaling. I was so happy I might have even been whistling.

I climbed atop that odd exterior door frame and stood erect. Next, I reached up to the window sill and began hauling myself up to it. Once I got my hands over the ledge of the kitchen window I began pulling myself up, as usual. I placed my left foot on the building almost waist high to continue propelling off of the boost I made from pushing off the locker with my right. Whenever I got both of my elbows over the ledge, I knew I was in. After getting my elbows up I always looked up, just to double check to make sure there was nothing I could knock over on the counter. I tried to be preemptively thorough, you know? I couldn't bank on any clean up time once I got in. It would be much better to not make messes at all and breaking something was a death sentence. Nah, being thorough would be best. So, I got my elbows up and checked to see if the coast was clear.

It wasn't.

CHAPTER 11

INTO THE FIRE

"GOT to be more careful! You scared the life out of me. What in the Sam Hill are you doing hanging out of my darned window, Busara?" Ma fired off.

(Oh shit! Oh shit! Oh shit! Oh shit!)

"Get yo' butt down and get in here!"
"Yes, ma'am!"

I proceeded to climb through the window.

"No you don't! Take your narrow behind back down the way you came up here and go through the door like a normal person. Thanks for showing everybody in the neighborhood how to break into my house." She barked.
"…like you ain't got no dad-blasted sense!"

I reversed course as fast as I could.

"And hurry up!" She shouted.
"Yes, ma'am." I said.

My voice cracked a bit when I responded that time. We all know that sound as the onset of tears. They did not work in my favor.

"Don't you dare start all that crying or I'll give you something to cry about! That's not working today." She yelled out the window.

Honestly, I don't know why she added "today". There was never a time that crying prevented an inevitable ass whipping. Usually, like the night in question, it intensified how angry she was.

"What... what is that down there? Are those milk crates?!"
"Y-y-yes, ma'am." I said into the wall as I descended.
"Doggone it... get those darned things from under my window! You have lost your ever-loving mind."

She missed nothing. Nothing at all.

I didn't cry, though. The voice crack was real but something about me, innately, wasn't going to release the water works. It just wasn't going to happen that night. Well, at least not without the extreme duress of some painful device against my backside. No, she would have to earn my tears from then on. I was just in a different space.

Not a different space of fear, though. Nah, I wasn't trippin' that hard. I was still terrified. So much so that I didn't even bother climbing all the way down. I jumped from the top of the mystery door, tossed the crates as far as I could and ran all the way to our front door.

Now, mind you, I ran at top speed. Hell, I almost slipped rounding the corner in front of our building. When I walked in the living room she was already sitting on the couch with an extension cord in one hand

and a glass of orange juice in the other. She looked as composed as I had ever seen her.

She was on fire.

"Close that door and sit yo' butt down."
Her words were almost whispers. Then she paused.
"It's a lot easier walking in a house through the front door, isn't it?!"

Ladies and gentlemen, I present to you the infamous "trapdoor question". If you find yourself in this place just know that you are assed-out. There is no such thing as a correct answer. Whatever my response would be to that question it was going to cost me. Painfully. If I said 'no' she would have skipped the 'interview' and gone straight to kicking my butt. If I said 'yes' I would have been calling myself stupid and she would have brought that point home with a multitude of embarrassing tropes and a collection of old bad choices that I made. Then kick my butt after working herself up. The only rational choice to make in this case would be for me to keep my mouth shut, wait it out and hope she'd let it be rhetorical.

Fortunately for me, she intended it that way.

"Where have you been? Where you coming from, Busara?"

I stood there… trying to keep my composure. A million things were running through my head. I was trying to think of a way out of it but I struggled with the idea of lying. Of course, if she caught me in lies I'd be in more trouble but that wasn't my concern. I felt like a lie would make me smaller somehow. Like it was less than a man to lie and I wasn't willing to…

"Did you hear me? I said, where have you been? Busara Andre
Dizzy! You better answer me right now!"

"Yes, ma'am. I, um,… I was at a meeting."

"A meeting? What meeting, Busara?" She was befuddled.

"With D Smooth and Nardy and them." It was the first thing
that came to mind. It just fell out.

"What in the world is a 'D Smooth'?"

"He's one of my brothers, um, the guys in Kowrie. The group
I'm in."

"You not in no doggone group! I done already told you, you
can't be in no groups, dang nabbit. That's over right now."
She took a breath.

"What 'group' are we talking about anyways? Is it that thing
that was in your pocket a few weeks ago?"

(How does she do that? She's always on it.)

"Yes ma'am. It's… it's called the Kowrie Group."

"The what group? What kind of language is that? It's not
English, I know that. So, that's the Afrocentric group you
were talking about?"

"Uh, yes ma'am. Sorta."

"Mm-hm. I already told you, you don't need no Black
consciousness group, Busara. You were born Black and every
day the good Lord allows you to wake up you're conscious.
That's all the Black consciousness you need." She changed
gears and levels of anger.

"What kind of damned school group meets until 10:00 at
night?"

(Damn it! Knew that would come back and bite me in the ass.
Instincts, man. Instincts.)

"Ma. I... um, I don't go... it's, uh, it's not a school thing."
"Oh, it's not? So, you not only left the house without permission but you lied to me, too. Right? Okay." She let that linger
for a minute. Read that as extra ass whippings.
"Then where do you go?" She squeezed out between her
teeth.
"Ma it's... I..."
"It's what? You what? Don't act like you can't talk now. You
were so smooth with the 'it's a school group' -thing you could
have sold dress shoes to a cobbler. You better open your mouth
and tell me where you were going."
"Yes, ma'am. The meetings are at St. Stephens. In the community rooms."
"At the church, huh? Hm." She paused in thought. "Is that
true, Busara?"

She looked square in my mouth like she was measuring every letter
of every word that left my mouth. I answered as definitively as I could.

"Yes, ma'am. They're down the street at Saint Stephens. If you
go any Tuesday or Thursday you'll see them there."
She silently stared at me. Lifetimes passed in mere seconds.
She sat back and began thinking to herself aloud, "...and at
least it's at a church, it can't be that bad."

She took another second or two in thought before she looked up and
saw me watching. It appeared to trigger something.

"How long you been going to those meetings, Busara?"

(Oh shit! Totally didn't think she would ask… she's really gonna kill me. I… man… fuck it.)

"Busara?!" She insisted
"A… about four weeks."
"Four weeks… four weeks!? What, since you had that permission slip?"

I nodded silently. She, conversely, was not silent at all.

"You've been leaving my house empty, window wide open with steps that *you* put under it, showing everybody how to break in my house… for four weeks?!"

I silently nodded again. I stayed as quiet as I can get away with. She didn't need any help being angry at that point.

"I just can't believe you out here de-mon-stra-ting how to get into my house! But I better believe it because you were doing it. Weren't you?"

More nodding. Questions are the worst. They hammered the misery right in.

"Here I am, worried about you every time I leave to go to work or church. Now I got to worry if somebody saw you crawling in and out of here like you Spiderman or somebody! You running loose in this neighborhood at all times of night.

Someone could have seen you, Busara. Look at you – you're dressed like a burglar in your all black. What if somebody shot you? Huh? What if they thought *you* were trying to break into these projects and steal something and they just shot you? Did you ever think about that?"

(Oh damn! I never thought like that. I live here. It didn't cross my mind that someone could think I didn't. And all those gunshots every night…)

"Huh?" She insisted.
"N… no ma'am."
"Shoot! You know what… just go to your room. I'll meet you there. And I really hope it was worth the price you're about to pay for it. Get your butt out of my face."

I hotfooted it up the stairs to my room. I took the route around the living room table as far away from my mother's reach as possible. I didn't want her to change her mind and catch me before I got up there.

There's no need to get graphic on the aftermath. Otherwise we could go several chapters drowning in the minutia of why you don't piss off my mom. I intimately knew that to be true and you want to just trust me on that. No, we won't go there. Suffice it to say, though, that this wasn't one of those times she 'kicked my butt a little bit more'. 'Little' had nothing to do with it but that 'more' part was way too real. I think she was trying to beat my connection to the 'Group out of me. She could certainly stop me from going, and she did, but she didn't know that disconnecting me wasn't possible. She would have had to take a part of me to do that. Ma fell just short, though, because it definitely felt like parts of my ass were left on that belt.

Not sure if you noticed or not but my mother did not curse. No matter how angry she was there was always some decorum to her conversation. She was a true Christian woman and her principles were steadfast. I told you before that she had a high value for words and their strength. Yes, she was upset that I had betrayed her trust, disobeyed her rules and lied to her. She was surely livid. But her character prevailed over momentary frustration.

It was within her stringent spiritual belief that she had to maintain a chased heart and mind. That meant she also had to congruently filter her speech. Her commitment to her spirituality had no limits and it was omnipresent. Hence, neither situations nor circumstances ever took my mom out of character. Unfortunately for me, that didn't mean you couldn't bring out her fury.

And I foolishly brought it out. Her child rearing technique was old testament where "sparing the rod" meant "spoiling the child". I can fervently assure you, I wasn't spoiled. She had just exercised that belief on me in full.

Afterwards, I laid in bed (as best I could lie down amidst many much-worse-than-low-level pains) with a million things running through my head. I couldn't stop thinking about the fish that got away - the Gum Boot Dance. If I had just lasted one more week...

CHAPTER 12

BREAKING NOT BROKEN

So, it's clear that I wasn't precisely an angel. Halos would not have found a home on my head. Shit, I still rarely wear hats. I wasn't obstreperous though, I didn't have fits or tantrums or pout to get my way. The adventurous defiance of joining Kowrie was literally about my manhood, not childishness. No other situation in my life was ever like that, either.

It cannot go unsaid: I was super bummed about leaving Kowrie. I had truly connected with the group. The more I learned about its roots and purpose the more I felt I was learning about me. Sadly, one of the factors of maturity is learning to move on. My mother was painfully insistent that I didn't have a choice. So, I moved on.

They say the best way to get over an old love is a new one. For me, I was looking for something to occupy my focus and I turned to the clarinet. I didn't pick this instrument, though. I don't know what your middle school was like but at mine the instrumental music teacher handed you an instrument then started teaching it to you. The classes were split by section: first and fifth periods were brass, second and sixth periods were woodwinds and third period was strings. I landed in his class on second period so he put a clarinet in my hands and that was that. At least I didn't get stuck playing a recorder.

Students typically just shrug their shoulders, take what's handed to them and try to get a good grade. I was no different. After I lost Kowrie (that's how it felt), I started learning the scales on the clarinet, learned to read music a bit and got pretty comfortable with it. Ultimately, I taught myself a solo version of Star Wars. Before figuring that out, playing the clarinet was just 'meh'. When I learned how to rock that Star Wars piece, though, I was amped! In the early 80's Star Wars was everything. I was the man because I was able to flex that on anybody. I was pretty proud of myself.

That was an incredibly short-lived passion. Before I could really get into the clarinet someone had stolen it. Let me unpack that: some pre-teenage criminal stole my clarinet! I was on pins and needles trying to figure out how to tell my mom.

When the school assigned you an instrument your parents would have to sign for the responsibility. It was in my custody when it was lost so my mom would have had to pay for it. When she had to pay for it then I would have to pay for it, you know what I'm sayin'? I was NOT looking forward to delivering that news.

So, I held out a day. I told my teacher I had left it at home and that earned me a zero for the day. That was the least of my concerns, I was trying to give myself time to find it. Actually, I was just stalling. I had no faith that it was going to be recovered.

Fortunately for me, the idiot middle schooler who stole the clarinet soon figured out he wasn't a fence. He couldn't get any value for it, and apparently he wasn't himself a woodwinds player, so he left it sitting somewhere. Moron.

In a super dramatic twist, the guy who then found it was the brother of a girl I went to private school with years earlier. She told me he had it the next day because he had brought it home. So, I went to their house to retrieve it. Her brother was playing a tough asshole until she intervened and got him to give it back. I'm glad she was there because dude was a huge eighth grader and I was still in my fifth grade body. Didn't matter: if we had to go those rounds it just would've gone down. I would've taken ten of anybody's ass whippings over the idea of getting one from Ma. Fortunately, I didn't have to test that theory to get the clarinet back.

Once that semester was over I was done with that thing. That clarinet only represented a way to get in trouble to me. I didn't like it enough to assume any level of risk so it was done. I got my counselor to get me into gym the next semester and that was the end of my first instrumental music stint. I started playing basketball in school and Ma didn't reject it. So, that became my thing.

Outside of my Kowrie Group anomaly, I was basically terrified of my mother as a kid. That definitely kept me in line but I was still a kid. I did stupid things like any little kids do. Ma didn't just 'kick my butt a little more' because she got bored. I would cut up sometimes and everyone would know when I got in trouble because our neighborhood was that kind of tight. Sorta like Mama's town back in the day except we had street lights and A/C. Of course, the 'Neighborhood Network' was always in full effect, too.

Speaking of Mama, I want you to focus on the big picture. What does my family gene mean? I told you my Mama made stuff happen. More than just working a job, if she had a need then she created the supply: Mama built a frickin' log cabin, for Heaven's sake! Ma worked religiously to provide for our home. She saw a need and went to work reforming her life. Y'all already know Bubba was a hustler extraordinaire. Yeah it's true that he was pressed to just have some money to eat, that was a definite motivator. It still doesn't lessen the fact that he drove a truck long enough to retire and probably built a measurable percentage of St. Louis with his side hustles. Bubba was a go-getter! And I grew up with an uncle who owned the most prestigious funeral parlor in the region. He was featured in Jet magazine a couple times and everything.

Listen: my uncle's funeral parlor did some extra 'thangs'. They once buried a famous musician in a baby grand piano. That got them in the Jet the first time. Then they were published again for funeralizing a guy standing up. It was one of the guy's last wishes because he 'didn't want people looking down on him'. People have some real issues, y'all.

The compendium of all that family history is: hustling is a family trait. It makes total sense that I would be industrious from the start. And, yeah, I was. The empty space created by leaving the Kowrie Group put me on that path over the next couple years. I took that commitment-energy and channeled it into being industrious.

When other kids were playing I was finding a way to make money. See, Ma was our only provider and she didn't have a lot of expendable income. A lot of those "no's" that I got so frequently were due to our fiscal disposition. Straight up? I wanted more yesses, y'all! So, I decided I would make my own money. My approach was serious and I was judicious in evaluating what was working for me.

Case in point: my first hustle. Selling pencils.

I was in elementary school when Ma had bought me a 12-pack of Snoopy pencils because I was nailing grades. I was proud as hell when I walked up into the school with them. A kid in my class thought they were so cool he offered to buy one. That's when I started offering to sell them.

A whole pack costed about $.89. I sold each pencil for a dime. I reupped every time I ran out, I even started stocking them once I got my profits up. I really liked those pencils from the start. They got boosted into the love category when they made money for me.

Marketing made the business. I played the pencils up, like they were the best thing in school. If you didn't have one of these Snoopies then you weren't cool. This created the trend where everyone wanted to have one of my pencils. I started selling them for a quarter each before long.

I made a killing! It was an elementary school-level killing (overall I may have made $30-40 profit that school year) but my early grasp of supply, demand, profit and entrepreneurship was invaluable. They were powerful lessons to learn at such a young age. That venture worked out sensationally for me. My next one... not so much.

The following summer I tried collecting aluminum cans. It was a lot of work on the front end: scrounging for cans, finding enough to think it was worth the effort, cleaning them, crushing them, placing them in a bag and toting them to the recycling center. The return, though, was paltry. I'd spend a whole day or two collecting then take in several pounds of aluminum only to get a couple dollars.

My cost/benefit analysis said that wasn't working.

The need to create my own pocket budget built my eye for opportunities. I could see demands that were bereft of a supply. The key for me to get involved in such shortages was finding a way for me to capitalize on the need. I lived in the lower Midwest and we had serious seasonal weather. The winters were filled with snow and the greenery of spring brought all kinds of landscaping opportunities. Unfortunately, I lived in housing projects where grown people were full-time employees who covered every version of landscaping need. So, those hustles (shoveling snow and cutting grass) were basically not afforded me. I still managed to recognize a need.

My first gig ever? Two years later at thirteen years old. Thirteen! One-three. Y'all know the 70's and 80's were a different time. A working 13 year old in this contemporary climate means prison sentences for somebody. But I was getting paid. And I created the job.

We lived near a retirement home. I walked past there often and the grass was normally well-kempt and expertly groomed. Their grounds crew was one guy who was super sharp at his job. The home was the nicest, best kept and best managed building in all the projects. It was both gated and secure. It was as if some different people lived there and managed the facility than those who managed the rest of the projects. It was totally disconnected in stature.

One day, I noticed it wasn't so sharp. It wasn't wild or completely unkempt but it looked off from normal. I thought maybe the dude who took care of it had quit or something. I saw opportunity! I thought, they needed someone to take care of their landscaping, I needed some money and I had a whole summer to occupy. Seemed like a match to me. I decided to try my luck. What did I have to lose, right?

You would've been proud of me. I certainly was. I walked into the place on the humble and shot my shot. I had no idea what I was going to say, I didn't know how to go about getting a job and I had no idea who could help me get it done. I couldn't even make a plan because I was too far out of my element to form one.

So? I was thirteen, it was time to wing some shit! Without bragging, I made the best sales pitch of my life. Of course, it was the only sales pitch I ever made at that point but don't concentrate on the wrong details.

I walked into the senior citizens home with a smile. The office door was open so I strolled into it as if I belonged there. More accurately, I tried not to look lost. I'm sure I did anyway.

When I walked in a young lady greeted me. She had just hung up the phone. She smiled at me and it made my day.

> "Well, hello young sir! How are you doing today?" She said through a wonderful smile. It felt like an angel was talking to me.
>
> "I'm great, ma'am. How are you today?" I replied with all my teeth showing.

"I am great, too. Thank you. What can I do for you today, sir?"
She offered kindly.

"Well, is your manager in, ma'am?"

I didn't really know what to say but I had seen a lot of movies where people asked for managers. I figured that's how you get things done. So, it's the play I rolled with.

"Yes she is. Can I tell her who is inquiring?" She said, almost laughing.

I put on my professional hat. Not actually a 'hat', I never really wore hats like that, I'm not a hat fan, but you know what I'm saying. Don't get technical on me now. I hit her hard with the James Bond, also the most frequent introduction I'd seen on TV.

"Yes, ma'am. I'm Dizzy. Busara Dizzy. Glad to meet you." I stuck my hand out and she shook it.

She looked like she would burst into laughter at any minute.

"Well, Mr. Dizzy, Busara Dizzy, I'm Madison, Kelly Madison. I'm the manager here. What do you need, Mr. Dizzy?" She was actually chuckling now.

I thought it was a good thing. Happy is always good, right? So I rolled with it.

"Well, um, Ms. Madison, it looks like the yard is growing some character outside your building. It appears you could use a hand out there. And I have two."

I emphasized the point by putting my hands up. She could no longer contain herself. She burst out with a hearty laugh that made me smile even harder.

"It appears you do, Mr. Dizzy. What do you have in mind?"

Whatever was going on in her life, I had arrived at the perfect time. She was happy from the minute I walked in until I left out the door with my first job. I don't think I've had that easy a time selling anything since then. Hell, I've had a harder time giving things away than I did getting that job. I'm gonna quote Cube when I say, "it was a good day."

Turns out, the maintenance guy was only out sick. And he hadn't been out long. My characterization of the yard needing 'a hand' was an exaggeration, for sure. That's probably why the young manager lady was laughing. Still, you she gave me love and my first job.

The groundskeeper had returned the day I got started and I was turned over to his supervision. He kept me busy and I operated like his assistant for the rest of that summer. The maintenance guy was an absolute character. He was animated and always affable. I liked working with the guy, he was cool as shit. Never sweated me. I went to work happy daily like, "I got a job!" I was 13, I didn't have enough experience to know jobs suck. Ignorance is bliss, man.

I worked for anywhere between seven to nine weeks. When the summer was over they gave me one fat check! It was fat to me because it was mine and it was in the hundreds. I was rich! Ma made arrangements for me to cash it and I was as happy as a kid in the candy store with a pocket full of money. And I would know how that felt because that's exactly what I did: I went to the candy store with a pocket full of money!

Ma and Mama were so proud of me. I was proud of me, too! It was a terrific feeling going back to school after working. (Especially with a few fresh items I bought myself – baller!) The thing that stuck with me most, though, was success. I like that I achieved my goal by walking in that building and talking to that lady. It taught me to be brave. I like that I had my own money. It taught me some principles of freedom.

Oh, and I loved the power I had with my own money, that I could make choices. That's when it hit me: a dollar represents a choice. The more dollars I have the more choices I can make. That's what power is - making choices! Once I had that 'eureka' moment I knew I had unleashed something within me. I had to be in that spot again.

So, I had these two homies, like, my real dogs. My man Word and my dude Gene. Different Gene. Mel and Mike would also hang with us. I can't forget Dave, he was down too. Dave was like the guru on all things we got into. He was kind of a researcher like that, he wanted to know stuff so he would share it with us like he was the 'source'. He was the 'Google' for my crew.

Now, in retrospect Dave could've been completely fabricating shit. If he was we wouldn't have known. He was literally talking about stuff we didn't know so he could've pulled wool over our eyes and we would've been thrilled while he did it. He was kinda out there, too. He called himself 'Storm'. To my recollection no one else did. That made it really weird.

My real dudes, though, were Gene and Word. We did all the neighborhood things together. We played all the games together, ate new candies together, talked about sports, you name it. We made up new games to play and stuff, too.

We played a game of basketball on the monkey bars. What you had to do was get the basketball through any hole in the monkey bars and that would be two points. Any hole. That would earn you three free throws on the actual basketball court. The first man to 32 would win. It was a crazy fun game and I had a blast with my guys. We did all kinds of kid stuff together.

All of our developmental phases were spent together. We were growing kids, that's how that works. So, when kung fu got popular we were into that together. Everybody wanted to be Bruce Lee, of course. Then, for some reason, we were digging on Kizz. Yeah, the rock band. Sticking our tongues out and nodding our heads like crazy was our thing. Every one of us swore we had the best air guitar solo! It was a challenge that was begging to happen but never really materialized (pun intended). We were really feeling Kizz for a good little while.

Then "Breakin'" the movie came out. What?!? Immediately it was on! Word became Big Word, Gene became Thrust and I was Jay Dog. We were totally sold out for some breakdancing. There was another dude, Mike, who was down from the start. Once we started to perform, though, he had a major case of stage fright. We later realized that he was developmentally disabled. Oops. After learning that we felt kinda bad for putting him out there.

Ultimately, we started putting it together. We made a routine sorta like what they did on the movie "Beat Street", which came out a little later. We had this routine where we all bust out the same moves. We were cold! We would try to look exactly the same so it would look crisp and smooth at the same time. Then, of course, we would break off and rock our solo specialties.

Big Word did the Turbo Walk and Thrust would do all the floor work (kamikaze, backspin, etc.). I did the Boogaloo like Rerun from "What's Happenin'". Real fans know him as Shabba Doo but I won't be mad at you for slippin'. I would top off my skill set with a Colt 45: drop it down low on one knee then spin back up. We were tight.

We got serious with it in no time and decided we needed a look. The culture demanded that you had a few things: a name, some flavor and proof of your skills were at the top of the list. So, we went with what we thought was the rough look.

Our 'uniform' had some serious edge to it.

Stage names?	Check!
Muscles shirts?	Check!
Studded wristbands?	Check!
Parachute pants?	Check!
Ear clip (w/hanging feather)?	Check!
Cardboard/linoleum tile?	Check!
Asian bandana (complete w/writing)?	Check!
Boom Box?	Damned right!

The funniest one on the list is the bandana. We tried to have, like, a tough vibe. What possessed us to get headbands that made us look like Ralph Macchio? To symbolize 'tough'? I have no idea. They were popular, though. I also cannot tell you why that was true. But when we rolled up with the cardboard and the roach clips hanging from our ears we looked ready for business. We were killing it! At least, we thought we were. We may have looked like orphans or something to old people (carrying cardboard around and stuff) but we felt great about it. We were ready!

Battles were the thing. Actually, battles were everything in the culture. You're not any good if you can't prove it by beating somebody in a direct challenge. It was a standard of the culture. So, we battled all the time. The biggest stand-off we had, that I can remember, was against some dudes named Kevin Baldwin and Puddinhead.

A big crowd gathered around to see us, the Street Side Breakers, take them on. That doesn't mean the people were there *just* to see *US* in a battle. That would be mad arrogant and blithely untrue. They were there to see breakdancing, so they crowded around us when we got started. To me, that made it seem like it was important.

The crowd was so big that it felt like I was in a concert or something. I couldn't see the end of it from where I was standing, but I wasn't that tall so… whatever. It was a lot a people, y'all. To me, they were there to see us. So, I felt like a celebrity for no damned reason. Dawg, it was off the fucking chain! (That's a slightly-less-than-contemporary colloquialism for 'totally awesome').

We were handling those dudes until Puddinhead pulled out his secret weapon. This dude would do a Waterwave with a lit cigarette in his mouth, flip the cigarette into his mouth then reverse the wave and bring it out, still lit, while blowing smoke from his nose. Grown folk move, right there. He wowed the crowd with that, for sure. It was tough to beat. I would be lying to you if I told you we won that battle. Instead, I just won't say who the winners were. This ain't their story!

But we wowed the crowd, too! On a regular basis we had people screaming, applauding and congratulating us and stuff. The best part of it? We were rocking together out in the neighborhood pretty often. People would stop and watch to check us out, we were pretty good.

So, one day we went down to the stadium, cardboarded up. We got a good spot not far from the exits of the Cardinals game and set up shop. We had 'Rock It' by Herbie Hancock cranking out of the boom box and went to work. As soon as that first "waymp-waymp, waymp-waymp…" came through the speakers it was automatically a party. We became adept at keeping that party going.

Side note: boom boxes were expensive as hell. Not just to buy the thing but you needed a trunk-full of D batteries to make it work. Those D batteries were the most expensive ones on the market and you had to have an army of them! They might as well have been hand weights because they added an easy ten pounds to the radio. You had to do a workout just to carry the damned thing all the time. It was crazy.

So, the music was blaring, we were dressed out like 'Beat Street' extras (or a whole crew of Ozone impersonators) and we were showing all our skills. We put a shoebox down on the ground while we did our thing hoping we might get a few bucks. While we were doing our routine, in the middle of a Waterwave line, I saw white people walking by throwing money in the shoebox.

And they kept tossing it in!

When I saw that I started waving harder than a mutha fucka! Damned near yanked Big Word's arm out of socket. I was like...

"Man, you see them put that money in there???!!!"

I was dancing my ass off, y'hear me? From the second they started putting money in the box I did everything extra hard. So, we used to do the Airplane Spin. Thrust would put his legs around my waist and I would helicopter him in a circle, his arms flared out to the audience like airplane wings. We made it look really cool.

This time when we did it, I got crazy excited while we were spinning because the people kept throwing money in the shoebox. It was like Candy Crush, I kept hearing the change go "jingling, jingling, jingling". The hustler gene was activated and I was hype! I was saying,

"Daaaaamn!"

We were making a lot of money and I was amped! I started spinning faster and faster until I heard this faint voice saying,

"BuuuSaaaaRaaaa... aaaaaaaaaaah!"

When I finally let Thrust down he had scars and shit on his forehead. His forearms were all scuffed up, he even had a few small pebbles embedded in his skin. His hair seemed a little extra… uh, blown? It was wild as hell. I swear there were a few pieces of gravel in his clothes. He had hit the ground a couple times coming around the circle, bouncing and skipping off of it because I was spinning like crazy listening to those coins drop.

Dude was NOT happy.

Normally, once I set Thrust down he would bust a pose: he'd lie on the ground with his legs crossed, one of his arms on his hip, his chin leaning on his propped up arm like, "try to do that!" He had it so cold that you could virtually hear the sound effects when he came to a snappy stop and locked into it like a mannequin – "pa-dow!" He really had that down to a science.

But this time? He rolled to a raggedy, uncoordinated stop and he looked worn the hell out. Thrust was breathing heavily as hell. He started removing the rocks and stuff, trying to dust himself off. His eyes had red streaks in them like he desperately needed some Visine or something. Thrust was staring at me like, "mutha fucka! What did you just do? Are you fucking trying to kill me?!?" He wasn't insane enough to volunteer for any more of those damned Airplane Spins. You can believe that.

Oh, but I was inspired! I was on fire! The shoebox was packed with money! We couldn't see the bottom of the box and could barely see the sides. Seeing all of that money put a Cheshire Cat-sized smile on all of our faces.

We were all proud of how we had scored with that one performance. Hell, we even made enough to buy batteries for that damned shoulder jukebox – twice! All jokes aside, we made a horde of money that day. We couldn't stop high-fiving each other. We were successful beyond anything we expected.

Another thing I didn't expect was my mother's response. Ma was not thrilled when I got home and told her what we did. She seemed almost disgusted.

> "Man, Black folks been dancing for money and performing for white folks forever. I don't want that for you." She explained, "I don't want you to become 'Mr. Entertainer', 'Mr. Shoe Shine Boy', or, you know, 'Mr. Buffoon' for the white folks. Don't do that. You better use your brain to figure out how to get what you need in life."

That may seem rough because I was on a high of being successful. But successful at what? Everything she said was right. I didn't like what she said as a 13 year old, of course, but she wasn't 13. She saw the real picture and wanted me to be, knew I already *was* greater than that. I more than respect that she was that woman, I'm thankful. It's where I needed to be mentally and she helped me see that.

I didn't fully see it then, though. In the moment, I was straight frustrated. I wanted to get my hustle on and make some money off of those people. Kowrie had fortunately taught me some insight to my value as a Black man, so, I partially understood where my mom was coming from. Still, I was determined to hustle somehow. Maybe it was just in my blood or maybe the ancestors were telling me to keep going because they knew what was coming. Either way, I stayed on the grind. And the grind kept working for me, in more ways than I knew.

CHAPTER 13

PROVIDENCE

So, the 'going downtown, making some money'-thing was out. My entrepreneur vibe had to take a raincheck on that one. She didn't say I couldn't breakdance, though. So, we continued rehearsing and stuff. We still had frequent battles against other crews. Sometimes people would come to our practices and invite us to different things. When talent shows came up we would definitely rock those. We, or more accurately I, just couldn't hustle on the street. I accepted that, not like I had a choice but... you know. I took it in stride.

Street Side was really good because we worked hard at perfecting our craft. It didn't hurt, at all, that our rehearsals were live as hell! We would practice out in the open in the back of my building. There was a cyclone fence between the Peabody's and the junkyard behind us. Next to the fence was the basketball court with the monkey bars where we made up that shooting game I told you about. It made for a great place to practice because it was like a makeshift venue.

Half the neighborhood would come listen to the music and watch us put some work in. We'd drop some cardboard, crank up the radio and put our performances together right there in front of everybody. Even just practicing made us popular, that was one of the perks. We were like the unofficial breakdancing crew of the Peabody's! We always got love from the 'hood and it kept us going.

Amidst the practicing and the performing, we stayed incredibly visible. Our crew was building a substantial following and we kept battling! We took on challengers as often as we could and whenever the opportunity presented itself. And, as the Peabody breaking ambassadors, the projects had our back. They supported us when we had gigs and battles. Through serving crews, we built a really strong reputation. That rep got us into more than a few shows and kept us active in town.

Sometimes I have to retrospectively check my takes. Like right now. We were one of many breakdancing crews in the Peabody's. I mean, there were a whole lot of crews! We definitely were not heralded as like the 'official break dancers' of the projects, that was taking it too far. We got a lot of support, sure, but that was relative. If 50 people happened to be around watching us that was a hell of a lot to me. I was just fricking 13. When you're that young, and innocently narcissistic, 50 people focused on you feels like the whole world.

Realistically, though, the number fifty is not an exorbitant amount of people. And "half the neighborhood"? There were easily hundreds of people living in the Peabody's – 50 is not half of hundreds. There *was* more than enough to get me geeked to go, I'll tell you that. The concert vibe was happening for me.

And, I don't even think I ever heard anyone refer to us as the best in the 'hood. Nobody called us the worst, either. Just to be honest with you, we were probably middle of the road. We never got embarrassed by someone just killing us in a battle so we had reason to think we were good. The 'hood never really gave us any kind of distinction, either. Not really. They just got free shows when we practiced so they gave us love. Makes a lot of sense to me.

I don't want to be misleading in my assessments, is all. Playing it like we were the dopest thing going would be a fun embellishment but it's not at all historically correct. I gotta rep the Peabody's the right way. So, no, we were not the 'hood breaking ambassadors but we always represented. We were out there constantly and that did get us some attention.

Enter Chuck Cantrell. Chuck was in his young twenties and, to me, an anomaly of the projects. His speech didn't seem like he belonged in the Peabody's. It wasn't an outcast type of thing, or anything like that. He was just really polished for a young cat in the 'hood.

That's not to say the projects were filled with idiots because that would be bullshit. I've known plenty intelligent people from the Peabody's, including yours truly. But there is a particular verbal twang that generally shines through. You kinda know when people are from our neck of the woods by the way they talk. Chuck didn't have that.

He was from a highly educated family and seemed to have congruently high aspirations. Chuck was just a different-level guy than who you normally ran into in the projects. It was weird that he was around at all. He saw us rehearsing frequently and took an interest in pushing us further.

Ultimately, he took on a role as our undeclared manager. Chuck worked diligently to get us signed into different shows and he kept us performing. He wasn't a part of our rehearsals and never really had any input in how we did our thing. That's not how he operated. He knew that wasn't his area and didn't even try to put his hand in it. He trusted that we could rock crowds and kept getting us stages to do it on.

We never paid him anything because we weren't making money and he didn't ask for any. That's one of those things that made Chuck exceptional: he dedicated his time to us simply because he wanted to see us succeed. He had a community focus and invested himself in the betterment of young people. How he helped us was just a small portion of that commitment.

Chuck had some business background and he was a pretty sharp guy. I don't know what degree he had earned at Mizzou but he had solid business skills. He had organized a calendar for us and handled all of our affairs as if our dance crew were a business. I think his most effective skill, though, was networking. Chuck had the gift of gab and he let it ride for us. He did a great job connecting with people who could connect us to performance opportunities. This is how he kept us working. We were a helluva team: Chuck talked to the people, the Street Side Breakers rocked them. We were an '80's power team.

Ma had been slowly but surely easing up on my constraints. I had just turned 13 and her grip was steadily loosening. The work we were doing with Street Side Breakers pulled me out of the house more and more and she allowed it to roll. Each yes was more surprising than the last but I continued asking. I was *always* respectful and asked permission, of course. I had no designs on ruining that flow or slowing it.

Before I realized it, I was away from the house as much as I spent time there. Chuck was a large part of that. She knew we were in the hands of a college grad from a good family and that we weren't "shuckin' and jivin'" for white people so she didn't stop me.

So, I dug in with all I had. I was proud to be a part of something I helped build. It was a major plus that it garnered me some degree of freedom.

Freedom.

Having the levity to operate changed the world for me. It was a sheer privilege that I was able to move around like that. Certainly the freedom alone was huge but being able to rock stages because of it took me over the top. I was living a dream.

My fellas and I put our crew together from just vibing a trend and sticking with it. We achieved some levels of success with it locally by building a brand. Being guided by Chuck was the best external thing that happened to our crew. It was ironic: I was forced to leave a group I valued highly after watching them 'dance' then created a dance crew with high value for me. Total different types of entities and purposes, obviously, but the parallels were there. Then they melded.

Just after I got into high school, Chuck got us invited to the St. Stephens Talent Show. We had never rocked on their stage before because we weren't a serious crew the prior year. Yes, we were 'hood popular' but you have to understand - the Talent Show was a major event in our neighborhood. I told you earlier, it was *that thing*! Everybody was there and it was always live.

We were dancing vets by then, sure, but we didn't have the clout to get invited. There were lots of breaking crews in the 'hood, standing out for this show was hard to do. To make it a shade more difficult, none of us in the crew really sought gigs out. Before Chuck, we just got in shows that came at us. We never committed real effort to try to get in the 'Show, per se. And, honestly, we were a bit intimidated by it.

To be completely transparent, I don't think I fully applied myself because the money wasn't there. Once Ma stopped us from rocking the stadium it just became a thing to do for fun. I would give my all at being good but I didn't feel a future or current cash in pushing it. So, I didn't.

Then we got Chuck. He put that work in, used his networking tools and got us the kind of attention we needed. He's the reason we got invited. You know when he told us he got us in that we were geeked, right? Man, I jumped up and down like we had just hit the lottery for millions. We knew that put us on that next level. It made us feel like we were *that crew*, y'know?

So, we're at St. Stephens but we're not hitting the stage yet. Our confidence was colossal, we rocked our Street Side Breakers uniforms with pride. Quietly though, we looked like we were either going to dance behind Michael on the "Beat It" music video or beat up some small kids. It was a tossup. Chilling with the crowd, we were waiting for our turn to be called. There were vendors everywhere selling goodies and the smell in the air was straight delicious. I distinctly remember reaching out to grab the $1 Sno Cone I had just bought when...

THWOOOMM!!!

I never considered myself a 'jumpy' person. I wasn't particularly easy to startle. There is only one situation I had experienced in my life that tested all of that, frequently. I knew it was the only thing that could do it again. This talent show is where it initially captivated me and I knew what the sound was when I heard it. That still didn't stop it from rattling me and I was ecstatic that it did. Shit, I wasn't even mad about dropping my Sno Cone. If you know how difficult it was for a St. Louis teenager in the Peabody's to acquire dollars in 1983 then you know that's saying something. (Dude gave me another Sno Cone anyways, it was a church function for crying out loud).

Again, I just about jumped out of my bones when Kowrie made the stage quake. I told you, it was like that teacher slamming a book on the floor. That's an incredibly fitting analogy because the sound on the stage at that first talent show had awakened me. That awakening is what gave me the bravery to defy my mom. It changed how I saw many things in life to that point. It also greatly influenced how I received and processed information from that point forward. Everything about my perspective regarding the country I lived in, even who I was and where I come from, was irrevocably altered from my Kowrie Group experience. When I first came across them I thought I had stumbled across the best thing in my life.

It was serendipitous to be in that moment again.

Seeing those guys on stage again gripped me more than it did the first time. I had a much greater appreciation knowing how much went into what they did and where it derived. I had spent quality time with the group. It mattered. Even though I fell short of learning the African Gum Boot Dance, I felt like I was out there with them. I didn't brag to my fellas about it or anything, but I felt a deep sense of pride about being connected to them. I was cheering on my brothers, y'know?

I wanted to go kick it with the guys but I was more than a bit ashamed. I had bailed on the meetings without any notice or goodbyes. Nardy had most likely told them my mother took me out of the group. He had asked me the following Friday after I missed that first meeting and I told him the situation. If you thought he would have been an ass about it, well, that makes total sense. Before I told him, I thought so, too. I mean, he was the guy who wouldn't willingly give me the info to get in, right? But we would have been wrong. He and I were brothers in the 'Group. That was real for him. When I told him what was up, he was sad I couldn't roll. That made it even tougher for me.

I automatically thought that the first thing some of the brothers would do was invite me back. At the very least they would have made me feel welcome. That's just how they were. Nearly three years had passed but I was still pretty certain that Ma wouldn't let me join again. So, I spared myself some degree of anguish by not reconnecting. I didn't want to have to face telling them no and that I couldn't return. It felt like I would've been pouring salt into my wound. That's why I didn't go holler at them when they got off stage.

After they sent their shockwave through the audience, my Street Side Breakers crew rocked the stage several acts later. I was completely charged up by seeing the Kowrie Group there and I took it on the stage with me. We didn't stop traffic like they did but we had heads knocking. Seriously, "Rock It" is a straight classic! It's kind of a cheat, actually. Anybody who played that song in the 80's was going to have people dancing. That's why some really smart guy on our team picked that song for us to perform on. (I'll let you guess who it was). The music was thumping, the crowd was partying and my crew was killing it on the stage. My adrenaline shot so far through the roof that it turned into a courage pill or something. Whatever it was, I got determined to find the Kowrie crew when we got off stage.

I looked all over the church grounds for them. I thought I might be able to catch a few of the guys grabbing something to eat or playing a game so I checked those areas. Not one of them could be found. I ran into one of the parishioners during my search and asked if he knew where I could find anyone from Kowrie. He told me they had another engagement for the night. They had already left the venue.

That sucked. I had missed my shot to kick it with them for a bit. That made me feel pretty crunchy about waiting.

I was entirely dejected leaving the church because it occurred to me that I might have been there for a reason. Maybe I was *supposed* to reconnect with the Organization. It still meant a lot to me, it was the deepest thing I had ever experienced in my young life. I thought that maybe I had, again, missed my window. There's was just something about the Kowrie Group for me that was... it just resonated with my soul. It was the kind of deep that would not easily be forgotten. Fortunately, I was a teenager so my life had the fluidity to move on pretty rapidly. Ultimately, even though I really didn't like the thought, I'd be fine without the 'Group. Or so I thought.

One Tuesday afternoon a few weeks later, Chuck came to our practice and told us he had a meeting for us to go to at 7:15. He said it would more than improve our performances but also prepare us for everything we would want to do. We were all inspired and talked to our parents. I was surprised when Ma said it was okay. I told her it was for Street Side and it wasn't going to cost anything. She watched me grow in my commitment and she respected it. So, she didn't trip.

I did, though! I was completely trippin' on her answer. I was happy as hell anytime I was allowed to get free. For any reason! This was a glaring statement for me. I was growing up and I was proud to be able to see it. I don't know where my open introspection came from but I've always had it. I think it helped me value life in the moment. It was clear to me that my own maturity was rapidly unfolding in that moment – life was progressing for me. Whatever Chuck had in mind wasn't remotely as important to me as being free to do it. This was a milestone that I was fortunate enough to feel when it happened. It emboldened me on my path to manhood. I was definitely feeling myself.

Conversely, the meeting wasn't handled like a huge deal. Chuck told us it was a thing, we all got permission and were set to jet a few hours later. He said the meeting spot wasn't far but he wanted us to go together. The plan was to meet at our practicing basketball court and go from there.

My whole crew was excited! This dude had only delivered for us to that point, so we had every reason to trust it would be good for us. None of us even questioned it. We didn't know what was going on but we were always down to do something different. The whole crew was at the court early. When Chuck arrived we rolled right out.

That ride was brief. A few minutes later we were just around the corner at St. Stephens. He *did* say it wasn't far. There were no signs of activity when we arrived so, at first, it struck me as a little strange. That only lasted until we walked to the community center entrance. Then I knew exactly why we were there.

I was returning to a Kowrie Group meeting!

(HELL YEAH!)

Walking into that room felt... righteous. I knew I belonged there when I went the first time and not one thing had changed. It was like coming home after a long journey without a compass or a guide. I had returned without trying. Providence had brought me back!

It took everything in my soul for me to contain my excitement in front of the fellas. What's really funny is that, even though my mind was ready to explode my mouth didn't. Maybe I was suffering from a mild level of shock but words were not forthcoming. I just rolled with the program in silent elation.

Mind you, when we got in the meeting I didn't try to join the ceremonies. That felt like it would be disrespectful, especially because I was still dealing with a degree of guilt. So, I just stood as an observer with my Street Side crew and Chuck.

It was kind of weird that Chuck didn't join the ceremonies, either. He was the one who took us there and he seemed pretty familiar with the things that took place. That struck me as sort of odd. I didn't get the impression that he was part of Kowrie, though. He seemed more like some type of a liaison recruiter or something. That made it even more meaningful that he introduced young people to the group. It was genuinely because he cared and worked to empower the youth.

Chuck appeared to live by one of the Kowrie mottos 'it takes an entire village to raise one child'. I've seen that as an indigenous people's quote but we know all of history to be *our* history. Our villages were the first known to man, our ways to build them were the nascence of mankind. Still, I can concede that many cultures share in the wisdom of community. So, let's not get wrapped around the axle about the origin and miss the point. Chuck's choice to expose us to the organization was an attempt at surrounding us with a village. There was no form of gain in it for him aside from seeing us built up. There's a special kind of honor in that.

The entire session was fantastic. Throughout the course of the evening, I was able to preface or clarify a few things for Word and Thrust. They were taught how the meetings began and ended and how to request to speak. I helped guide them through a few spots, give some background on a few others. There was a quiet pride for me in the responsibility of providing some inside understanding. It was a cool flip on my first experiences because I was taking on a form of big brother role. Don't read that to say I was the 'expert'. I was far from versed in all things Kowrie. Still, I was able to add value to their experience and that was next level stuff. Of course, I have a little sister, and she's the best. Having 'little brothers' hit differently. It was greatly rewarding to be in the circle again. Even if it was for just a night.

That wasn't the program though. Of course they were going to invite us back, and they did. Part of the allure of the Kowrie Group was being openly welcomed, despite the mantra of steady skepticism, secrecy and caution. So, as the meeting was wrapping up they extended the invitation.

Mwalimu had no plans of letting me go unnoticed.

"We're delighted that you young brothers joined us this evening. We want to invite you back in hopes that you would join us and add to the strength of our community." Mwalimu said.

Then he looked at me.

"Mr. Dizzy, it appears we were both right. After some technical difficulties, and a few years, you managed to make it back. I think you do belong here. It seems the ancestors have plans for you." He smiled as he walked to Mama Mlinzi and grabbed some papers.

"Gentlemen, we will need these forms filled out by your parents in order for you to return." Again, he zoomed in on me.

"Mr. Dizzy, I advise you to bring your mom to our session. Please let her know that we extend her an invitation."

"Yes, sir." I said.

"This is also the only way you can return."

"Um, yes sir."

When the meeting was over I walked out of that building on fire anew! Everything that the Kowrie Group was made me feel alive. Empowered.

Manly.

I was going to talk to Ma the minute I got home. Mwalimu's idea was brilliant, I knew it was the thing to do the minute he said it: ask Ma to come to a meeting. Since it was also the bar to returning, I had my work cut out for me. I was good with that.

Just like I'm trying to explain it now, the Kowrie Group was vastly more than words can depict. There is a genuine depth of purpose and community that permeated every facet of the organization. It could only be understood in its presence because it created an omnipresent aura of that exact strength and unity.

While that consistent Kowrie reality was both powerful and palpable it was not explainable. Some things in life just don't translate into words. The Kowrie Group was one of those things. Though the function of the 'Group was measurably effective, its value was beyond calculation. It was impossible to convey with paltry words like 'Black awareness'. Understanding that makes me proud that I had never used those words to describe it. The Kowrie Group was so much more.

I believe this is why Chuck didn't try to explain it to us before he took us. Kowrie was its own best selling point. I believed the approach that Mwalimu suggested would work on Ma for that exact reason: get her to come to a meeting and the 'Group would do the rest. Clearly she would see the value with her own eyes and everything would be good.

Ma could meet the mothers and ask questions that I wouldn't be able to effectively answer. Mwalimu could talk to her and she'd better understand the value of the organization's leadership. She would see for herself that the Kowrie Group was awesome. There were also a few mitigating circumstances in my favor: I was a little bit older, it took place in a church, there were moms present – I couldn't lose. Right?

I stayed optimistic on the ride home. This was a huge moment for me and I really wanted it to go well. I was single-minded in my purpose but that didn't stop me from processing my odds.

I was a pretty grounded dude so my excitement didn't make me delusional. It was painfully true that I had thoroughly tarnished the whole process with her by sneaking out. That's also simultaneously how I learned Kowrie's value to me, though. So, while I did have remorse for disobeying my mother and causing the tension about my 'Group involvement, I was beyond proud of my bravery to investigate the organization in the first place. I was still ecstatic about having the nuts to pull that off. I guess it's also fortunate I had a strong enough backside to handle those repercussions. That just seems weird to say out loud.

It no longer mattered how my 11-year-old-self handled things, though, I couldn't take it back. Life always and only moves forward from where we are. Countless scenarios played out in my head on that brief ride home. Very few of them were successful visions. I was already sold on rapping to mom about it, so the bad insights had no bearing on the task at hand. Ma was getting an invitation to a Kowrie meeting, how it went was up to her. My optimism was real but I was prepared for failure, too.

It continues to be funny to me how far your mind can travel in very little time.

When I got home I ran into the house to talk to Ma. Honestly, it was much less than an optimal time to discuss it because it was late. It just couldn't wait, it had to be done as soon as it could be done. I had enough lessons about shooting my shot that I realized the ball was again in my hands: I had to take the J!

How I approached my mother usually made a huge impact on my success. She preferred that I was direct, delivering with confidence was a plus. Being respectful was a given, of course, but she wanted me to assert myself. Whenever I beat around the bush to ask for something it was much more likely going to be a 'no'. Straight up. The issue didn't matter. She said there was no room in America for a timid Black man. Those are the words of life.

I thought of the most mature approach I could have. If I handled it like a meeting and got her to singularly focus on our conversation that would likely give me the best odds. So, I asked her if she could sit down with me so we could talk. She smiled at me and agreed. That's the exact kind of start I was looking for.

We sat together on the couch. She got settled and looked at me patiently.

She said, "what's on your mind, Man?"

"Ma, the meeting we attended tonight was at the Kowrie Group." I said.

"That's the name of that Black awareness group, right?" She responded.

She wasn't exactly pleased but she had not hardened on her stance yet. Seemed like an opening.

"Yes, ma'am." I said pensively.

"But that's not a good description of what it is. The Kowrie Group has helped me better understand myself from the standpoint of manhood. It reinforces self-respect through the respect of our elders and our ancestors. I've met guys there that I can call my brothers."

I offered the next bit carefully.

"Now, Ma, I do apologize for how it went before. I do. I was wrong, I should have been better than that. But... please don't be mad at me, but I felt like I needed to go. I don't think Chuck taking me back there, when he didn't know I was involved at all, was any kind of coincidence. It seems like it was supposed to happen. Like I should be there and it seems right to me."

She sat looking at me for a minute in thought.

"But here's the thing, Ma," I continued, "I don't want you to take my word for it. I am asking you to come with me and see it for yourself. I can't explain it as well as you being there to see it."

I gave it a minute to sink in. I was also building courage.

"So, what do you think, Ma? Can we go to a meeting together?"

She took a minute while she examined me. Her intensity felt like she was either reading a book in my eyes or waiting to see me fall apart or back out or something. What I think was actually happening is she was weighing my sincerity. All I could do was sit patiently and wait for her.

It didn't take long before she let it out.

"This really means something to you, Man?" She said.
"Yes ma'am! I just... I feel like it's something I gotta do, Ma."
I argued.

"Well, Man, I believe that. I believe it really is important to you. And I guess it's time for you to do some things. I just... when are the meetings, Man? You went when I was at choir practice and you know I'm not skipping that."

"Today is Tuesday, Ma. They have them every Tuesday and Thursday."

I, again, paused for affect.

"We can go next Tuesday, if that's okay."

She seemed iffy. I figured I should put a cherry on top. I had to seal the deal.

"If we go on Tuesday you won't have to miss anything. And you can see for yourself. It's also at St. Stephens so we'll even be at church. It's all upside, Ma."

My mom had lived a life with hustlers. I've told you about my grand-mother, my father and part of my paternal tree. She was used to the hustle. I think she liked to see the fight in me. Ma wanted me to have the effort to get what I wanted and the fervor to see it through. Right then, a half-smile crossed her face that said she was looking at what she wanted to see.

"You're laying it on thick, hunh? I love the Lord, you know I do, but I go to church enough."

We both laughed.

"We can do that, Busara. We can go to your meeting."

Then she instantly changed gears.

"You just need to know, if I don't like what I see I'm still going to say no." She authoritatively said.

"Yes, ma'am. I know that. And I respect it."

I was as serious as A.I.D.S. when I said it. She saw it.

"Okay, Mr. Serious, we'll go and see what happens."

Have you ever been completely overjoyed? I'm not sure if I had, either, but I'm sure the feeling that overcame me was close. I got up and gave her a hug. She let out a bit of a chuckle.

"Thank you, Ma!" I said.

"Aw, you're welcome, Man. Now, don't do anything crazy for the next week. I don't want you to ruin it." She warned.

I threw my hands up and said, "no ma'am! I won't mess this up!"

"You bet'not." She sternly said. Then she sweetened, "Okay. Now, go on to bed. You got school in the morning."

"Yes, ma'am. I love you, Ma."

"I love you too. Good night, Man."

"Good night, Ma."

Dawg, I was gonna go to my first Kowrie Group meeting without sneaking! Straight up, it's not a thing I thought would ever happen. A little growing up, a little bravery and a straight and honest approach opened the door for me. I had to wait a week to find out if I could keep a set of keys. Believe, it was a long week.

CHAPTER 14

ENTRANCE EXAM

The minute Ma got home from work that following Tuesday I over-emphasized our need to be early. I filled her in on how the process worked: the meeting started at 7:30:00 – not a second before or after. I told her that all the members arrived early for every session, the only people who were ever late were new *and* that tardiness meant pushups for me. That would constitute being the wrong kind of stand out and I refused to be that guy. I didn't say it exactly like that to my momma, of course, but that's the point that was delivered.

Then I looked her in the eye and stressed to her:

> "Most importantly, Ma, a man has to be dependable and that
> means being punctual. There is no honor in being late."

I distinctly remember that she had an intense look on her face while she listened to me. You could even call it disbelief but it also looked like pride. Ma cracked an awkward yet thoughtful smile then agreed to be early. I would pay real money to know what she was thinking that day but I never asked her. We left the house at 7:10. After dropping off my little sister, we arrived at St. Stephens at 7:22.

The first faces I saw when we walked in to St. Stephens were Thrust and Big Word. The Kowrie brothers were rapping to them when we walked in. I had put my crew members up on game (that means 'I had informed of the situation') and told them that being late was bad juju. I was glad to see that they listened to the point of arriving before me.

I had to remind them about not wearing logos and the philosophy behind it because one of them showed up with a Polo jacket. The logo on it was so big you could almost make out the jockey's face. He was about to freak out about it but I assured him it was cool. It was a damned jacket, man. He could just take it off, so it was no big deal. I told him to just place it in the visitors area and not to put it back on until we were leaving.

What I forgot to tell them about was the unwritten code to just wear all black. Wearing black was an easy reminder to refrain from wearing labels while helping us stay unified at the same time. When they saw the sea of black clothing from all the brothers in the building I was certain they wouldn't forget for the next session, if they returned.

Ma thought that the rule banning European brands was remarkable. She remembered when I was talking about not wearing brand names at home and added the two together. She thought it was pretty deep.

I got Ma a seat in the visitors area. I told her that the 'on-the-second' thing was real and that they used the wall clock for accuracy. She said she was going to watch it and see. I made a mental note to try to catch her reaction. I thought it might be funny to see her get startled. Well, not as much 'funny' as rare. She was, typically, an absolute rock in a storm. Seeing her get rattled would be real different.

The fellas and I continued meandering about as we kicked it. I introduced Big Word and Thrust to all of the Kowrie brothers I knew. They all carried on like they were the best of homies. Then 7:30 came.

"NDANI!"

As is the standard, the instant yet silent pandemonium ensued. Conversations stopped on a dime. The young brothers hustled to their positions in formation without another word spoken. I snuck a glimpse of Ma on my way to formation. I didn't catch her precisely on the command to 'fall in' but, by the way she was still clutching her purse, I was free to assume she was hit by it the same way I was. It's a powerful command that catalyzes hypertensive activity in the whole room. The energy itself can definitely spark a shock to your system. Quietly, I hated missing her full response.

Ma patiently watched as we went through all the opening phases of ceremony. We opened with 7 Strong Harambee, did the news reports and sat through the breathing exercise. She then watched as Mwalimu handed out assignments. I saw her face contort as the brothers requested permission to speak before they assumed their responsibilities. Watching her try to process the information reminded me of my first time. It was an awful lot to digest. She was engaged, though, and stayed quietly observant the whole time.

Candidly, I know I didn't explain 7 Strong Harambe and I won't. There are some things I am bound to keep protected. Hence, I won't divulge all things Kowrie because I can't. Painting in broad strokes is as far as I can go with some elements of the Organization. This is one such situation where the details will not be forthcoming.

When we broke off into groups, Ma spent time with the elders. She talked at length with Mwalimu and the elder sisters. I wondered what she had learned and what she went through with them.

(What kind of questions did she ask? What kind of information did they tell her? Was it stuff that I knew? What things did she learn that I didn't know about? What did she think about the Kowrie Group and all the things she learned over the course of the night ...will she say yes, I can join?)

I looked for her when we returned from groups for dismissal. I wanted to read the look on her face, see if the 'Group was working on her.

She gave up nothing.

Her expressions were non-committal and emotionless. Truly, I didn't get one clue by looking at her. I swear, I would've loved to take Ma to Vegas. Quietly, that woman would have murdered a poker table and we would've gotten paid!

Straight up though, that never would've happened. Her devout Christianity would have had nothing to do with gambling or Vegas. Well, she might have taken that trip to Nevada with me but gambling wasn't going down. Her control of her facial reactions was just a microcosm of her extensive and steadfast disciplines.

Mwalimu wrapped up the meeting with the normal processes. He addressed my mother directly because she was the only parent in the building. He took a parting shot at me while doing so. I guess I had it coming because I avoided turning in the permission slip for four weeks.

"Again, thank you for visiting us, Ms. Dizzy. It was a joy having you here. Busara is a bright young leader in the making. We'd love to have him with us. I know if he returns this time it's because he received your permission. We'll still need him to bring the permission slip with him. We dot I's and cross T's here and there are no exceptions. If you ever have any questions for us we will always be available to you." Mwalimu said to Ma.

"Thank you," Ma said humbly.

Ma silently nodded in agreement while he was talking. It was one of those "you damned right" -type of vibes. I was really hoping I wouldn't hear more on it later. I knew I would.

'Later' felt like a whole lot later. The walk to the car to go pick up Lori took forever. Seriously, it seemed like we parked in another town and took the long way to get to it. She didn't say a word before we got in the ride. In the car, she still wasn't talking. Her silence was not helping my life. I needed to know where we were, how it went and if I was getting in the organization. Every ticking second felt like an hour.

I tried to start the narrative.

> "So, what do you think, Ma?" I asked desperately.
> "Don't you ever go sneaking out the house like that again, Busara Andre Dizzy! You understand me?" She sternly and immediately fired back at me.
> "Yes, ma'am," I meekly replied.

(Aw man.)

Have you ever watched someone work through their own thought processes and could tell they had a lot going on? This was that moment. She was in her own world of thought. Occasionally, she verbalized her thoughts aloud which let me in on where she was mentally. For real though, her conversation didn't really include me. Until she aimed it directly at me, of course.

> "You had me giving those people 'what for' for nothing. They told me they asked for your permission slip every time you came. And they even gave you new ones to make sure you would turn one in! Is that true?"

"Yes ma'am. They did."

"Mm-hm. Don't you do nothing like that again, you hear me?"
She again asserted herself sternly.

"Yes ma'am."

When I responded I spoke 'just over my breath', as the old folks would say, because I was waylaid. Before she started talking I had a sense that it had gone really well. I thought she would have nothing but respect or admiration for the process. It's a great organization. She got to see it with her own eyes. I was super optimistic about my odds. What went wrong?

She was not at all in the space I thought she would be. This point was graphically laid out for me.

"That's not enough, Busara! What you did was dangerous and stupid. You risked your own safety and your whole family's safety by jumping out of my window like that. Weeks in a row! What if you fell, Busara? You climbing in or out of that window and you slip. Hunh? What then? You lying on the concrete in the alley, I'm at church and our house is wide open. What then, huh?"

I sat there with no words. I didn't see that conversation coming but it hit with a new weight. It never crossed my mind that I could fall. I was never scared getting out of or into the window but I certainly could have slipped. I could've landed on my back or some other craziness. Then who would've helped me? In the alley. It was pretty dumb. I felt really small.

"What about your family, huh? What about our house, Busara? Someone could have watched you climbing down, waited until you turned the corner then followed your path

203

back up. They let a few friends in the front door and clean us out. Take all your stuff, your baby sister's things and everything in the house. You return, happy from your meeting, to four empty walls. And a hos-tile momma! What then?"

With every one of her words I literally felt myself shrinking. At the same time my shoulders felt heavier. A lot heavier.

"What about you? What about your life, Man? What were you risking for you being out there? By yourself. Late at night. Those same people could've knocked you upside your head to get into my house. Into our house! Like I said back then, you could have been robbed or kidnapped or shot at any point on your route there or back. There are way more things out here on these streets that work against you than ones that will work for you. You have to think about what's immediately in front of your face *and* the things you can't see! The things that are coming, will come or that can reveal themselves. You have to ask yourself, "when I make this choice what are the possible consequences?" This has to be part of how you make decisions, Busara, because every choice you make will have repercussions. Every one of them! Cause and effect, Man. You are becoming a young man, real life is in your face *right now*. You can't do stupid little stuff that will risk your life or people you care about without thinking."

We came to a stop sign and she looked directly in my face.

"There is never a time for you to make decisions without thinking. Never. You understand me?"

I sulkily said, "yes ma'am".

We spent an eternity at that stop sign. It felt like it, anyways. She didn't look like she was concerned about moving.

"Now, when I tell you no, Busara Andre Dizzy, it's just no. I have my reasons. You may not understand them or like them but they're for your best interest. And you don't have to understand or agree to respect what I tell you. But you will respect me. You ask and you deal with the answer. It doesn't matter if that's a yes or a no, you take the one I give you. Do we understand each other?"

"Yes ma'am."

"Do we understand each other, Busara?"

"Yes ma'am, we do."

She peered into my eyes as if she was reading my soul. That's that thing she always did when she was looking for truth. We pulled off from the stop sign moments later but it felt like a lifetime. An incredibly cumbersome lifetime.

That car ride got real dark.

We drove the next block or so without a sound being made. She stayed quiet long enough to allow my lessons to sink in. Long enough for me to come to grips with the gravity of those choices I made and the dangers in them. Not sure if it was intentional but it was effective none the less. When she next spoke it was out of the blue.

"That is one noisy group of people." She replied. "Like to gave me a heart attack."

(Maybe I should ...)

"Me too, Ma. I felt the same way," I admitted.

"But it's also really quiet. I've never been in anything like that." She continues, "that was really something, Man. Shoot, they mean business with that time thing, don't they? It's just like you said, at 7:30 on the dot! That was really impressive."

"Um, yes, ma'am. On the dot."

She was extremely excited. I was taken aback.

"After seeing that, you bet' not ever be late waking up for church on Sunday again." She threw out.

"Yes, ma'am."

My response was part sheepish and part surprise. I hadn't seen that coming. I should have but I didn't. It never crossed my mind to disagree, though. I just wanted to support her line of thinking at this point. Anything to get her mind off of me sneaking out of the house.

And, believe, I was thrilled that my read wasn't wrong. It definitely went well.

"Oh, and your report was great! That was a lot of information. Can you keep doing those *and* your school work?" She asked.

"Yes, ma'am. I can, no problem." I said from experience (without mentioning that experience, obviously).

"Okay, Man. That just seems like a lot."

I was thinking about telling her that I just watched the news more often. That the stories come from world events and that I had learned that I was interested in those things. But the number one rule of criminality is...

1) Offer as little information as possible.

She would have heard what I said and started thinking. Guaranteed. Likely it would have inspired memories which would go something like, "...yep, I wondered why you got interested in the news all of a sudden. I should've known you were up to something when I saw it." You know she misses nothing. That recollection would have made her focus on the wrong set of details. I would have been in trouble all over again.

Nah, it's just better to stick with rule number one and mitigate the risk. Offer nothing that isn't asked for and very little of that. Hell, even then only offer mandatory portions. Basically, be brief or be quiet.

By the way, rule two changes depending on the school of dirty deeds you go to. Number one is universal, though. If you do some dirt be consistent enough to shut up about it. Tell nothing and stay quiet. That's a tip you get for free. You gotta pay some dues for the rest of that list.

Ma took a breath and kept rolling.

"And I heard you speaking that language, Man! What is that, Busara?" She asked with great interest. "What language was that?"

"There are actually two languages we speak in the Kowrie Group, Kiswahili and Zulu. Most of the words are Kiswahili."

I was trying to be slick by saying, "...*we* speak in the Kowrie Group". It was a suggestive play to already assume that I was in the group. Subliminal messages are supposed to be the most potent. I was trying to run that game at a young age. She had her mind fully occupied with her own mental notes from the meeting. I thought she might not even notice.

"'We', huh?" She sarcastically said. "So, you learning French, too?"

That second bit of sarcasm was playful. Thank goodness. I should've known better than to think I could slide anything past her. I already knew.

"Two languages? What in the world? Well, that's really special, Man. That's a tough program. You sure you can do all of that and it won't affect your schoolwork?"
I tried to argue my case, "yes, ma'am. You know I'm good at school work. I can do it. I'll make sure I do."
"Mm-hm."

I could literally see her mind working.

"It was the sweetest thing to see the young guys asking for permission to speak and accepting their responsibilities and all that. Um-hm. I'm glad I got to see that. That is really something else."

I kept looking for the opening but I didn't want to rush it. She was on a roll with affirmations. So, I decided to just let her ride with them for a minute. It appeared to me that she was making an argument for me. I thought I should let her.

> "I really like that they keep y'all from wearing all those name brands. That's my kind of thing, there! Ain't no reason to give those people all your money when they don't care anything about you. They're not going to do a thing for you or your community, they don't deserve your money like that. Support your own people." She chuckles. "I hear that!"

Self-incrimination isn't the only reason to stay silent. Sometimes you just have to let things develop around you. You can watch them work in your favor without any effort on your part. This was one of those times. But I was young, man. Running my mouth was going to happen.

> "And they had y'all meditating and stuff," she blurted out.
> "It's called breathing exercises, Ma, but it works the same way. It helps clear our heads for the lessons." I decided to clarify it for her. More insight couldn't hurt.
> "Mm. Well, I would call it prayer. But that's only if you're using it right. You gotta be calling on the Lord for that." She thought aloud. "Meditating. That shole is a lot."

She paused.

> "And that man, Woweeloo, he's pretty sharp. Is he always there?"
> "Yes, Ma. That's Mwalimu and he's the kadamu, that means leader. He's always there."

"Look at you! 'Wahleemoo', 'koodeyemoo', go on then, Man! Well, he was nice and the ladies, the teachers, they were nice and smart, too. You may have found something, Busara."

She took another pause.

"That group sure is well put together. It looks like a great thing for young men. I'm really impressed."

There wouldn't be a more clear opening or better time to close the deal. I had to take it.

"So can I do it, Ma?"

She glanced at me then focused back on the road. We were pulling up to the neighbor's place to get my sister. Ma parked the car then looked at me.

"You were right, Man. It is more than a Black awareness group. That's good ole fashioned empowerment in that group. This is a big deal. I already see some of the effects its having on you and, to be totally honest with you, I like what I'm seeing. I think it'll be good for you. So, yes you can do it."

I'm sure she could see me bursting with joy inside. Her response to that was to make sure we had a contracted agreement. That agreement was going to have terms.

"The minute your grades start to suffer it's over. You understand?" She said.

"Yes, ma'am. But I can do this, Ma. I'll make sure my grades will always be great. I promise," I argued.

"They better!" She punctuated the point.

Ma got quiet again and I could feel it. She formed a hyperintense look in her eyes then kind of cocked her head to the side. The whole time she was staring in my face. She was looking through me more so than at me.

"Listen to me, Busara. I understand this to be a 'manhood training', for lack of a better definition. I think it's really good for you. I think it's great. Whatever they can show you and help you develop is terrific. All of that said, it will not make you the man of my house. Just because you're going through man training does not mean I'm going to give you permission to run my house as a man. I'm not. You understand that?"

"Yes, ma'am." I replied.

This was the least shocking thing she said. Honestly, it wasn't a thing I considered but, like I've repeated numerous times, she missed nothing. Even the things that had not yet developed.

"I'm proud of you and I think you'll do well. And we'll leave it at that. Okay?"

"Okay, Ma. Thank you!" I said firmly through a smile.

And that was it! I was officially sanctioned to go to Kowrie meetings! Most people would just say I was "allowed" to go or that I had "permission". I was feeling the officialness of the occurrence so… it was 'sanctioned'.

When I heard her say 'yes' my chest swelled up and I felt like a statesman so describing it as sanctioned was more fitting.

(YEEEEEAAAAAHHHHH!!!!)

CHAPTER 15

LEGACY

It was official: Ma said yes and I was a member of the Kowrie Group.
I was fired up for that shit. Man, listen, this is where the nitty got gritty!
Once I was in, though, what did that mean? Plainly, it meant everything
to me. Oddly, I'm going to struggle a bit trying to explain it beyond that.
It is a profound and important organization. Believe me, I have plenty to
say about it. However, there are many more things about Kowrie that I
can't tell you than the things that I can. So, this may be a little tricky.

The Kowrie Group is exclusive, largely secretive and incredibly paranoid because of deadly lessons learned. Real talk. It's a unique situation
where the precedence for the shroud of secrecy around the 'Group is also
the basis and inspiration for the foundation of the organization. There's
some really deep history with this one, y'all.

The good thing is that even though I am limited in the detail I can
share about Kowrie, I can simultaneously tell you why it was created and
the reason for the mystique. This information I'm going to share is more
than just my history, it's Black history. That's because everything about
Kowrie is much bigger than the sum of its parts. I need y'all to take a bit
of a walk with me to fully grasp it all.

Back in the 1960's, a brewing Black independence explosion erupted
in America. There was a massive equal rights movement that had captured
the entire world's attention. It was a necessary fight because Black America

was still facing post-slavery, Jim Crow system-inspired racism, inequality, oppression and persecution. The same stuff we face today.

I digress.

American social life was rife with blatant injustice, imbalance and intolerable racism. Quietly, it's still not much different now. Very dissimilar to our current social climate, the 1950's saw an uprising to counter and eliminate those barriers that spilled into the 60's. The rejection of those debilitating principles also paved the way for those who wouldn't be placated by simply being regarded as equal. That sect of Black people saw the need to counter our excruciating American past with an emboldened future. Hence, an overt fervor for Black empowerment also had its emergence during that time.

These thrusts for equality and empowerment were most popularly fomented by the works of Dr. Martin Luther King, Jr. and el-Hajj Malik el-Shabazz (Malcolm X), respectively. Their efforts took center stage for the world to see. They had vastly different receptions from the world due to their disparate approaches to achieving the same goal – social balance. The successes and failures of their campaigns became a varied assortment of lessons for all onlookers, particularly budding ones with similar interests. It was also an education for their enemies.

Dr. King, Jr. waged a Christian faith-based non-violent campaign of civil disobedience in hopes to remake the American society into an ideal nation of equality. Basically, he was trying to make America own the shit they were selling about 'liberty and justice for all'. Truth is, Black people had only the façade of liberty while we have consistently been the targeted victims of America's injustices. As a devout and practicing minister, he believed that by turning the other cheek he could appeal to the 'better angels' of his oppressors. He would learn, and be steadily reminded, that such angels were in hiding and were spectacularly difficult to locate. Very often it would seem as if those voices of conscience didn't exist at all.

Any sane person will agree that human equality is existential, right? Every human being has the right to live without oppression or persecution. Still, getting the white American establishment to acknowledge that fact and enact equitable legislation was a painfully mountainous task. Dr. King and his followers paid astronomically steep prices fighting for what many believed to be self-evident. Further, said balancing legislation would guarantee no shift in human practice that would positively impact society. But that's a deeper argument for another time.

American reality was not only non-equitable, it was shitty. Dr. King's peaceful resistance campaign was frequently treated much less than humanely. He and his followers were beaten, imprisoned and slaughtered for their amicable and honorable efforts. Dogs were unleashed on the non-violent marchers, viciously ravaging them on the open streets. Fire hoses, with pressure so hard that it felt like they could remove flesh, were turned on men, women and children peaceful protestors. Baton-wielding policemen clubbed them relentlessly, ruthlessly bludgeoning them until they were bloodied, broken and murdered. This was the typical American government reception for Black people committed to peace while seeking equality. Again, our present societal norms continue to echo those atrocities.

Stunningly, Dr. King and his passive efforts are now fondly framed in text books. They literally murdered them in the open streets back then but glowingly praise the movement now. You even hear white politicians quoting Dr. King, as if they would have been among his followers.

Fuck them.

Many believe Dr. King receives this exaltation because his methods posed little risk or endangerment to white society. It allowed the agents of the state (the police) to brutalize and murder unarmed Black people without reprisal. The 'without reprisal' part is key. The psychological message they endorsed was 'do no harm to white people' – harming Black people was fine, though. The fight to sustain the reality that Black lives must also be preserved continues. Even in our peaceful cries for decency the government's response came off as 'don't harm us and we *might* listen'.

Might.

The issue there is, few times in recorded history have bullies let up because they were asked nicely. Typically, the bully will move from just taking your dessert to eating your whole lunch *and* taking any money in your pocket. And, make no mistake, the American government has always bullied Black people. Merely asking them to change had little chance of ever working. The truth is, you have to punch a bully in the mouth to get him to back the fuck up.

This brings me to brother el-Hajj Malik el-Shabazz also popularly known as Malcolm X. Brother Malcolm began his civil fight under the auspices of the Nation of Islam. He embodied a doctrine of empowerment that stood in stark defiance of American government. He's affectionately remembered by one of his more cherished quotes, "by any means necessary". He believed that freedom and justice were too expensive to live without, so they had to be acquired by whatever measures it would take. If you had to kill people trying to kill you then they had to die. Period. Still, it was not a violent approach it just wasn't non-violent, either.

Black people receiving his message had emotional whirlwinds prevailing in their days. They were both debilitated from getting their asses whipped and infuriated from watching our people be abused. Malcolm's self-respecting and self-preserving stance had great resonance with the battle-worn Black population. It asserted that our inherent right to live, our value as human beings meant we had no business allowing ourselves to be abused. Both his message and its popularity were every problem for the white American establishment.

The Nation of Islam often made shows of force in the community for Black people. When they were alerted to police brutality in progress they would arrive to scenes, in force, to end it. They were largely successful just by showing as a disciplined, unified front of massive numbers. Donned in suits and ties, they utilized the subliminal American image of authority against them. They had the knowledge of law and employed a respectful decorum that precluded disrespect. While the lawmen who dealt with them truly hated being challenged, they often complied with the Nation's requests.

Malcolm X was the face of that movement. He reinvigorated a rise in Black confidence and in Black power. In doing so, el-Hajj Malik el-Shabazz was directly contradicting what the government wanted to see.

Dr. King and Malcolm X approached the same set of challenges, for the same group of people, from opposite ends of the spectrum. Much of that is a result of their extremely diverse backgrounds. Dr. King was the son of a Baptist minister. He grew up in the church and followed in his father's footsteps. Malcolm X grew up mostly without his father present, roaming through the foster home system. He broke a multitude of laws and landed in prison before discovering the Nation of Islam and finding his purpose. The life approaches of these gentlemen were byproducts of their immediate environments which were extraordinarily different. What those gentlemen had in common, though, was uplifting Black people. And they were both assassinated for it.

The American bureaucracy, and thereby white people, believed that any Black empowerment was a threat to the American way of life. It is now written and easily accessible fact that both men were undone by the same government program; COINTELPRO – the U.S. government's nefarious Counterintelligence Program. The FBI launched an operation to ruin any and all progress that any Black heroes were achieving. The government planted agents and informants that were able to infiltrate both camps. Through dishonesty and deceit, they were able to sew discord and chaos that would hamper, prevent and outright destroy the equality and liberation agendas. It was an elaborate and underhanded scheme that often disregarded the law to achieve their heinous ends.

Ultimately, the government's racist and illegal activities were able to remove both men. I gotta note: there is scarce concrete evidence that they are explicitly responsible for either assassination. But their cataloged involvement as saboteurs suggests it was entirely aligned with their efforts to destroy the two men. There's even contemporary proof, via a recently deceased police department plant, that the CIA and FBI coordinated locally to have Malcom X assassinated. It's what we, as Black people, have known all along. Fortunately for us, they weren't able to stomp out their legacies.

Within the span of a few years, both men were murdered. It devastated the hearts of the Black community. There was great sadness and intense righteous indignation about our heroes' assassinations. Black people were mad as shit, y'all. From those smoldering coals of fury, the Black Panther Party arose.

Not long after the murder of Malcolm X in 1965, Huey Newton teamed with Bobby Seale in Oakland, California to form the Black Panther Party for Self-Defense (BPP) in October, 1966. They were not only inspired by the work of el-Hajj Malik el-Shabazz but believed their Party to be an extension of it. These are Huey's words on the topic:

> "...therefore, the words on this page cannot convey the effect that Malcolm has had on the Black Panther Party, although, as far as I am concerned, our Party is the testament to his life work." (6)

Bobby and Huey worked feverishly to honor that statement.

Where Dr. King and Malcolm X fought for acknowledgment and freedoms, the BPP embodied the progress of those lessons then worked to empower Black people directly. The BPP was forthright and deliberate in challenging the American system and the jaded authority within it. Taking up that mantle for Black equality earned the Black Panther Party an immediate target on their backs.

The Black Panther Party is most notably, and almost singularly, remembered for taking up arms directly against the police. Their just cause for doing so was to end the police *standard* of brutality against Black people. Like Malcolm and the Nation of Islam, the Black Panthers arrived at police confrontations with a unified physical presence. Their show of force, though, included a language of intimidation that white Americans previously thought was exclusively theirs: guns. The Party employed the open carry laws to their fullest extent. They shook white people by utilizing their own methods, and laws, against them. It shook them so much that Californian legislators changed the gun laws to specifically stop the Black Panthers.

The media focus squarely targeted 'Black people with guns' and villainized the organization. This was the way the government wanted it. 'The Black Panthers are gun-toting cop killers'. 'The BPP is a terrorist organization'. 'Those scary Black people want to take over America'. This is the type of mischaracterized red meat frequently wagged in front of Americans to vilify the movement.

There was no mention of innocent Black people who were beaten to a pulp by wards of the state. Not a blurb on the innocent Black lives lost at the hands of racist and hateful cops, or any of the vast assortment of prominent white hate groups. No mention of the reason, the purpose or the need for Black people to protect themselves in that way. It was just context-absent demonizing that branded the Black Panther Party. The government controlled the messaging and that's how they wanted the Panthers framed.

The media purported the government's narratives that misrepresented the Black Panther Party as some sort of villains. That psychological warfare was about devaluing their lives to justify the number of laws the government broke to take them down. But I'm here to tell you, there was no justification for what the FBI did to the BPP. The Black Panthers were a law-abiding organization. They studied the law, in fact, to make sure the movements they made were in accordance with them. These are well-recorded facts.

So, yes, it is true that the BPP openly carried weapons. It is also true that they confronted law enforcement with those weapons on behalf of the Black community. Absolutely! Every Black person should revel in pride about that fact. They were within their governmental and human rights to defend themselves and their community. Shit, 'self-defense' was in the organization's name! The true reveal is: Black people with guns weren't the main issue. I mean, America certainly wanted to end any power or authority the guns provided Black people but it wasn't their only concern. The government saw the Black Panthers as a threat because they were so much more than simply armed sentries.

What the FBI thought was much more inherently dangerous was liberated Black minds. This was the true work of the Black Panther Party. The BPP constructed systems to elevate the Black community called 'Survival Programs'. The most notable of them was the free breakfast program. Bobby Seale was quoted saying, "no child should run around in school hungry" and the Party did their share to change that. The program they created had an indelible impression on the entire Black community by investing in our children.

Black Panther members fed children in the morning before school while educating them. Black kids were taught liberation lessons, 'Party messaging and Black history. This is what bonded the BPP to the community and drew broad support for their cause. It was such a potent work that then FBI director Edgar Hoover said it was, "the greatest threat to efforts by authorities to neutralize the BPP and destroy what it stands for". (7) He said that because he knew the Party stood for Black unity, a thing they feared much more than anarchy.

The BPP's value to Black families was exponentially multiplied by their full accompaniment of free community services. They were uniquely adept at directly addressing a massive assortment of immediate community needs.

In addition to meals for kids, they provided clothing for the people. Quality education was the cynosure for the Party so they offered a wide-array of courses in varied subjects. The Panthers taught political and economic classes. As an interesting twist, they simultaneously had lessons on self-defense and first aid. I guess you needed to know how to help people after you beat them up. Accordingly, family members of inmates also received free transportation from the BPP to upstate prisons for visits.(8)

One of their major works, among many valued services, was an entire medical clinic system. It was a network that extended across 13 states and it was absolutely free. It was a community-based health care program that was the first of its kind. Their connection to the Civil Rights Movement helped establish the Medical Committee for Human Rights.(9)

There has always been a disparity between the health emergencies of Black people and the system's response to it. So, the BPP created and maintained an emergency-response ambulance program. In order to counter the drug invasion, the BPP helped to get people clean with a drug and alcohol rehabilitation program. They even tested the community for sickle cell disease. These were very valuable services for the community, making the Black Panthers highly cherished.

The list of amazing things the Black Panthers did for the Black community is roaringly long. While those things made them champions in the Black community, it made them despised enemies of the American government.

Retrospectively, it is arguable that some of the BPP error was in their transparency. Just as Dr. King and brother el-Shabazz before them. It was vividly clear that they were improving their communities because both their work and its results were in the open for all to see.

Ironically, it was their visibility that also made them effective. The more success their systems realized, the more inspirational and transformative they were for the Black people in those communities. More than merely stating they had the freedom to operate, the Black Panther Party was effectuating strength, pride and unity through their actions. This conspicuous reform was both their greatest asset and the knell of their doom.

According to government documents, that you can research right now, their manifest successes landed the BPP on the FBI's most wanted (or hated) list as the greatest threat to the pro-white oppressive America system. Black people were, again, becoming unified and motivated. That scared white America shitless.

Unfortunately, the government already had a tool in place to eliminate the threats that true freedom and equality posed to the racist and oppressive American system. Once again COINTELPRO was unleashed on Black freedom fighters. The FBI had also learned some lessons and they had the full of weight of the American bureaucracy to support their lawlessness. They intensified their divisive, destructive and murderous tactics with the Black Panther Party.

The COINTELPRO operation was singularly responsible for the demise of the Black Panther Party. Through their surveillance, informants and infiltration, they were able to pit the party against itself. They also framed them for crimes and murdered several members. All of the key leadership, from both coasts, were imprisoned, murdered or became refugees who escaped the country.

Now, despite what it may have read like, this ain't a history lesson. It's a lineage lesson. Everything I've told you is causal; uniquely connected and escalating in its development leading to the Kowrie Group. Dr. King's non-violent approach was asking the government to legislate decency. El-Hajj Malik demanded liberty and was prepared to take it, if necessary, at the pains of our oppressors.

They murdered Malcolm to end his messaging. Many believe the Feds did so to defer Black people to Dr. King's non-violent approach. Not long after Malcolm's murder, Dr. King began to redirect his message, calling for a more assertive stance. They then murdered him, too. The Black Panther Party was forged within the fires of those liberation movements. They publicly organized and orchestrated a literal restructuring for facets of our communities. They were empowered and inspired by the efforts of their predecessors. And, like their predecessors, they were targeted and dismantled by the COINTELPRO operation.

While the BPP was constructively impacting local Black life, a group of brothers and sisters studying at Berkley took notice. They watched both the rising success and the public dismantling of the Panthers. These visionary Black people valued everything the Panthers were able to do, despised what was being done to them and had a vision to take the empowerment movement a step further.

Those aforementioned brothers and sisters became the group of men and women scholars who founded United Simba (US). US realized several consistencies in the fates of their predecessors. Each of the preceding Black liberation fighter groups were visible and filled with adults from a vast spectrum of the community. All three of them were infiltrated and it became their undoing. US devised a way to prevent the same pitfalls while furthering the gains.

United Simba decided to build a school of young revolutionaries. This would allow them to shield young minds from propagandized programming by white America while preparing them to prosper in life as free and empowered Black people. A youthful program would largely insulate the group from infiltrators. And, most importantly, it would build an empowered village of young people. All under the radar. The founders were a brilliant group of young Black people. These men and women had watched the progression of development from their predecessors and improved on those models. They borrowed a sense of structure from the Black Panthers' sensational organizing work. Malcom X's direct fight against European aggrandizement inspired them to replace it altogether. In fact, five specific points from Malcolm X's life became United Simba mandates. The US founders incorporated those lesson as they structured a system built on African traditions, language, culture and customs.

The United Simba concept was to take the traditions of our ancestral past and reasonably, rationally and thoughtfully implement as much as possible in contemporary life to pick up where slavery and the middle passage interrupted our development.

The distrust built by Cointelpro, and every government operation that preceded it, laid the foundation for an extremely skeptical US doctrine. The progression of the tectonic American Black independence history embodies a great degree of sour irony. The federal government's treachery indirectly fashioned the very thing they were trying to prevent: a machine of prideful independent Black thought. United Simba was that machine.

While the word 'simba' directly translates to 'power', it also means lion. The term lion is often simply perceived to mean males. In the course of its development, the organization changed its name to become more inclusive. The scholarly leadership of the group decided to utilize another historical piece from the ancestors to represent their resolve.

Cowrie shells were once considered as currency or a form of exchange on the continent and became known as a symbol of wealth. They carried a value and represented some measure of power. The organization purposed itself as a means of empowerment in the same way one could enrich themselves to positions of power on the homeland by acquiring cowrie shells. So, they took on the symbolism of that universal medium of the continent in creating their name – The Kowrie Group.

This history illustrates for you why I am limited in what I can share with you. There are a few outlining principles that can provide some insight and a degree of understanding of the power of the organization. The ones I am free to share are fundamental in the Black experience and help us build a greater future as a people.

One of the major lessons established from the fall of our heroes was to not have heroes. This was not to disparage or disrespect the incredible work and sacrifices of our powerful ancestors. Our people will forever be indebted to brothers Martin and Malcolm for all their selfless efforts. It cost them both their lives. We can only have tremendous appreciation, respect, and reverence for their works.

Refusing to worship heroes was a principle focused on preserving the empowerment movement and protecting our people. Hero worship was discouraged because it made the movement easy for enemies to conquer. "Cut off the head of the snake", and all that. Instead, a broad and strong coalition filled with capable and educated leaders was the crux of the Kowrie preservation plan. This was a founding tenet of the organization.

However, it was also foundational to respect and honor past achievements, specifically the achievements of the elders. In true rejection of American white-washing, the 'Group focused on African heroes and heroines. This worked to build depths of pride and self-worth by educating our youth to stay connected to the greatness of our ancestors. Even in this effort, much of the focus was on how our people thrived together as opposed to individuals.

The Kowrie Group emphasized the need to build a collective vocation in order to elevate Black people to excellence. The charge for every 'Group member was to become an expert in your chosen field of work. The ultimate goal of the charge was to return to the fold and utilize your acumen to strengthen the village. Their method to manifest this broad and elaborate vision was to build success-driven behavior, personal development and high-quality character traits. The Kowrie scholars scientifically engineered a system to achieve those ends.

All success requires goals to be achieved and goals demand targets to pursue. With this in mind, the organization had a hierarchy built on achievement and every level had to be earned. Excellence was the mark you had to reach for every test. Perfection! For every test. If you didn't have a one hundred percent grasp of required information then, to the Kowrie Group, you didn't know it. You certainly couldn't teach what you don't know, right? Wielding information that you cannot share to empower more brothers and sisters means that you hold useless information. That was not allowed in the 'Group. These measures seeded and standardized a demand for excellence within the young people it led.

All tests weren't singularly knowledge driven, either. We had camp that we attended. You had to learn self-preservation techniques in the wilderness. After the experiential education, we were tested for our environment survival skills, too. The Kowrie Group was training self-sufficient warriors. And you had to have a perfect score to pass the field skills test just like every other requirement.

The Kowrie Group was founded with a uniquely proven distrust and disrespect for the government. I've repeated this fact multiple times because it is germane to Kowrie's origin. This is why it is an anti-establishment organization that took great pains to preserve itself. So much so that members were instructed to keep their cars running at gas stations, lest police cars, federal plants or informants sneak up on you. Yeah, that level of paranoia.

Every 'Group communique was personal. There were no advertisements, no news interviews and no company newspapers. Whatever you learned about Kowrie you were going to get directly from a person or you weren't going to get it. The organization was intensely frugal about sharing information. Security briefs were a programmed standard in meetings and information wasn't shared outside of the group. Trust was at a premium and it was completely reserved for those within the organization. Even with that, everything within the group was constantly reviewed with a cautionary eye for the most minute detail.

Make no mistake, the Kowrie Group was built from the pains of necessity. It still focused forward on the beauty and strengths of our people. Moreover, it was engineered to locate and accentuate the inner strengths of each of the members. There were many processes and responsibilities assigned to members to help each person better locate their passions and proficiencies. This is one of the many ways that the 'Group helped its members identify which life arena they wanted to master.

The Kowrie Group mandate also required you to build, develop and prosper. It wasn't tolerant of stagnation. There was an obligation to steadily grow and improve to contribute to the mission, to the village, to our people. Kowrie's system of expectation created a culture filled with devout work ethic, staunch accountability and unflinching integrity.

The organization also provided a climate where all things African were the norm. We were learning, executing and conducting ourselves in the ways of our ancestors to teach us our own culture. This helped exacerbate our strengths from the depths of our heritage and to empower us as the Africans we truly are. It was one of many facets employed to cancel out the otherwise omnipresent gentrification of European culture.

From birth, everything surrounding us in America has been teaching us, worse, *programming* us to devalue ourselves as Black people. American media, entertainments, even the school books steadily reinforce an asinine theory that the white man is every man. There is a foolish and consistent drubbing that the white man is every hero, every good guy, every brilliant person, every strong guy, every secret agent, everything attractive, everything powerful, every moral standard, the answer to every question, the remedy for every issue and the master of every culture. We have constant streams of media messages where the white man invades some foreign culture, learns it and masters it better than the indigenous people in three scenes. All the while we're mere footnotes or, often, worse. We're the lackeys, the criminals, the gangsters, we're drug dealers or drug takers or just the background subordinates taking orders. Erstwhile, the white man is always the lead character who is the beacon of morality and righteousness and compassion and dignity.

Bullshit.

These unyielding, unending subliminal messages build a base of intended misunderstanding within everyone subjected to it. The ability to reject it is manifest in recognizing it, particularly before being mesmerized and immobilized by it. We were taught to resolutely rebuke those lies in the face of the truth: the African is the first man. There's no need to exacerbate that point, the truth speaks volumes on its own.

All of humanity comes from the strength and beauty of our DNA. The Kowrie Group was built with a focus on eliminating the derogatory impact Europeans have had on our people. This was a replete philosophy, that's why something as simple as wearing clothing brands was not overlooked. We had to deprogram centuries of denigratory life in order to reprogram with self-love. They were teaching us to be conscious of our own greatness.

They were also teaching us to be suspicious of the government and to trust nothing we were sold. We could not allow or accept any of the subliminal programming that devalues us. As Black people in America we *only* have reason to distrust the establishment, its literally our history in the country. Living life by their rules of 'civilized society' always works to our detriment. It's one of the multitudinous ways that the deck has been stacked against us. As I've illustrated, the Kowrie Group was specifically conceived from the most contemporary egregious transgressions *against* the efforts of our people. We were butchered in droves for having the audacity to fight for equity. This is not a lesson that can ever be discounted.

So, the 'bring-back-greatness' doctrine is how the organization began. However, a 'make-it-spread' push caused it to grow rapidly. Some of those scholars went off to places like Howard and Hampton Universities installing Kowrie branches to broaden the reach. The 'Group soon reorganized all over the country in different pockets. They planted roots in many of the urban centers of the country to help systematize Black Power efforts wherever they were.

Even with that, there was a system in place. In an ironic twist, part of the Kowrie psyops game was to ostentatiously announce their foray into a new city. They would formally approach the government (Mayor's office, Department of Commerce, etc.) and introduce themselves. Instead of allowing a whispering stink to brew from the baffles of obscurity, our elders loudly proclaimed their arrival as to ward off any suspicion should any utterings arise.

Presenting themselves in suit and tie left the bureaucrats to wrongly assume it was a standard networking opportunity for future funding. They would make this false assumption because it's from their playbook. We let them think that. So, when they didn't see or hear from us again they'd be pleased. This created a perfect cover to operate under.

Though the foundations were the same, each Kowrie office had its own signature. Remember, the premise of development was 'become an expert, bring it home'. So, the leaders in the differing cities built their offices through their professional eyes. One city was built on self-defense. Another city was spectacular at community organizing. Our branch in St. Louis was heavily infused with the arts. This is why the Boot Dance drew me in. The St. Louis group did it with extra stank because it was their specialty.

I can imagine that you're in the same place I was when I learned all of this. It blew me away to learn that I was directly connected to Malcolm X and the Black Panther Party. More than that, the roots of the 'Group reached all the way back to the royalty of Shaka Zulu with his cultured and disciplined empowerment. As part of the Kowrie Group, I was a revolutionary descendant of all of them. The more I learned, the more I became involved, the more it gripped me. I was more than happy that it found me.

It cannot be countenanced that Ma and Mama helped shape my character. Through their love, dedication, leadership, and individual greatness, they both helped form me into a morally sound person. They helped me understand that anything you wanted to achieve required commitment. They taught me that my expectation level should be tightly tethered to my effort. 'What you earn you will have' was a functional family mantra. They both taught me this lesson with special emphasis on an empowered character.

The Kowrie Group armed me with the essentials of manhood and leadership. The combination of mentorship and brotherhood taught me more than pride and ownership, but I earned a sense of belonging. They helped me understand my responsibility to the community and to our people.

And all of that was just the stuff I *can* tell you! Straight up? Kowrie is a bad ass group. The best thing about it? They weren't finished teaching me things.

CHAPTER 16
GROWING PAINS

South. African. Gum. Boot. Dance. In case y'all are wondering, I stomped my foot with every word! South. African. Gum. Boot. Dance. You stomped with me the second time, didn't you? You damned right! It moves you like that, dawg.

I ultimately earned the right to do the South African Gum Boot Dance and that's exactly what happened. I did that shit! I took all my breakdancing skills, the anticipated excitement I had stored up for a few years and my learned passion for what the Boot Dance meant to fuel the sweat equity I put into the rehearsals. I was more than determined to be spectacular at it.

When I was finally able to wear that Kowrie lion monogram and get up on a stage... man, you couldn't tell me a damned thing! I wanted every part of it from the minute I had seen it and my moment had finally arrived. I gotta tell y'all, it felt righteous.

It would have been sweeter if my guys had stayed in the organization. Street Side Breakers was over for me once I joined Kowrie, particularly because my guys were initially there with me. It was a huge point of pride to lead them through the parts of the 'Group that I knew well and to clue them in when they weren't certain. It was dope to be responsible for some little brothers for a minute.

That changed pretty quickly, though. Big Word and Thrust only went for a few meetings before they just stopped going. Unfortunately, they didn't make it to the Gum Boot Dance. I think that definitely would have kept them involved. Those dudes were dancers like me, it would have certainly made a difference. We were still tight after that, of course. My dudes are my dudes, y'know? Loyalty is real. We just didn't run together the same once they left the 'Group.

By the time I got a chance to sniff the Gum Boot Dance, The Kowrie Group had shown me volumes more than I can explain. Many of which still can't be told. So, I was immersed much more deeply into the program than just the Gum Boot Dance. The 'Dance was still my thing though, y'hurr me? I could feel my entire soul rejoicing whenever we prepared to practice it. Yes, just the preparation got me fired up. It was undoubtedly a next level experience.

My love for the Gum Boot Dance never overshadowed the depth of what Kowrie represented. Of course, I was more than enchanted by the fact that we were true descendants of Shaka. Of the Black Panthers. Of Martin. Of Malcolm! But I was still a teenager. From the moment that first THWOOM hit me... I knew I was going to do that shit. Period. And I was a break dancer, too? Please believe, I was more than ready when I finally earned the right to do those moves, to perform with my brothers. I cut loose like it was personally made for me. The moves, the shouting, the rhythms, the brotherhood, the meaning... dawg, every bit of the process resonated with me on a spiritual level.

It did not, however, resonate with everyone. One of my first Gum Boot Dance performances was in a neighborhood called Kenlock. It was a forgotten Black community near the airport. It was sadly indigent, full of poverty and desperation.

A guy from Kenlock had seen one of our performances and invited that neighborhood. He was a dude who smoked weed and drank but was trying to get his world together. Mwalimu believed these were the areas we were needed most, especially when the brother who invited us was struggling. They booked us and we went over there to brighten their spirits.

We arrived at a pavilion that he had arranged for us. It was a covered area, like a gazebo, but there was no elevated stage. It robbed us of our ability to shock them into attention. Our opening stomp sounded like "PAT!" That didn't remotely have the same affect.

The worst thing was how we were received.

We got booed.

They were laughing and pointing at us. Many of the adults called us 'African Booty Scratchers' and talked shit about every traditional element of our presentation. Even the speech! They mocked the Swahili commands that were given, the moves we made... everything. Almost the entire Kenlock community was filled with disrespect for everything we were and all the work we were doing. It could have been heartbreaking.

I dealt with it in the true understanding of Kowrie. That experience encapsulated why the 'Group existed. It was formed to strengthen all of our people, of course. But that was because we were broken. The Kowrie Group was a tool for repair because we needed a lot of it. Harriet Tubman had to shoot some Black people because they couldn't stop being slaves. Some of the enslaved Black people didn't want to be free, they were too afraid to embrace their own power. This was the premise of the situation we faced.

Those people were so deeply lost in their programming, so far removed from receiving the idea of Black magnificence that they just couldn't accept us. They couldn't love the authentic thing because the colonization of whiteness was too deep with them. It was a true lesson in the need to deprogram in order to reprogram.

That whole community needed self-love repair. There was a culture of self-hate that we couldn't penetrate in a day. The Kowrie Group was built to institutionalize Black love from the root. It educated and culturalized our children for Black strength and unity. The whole plan was to circumvent colonized thinking before it could sink in. Even so, it couldn't reach everyone. It was guaranteed to miss some of us who needed it the most. Kenlock was that situation.

I personally needed that lesson. No matter how pure, positive or productive a thing may be, everybody that could benefit from it wouldn't support it. Things you love and respect with all your heart may be despised and mocked with the same fervor. The 'Group was so much stronger than that momentary challenge that the lesson was learned and bypassed in mere days. At the very next meeting we were back to business as usual. Somehow, it made me feel invincible instead of vulnerable. We rolled through that experience even more encouraged that what we were and the things we did were necessary. Just one more reason I whole-heartedly embraced the Organization.

What I loved most about the 'Group is it's seemingly bottomless depth. No matter how satisfied you are with the program there is always more.

So, I told you that the arts were our thing, a specific focal point at our branch of Kowrie. Our key influencers were a virtuosic group of performers. Case in point: there was a woman from East St. Louis who became a world-renowned dancer. She had graced the stages in France, Italy, hell, she performed all over the world. When she arrived at a particular point in her career, she studied heavily in Haiti. She also spent a great deal of time in Africa to learn different dancing techniques and the culture behind them.

Through her studies, she fused all that she had learned abroad with ballet disciplines and created a brand new dancing technique. It became wildly popular in the dancing profession. She was also a loyal sister. She embodied the community-building principle of the 'Group; go forward to master your craft, bring it back to enrich the village. Her return to St. Louis was most pronounced by her creation of the CD Dance Conference. She was a beautiful and truly amazing sister. The famous Eartha Kitt trained under this magnificent woman. When she arrived to teach us my mind was completely blown. As a cat (pun intended) who was big on dancing, it couldn't get any better than having her as an instructor. Or, at least, that's what I thought.

She brought with her instructors from all over the world to learn, then aid in teaching, her technique. In that number, the then Senegalese chief choreographer arrived in East St. Louis to join her efforts. Upon being introduced to Kowrie and the work we did, he committed to helping us perfect our performances. So, for the Gum Boot Dance lessons, we were educated by a masterful Senegalese instructor. He educated us on every move, every purpose for them and the depth of the culture behind them.

In true Kowrie Group fashion, you could not perform anything without a thorough understanding of what you were doing. Every Kowrie lesson was taught with the expectation that you would be able to pass it on. That's precisely what happened at our performances: we taught the audiences all of the history, purpose and culture while we were on stage. They were doing that the first day I saw it but I was too shellshocked to catch it all. It had come full circle when it became my responsibility to educate people on it.

The dancing really grabbed me. I started taking classes with the lady and found there were few other students. And by 'few' I mean one other student. She was such a thoroughbred, though, that she didn't quit on us. She simply drove us harder and taught us more. Ultimately this lead to an opportunity I could not have seen opening for me.

In learning the African dances she would bring in a troupe of drummers so that the entire experience was authentic. I was captivated by the experience and completely engaged with the whole process. My fascination landed me in the drum troupe where I learned to play the djimbe and the conga drums. But that wasn't an immediate transition. Let me explain:

Initially, the dancing rehearsals took place while guys were mouthing the drum sounds. For some reason, they didn't have access to their actual drums for a while. So, they just made the sounds orally, it came off like super elaborate beat boxing sessions. I thought it was cool. The instructor taught me all the rhythms vocally. He would sound them out so I mimicked him doing it. That was my learning by ear experience. It was kinda weird but I still thought it was pretty tight. And it was convenient, I was able to practice it anywhere.

When they finally brought the drums to play on I was fucking geeked! The sounds of the drums completely changed the impact of the dances. It also changed the attendance. More people showed up to play the drums, just because they were fucking cool. Still, very few people joined in on the dancing. Fortunately for me, I did both.

Kowrie was not only my thing but it kinda became Ma's thing, too! There was a really popular radio program back then hosted by Robin Boyce. Ms. Boyce interviewed the 'Group to tell the community about what we were doing. She summed it up by saying,

> "I want to let all my listeners know that these young men are in my studio and I am totally impressed."

Ma and her friends were avid show listeners. Once she heard that on air it pushed her over the top. From then on I would catch her talking to people with pride about the Kowrie Group and about me being in it. Likewise, that's when the windfall came for her. I would ask her to 'sign this'. 'Can I have money for that?' I was always in her face and she beamed about it.

My mother didn't need more reasons to have love for the 'Group but she got them anyway. I was learning verbiage from two different languages then I started dancing and playing the drums? I'm not sure if she liked it more because of the qualities it taught me or because she was right in letting me do it. I'm kidding, she was too beautiful to be that full of herself. She loved to see me thrive. The Kowrie Group was truly helping me do that. Ma enjoyed seeing that.

She never stopped being Ma, though. She was stern about wanting me in the house before 10:00. And she made certain I had a key, we both tried to leave the breaking-in stuff as a distant memory. Ma was always assertively positive. She increased my pride in the 'Group with how she felt about me being in it.

Let's count the score: I joined the Kowrie Group because of a dance, was mentored to be a warrior who turned into a musician. Who saw all of that shit coming? Not me but I'm glad as hell it did.

So, yeah, I was entirely sold out for the 'Group. It was everything I've told you about and a whole lot more. While it's true that the Kowrie Group was foundational for my life and character, it wasn't my whole life.

I realize I've largely left the church out of the conversation. That's a true error, it's damned near blasphemous, even. If the Kowrie Group was the cement for my foundation then the church was the rebar. Before I joined, better yet, long before I knew about the 'Group, the fabric of my person was being built by my belief system.

Going to church with Ma was, in itself, a religion. Yes, the actual 'going' was religious on its own. In fact, it's way easier to tell you when we weren't in the church as I was growing up than telling you when we went. It only changed a little as I entered my teens.

Choir was big with me. Never would I brag on my voice, but I can hold a tone pretty nicely. If you make me drop that baritone on you though, I might rattle your chest. Jus' sayin'. I thoroughly enjoyed doing it and it was fulfilling to invoke spirits with song. It could be stirring and uplifting. Every time we sang I had a great feeling about it.

So, I continued to sing in the choir until I left for college. That was a much bigger commitment than it probably sounds like. I was in church so often I don't know how I did anything else. We had youth and young adult choir rehearsals on the third Sundays. Male choir rehearsed on fourth Sundays and the 'all choir' (the one for everyone in the church) rehearsed on first Sundays. I was definitely there every Wednesday for bible study and, before the 'Group, I went to Ma's choir rehearsals on Thursdays, too. Of course, Sunday morning services always found my butt in the pews. I was almost always there on Sunday evenings, too, due to Ma's rehearsals and performances. So, basically, my entire Sundays until I left for college, from breakfast to dinner, were spent around the sanctuary.

There were really good people in my church. I'm sure it had drama like every other large gathering of human beings but it was good for and to me back then. I was also on the junior deacon board. This put me in close proximity to many male mentors from the church. I apprenticed under senior men carrying the spirits of old. Their souls had been through some shit. Those moments were as if being directly connected to the ancestors. It was a powerful thing to have people breathe on me and let myself simply be guided by the spirit. They would casually share life wisdom and feed my soul with positive affirmations and vision.

We're talking old school, too. There was no 'Kids' Church' or any separation of the congregation in that way. Because of that, I couldn't always understand the words or even the depths of the messaging but I would be carried away by the spirits that were present. We worshipped together. We learned together. We cried in prayers together. I would go to church and let my spirit simply exhaust. I was free to expend the energy within me because it was a safe space, a loving space. The harmony that existed there was terrific, I greatly appreciated it.

The advent of the 'Kids' Church' era continues to be grossly disappointing. It was a loss of a valuable mentoring facet for our young people. There was a wealth of life that got passed on in general church that largely ended when kids were separated. You can argue that the gospel was put into kid-sized pieces to be more easily digestible and I would agree that's true. I simply don't think that's better. There's a level of aspiration missing from that. It can be a great thing when you work for understanding, it builds character and adds another element of strength to the growth. Conversely, having things fed to you your way builds an anticipation of privilege. That's a subliminal lesson that is difficult to overcome.

The parenting factor is in that mix, too. The more people are able to unleash their kids on others the more lax they tend to be with disciplinary guidelines. When their kids are in school all day then in church for a whole weekend, parents have less direct influence. That's not ideal. Now, I'm not suggesting being a disciplinarian, but 'home training' is a thing. Sitting in church with your parents causes a myriad of things to organically develop. The vast majority of which are positive.

I think, in my own humble opinion, it's better to earn an understanding than to have things handed to you. A spiritual community can do wonders in awakening your ancestral connection. It's an entity that exists for us all collectively and singularly. I'm sure it's more easily accessed by sharing through embodiment as opposed to solo pursuits. And the levels of fellowship achieved by keeping us all together are good for everyone. It's a way to keep our entire village moving on one accord.

Church, school then the Kowrie Group, that's the order of my introduction to these foundational pillars. The church was the longest constant for me until college. However those winds have changed for me, I still very much appreciate that Ma guided me the way she did. Church was a sustained and dedicated activity while I was in school.

Let me digress.

I was still a teenager in high school and that was getting interesting, too. It became so interesting, in fact, that my commitment and responsibilities within the 'Group were tested. More than a few times.

In 1983, I walked through the doors of McKinley High as a freshman. Ma had become more liberal in giving me the room to operate. So much so that she allowed me to choose if I would continue in private schools or if I was going to public school. And that, ladies and gentlemen, was the end of my parochial career.

My reception was a lot smoother than it could have been. Mind you, I was a freshman at 13 because I was double promoted. The whole 'big fish in a little bowl' experience as an eighth grader had instantly turned into the 'little fish in a lake' all over again. That's kinda what we all go through, right? Personally, I was simply hoping I didn't sit in front of another 19 year old burglar like I did in the sixth grade. I'd had enough of full beards and feet in my ass for a lifetime. Anything better than that would be a 'W'. Nah, I'm being way too modest. By the time I made it to high school I was dripping with personal confidence.

Except with women.

Being in the Kowrie Group made us popular with girls and plenty guys ran through women like they were Pitfall Harry. Just running through screen after screen, ducking and jumping and swinging and shit, y'know? Having a good ass time. (Look up the video game 'Pitfall' on Atari, you'll get it). I just wasn't that guy. Charm wasn't the highest quality on my list of character traits.

And, being a son of a single mom, I had a serious take on family life. My father was promiscuous, I attributed that to his absence in my early life. My perspective told me that it wasn't a point to emulate. So, I was in no rush to 'play the field' or build a harem. Sure, I kicked it with a few young ladies but it was always one at a time and it was not a focal point. That never became a major cog in my high school career.

It could have, though. Which simply means I had that level of clout. Being a member of the 'Group put me in a socially comfortable space. All the cool cats were my dudes, which certainly increased my social credit score. I was a member in that rare thing (Kowrie), I played drums and I could move on a dance floor with the best of them. I was riding high for the next level. And that's how I walked in the high school doors.

But the 'Group really wasn't the reason for my ease. I walked in there super confident off the rip. I can't exactly place why I felt so comfortable but I was. There was no anxiety or anxiousness. Shit, I remember going to freshmen orientation feeling like I was walking into my living room at home or something. I'm telling you, I was comfortable, dawg.

Maybe being double promo…, no, being double promoted definitely gave me some self-confidence. There was a pride in skipping a grade, I felt… smart. There was no doubt in my mind that I was prepared for high school. My entire approach was like, "okay. Let's get this done." So, I kind of walked in with a swagger bigger than my station. I also made a few moves early that boosted my standing. Let me take you back just a bit to lay it out for you.

I was able to play basketball in middle school. It wasn't an outside program, though. Y'all know moms was saying no to all of those. But in the 8th grade, she decided that an in-school team was cool and she let me rock it.

So, one of my few real homies in middle school was Tank. Man, Tank was a mutha fucka. Whatever crew he was going to be in he was going to be 'That Mutha Fucka'. He was wilder, crazier and scarier than that daily-shaving burglar in my sixth grade class. He was my dawg in school, though. Everybody else at school acted as though he was, like, a murderer or something. They were terrified of this dude. I had none of that. We were on the basketball team together and we hung out. He was just my dude at school.

After graduating from Holy Guard of Angels middle school with about 15 other classmates, we both went to McKinley. I had planned on playing basketball when the season came but the school year always starts with football. I had never played organized 'ball. I wanted to play, badly as hell, but it just hadn't happened. Consequently, I didn't really competently know much about organized football. The season was already in full swing by the time the semester started. I had missed camp, and probably a game, before it was brought to my attention.

You know who *did* play football? Tank. Tank was a football playing mutha fucker. This wound up being bad for me because he was one of those dudes who couldn't spell the word 'filter'. He always said what the fuck he wanted to say whenever the fuck he wanted to say it. Likewise, one day he saw me when he had his pads in hand. There were a whole bunch of people standing around, just hanging out. It was a chilled vibe in the hallway, nothing major was happening. He felt like ending that shit.

"Hey Busara! You coming out here to play or what, dawg?" he threw out.

I didn't respond rapidly enough so he decided he needed to take that shit to the next level.

"Busara! You coming out to play football or you gone keep running around like a silly imbecile?"

Now, I wasn't inclined to front on my guy. I mean, I wasn't afraid of him at all but I didn't exactly want to fight his ass, either. So, I refused my first thought of asking him how to spell 'imbecile' and tried to redirect the conversation. There were girls around, I had to say something.

"Uh, yeah man. I'm trying to get out there. I just gotta take the physical and do some other stuff."

I mumbled out that lame set of excuses, hoping he would just drop it. They really were the truth, though. I was way behind the curve trying to get started so I had the whole slate of prerequisites to do to get on the team. I figured he would simply move on.

Nope.

"Oh, so you gone pick silly imbecile, huh? Silly imbecile it is, I guess." Tank said.

Just to make sure he brought the point all the way home he continued.

"Busara, the Silly Imbecile. That's him."

Was it really necessary for him to triple dip with the shit, though? I mean, I'm sure one 'silly imbecile' per semester would have been enough. I got four of them mutha fuckas in a single conversation. There's gotta be a written limit somewhere. Maybe his redundancy might have been because his vocabulary was light on intelligent sounding insults. I wasn't picking that fight. I just hoped that the dude wasn't going to 'silly imbecile' me to death for my first semester in high school. That would have been no bueno.

Football didn't work out for me my freshman year. I started the process too late to join the squad. I was more than a little salty (unhappy) about it. Organized football had been on my to-do list for a minute. Once I was actually allowed to do it, a technicality kept me from finally getting it done. It was my responsibility to make it happen and I didn't. Shit happens, man. What made it cool was I realized that nothing would stop me the next year. So, there was a little bit of a silver lining for me.

I did make it out to the field to see Tank and he was...

K I L L I N G P E O P L E!

He was at practice, just, terrorizing his teammates. In practice! Yeah, he was killing the dudes on *his* team! Killing them! He was running around out there like a collegiate senior linebacker pissed off at a bunch of fourth graders because they were wearing his team uniform. It was like watching a high school version of Billy Madison blasting kids in the heads with dodgeballs or something. He was a merciless brute. Quietly? I enjoyed the hell out of watching it.

Here's the really crazy reveal: it turns out good ole Tank was an *actual* killer! This dude was in the projects doing all manner of, uh, legally unbecoming misdeeds. My dog was fucking crazy, y'all. It became apparent that all of our schoolmates who ran around in fear of the guy just knew shit I didn't.

Maybe the football players knew, too! It's possible that they were letting him ravage them so they wouldn't be shot or something. I don't know. Again, he was just my guy at school – I wasn't too acquainted with the dark side and it never came my way. But, from all I now know, he could have been burying people on Sundays and it wouldn't have been out of character. That's crazy as hell.

Let me just say for the record: Tank was my guy. Is! Is my guy. We still cool, Tank. (Don't kill me).

I was able to get on the basketball squad that year and it really worked out. It didn't hurt my social standing at all. Personally, I think hooping can be more popularizing than football. There are fewer guys playing and people can always see your face. The crowd is also closer to you so the view is better, more intimate. You play offense and defense so you spend more time being visible in the game, too. I just think, if you get playing time, basketball affords you more social options.

Of course, an exceptional personal skill set can eclipse either sport. If you are the baddest dude on the squad, whatever squad that is, then you'll get mad props regardless. I wasn't exactly *that* guy but I did alright.

Being a jock came with obligations. The Kowrie Group was a living obligation. These things did not happily coexist in the same space. Our hoop practices and games included Tuesday and Thursday nights. Kowrie meetings were on Tuesday and Thursday nights. There were basketball tournaments on Saturdays. The 'Group had events on Saturdays. When you missed practices you couldn't play in games. If you were ever short with Kow… you just didn't do 'being short' with Kowrie. That wasn't going to happen.

The level of expectation in the Kowrie Group and the demand on your manhood did not accept excuses. Not even for legitimate conflicts. So, I was a man about it. I sat down with leadership and let them know the compendium of my obligations. They weren't entirely flexible and I didn't expect them to be. Still, we worked out enough of an understanding that things were operable. I made it through my freshman year without too much anguish.

Academically, I was surprised… or maybe my arrogance took a hit. The lessons were a leap from what we had been learning. They challenged me enough to make me fully engage in order to succeed. I should have expected that but I didn't. It was a self-imposed burden.

I had a vision for my entire high school career. I wanted to knock out all my challenging classes as an underclassman so I could skate in my senior year. That way I could skate on fluff classes, enjoy my senior year and prepare for the next level without stress. It was a good plan, except it kicked my ass early. Go figure.

So, I took a while adjusting to make sure I could master what I faced. Excelling was a given, regardless. That was the level of my commitment and expectation. It just took more for me to do it than I thought it would.

Fortunately for me, Ma had paid for me to get a great educational foundation. That private school curriculum was the real deal. I was certainly prepared for everything McKinley threw at me, but I had to put in the work to maintain it. It definitely made me pay attention to paradigm shifts.

Then came football. In my sophomore year I slapped on the pads and got between those line, man. I missed the chance to ride with Tank. For some reason, he moved on to JROTC that year. That seemed pretty weird to me because, well, sometimes you just think you know a guy. It didn't, at all, seem like he would've rocked that. But you can bet your ass there were more than a few brothers who were happier about going to football practice without Tank on the field.

That's not to say that the squad was short on beasts. We weren't! I hadn't told you about my guy Big Lou before but that's because before football we weren't tight. At all. Actually, the relationship was damned near adversarial. Fortunately, it wasn't personal. It was like a... uh, community beef. I may have to explain that a bit.

See, Big Lou lived in the Webbes. That was a large collection of high-rise government projects that were a block away from ours. Everything I knew about the Webbes was that I didn't really wanna know more about the Webbes. It was rough, man. I say that as a man who lived in the projects my whole childhood.

It was so bad in there that we would just avoid it altogether. Even when we had to go on the opposite side of the Webbes we just went around it. None of us were trying to go through there. Why? Dawg, nobody wanted to see old bastards arguing and fighting over a game of craps. Grimy people would be just standing around drinking 40's and shit. They looked like they had scheduled appointments with trouble and were waiting for it to show up.

It was also 'Night of the Living Baseheads' in the daytime. They were around begging and trying to get over on you. Most of them looked like any contact would result in you catching something. They would also shamelessly shoot their drugs in the open corners of buildings. Man, fuck that. Their counterparts, drug dealers with guns, were just standing around, posted up. And there was always some random dude running around with no shirt on, yelling out craziness. It was like a circus in there sometimes.

That place was just troublesome and perilous growing up. I knew I was a good kid and that wasn't my mix. So, I just stayed out of there. Everything about that project's world just told me it wasn't the place to be. I may not be the wisest dude in the world but I'm not hardheaded, either. I didn't really know anybody to be rolling in there to holler at anyways, so it remained a no-fly zone. That's just what was up.

Until I got older. Playing on the McKinley football team changed all of that. Once Big Lou and I were on the same team that's exactly what it was – we were on the same team. Big Lou was a good dude and we got really cool. He was different though.

From my understanding, he hadn't played the year before. He transferred from the V and the rules wouldn't allow him to play. So, my sophomore year was both of our first seasons on the team, even though he was a junior.

Big Lou was like... the young uncle on your dad's side, y'know? He just had a maturity that the rest of us didn't. So, he could do crazy shit with us but he also drew the line when things went too far. He'd pull your coattails if you were doing something too dumb. Like I said, he was like an uncle. He was a grown man before any of us were even on that at all. Well, I sorta fit that mold, too. Maturity is one of the major things we had in common. His was just... different. It seemed more... crucial, somehow. Thusly, I regarded him as a big brother. Most of us did.

Our team was awesome. I played my ass off my first year. Just like hooping, though, football came with responsibilities. Many of those conflicted with Kowrie, too. I did the thing I know to do, I went directly to leadership. They did the thing they always do, they expected me to perform.

You may erroneously believe that they were huge proponents of school. And that their advocacy for classrooms would manifest their support for me in school sports. I started this idea by telling you that outlook was erroneous. I hope you were paying attention.

The Kowrie Group believed in *education*. Deeply. Devoutly. The whole Kowrie system was based on educating us. But not the things the government sanctioned for us to be taught. They certainly didn't hold any value in games that required us to risk our bodies and our health for entertainment. They rejected the reality that America still wished to relegate our value to our brawn and not the depth of our brilliance. No, they didn't celebrate that we were mere cattle to be brutalized at high speeds to pleasure the horde.

We spent most of our time in Kowrie deprogramming systemic indoctrination. We learned to reject the fictitious suggestion that our history on planet earth began as slaves. We were taught to loathe the despicable implications that slavery somehow makes us of less, not more, value. We were trained to defy the fraudulent practice that we must leap to the standards they've set for us to be acknowledged. All of this is rooted and continues in public education. Everything the 'Group represents works to counter every one of those fallacious American habitudes. No, the Organization has no love for the public schooling system.

That said, none of the leadership at Kowrie had any empathy for my games.

"We have a show, you have responsibility, be here."

"We have an event, you have a responsibility. Be there."

"The books don't sell themselves. We'll see you at the store."

That sums up how they handled most things.

Honor your commitments.

Don't make new commitments that compromise your existing ones.

Don't believe the 'Group will compromise when you do.

Honor doesn't compromise.

They were tough standards to live up to. No matter how difficult they were for me at times, I still appreciated them. I just really vibed with the 'Group on that level. So, it was tough but I made it happen.

You may have noticed that I haven't mentioned classwork in high school. It's not because it wasn't a priority but because it was simply standard. I handled it, that was the rule. It wasn't much of a challenge so it didn't require much focus to satisfactorily achieve in it. I was also torn by my Kowrie principles on what impact it would have on my mentality. So, I nailed it in order to keep it from becoming an issue.

Ma was the steadying factor with that. I had to perform on a particular level in school to keep the things in my life the way I wanted them. This is an arena she and the 'Group weren't precisely eye-to-eye on. And it was okay, I had to do what had to be done. With Ma, that was handling school to maintain the status quo. I did that.

So, I had joined the football team and did very well. I rocked the basketball squad successfully. My grades were killer and I was continuing to advance in the Kowrie Group. I had this high school thing on lock! Every reason I thought I had to be confident going in to the school was validated. The sailing was definitely smooth and I was certain it would continue. You know that's a recipe for some shit to happen, right?

Well, shit happened.

CHAPTER 17

BALLER

In the summer of 1986, life was going extremely well for me. I had a terrific sophomore year, it was my inaugural year for playing football on a team. And I killed it! I got to kick it with my fellas and I had met a girl at school. That was going well. Man, life was good!

The actual summertime was Kowrie season, though. It felt like I was doing something with the organization every day. If it wasn't a meeting, it was a performance. I might have had a dance or drumming rehearsal. When I wasn't doing any of those then there was work for me in the book store. The only thing I appreciated as much as making money in the summer was getting wiser. With the 'Group, I felt both of those were a constant.

Our leadership was mentoring me to take the lead so I was assigned more responsibilities more frequently. D Smooth was the 'big brother' I followed when I got in. I had progressed to the point where we were in leadership training together, which was awesome. Our leaders began steadily showing more confidence in us. So, not only was Kowrie incredibly important to me, I was feeling more valuable to the 'Group. That was a certain boon for my confidence.

Warrior training never stops, though. The summer was when we hit camps really hard and did our wilderness training. The key focus there was preparing us for everything in the ways of our ancestors. You were going to learn how to work in the traditions of our people. We got deep into the nitty gritty of how things are traditionally done and the meaning behind them.

What we were doing was a severely condensed version of the traditional rites of passage. We only went out to the woods for an extended weekend. We learned to utilize our surroundings to live off the land. On the continent, this process took six or seven years! You would leave out into the wilderness as a preteen (from ten to twelve years old) and return accepted as a man by the village. Knowing the gravity of what we were doing gave me a unique appreciation for whom we are as a people. I loved being a part of something bigger than me. All the things I did in the Kowrie Group felt like that.

That's why summers were my favorite season for quite a few years. The Kowrie Group was a dope world to be in. The summer of 1986 felt like everything was coming together for me. Then I caught an insanely unfortunate wrinkle just a few weeks before the eleventh grade.

We moved.

Ma pulled us out of the Peabody's on the south side of St. Louis and we moved to the JVL. That's an area called Jeff Vander Lou. Our new house put me about five blocks away from our rival school, Vashon High. That meant I lived across town from McKinley.

Dawg! I was about to be a junior and I had made a name for myself at school. I stood a chance at being a captain on the football team before being a senior. That was huge! I was super comfortable on the hooping squad. I got plenty playing time and I was making waves. There was no way I was going to trade all of that for sitting out a year to play at our arch rival. Naw! Hell naw!

You know I had to talk to Ma about it. She said she understood that is was tough on me but moving was what we had to do. She told me if I wanted to go to McKinley badly enough I still could. It just meant that I would have to get up extra early and hop on the bus every day. She'd be gone to work before I needed to get to school and couldn't get me there. So, again, the choice was mine: wake up early and hit the bus stop or go to school around the corner.

At Vashon High. Our hated rival.

Man, I got my happy ass up and took a bus trek every morning for the last two years of high school. That was a false option to begin with. I wasn't about to give up on football when I had just gotten started. Even though I probably knew more than a few people at Vashon that still wasn't my high school. Nah, I was rocking with McKinley and that was what it was going to be.

That didn't turn out to be the worst thing. I'd get to the old hood early and catch the fellas walking to school. We rolled together like we used to, so it wasn't that big of a deal. Well, aside from the early ass wake up. Felt like I was in the military or some shit. Even that wasn't foreign to me. I woke up early on the regular because of Ma's work shifts. You could say I had been preparing for the neighborhood switch. Again, it was just another feather in my cap of discipline. Doing what I had to do was a sound foundation in my life.

Even when I was home on the weekend it was cool. I loved my little sister. She got more time from me on the weekends because I was rarely home during the week. Getting a chance to kick it with her was like a treat. It also caused us to not be as close as I probably would have liked.

And, my main guy, Roostah, lived around the corner in the Blumeyer Projects. He was someone I kicked it with when I was in the new neighborhood. Roostah even transferred from the V and went to McKinley, too. Whenever he got up early, we would roll to school together. Sometimes, on the days I didn't have Kowrie meetings, we would roll back to the crib together.

Until this conversation, I hadn't really considered that I was never really alone. That was true even after we changed neighborhoods. There was always someone around me whom I trusted. I had a bunch of options, actually. Connecting with people was one of those ways I found to adjust to my frustration. Change is life, I learned to live with that. Our new domicile was one of those lessons.

This new neighborhood also changed the dynamic with my 'Group meetings. The church wasn't around the corner from my house any more. It required some extra effort to make meetings happen for me. So, I went directly from the school, usually after practice, to the meetings. It was inconvenient as hell but I got it done. The Kowrie Group leadership helped a lot, too. They would pick me up and take me home for events and stuff. Commitment finds a way to perform in the things you value. I simply went about the business of handling my affairs in such a way that would make me successful. Thankfully, I had quality assets to help me.

Kowrie worked perfectly for me after school. The days I didn't have meetings I would put together my news report. I always tried to have the most interesting story with thorough details. The in-betweens and the bus rides are where I destroyed my studying. In the windows of my carefully scheduled program, and on the open weekends, I would get to hang out a little bit.

So, I planned it all out daily. My bus ride to school ended in connecting with the crew. Some days I rolled with D Smooth, particularly when we had 'Group meetings. Other times I would hit up Lou and roll with him. I managed to stay tight with my whole crew even though I lived in a different 'hood.

At the top of my hang out list was my dawg, Roostah. I told y'all he lived in the Blumeyer, he stayed there with his Aunt. Most days I would grab him then we would walk to school together spitting Run DMC songs and stuff. We would kick their lyrics word for word, I was always DMC. It was fun as hell. Roostah was my dude, we ran hard together.

He sort of represented a double life for me. Moms kept me in church, Kowrie kept me engaged in cultural empowerment and other constructive things. As a consequence, I was always reserved and calculated. But Roostah was wild as shit! If you looked up 'unruly' in a dictionary I swear you would find just a picture of his middle finger. He wasn't really tamable and his motor stayed on ten. There's reason for all of it, though.

Roostah's mom frequently had problems with the law. She had been caught shoplifting and some other things. Consequently, she spent all of our high school years in prison. He didn't have a relationship with his father to speak of, so he had no core family options. That's why he lived with his aunt. So, his home life was crazy rocky. That played a huge role in everything he did.

He had a hard time in school. His lack of appreciation for authority caused several reroutes in his life. Such as, he went to Vashon as a freshman but got kicked out for some shit. I don't really remember why but, knowing him, it could have been some of anything.

That landed him at McKinley High with Big Lou and me. He ran hard with Big Lou from the start. They boxed together at the same gym and everything. So, they were already homies. Because I got tight with Lou, we just became our own running crew of sorts. Being the big brother he was to all of us, Lou kept Roostah grounded. In fact, Lou was the one who gave him that nickname. He said he was wild like a crazy rooster, ready to fight all the time. The crazy thing is that shit fits him perfectly. Anyways, that's how I got tight with him, just hanging with Lou. Once we found out we lived in the same 'hood it boosted our connection.

Roostah had some real life frustrations. Acting out some emotional tensions made him certifiably wild. He simply didn't acknowledge authority or rules, they weren't his thing. He respected Lou, though. I think it was because Lou operated on his level and it was obvious that Lou cared about him. Like me, Roostah didn't have a big brother. It was kind of a comfort to have Big Lou around.

Don't get it twisted, Roostah still did crazy stuff even while he was hanging out with Lou. That was kind of the wavelength he operated on so you had to expect it. Roostah wasn't about to stop doing wild stuff altogether, that just wasn't going to happen. Shit, Lou wasn't an angel, either! Quietly, they did some crazy things together. That was just part of where we lived and how stuff worked. But, Lou would keep him from doing life-changing-type stupid things. He would basically keep him from doing shit he would go to jail for or get killed over. Basically, Lou did what he could to keep Roostah from going too far with things.

Well, Big Lou left high school a year before us. Roostah's aunt pulled me to the side not long after that. She knew that having that big brother presence around had settled him down a bit and, with Lou gone, a void was created. She thought Roostah could use a friend and maybe I could help keep him out of trouble. He was my guy anyways so it was cool with me. I also took that compliment for what it was, she thought I was well put together. It's always an honor to be regarded in such a way by an elder. That was no small source of pride.

Thing is, I knew Roostah to be a cool ass dude. Yeah, he did crazy shit pretty often but he was still a good person. We each adjusted to our environments differently – he became jovially aggressive to deal with his tests. He wasn't one of those guys trying to hurt people really, he was just carelessly calloused about how he had fun. That's how I saw it and I understood it. I never judged him or tripped on him. But that's a neo-social idea anyways. "Judging people." Back in our day, it was called critique or constructive criticism. I guess that's because we weren't whiny ass babies, but that's a different subject for another conversation.

I guess his aunt was right with the influence thing. Roostah didn't really do crazy shit with me. I wasn't a cat who tried to tell him what to do or anything like that. But, I guess, from the stuff he saw me doing all the time, he didn't feel comfortable going too far out there when he was around me. I'm going to call that being a positive influence because there's no need to overdo it by giving me too much credit. We were also a bit older so his own maturity likely played a huge role in that, too.

Roostah had serious challenges staying in one school his whole educational career. The fact that he arrived at McKinley and stayed until graduating was notable. I would like to think that rolling with Lou and me helped. I'm just glad my brother was able to continue moving forward in life. Whether I had personally helped that or not was very unimportant.

My reference to 'double life' was because Roostah's ways were contrary to my Kowrie world and my general approach to life. Most of my younger motivations were about NOT getting in trouble. He was straight looking for it. Now, I didn't do crazy stuff with him because he was doing it, I wasn't that kind of impressionable. But, many people make you guilty by association. It wasn't a consistent look for me to be in the 'Group and run with one of the wildest kids going.

Fortunately, I had balance. The Kowrie Group was building warriors and leaders. I embraced those lessons in equal measure and I believe they had significant impact on my character. I was able to lead a bit without even trying because it was my training. I was stern enough in my ways that I had a sobering impact on Roostah. Yet, Roostah was liberated enough to keep things live and interesting.

So, in some ways, it worked for both of us. Roostah was fun as hell to be around. He didn't carry the burdens of rules or trying to impress people, so he was carefree. I was focused on success which kept him/us from getting in deep shit. We had fun but didn't fuck up our own situations doing it. Our seeming opposites created a working balance. That was probably what both of our lives needed. So, despite football, basketball, the Kowrie Group and schoolwork, I made time to hang out with him. I mean, if you don't make time for friends what kind of person are you?

Retrospectively, my organization skills allowed me to fit a lot of things in my daily life without sweating too much. Managing my world became a testament to planning. I handled the travelling without any major hassles, it was maximized by conquering homework assignments while riding the bus. I was killing football at the beginning of the school year. Basketball got completely worked over right afterwards. Kowrie was my life season and schoolwork was virtually mastered. I even managed to date.

So, I was seeing a particularly gorgeous young lady. We actually kicked it pretty tough through a big chunk of high school. I met her as a sophomore and we were a cool pair. It wasn't too serious, there weren't any marriage conversations or any craziness like that. Hell, we weren't even sexual. It was just about having attractive and pleasant company.

Believe me, I'm not downplaying it or trying to play the consummate gentleman role. The truth is, I had serious fears about women, or more importantly, about the repercussions of sex. The first of which is; I was terrified of being a father! There were cats all around me becoming teenage fathers and I couldn't bear thinking about that path for me. I missed out on a large chunk of my dad in my life. I figured being a young father would cause that exact situation or worse. Everything in me was committed to preventing that.

Trying to abstain wasn't as easy as it sounds. Our school was very sexually active. Those gals were as aggressive as guys a lot of the times. So, I wasn't celibate because I didn't have offers. There were a lot more than a few opportunities literally *thrown* my way (you know what I'm sayin'). Shit, I was a successful jock! I just wasn't trying to do all of that. Hell, I know a person or two that conceived children the first time they had sex.

Picture that: dudes were babies with a baby. They had to work part-time jobs after school, buy diapers and focus on a child of their own as a child. Baby mamas were a test, grandparents could be even tougher. Then, she may want to kick it with another dude and you got beef with some other young punk who just wants to hit but doesn't give a damn about your kid. Illnesses, doctor's visits and always trying to be available for stuff like 'baby's firsts' when you're still trying to figure out who you are was a no.

Didn't want any parts of that.

Sexual diseases are real, too! Don't think I was sleeping on that. Crabs were super popular back then. It makes my flesh crawl just thinking about having little critters dancing in my drawls. That didn't even slow mutha fuckas down. Dudes were burning in high school like it was a fad or something. They played stupid games like comparing how many women they had run through before they crapped out and shit. My thing was, they were playing that dumb ass game whether they were trying to or not. Y'know what I'm sayin'? Not me! What I look like living the rest of my life with a cauliflower-sized dick? Or dealing with that 'fiery sensation' when I urinate? Or running around like a leaky faucet for no damned reason?

Nope.

My commitment was physical. I had copped some condoms and kept one on me at all times. You should take that literally: I had that same one on me at all times. I wasn't actually sexually active and wasn't going to be. So, that thing made my wallet look like a 3" speaker. My girl and I were cool and I really liked her. Having sex still wasn't on my agenda, at all. I told y'all that and, damn it, I meant it.

Still, in the off chance that we got into a situation, I just wanted to be ready. It made much more sense to be responsibly ready than sorry. I was serious about my life so it was that kind of important to me. Since 'ready' never became necessary, it stayed in my pocket like it was some form of anti-daddy shield. I gave a whole new meaning to the name 'Trojan Man'.

If somebody had given me that commercial jingle as my theme music it would have definitely been fitting.

Particularly considering my tests, junior year was everything I could hope for. The football coach made me one of the captains and I was super geeked. I was a fucking football captain in the eleventh grade! Thinking it was possible didn't mean it was going to happen. I was hype as hell when it did. There was a senior or two who totally wasn't happy about it, and that's putting it mildly. That made sense to me but I was still fucking geeked.

I think Big Lou was hot but he didn't trip on me. He was a captain, too, of course. He was like having a coach on the field the year before and the coach was clearly connected to him. So, everybody saw that coming. I'm telling y'all, he wasn't feeling me being a captain too, though. You know how people have that stank-vibe but even they don't think it's a big enough of a deal to say something about it? It was like that. He didn't actually say anything and I wasn't going to ask him shit. It was just a thing. He was still my dude, though, so we overlooked that and kicked butt together on the field.

Being a football captain was a banging start to the year but I knew I needed to set my horizon higher. In the eleventh grade, there isn't much high school left. It was time to begin planning the next steps for my immediate future. The issue there was, who in the hell knew what those steps were? Not me. Hell, I didn't even know which direction I really wanted to go. Did I have ambition? Yeah. Was I driven? Hell yeah. That didn't mean I had a path figured out. I didn't. A plan had to be created.

We can get this out the way directly, I refused to go to the military. I can sum that reasoning up for you in one word: Kowrie! Donating my skills and value to a system that gives not a single damn about my life would have been wasting every minute I was connected to the 'Group. Even in the 1980's, the military was still largely racist with career choices and promotion rates. Nah, that wasn't going to be my world. That shit was dead.

College made sense, I guess. Sorta. Actually, once you weigh in the debt accrued and the likely careers you'll land in, it usually takes decades before you get free of fiduciary burdening. So, really, nah. That was definitely not working for my logic. I had to get my school finances covered. My life focus was to find ways to win right out of the gate and set myself up for success. It was my commitment in Kowrie and I took it, like all things in the 'Group, with all seriousness.

So, one day I strolled to the counselors office. I was there to see if one of them they could help me with an understanding of the university world. Candidly, I knew nothing about college. I hadn't filled out applications, didn't know what it was to be accepted and had a super loose grasp of scholarships. Those are all key essential understandings for successfully going to a university somewhere. I needed some damned help.

While waiting for a counselor, I started skimming through information on an opportunity bulletin board. It was a cool feature in the office. I took a gander with no expectation that there would be something useful on the wall. I wasn't pessimistic, per se, I just didn't think something useful would magically adorn the board.

There were all types of flyers and pamphlets and such. Every branch of the military generously represented themselves in multiple forms of literature.

Garbage.

I expected to see that and dismissed it accordingly. There was a litany of college information documents, too. Again, they were largely summarily dismissed. I was looking for means not the tool. Then I saw something pretty unique was posted up there, too. I almost missed it in the sea of endless advertisements on how to spend money.

In the center of the board was a flyer that featured the Minority Youth Entrepreneurship Program. It was a program where young minds would be specially trained in business. Students were going to be housed on the University of St. Louis campus for eight weeks. It included courses that were designed to help the students thrive in real-world careers. There were weekly planned field trips to businesses for on-the-job training. They were selecting 25 Black students from St. Louis high schools. I got to the bottom line of the flyer and my mouth dropped open: every week those students would receive a $500 stipend *AND* a big check at the end! All you had to do was write a one-page essay in order to apply.

Man, if I didn't snatch that damned flyer off that wall...

That program said I could go to a university campus, learn business skills and get paid while I did it. Done. I didn't know who the entrepreneurs were but I knew the entrepreneur I was. My uncle had told me when I was much younger that entrepreneurism was a way of life. All my influencers were self-starters. The way I was hungry for success, it was clear to me that I wasn't going to work for someone to get there. I knew entrepreneurism was for me. This opportunity was right up my alley. I got busy writing and submitted the essay before the week was out. I believe it was a Friday when I saw it.

I figured it would take a while to hear from the summer entrepreneurship opportunity. So, I carried on as usual. And it was a test! I made the best of it because there was no other way. Those long rides in to school were great for keeping me ahead of my schoolwork. Football was straight banging, being a captain was the shit.

One of the incidental effects of living far away from my old 'hood is that I got even cooler with D Smooth. We would kick it before 'Group meetings since I was sorta stuck over there. Because of that, he and I excelled within the Kowrie community. We got promoted through the system really rapidly. We both took on more responsibilities and we were regarded with a larger measure of reverence. Teaching classes was cool and leading segments of the meetings felt super important. I could damned near feel the manhood swelling in my chest when I was there.

Unfortunately, the 'Clash of the Programs' continued. My school activities were steadily a test for my Kowrie life. The rise in my 'Group responsibilities made my school success more of an interposing demand on my time. It was a serious seesaw. From time to time I would shift priorities. Not because the 'Group was ever less important, no sir, but because I was a teenager. I wanted to do shit, man. So, I had a few tests that were less than terrific.

I became one of the captains as a junior because, quietly, I was an absolute beast on the field. No shit. So much so that I moved from the lineman positions on both sides of the ball to being a defensive back on defense and a halfback on offense that year. Our coach was typical for a high school coach. He valued wins above most things. So, when he had horses (dudes he knew could flat out play) he would have them playing ironman ball. That means some of my teammates played on offense and defense. Of course, I was one of them. This would definitely wear us out but the thought process is that we 'were young' and we 'could handle it'.

This is precisely why the Kowrie Group didn't have a whole lot of love for the sports world. Our health came second to results. That's not meant to cast aspersions on our coach. He was a good man. That's just how that system went. When you played ball you were a useful tool. Period.

Anyways, I was a MONSTER on that D line! I made it my personal mission to introduce myself and become closely acquainted with every running back we played. That's a very nice way to say I was trying to kill the guy every down. My track record for doing so was pretty damned successful. I got entirely familiar with lot of running backs that didn't want to know me. Seriously, I was a run-stuffing machine, y'hurr me?

Our last game of the season was on a Friday night. Night games were always the best. They felt like spotlights were on you and it seemed to make the crowds more raucous. They were often much colder so you played with a different aggression. We were mad as hell that we were cold, that provided some tackling fuel. We did everything we could to take that anger out on the other team.

At most night games, you could see everyone breathing on the field. Its presence was so big that it looked like steam rising from the ground all game. Every player was sportin' a peeved expression because we were fucking cold. So, when you saw those vapors coming out of a dude's face, it was like a raging bull was ready to charge at you. That created sort of a grim ambiance of tension and hostility. Day games rarely gave you that. Night games had a different energy that just seemed to take it to another level.

Well, this particular night was a championship game. We had kicked butt all season and we were trying to get to the state championships. That's how we earned the privilege to be playing in December, our record was wicked and our team was even more so. The football field bore all of the magic of a winning season for both teams. When championships are on the line, there was a prevailing electricity out on that grass that's difficult to describe. I swear my guys wouldn't eat all week so we would hit the field hungry in every way.

(They ate, though. High school athletes are some of the most gluttonous kids you'll ever see. Don't get me lying, them mutha fuckas ate. I was definitely exaggerating).

Here's where it gets hairy. Earlier in the year, we had planned a Kowrie Group retreat over the winter break. This was an annual week-long trip. It came a week earlier this particular year due to a simple switch in logistics. No one foresaw that I would still be playing football into

December. Few teams were. The 'Group wouldn't have planned group events around my individual game, anyways. No self-respecting organization would have. However, I was out there balling and it created a situation for me.

The Kowrie Group had scheduled to depart Friday night to get to our site in the wee hours of morning on Saturday. This wasn't anomalous, it's a part of the process and the tests we had to face. These things are typically no big deal except I was still playing this particular year. The night game had real chances of preventing me from getting on that bus. As one of the prominent young leaders, I would send all the wrong signals if I were in any way less than punctual. This was the clear threat that my game posed that night.

Speaking of which, I was in rare form. I had teamed up with the football field and we were sandwiching the hell out of their running backs. Thinking back on it, I remember it as if I smacked those dudes for a loss on every possession they had. I'm sure it wasn't remotely close to that often but that's what it felt like.

It was more than just a defensive night. I made seriously key lead blocks on offense that broke our running back open for a pair of scores. That's right, not just one but two touchdowns! I was killing it out there and the results were vividly plain. Our opponents hated facing me on that field that night and that's exactly how I would have planned it. The home team was loving me and I felt invincible.

That's because I wasn't stopped! We pummeled that team to the tune of some ridiculous point differential. I was heralded by all my teammates for balling my ass off. It was such a studly performance that I saw the small local press core waiting for me when I was leaving the field.

Standing in front of that press core was Chuck Cantrell. Chuck was my ride to the Kowrie buses and he wasn't in any sort of waiting mood. Before I even got close he walked up to me.

"Let's go." Chuck said with authority.

"Did you see the game, man? I was killing it!" I was yelling.

Yeah, I was yelling my damned head off.

I could barely get the words out. My adrenaline was on 300.

"I did see you," Chuck said. "You were awesome, that was a great job. Now let's go."

He turned me the opposite direction of the bulk of the crowd and immediately began ushering me away.

There were people all over the place. The whole campus was filled with excitement. We were going to the state championship! There was yelling and laughter everywhere. Cars were blaring their horns and flashing their lights. Some of them were cranking out music with their doors flung open. People stood in the risers shaking pom poms, singing songs and yelling out school chants. It was an instant party.

A few girls came up to kiss me. Fellas were walking by trying to give me dap. It was crazy as shit, man. I felt like a celebrity. Hell, everyone was treating me like a celebrity. Everyone except Chuck.

Chuck had, oddly in some respectful way, grabbed my arm and started leading me off the field.

"Hey Chuck, where we going man?" I pleaded.

"You know the 'Group has to roll out tonight. It's about that time right now. We can't have them waiting on us." Chuck responded.

Right then, a reporter stepped up and tried to shove a handheld recorder in my face. He was walking in lockstep with us as best he could.

Chuck was really trying to get me out of there so we were booking. The reporter was in a half-trot just trying to keep up.

> "Hey champ! You had a magnificent game out there. I'm Billy Bell from the Post-Dispatch, you wanna talk to me about it?" The reporter said.
> "Oh, uh, yeah!" I said.
> "He does but he can't. He has somewhere to go." Chuck rebuked the guy.

Something about Chuck's tone made the reporter stop walking with us. I would assume it's because Chuck wasn't bullshitting. He meant that we were leaving without telling that dude a damn thing.

I felt a weird rejection. It seemed like *I* had been shot down. I couldn't rush off in silence like that without saying something about it.

> "Why can't I talk to the guy for a minute, Chuck?" I asked.

Chuck didn't break stride trying to fight through the masses.

> "Just like this game, the press wants you for what they can get out of you. Believe, whenever you need them to share a truth on your behalf they'll find a more important story for them to tell. Just like they don't exist for your strife, you're not here for their headlines."

I ain't gone lie, dawg, it wasn't my best moment. I could understand where he was coming from but I had just won a huge game, man. I wanted to revel in that shit for a bit. Kick it with some folks. Get my face on the front of the paper. Or a few pages in, whatever. Give me some bragging rights for my children in the far future, you know?

My training, my research and everything I knew about the media told me he was more than right about the press, though. It's about how its set up. They want the saucy stuff, the things they think will make people read or watch them so they can sell ads. Normally, that would be some stereotypical black eye for our people. Real news? Anything positive about our people? Nah, they didn't have a habit of sharing that. Black positivity didn't fit the American narrative for us so it wasn't "marketable". If they couldn't sell it they wouldn't tell it. Those mutha fuckas didn't care two shakes of a rat's ass about my plight or my fight. They just wanted to sell copy. That truth got my mind right and I stopped being salty.

There was no time to pout about it, anyway. I was a Kowrie Group leader heading into a situation where my leadership would be demanded. I had to gather myself and handle the business my honor was committed to delivering.

I took a last glance at the reporter while leaving the field with Chuck.

That kind of scheduling conflict wasn't as rare as I would have liked it to be. That night, Chuck was a true representation of the Kowrie approach. All business, no frills. Sometimes it was a tough weight on my teenage life. Fortunately, I was grounded in and by the Kowrie Group, so, I just handled it. The way it was helping to form my manhood, man, I valued it more than all my school involvements combined. Honestly, the character-building that took place in the 'Group is what made those rough times a lot more bearable.

Fortunately, I didn't have any other major conflicts that school year. The spring semester proved to be one of the easiest and most fun of my high school career. When the spring semester ended, I was riding high. Everything in my world was working for me. It was an incredible inspiration just knowing that I was about to be done with that phase of life.

By the way, y'all remember that entrepreneurship program I told you about? They sent me a letter.

CHAPTER 18

BUSINESS 101

When the letter came from the Minority Youth Entrepreneurship Program, I had forgotten about my application. It's not that it took a long time, either. My life agenda was so demanding that I didn't spend a lot of time pondering things that weren't on my immediate horizon. I sorta figured that they would only send correspondence to people who made it in. So, I prepared myself for not being accepted by taking it off my radar.

That was kind of crazy because I thought enough about it to tell Ma. Well, I had to tell her because I would be leaving for several weeks if they accepted me. She would have to give me permission and all that so I wanted her to have the heads up. My experience with Ma had told me that being preemptive with information was the best way to handle situations. She was much more amenable that way.

Those aren't the only reasons I told her about it. I was excited! That summer camp would be a dope opportunity. The fortuitousness of ever reading that posting was also fluky – looking at the wall wasn't part of any plan. It was total coincidence. I didn't expect anything at all while perusing the posted info. Yes, future moves were on my mind while going into the counselors office, that's true. So, that *would* make it serendipitous. Still, I had only heard of it because it was posted there.

The youth entrepreneurship program was open to all St. Louis high schools and they were only going to select 25 students. What are the odds something like that would work out for me? That's some shit that happens in movies and books, I just didn't even seriously consider it. It was basically a lottery ticket, y'know what I'm sayin'?

When I walked in the door that day, Ma walked up to me out of the kitchen and gave me a kiss.

"Hey, Man! How was your day?" She said.

"It was good, Ma. We did some more cool stuff in my production class," I responded.

"Yeah?" She asked, "like what?"

"We split into teams again and got to put together a really fresh skit about battle rapping. It was fun."

"Really? Were you rapping?" Ma asked.

"Nah. I was working the camera. I did get to bust a few moves in the background, show off my skills, y'know? What we made was like a music video. It was about 4 minutes long."

"That's nice, Man. I'm glad you enjoyed your day. Sounds like you had a good time." She said with a smile on her face.

"Yeah, it was a good time."

Part of what I didn't tell her was that my current crush was also in the class. I was again single and a blazing hot cheerleader was in TV Production with me. It was hard to have a bad day when I saw her every third period. Dawg, she was that one. I would've broken the abstinence code for her. It was like that.

Ma seemed to be in a good mood.

"How did your day go, Ma?" I asked.

"Oh, I had a good day, Man. Not a whole lot special but I don't need that. The Lord let me see another day, my babies are fed and happy. We're healthy. I'm good." She replied.

"Okay." I didn't have a comeback for all of that.

"Man, there's some mail for you on the table."

"Some mail?" I was caught off guard.

"Mm-hm. It's on the table, baby." She pointed as she turned back towards the kitchen.

I saw that the envelope was addressed from the Youth Entrepreneurship Program before picking it up off the table. My eyes about popped out of my head. It surprised me that it arrived at the house so fast. Then again, it was near the end of the semester. They had to get the word out so folks could make plans, if they were accepted.

That's when the thought of me actually going hit me.

(Am I really gonna get to do this shit?!)

"Hey Ma, this is for the entrepreneurship program."

"I know, Man. I saw it when I picked it up. I didn't want to spoil it for you, though. Open it, let's see what you got."

She walked back into the living room. We both sat on the couch and I ripped the thing open. I started reading it aloud to share it with Ma.

"Mr. Dizzy, thank you for applying for the Minority Youth Entrepreneurship Program. We were very impressed with your application, your essay in particular. We would be honored if you would join us in our inaugural year of the program..."

I popped up off the couch and my mouth flew wide open. I stared at Ma with my eyes ready to jump clean out of my skull.

"Well ain't that special? God is good." Ma said.

"I made it in! They accepted my application, Ma. I made it in! I made it in!"

It took all the discipline in my body not to literally jump up and down until I broke one of my limbs. I was out of my entire mind! It was official: I was about to get paid in the summer for getting educated about business. This was going to be dope! I just couldn't believe they picked me.

You'd have to understand the odds to grasp the gravity of this anomaly. The capacity of our school was somewhere around 2400-2500. Our school was at least half full in 1987, that means there were more than 1200 students in our hallways. McKinley was just one of ten schools they used for their selections. The entire student capacity of the project was 25 kids. Twenty-five of us selected from more than 12,000 students! Those are hellacious odds.

I don't even care what kind of thing it was – that was fuckin' awesome! Just to be selected while facing those numbers was a huge point of pride. The letter I wrote was my only representation and it was enough to get me in. That felt great.

Not every kid applied in all the schools, of course. Quietly, I have no idea how many applied and that's not the point. I just knew that I was rolling into a very profitable sounding program that maintained a rare acceptance rate. Going at all was marvelous so I pledged to make it work for me. Entrepreneurship was a definite part of my life path. My then-fluid plan included leveraging that program as a career springboard. It seemed like it would help me find my direction.

Ma and I sat there and read the rest of the details of the letter. Everything was provided for us. Our tutors would be entrepreneurs. Trips to businesses were at the expense of the program. The lodging and the meals were paid for. And the contest at the end came with a monetary prize. We also got a paycheck at the end of the course. I knew the program was going to be amazing!

It was dope that we would stay on campus at St. Louis University. I had been up there plenty because it was part of our community. The campus was wide open and they would frequently host activities for the people of St. Louis. We cut through the school a lot just hanging out because it wasn't far from the house. Hell, two summers before the entrepreneurship program, I attended the Rich Grawer basketball day camp at their gym. So I was familiar with the school.

That did not include the dormitories. I'd never been in those before. And I hadn't really spent consecutive days on campus other than the basketball camp for a weekend. But the youth entrepreneurship program would have us on campus for almost two months straight. I wanted to know what it would feel like to be a college student. Staying on campus that long would have to give me a really good idea. That only made sense, right? I couldn't wait!

There were still quite a few weeks left in school after we got the letter. Basketball season had just ended so I had a little more time on my hands than most of the rest of the year. My childhood fear of 'getting in trouble and ruining things' had become a programmed motivator for me. I attacked my school books and my Kowrie responsibilities until the summer came. I wanted to make certain that nothing would stop me from going to that camp.

The Kowrie leadership knew all about the program. I told them every detail I could iterate. They thought it was a great idea and supported me in doing it. Better yet, they challenged me to represent the 'Group. They charged me to excel by coming out of the contest victorious. I accepted that challenge with pride swelling in my chest.

I gave my word to continue attending every 'Group meeting that didn't disrupt the program commitment. They understood it to be a temporary opportunity and were very reasonable. That was almost shocking because typically they just didn't waiver for anything. Maybe I had earned that level of trust. It definitely helped that it was sponsored by Black people to lift the community. That's the primary function and concern for the Kowrie Group. So, I'm sure to them it was a complimentary effort. For me, it felt great not to be under any extra pressure. The summer couldn't arrive fast enough.

Everything was prepared for us when we arrived at the campus. There was a greeting team that gave us ID badges, passed out welcome packages and showed us to our rooms. When I got to my room I was blown away!

The first thing I saw was the huge window on one side of the room. It provided a perfect view of the Arch, just perfect. I'd seen that thing my whole life but it looked different through that window. As if that wasn't enough, the room was filled with perks: a few balloons, a real sports blazer, a full accompaniment of stationary and a briefcase to put it in. They even had a little satchel of candy on the nightstand that welcomed me by name. An absolute imprimatur of class.

I had been pondering going to college. That's how I found the flyer for this thing in the counselors office, of course. Standing in that dorm room changed that shit! Pondering was over. That place was awesome. There was also a resounding air of independence. It was the best and most resonating feature for me. I was ready to be cut free on a campus somewhere. If their intent was to create a level of expectation then it worked. The bar was set. This shit was fresh as hell!

The candy welcome had my name and my school on it with a really cool message. They had us bunking in pairs but I arrived before my roommate. I got curious about him and decided to see if he was from McKinley. I didn't know who else had made it. So, I looked over to the other guy's candy and saw he was from Watson High.

I just guessed the other kids from McKinley were probably in a room together. Or, maybe they split all of us up on purpose to get us acquainted with kids from other schools. I wasn't sweating it. Whoever my roommate was I figured I would just meet them later. And I would see the other McKinley kids later, too.

Walking into that dorm room changed everything. I mean, I was familiar with the campus but all my prior activity was outside. The basketball camp was in the gym, sure, but it felt like they were trying to keep us out of everything else while we were there. We didn't get to explore the campus and we got bagged lunches in the gym. The MYEP was in a different stratosphere than that camp and I loved every bit of it.

Like I had imagined, inside access to the school was different. We were treated differently. I got to see the innerworkings of the campus and it opened my eyes anew. It was super clean, neat and orderly. Everything was modernized, it was as if they had the best of everything ever made. The architecture all seemed... big. I swear I had hit another level of life. The best part about it? It felt like actually being in college. That was a sensationally empowering feeling. Like I told y'all, pondering was over.

They got us settled, they got us fed then it got started. We all met in one of the College of Business meeting rooms for orientation. There were 45 people in the room including all 25 students and the camp staff. I didn't see anybody from McKinley initially but it's not like I knew everybody in the school. We would all get introduced soon enough then I would find out who I was representing with.

The first people who talked to us in the meeting were the two founders. They were both incredibly successful business owners. Here's a rundown of their accomplishments:

One of them was a railroad owner. There was a casket manufacturer. One was an incredibly successful real estate investor. One was a railroad supply genius. This gentleman was the patent owner of tank cars: the train cars that are able to transport liquids. One of them earned a businessman of the year award. Lastly, one of their more unique claims is that one was an NFL veteran. Again, these are the accolades of just two gentlemen. They were the creators of the opportunity and they were wildly successful.

They greeted us, thanked us for coming then went to business. The two of them explained that every facet of this program was purposeful. We were getting paid to make the statement to us that we were valuable. They emphasized that we should never work for free. Doing so would decrease our value. Our time and effort are always worth someone paying for them. They explained that our instructors were all industry lions. It was made clear to us that the lessons we would receive in the program couldn't be purchased outside the platform.

The founders talked to us in tandem. They stood together in front of the room. Each had a cordless microphone in their hand.

> "Thank you for coming to the inaugural Minority Youth Entrepreneurship Program. Out of the entire St. Louis school system, the 25 of you were the only ones chosen to be here. That is a stellar accomplishment and we want to applaud you before we begin. Feel free to applaud yourselves. Welcome and congratulations!"

Everyone in the room clapped, some vigorously. Then I realized an odd detail: looking around the room, I saw we were in six groups. That meant one of the teams had five people while the rest had four. I thought it was odd but decided not to care. My team was four people and I would just have to make sure we had that hustle, you know. I was committed to winning regardless.

The other gentleman stepped forward.

"All of you help form the commencement of our program and we're excited to have every one of you kicking this off with us. You are some of the best and brightest that St. Louis has to offer and we want to offer you the best you can have."

The first gentleman again spoke.

"Speaking of which, your first lesson is a question from entre-preneurship 101 and I need you to answer it for me. As an entrepreneur, what is your greatest and most valuable asset?"

He looked around the room and one guy put his hand up. One of the founders addressed him.

"We appreciate you raising your hand. However, we want you to treat this like a business setting from now on. Find your way to voice your perspective without being rude, of course, but you're an adult to us. Interject your input when you see its necessary. Just be respectful. Okay? Alright. What do you have? What's your most valuable asset?"

The student stood to speak.

"Your employees."

Both of the founders smiled at the answer. One of them responded.

"Thank you for that answer. You are officially the first associ-
ate of the program to provide an answer to a question. Being
first is how you make your mark in this life, it's a character trait of the brave. Thank you for being that man. Now,
employees are definitely important. Taking care of them will
make you better than a good owner, it will make you a great
leader."

He paused to look around the room and ensure it sank in. He then
continued,

"Once you get to that phase. In order to get to that phase
someone has to do the work. Create a business. Find the
employees. Attract clients, manage all transactions and keep
your firm afloat. Who does that?"

He had laid it out so vividly that I was compelled to answer. So,
I did.

"We have to. We're our most valuable asset."

Both Founders again smiled. The second of them responded.

"That's right. Don't you ever forget it. Take care of you first.
Make sure you're always squared away. Everything else follows
that."

The other founder explained.

"That is our plan for you in this training. You will be the first priority and you'll be taken care of like the precious asset you are. Our purpose for this is to show you that you must acclimatize yourself to the type of success you want to achieve. It helps you set goals and it drives your 'why'."

(See? Setting standards. I'm with it.)

The second founder continued.

"This program is about empowering you to succeed in any phase of business you choose. All your lessons will come from successful entrepreneurs who specialize in the fields they'll tutor you in. We advise you to be hyper studios. Take notes. Ask questions. Make relationships. Pay attention to every word they say and everything they show you. Our number one goal is helping you succeed so you can do the same with young people one day. Do all you can to maximize this opportunity."

The first founder summed it all up.

"We have paired you in 6 teams with incredible chaperones. The interns with you are all college grads, most are working through MBA programs. They've come from all over the country: from here at SLU Law, Drake, Grambling and several others. Treat them and your teammates as your business partners because, as of this moment, they are. Get to know them and their strengths, you'll need to utilize them before this session is over. This program will be educational, it will be empowering and it will be fun. You will have a great time, we're here to make sure of it. So, without further ado…"

Both founders spoke at once.

"Welcome to the Minority Youth Entrepreneurship Program!"

We then were able to meet and greet everyone there. We spent that day getting to know our mentors, chaperones and peers. Everything we did was top notch and we were treated as if we were wealthy. In the evening, we shared individual stories at dinner. This included all of our mentors and chaperones. Everything was lavishly comfortable and casual to ease us into the system.

It was then that I learned why my roommate was a guy from Watson: no other students from McKinley made it in the program. It was just me! What?! Talk about being blown away… dawg, that fucked me up! I was so proud I didn't know what to do. My first thought, though, was to tell Ma. I knew she would be proud, maybe even as proud as I was. That was one hell of an honor.

My roommate was also the only kid from his school, too. We were put together because we had that in common. His name was Ronny Wright (that's what we'll call him for the purpose of this story). Ronny was supposed to be the smartest kid in the program. He was a cat who ran with that kind of confidence, too. I didn't appreciate the implication that anyone was directly smarter than me. So, it was an immediate competition for the both of us. That was probably the thing that made us the most cool with one another, the mutual respect.

The next morning was a Sunday. We were awakened at the crack of dawn and began classes. It was made clear to us that entrepreneurs don't get days off. The work doesn't get done if you don't ensure that it does. It is not a nine to five world. I took particular note of that fact.

Moving forward, we were trained by a veritable gourmet of business moguls. Every lesson we received came from an entrepreneur in that specific field. Accounting came from an accountant who had a decades-long successful firm. Our Marketing courses were taught by an advertising conglomerate's founder. Our manufacturing lessons took place at a plant – we toured with the CEO who was the founder. We even went to Carper Caskets. We learned about a casket manufacturer (and broker) to teach us that all business isn't sexy. A multitude of successful ones are born of necessity. And, yes, we were educated by the founder.

These powerful people took time to instruct us directly and they answered every question patiently. I felt the true magnitude of their station and it made an indelible impact on me. I saw myself in their places and added that as my motivation to achieve.

All portions of the program were competitive. This never abated. The teams were branded as businesses and we each chose a name for our partnerships. We stood off against the other 'firms' throughout the entire course. This lesson was to teach us marketplace awareness. In business, you're always in competition. This is when we learned what a SWOT analysis was. SWOT stands for Strengths, Weaknesses, Opportunities and Threats. You must honestly assess your product, its effectiveness and your success with it against your competitors because they are doing the same with you. A SWOT analysis is a tool to help you achieve the appropriate level of competitive understanding in order to attain your goals. Personally, I liked the premise of the SWOT analysis. It made a bunch of sense to me.

They taught us that markets have a measure. Your firm's share of that market determines the level of your success. Other firms will never help you succeed and will revel in your failure. They are uniquely motivated for this end because your losses have great potential to add to their success. You don't necessarily have to take aim at your opponents to best them, but never lose sight of the fact that they are your business foes. Always be committed to outperforming them or you may need to look for another business opportunity. This is another lesson that profoundly struck me.

Each segment of lessons had a major takeaway for me. We learned how to speak to groups, to motivate our teams. I definitely needed that skill. They emphasized that we should capitalize on opportunities when they presented themselves to us – if you recognize a need then build a business to fill it. When such opportunities don't present themselves, look to create them. They emphasized, though, that when we created a product or service for an existent need then we stood greater chances for success. All of these were catalogued in my mental rolodex. That information just resonated with me in such a way that I knew it would avail me much one day.

All of our lessons and efforts culminated into the contests of the program: an individual 100-question exam and a group business plan challenge. The highest individual score for the test won a scholarship. Separately, each firm had to come up with a winning concept and support it with a plan of execution. The winning firm members would also receive a scholarship.

This program played perfectly into my wheelhouse. The Kowrie Group made me an excellent test-taker. We literally had to be perfect to be acceptable. Actually, testing was sort of my frame of reference. It was a weird place from which to view performance but it demanded excellence as a rule. That worked for me. I also made plans for everything. It was my personal habit to better control the outcomes of my situations. The particular challenges of those competitions played well into my practices. I didn't think it was going to be easy but I certainly thought I was well prepared. I was stoked and ready to go.

The business plan concept had to be actionable. It had to be illustrative and functional. There was not a budget limit for the contest but the financial projections had to be comprehensive and profitable. Beyond that we were not given very many constraints.

Every student in the program was a St. Louisan. But, since I was the only person from McKinley, I was the only one from the neighborhood. The campus was just a few blocks from my house. I knew what it was like when they had events. I knew where the hotels were and that there weren't many in the area. My neighborhood dealt with the traffic jams from parents and visitors who came to campus for events.

It struck me that the school needed a hotel on campus. Building one was a practical and pertinent idea. We could include the school aspect where hospitality students could be interns and get experience. It also capitalized on where we were and would be easy to envision. Our chaperones were concurrently staying in the dorms because hotels were inconveniently far away for a daily commute. Certainly, the judges and mentors had the same situations or, at the very least, the information of their inconvenience. So, my idea capitalized on one of our key lessons: recognize a need and fill it. I discussed my observations with my firm and we chose to move on it.

We made a business plan to build a campus hotel. It would fill the need of visitors but would serve a much larger purpose for the university. It would be managed through the School of Hospitality and make it a much more comprehensive program. A school-managed hotel would bolster that program significantly while providing a profitable asset for the institution. It wasn't the sexiest idea but it was incredibly practical. And, again, it utilized one of the fundamentals we were taught in the program. We thought we had a slam dunk.

Unfortunately, the end had to come. We rolled into the last week of the program with the stakes high. I enjoyed myself immensely and had learned volumes. There were a bunch of things I knew would be pivotal lessons for my future. I was glad as hell they picked me.

Everything we had done over the course of the eight weeks all boiled down to the results of the final three days: team-written business plan scores, the personal business exam and the business plan presentations. My team was ready and I was definitely good to go. It was time to be about that business. Really though, isn't it always?

CHAPTER 19

FRUITION

All of our business plans were turned into the staff no later than the last Tuesday of the program for the judges to scrutinize before we delivered the presentations. This helped them research our proposals because they planned to judge them on that Thursday when we presented them live. We knew they would declare all winners that evening, which would mean the end of the program. It was an incredibly exciting week and a whole lot to prepare for.

The next day, Wednesday, we took the personal exam. I went into the testing space expecting to deliver a perfect score. My Kowrie training conditioned me to understand that was the only acceptable result. After we took it, I was certain I did well. When we all finished, or the time expired, we retreated into our firms to prepare for the business plan presentations the next day.

Like the rest of the program, our presentation evening was completely plush. The program had leased space at the Julius Hunter's Restaurant. The proprietor was a local Black TV broadcaster who had deep tenure on Channel 4 News. It was clear that the dude was setting a reputation with the place. The restaurant was impeccable. And it was completely sequitur that we would have the coup de grace at a Black-owned venue. The program was nothing if not thorough.

The venue was entirely decked out. There was fine linen on every table with monogrammed cloth napkins. Even the ceiling was adorned with exquisite chandeliers and they were complemented by crystal and glass everything everywhere which underpinned the elegance. All the servers wore shirts and ties to enhance the classy vibe. A snazzy live jazz band set the tone and made you feel like you had arrived. I'm telling you, these wealthy mutha fuckas knew how to live.

Accordingly, everyone arrived suited and booted. All of our parents were there in their Sunday best. Everybody looked sensational. Even our firms. We all wore the jackets that were provided to us. Each team arrived with an entirely different look than the other. I don't know about anyone else but I didn't expect that. Because my roommate and I had the same jackets I just assumed everybody would. I've never been so glad to be wrong. It was fresh as hell, dawg! All of the looks were hot and exclusive.

The blazers were custom made and donated to the system by a Black entrepreneur's clothing company. So, I was sporting a jacket that only four people in the world had. That's some posh shit to deal with as a teenager. Seriously, this program had covered all the bases and made us feel like gladiators. We were ready.

Each of our individual firms sat at separate and personally designated tables. We were accompanied by our chaperones, the grad students who helped cultivate our teams. After all, they had long become part of our firms and it was only fitting that they end the program with us. Our parents sat in a section behind us but they were more than comfortable. Centered in the front of the ballroom was a long table with three chairs. Off to either side of the table were a pair of huge projection screens. The room was prepared for the needs of the presenters. It was go time.

The judges took their seats at the front table to signal the beginning of the evening's festivities. Before each seat was a table microphone on a short, bendable stand. The three judges were the two founders and one of the tycoons who spent a lot of time on campus educating us. She was a chocolate woman with long legs. I truly appreciated her demeanor. She was intelligent and curt but very friendly. Totally reminded me of Ma. If I had to make an assessment, I would say she was a perfect accompaniment to the founders.

After greeting everyone, the first founder opened the evening with one of our last lessons.

> "I'm sure all of you have noticed that there are 25 young business minds here that have been split into six teams. There is no equal split for that. We could have simply made five teams and created a balance but we realized that would create a false model. All businesses don't have the same assets. In fact, incredibly few ever do. You must simply be successful with the assets you have – fairness isn't business."

The second founder chimed in.

> "A true testament to you all is that there hasn't been any complaints about this fact. Not one. We're certain you noticed it and you've carried on just the same. There were no extra expectations for the team with five members and no breaks for the teams who were shorter. Business doesn't do that so nor did we. Still, you all handled it with aplomb and performed amicably and admirably. We're extraordinarily proud of every one of you."

A round of applause ensued. Then the first founder again spoke.

> "Let's begin this evening by taking care of a little business."

There was a spattering of laughter.

"You have no idea how glad I am that someone got that joke. It means I'm not the only nerd here."

A louder chorus responded.

"So, the first phase of this business venture was educating our young entrepreneurs in training. This education was wide ranging. It wasn't just business practice but theory, as well. Like the beautiful trappings of this glorious venue, we wanted to put them in the frame of mind for success. You would be pleased to know, we've had a spectacularly prosperous inaugural class. These young people have bedazzled us with their brilliance and creativity. They have set the bar incredibly high for the program moving forward and should be wildly applauded for their accomplishments. Be proud of your children, family."

The room erupted with applause. He continued.

"But here's the next business reality: everybody doesn't win. Our events of the past few weeks have led to the competition of our program. All of business is competition so, of course, we've captured that here, as well. I'm going to let my partner take it from here."

The second founder leaned forward to his microphone.

"Likewise, the second phase of our program was a pair challenges. There was an individual challenge where our young
businesspeople tested on all the material we've covered in
the last two months. And there is a group project that you all
will witness this evening. In fact, thank you for being here to
share in it. This will be a terrific event and we're very much
looking forward to seeing these young people in action. We're
certain you are, too."

The room again came to life in applause. The partner continued.

"The individual exam was administered on yesterday. Those
results will be shared with you by the most brilliant woman
I know and the unofficial campus mom. Give her some love,
family."

The entire room gave her a rousing applause. Our campus mom then
addressed the audience.

"Thank all of you for that. It's been an honor and a pleasure working on this team and with all of your children.
Thank you."

The room again applauded her. She continued.

"Okay. So, each young business person was given a 100 question quiz on yesterday. It was comprised of ten questions from
each segment of the training we've covered in this program.
When we graded it this morning we were astounded by the
scores and decided to check it twice. You will be pleased to

291

know that each of your young people scored an 85 or above. That's twenty-five scores over 85%! That is a magnificent accomplishment."

Everyone began clapping.

"Yes, that is definitely worth celebrating. Please, give them another round."

I looked around and thought about how cool it was to be in a room full of smart people. It was a pretty dope moment.

She continued.

"Unfortunately for twenty-four of you, there is only one winner. Don't let that be discouraging to you. Just like in business, you can have great achievements without having all of the accolades. Every one of you leaving this program is a winner and your efforts have forwarded your careers. You have set a precedent here that will be difficult to top. You should truly be proud of yourselves."

The crowd again erupted.

"The winner of this first challenge did a marvelous job on the test. He is one of our two students here that singularly represented their school."

I looked over at Ronny. He was smiling broadly like he was Tom cat and he had just caught and ate Jerry. I thought to myself, "I guess he is the smartest dude here. Fuck!"

"This young man will receive the first ever Minority Youth Entrepreneurship Program scholarship. This is a monumental milestone that we hope to repeat countless times. But, without further ado, for a total score of 98%, we award our first scholarship to…"

I looked back at Ronny's table. He had started shaking hands with people. He put his hands on the arms of his chair, preparing to stand. Then I looked back to the judges table.

"… the young business mind out of McKinley High School, the only school represented from this neighborhood, Mr. Busara Dizzy!"

I sat there a minute… lost. I got stuck in thought.

(She just called my name. Why did she just say my name if he won? Wait… what?)

Everyone rose to their feet to applaud. I was actually the only person not standing. When I realized she meant I had won my next thought was about perfection.

(What? I got a 98? Don't know if I'll tell that to Mwalimu.)

One of the founders reached down to the mic and called me out.

"Come on up here, Mr. Dizzy. Claim your scholarship, young brother, before one of us gets tempted to put it in the bank."

I walked up to the desk through a sea of handclapping, handshakes, pats on the back and laughter. The energy was palpable: it felt like I had won for everyone. In a sense, that's precisely what it was. I carried the 'Group with me in all my efforts, so my win was assuredly representing us. Ma was there and she believed in me heading into this thing. She was all aglow with joy. It was certainly a win for team Dizzy.

Still, we were approaching that team competition, as well, and I was in that frame of mind. So, my firm was added in my victory, too. Our connection had rapidly grown during the camp and they were vigorously celebrating me at our table. It all felt so surreal. I had carried my world on my back and delivered for us. Man, I was proud as fuck.

Before it was all over with, we found out that Ronny got a 97. He was pissed and wouldn't let it go. Sorry if its petty, but I felt even better about beating him because he hated it so much. Hey, sometimes petty happens. Sue me.

When I got to the table, the three Black moguls shook my hand. They handed me an elaborate trophy and a billboard-sized check for the amount of the scholarship.

The second founder had grabbed his cordless mic off the stand and walked around the table to stand talking with me in front of it. He put his arm around me and addressed the room.

> "I am not remotely surprised that Mr. Dizzy is standing here right now. He was the second to answer questions in the program's history. He asked questions everywhere we went, participated with all his energy and stayed completely engaged the entire session. Let his presence in this spotlight be a testament to participation, persistence and perseverance. Congratulations, Mr. Dizzy."

The entire room stood to applaud me. I basked in that vibe for a minute. It was dope, y'all.

"Mr. Dizzy, you want to say a few words?"

He handed me the microphone and took a step back. I figured it would be difficult to talk through the massive cheesing smile on my grill. I took my shot anyways.

> "Thank you, sir. I want to extend that gratefulness to your partner, all the staff and especially our chaperone, Tyrone, as well. He was marvelous at looking out for us. Thank you to my firm, they're a great bunch of brilliant minds. I've learned a lot from each of them. I have to send a shout out to my childhood organization for making test prep a character trait and demanding perfection from me. They might be unhappy with my 98 but they would approve of the result.

The audience laughed a bit.

"Lastly, and most importantly…"

I picked Ma out of the crowd and spoke to her directly.

> "Ma, thank you for everything. Thank you for believing in me and supporting me in attending this program. You're the best. I love you."

Everyone again applauded as I handed the microphone back. The founder shook my hand and addressed the crowd.

"Thank you, Mr. Dizzy. You are the first recipient of a MYEP
scholarship in history. You should be incredibly proud, we're
all proud of you."

I walked back to my seat beaming with more than pride. It was the
most amazing of feelings.

While the founder walked back to his seat, the other founder began
speaking.

"The only fitting way to follow his individual greatness is to
host our groups and their powerful business presentations.
Throughout this process we've addressed their partnerships
as firms. They have all operated like businesses and have
achieved a great deal together. Their team bonds are visible
and we are very satisfied with their results. Tonight you'll get
to see their works firsthand. So, let's get this party started!"

When the presentations began, we found out that our competitors
had much more fantastic ideas than ours. One firm had a vision to combine
pizza deliveries with the VHS video service. (It was the 80's, Blockbuster
was king). Food and a movie was an interesting idea that capitalized on
marrying preexisting business factors. It was pretty impressive and looked
like it could be very profitable.

Another firm wanted to build a robotics company. Among them
were a pair of robotics students who wanted to bring their dreams to
fruition. They aimed to revolutionize the factory industry by boosting
efficient production through automation. It was an aggressively visionary
idea and it was impressive. Both plans were thorough and compelling.
Hell, I was excited just hearing about them. The founders and their team
had obviously chosen quality students because the competition was stiff.

I realize that I hadn't told you about my firm. Oh man, y'all were going to be cheated if I didn't drop this dime on you. We were no slouches! The oldest partner in our team was a senior who looked to be an accountant. We literally had the language of business on our side, y'all. Believe me, that was dope. One of our other partners was really huge on mechanical drawing and was aiming at a career in architecture. This was a sublime asset for creating our project visuals.

The last of our partners was a computer nerd. That comes in handy for any number of reasons. And, rounding out our four corners was me. I had been studious my whole life but that wasn't my major contribution, shit, all of us were pretty sharp. I had been uniquely mentored through the Kowrie program as a leader. It was my role to coordinate our talents and strengths to keep us flowing. We all fit our roles fantastically and worked like one big well-oiled machine. One of my partners said we were like an organism and it stuck.

To top it off, our chaperone was working on his MBA in marketing. Dude, need I say more? Our team was ironclad! Once we figured out how to get our individual strengths to coalesce it made us extremely confident in our product. We titled our hotel the Billiken Inn. Our marketing guru thought it would be best if we engendered the school's favor by utilizing their mascot in the title. It was such a natural that it sounded like it was already a thing. In fact, that was how we presented it – like it was already a thing! It was a powerful plan. We thought we had a real shot at winning.

Every firm did an exemplary job illustrating their plan. Once we were done, the restaurant served exquisitely delicious meals while the judges left to tally their scores. Dawg, I chowed down! Y'hurr me? I had a massive ribeye that tasted like they had turned the value of platinum into a food. Their hors d'oeuvres were super tasty and the side dishes were crazy flavorful. Man, they served bread that melted in your fingers then deliciously disintegrated on your tongue. And to wash it all down our glasses were filled with Shirley Temples that had pineapple hints and a maraschino cherry floating on a whipped cream cloud. Calling it an amazing restaurant is a drastic understatement. Dawg, I'm telling you, I loved that place.

The judges completed their deliberations just as I was finishing that glorious cut of meat. A hush fell over the dining room as they returned to their seats. It got so quiet that you could hear every fork that hit a plate and every delighted swallowing gulp. The building was filled with anticipation. We were all so eager to know who would win the first firm challenge. Every person in the room was tied together by the thick thread of tension in the air.

The second founder reopened the conversation.

"Alright, family, we're back. We hope you were able to enjoy your meals and the nonpareil ambiance of this remarkable restaurant. Please join us in thanking Mr. Hunter for hosting our festivities."

Everyone generously applauded. The founder continued.

"Now, I'm certain everyone is anxious to find out which firm will be the winner of the inaugural Minority Youth Entrepreneur Program business plan challenge. Right?"

The audience responds verbally and with handclapping. The Mom of the program took over.

"We know y'all are! We were, too. We were so anxious, in fact, that our deliberations were extremely difficult. We've had some excellent ideas, concepts and plans of execution presented to us tonight. These young people have been extraordinary. Please give them a hand."

The room again fills with joyful noise. She continues.

"So, though the choice was quite the challenge, we have reached a decision. There will be a singular firm that will receive the scholarships tonight. However, we want to make sure you all know, every last one of you, that if you're here, you're a winner."

Applause erupts anew. The second founder continues.

"This is also a high honor for us. This is the premier of this challenge, it's never been done before. Whichever one of us presents this award will be the pioneer, the first to ever do it. We struggled to decide which of us would deliver this momentous outcome. So, in the true nature of business we had a competition."

There is a low roar of laughter. The second founder continues.

"I know, right?"

He chuckled a bit then rolled on.

"Well, we went old school and decided to just draw straws. That's how we figured out who would go down in our history books as the presenter. And, maybe you've guessed because he's been silent since our return, but my partner drew the lucky long straw. So, give him some love family, he's ready to deliver the news."

The entire room went to its feet. The applause was robust and anticipatory. This was it.

The first founder leaned into his microphone.

"Thank you for that. And thank you, parents. Thank you for your support and belief in your children and for allowing them to spend these last few months with us. Certainly, there is nothing more precious to you than your children and you entrusted them to us. We sincerely appreciate that. They arrived as students, became business partners and will leave here as our friends. I can assure you that, as a rule, we take very good care of our friends. We believe we took good care of them here. Are we right, partners?"

Every student present vigorously agreed.

"Alright, that's great to hear. It was a joy having them. This entire process does not take place without your extraordinary kids. None of them could be here without you. On behalf of all of us here at MYEP, thank you for all you do."

The students all rose again and turned to face our parents as we applauded them. We had discussed it before the night arrived and I was really glad we did it. It was a classy move. If anyone deserved a standing ovation it was our parents. That's a thing we all agreed to.

The founder continued.

"So, let's get to it. We evaluated the presentations on several criterion: originality, practicality, feasibility, thoroughness and presentation. While a number of the firms expertly covered many of these areas, only one had a clear, concise and immediately actionable project. In that single regard, it stood tall above the others. I want to say one last time, thank all of you for the work you've done. We've had an excellent first cycle and you have convinced us that this must continue. Your efforts have been historic. Thank you all."

The applause that followed was real but pensive. You could tell that the room was eager to share in the verdict.

The founder grabbed the mic and stood up behind the table.

"That said, it's time to let it all hang out. This year's winning firm for the 1996 Minority Youth Entrepreneurship Program's business plan challenge is…"

He looked around the room scanning from face to face. There wasn't one person still eating. It was eerily and suddenly quiet, save the students' heartbeats thumping as loudly as a drum troupe. Every pair of eyes in the dining room were focused on the founder.

He baited us once more,

"Our inaugural champion is…"

Silence. No one moved. Not a sound was made. It felt like even the hands on the clock stood still, waiting to hear his words.

He shouted out ceremoniously,

"The Organism with the project called 'The Billiken Inn'. Give it up for them!

Mutha fucka! Whaaaat? Our table erupted! We jumped up and embraced one another. We did all the celebratory things: we shouted, raised our fists, high-fived, one of us even stood in place and ran in a circle at the same time. I wanted to dance a jig, and I don't even know what a jig is.

The second founder called out to us.

"Come on up here, The Organism. We've got a big ole check for you."

My firm partners began walking towards the founders at the table. I made a quick beeline to Ma. She stood when I got to her table and we hugged one another.

"I'm so proud of you, Man. I knew you could do it. A clean sweep, just amazing. So proud of you." She said.
"Thank you, Ma. Thank you for being you." I responded.
"Oh, you're welcome, Busara. You're welcome. I love you. Now, you get your butt up there before someone takes your money."

We both laughed.

"Yes, ma'am."

I trotted up to the founders' table and joined my firm. They presented us with a collection of towering trophies and one massive, grossly oversized check. Of course, they gave us each individual checks for our scholarships afterwards but the huge one was for the sake of ceremony. It was fresh as hell to be standing there with it. We took pictures with the founders and they closed out the ceremony.

It was a phenomenal summer! I walked into a training competition, learned invaluable lessons and business skills then walked away with everything it offered. If there were ever any self-confidence issues nestled in me, that summer ended them all. My inner-belief was at an all-time high. I decided that I liked it and would never let it wane.

I had just won everything, y'all. Everything!

Something deep within me decided that I would love to make that a habit.

CHAPTER 20
FINALS

Senior year.

Man, I walked back into that school like the lease had my name on it. As far as I was concerned it was Dizzy High. Hell, it was bad enough that I walked into the building brimming with confidence as a freshman. After the summer I had just gone through, it was damned near surprising that I still had to travel by foot. I was floating on sheer certainty. There wasn't a shard of self-doubt in my body. It was clear to me: Busara was that dude! I knew I could do anything.

I had a fantastic year on the football field. Basketball was a banner season for me, too. Between the two of those sports and my grades, I had reason to believe that I could attend any school I chose. Operating on the SLU campus had altered and enhanced my perspective on what they should be like. I was more than certain I would attend a school comparable to my desires and skill sets. My aim was to find one that would help me propel myself to a level of business mastery. It was time to take on the world. I'm telling you, that newly-bolstered confidence I had made everything work.

Well, not exactly everything.

I was thriving in Simba. D Smooth and I continued to be among the more prominent young leaders. Still, school activities were constant clashes with the itinerary. I managed them as best I could and kept major conflicts between my Kowrie schedule and school activities to a minimum. They still happened, though. So, not every single thing was smooth but most were.

Speaking of schools, it looked like I would go somewhere on a football scholarship. I had an onslaught of frivolous mail and questionnaires from schools arriving at the house. We had whole milk crates filled with college interest letters. The letters arrived in groups every day. They were low level probing questions which asked me all sorts of prospective student things. They had me asking my football coach to measure my 40 times and all kinds of stuff. It was a confusing time where I had more questions than answers. I didn't have someone inside my personal circle who knew much about college and how to navigate the process. But, I had good reason to believe I would get an assortment of offer letters, whatever that would mean.

I needed guidance, though. So I was always in the counselors office. If I wasn't in there every day it was awfully damned close. It became my in-school hangout. I rolled in there frequently trying to figure out my next steps. Remember, that's how I got into MYEP the previous summer, just visiting the counselors office. No one in there really provided any real help, though. That's why I needed to return so damned frequently. They were never of much assistance to me so quality answers were not forthcoming.

They could have probably saved me from doing a bunch of dumb things. Some universities were sending letters to my house that I had never heard of them. I had no idea why they were contacting me or how they knew about me. I certainly hadn't sent them anything inquiring about their schools. How in the hell did they even get my address? So, I started writing the schools back asking, 'why are you interested in me?' Man, I bet that was a first for a bunch of those universities. I needed to know what I needed to know, y'know?

So, I bandied about with schools for a while. One day my coach saw me in the counselors office. He pulled me aside and started talking to me about HBCUs. He told me he went to Knoxville College (KC) and asked if I had considered going to an HBCU. I hadn't particularly sought out any because I wasn't incredibly aware of them. I mean, of course I had heard of them but I wasn't personally connected to any. However, that fit my pro-Black outlook perfectly. So, I was more than interested. It seemed like it would be the perfect fit for me.

He then told me that Big Lou was already there. He had sent him there through his connections in the football team and the athletic department. I was concerned about paying for it and he said he could work on getting me a scholarship if I wanted to go there. He said KC was his school, and he loved it, but he didn't push it on me. Coach told me it was a good school but there were plenty others out there. I could probably have more than a few options, he said. He just made it clear that KC was his alma mater and he could help get me in there if I needed it.

I had a great degree of reverence for my coach. He was a good man and a powerful mentor. His recommendation carried a lot of weight with me. It didn't hurt that he could connect me with the football program, either. So, I said I was game and he told me he'd put the word in for me.

Amazingly, a recruiter came from KC soon after our conversation. His name was Stan Snow. He came regaling students in our high school with magnificent tales of a beacon of higher education, steeped in tradition. This campus, of which he spoke, was pristine and lavish. He pontificated about swimming pools and bowling alleys, as if the campus was located in an exclusive corner of Club Med. His flowery representations should have told me all I needed to know. Unfortunately, I was young and wide eyed. I would eventually learn why he was nicknamed 'Snow Job'. That mutha fucka.

Still, I had great respect for my coach. And, y'all already know, I was super tight with Big Lou', we were team captains together. Well, Big Lou came home on winter break. He told everyone about how live it was at KC and that we should join him. My guys Roostah and Donnie Don started talking about going to Knoxville to check it out. We rapped about it and decided to go visit during Spring Break. We talked to our parents and got it all set. We were heading to Knoxville.

Our families rented a 10-passenger van to make sure we could all go and save money together. It was a solid idea except for the driver decision. I'll get back to that. Roostah, Donnie Don, a handful of parents and I rolled in this van. It was a crew of moms and one father. He was part of a couple who went to check out the school for their daughter without bringing her. So, we had a small crew rolling down south. Everything was chilled.

I had a basketball game that Friday afternoon and we left after that. Here's where that driver selection wasn't so wise. There was only one father in the group and, in the 80's, it was going to be natural that he would drive. At least he would start it, if nothing else. So, that's what happened. He grabbed the wheel and went to rolling. We were on our way.

But on our way where? Man, it was obvious this dude had never travelled to Knoxville before. I doubt he had ever been to Tennessee at all. Seriously, he may not have ever left Missouri! He had no earthly idea where the hell he was going. And there wasn't any GPS or SIRI around to help him out. We had a road atlas but it didn't look like he could read that too well.

Even worse, he wasn't the listening type. Dudes that are stuck on the 'I'm a man and I know what I'm doing' -type shit never listen and he was one of them. They also usually don't have a clue about what they're doing. That was also him. He took some majorly unnecessary eastern route long before we began heading south. So, instead of taking six or seven hours to get there it took more than nine. I'm surprised we didn't land in New Jersey somewhere. No shit.

By the time we arrived on the Knoxville College campus, it was well after midnight. The parents had reached out to the school before the trip and had their accommodations set up for them. So, in the pitch black of night, we rolled right up to the President's house. It was the best spot on campus and it was their domicile for the evening. I thought that was pretty dope. It sounded all big and official and they got to live lavishly for the evening. Once we got them all set, we bailed.

We left looking for Big Lou. He told us where his room was and the dorm it was in before we had left from the crib. After hunting around on KC's campus for a while, we found the dorm and went to his room. He wasn't there but we ran into a dude named Poppy.

Now, I didn't know him well at the time. Yeah, I had seen him around before in the 'Lou but we weren't tight or anything. Fortunately, Roostah knew him from the V. I don't think it would have mattered, though. This dude just took us in and looked out because we were from the 'Lou. I found out from Roostah that his nickname was from a nickname. They teasingly called him 'Mr. Popular' because he both knew everybody at his school and they all liked him. So, it fit that he treated us the way he did.

Poppy immediately took us to a package store and bought some Little Kings (a popular beer at the time). We rolled back to the campus (they called it the Yard) and we got drunk off our asses in Big Lou's room. No, he wasn't there.

It's a good thing that my crew had fallen out on the way to Knoxville. We were tucked away in the corners of that van, knocked out. So, we weren't conscious while dude was fucking up the route. Whatever drama they went through trying to figure it out missed us, for the most part. I had an eye open here or there but I definitely got some winks in. So, because we were well rested, we were live and energized for a long ass night.

That mutha fucka Big Lou bounces into the room near 3:00a. He wasn't even tripping that we were in there without him. We could tell that was some college life shit because nobody really closed their room doors anyways. There were all kinds of people in the halls and stuff. Loud music was blaring from a few of the rooms. Everybody was walking around with something to drink in their hands. It was a fucking partying festival!

The occasional woman or two rolled through the hallway from time to time. Whenever they did, they moved quick and discreet-like. What was crazy about it is everybody was in on the caper. It was like dudes would instantly become lookouts if someone crept in the hallway with a lady. Now, the way I understand it, KC was a Presbyterian school. That meant there was no coed visitation allowed. That is to say, there were official rules against it... you know what I'm saying. Legislation aside, or spited, I can personally validate that a lot of visitation was happening. Dudes had visitors and stuff was getting 'visited'.

Anyways, he wasn't upset that we were in his room but we were absolutely tripping about the way his ass fell through the door. He rolled in with half a towel on his body and some Speedos talking about he went to a damned toga party. We were drunk as fuck and had a good ass time laughing at his ensemble. Man, he looked crazy as hell and we were fucking full! (That's a reference to both our livers and our bladders). Believe me when I tell you, we were to' up from the flo' up. (That's "torn up from the floor up – as in, we were drunk until we were of no use to anyone). Our drunk asses kicked it until just before the sun pierced the windows.

While we slept, the moms and dad took a joyride that morning. They went to investigate Knoxville. Its highly probable that they went to the mall or something but they were out acquainting themselves with the city. By the time we awoke and got to them they looked fresh and spry.

Not us.

We all had whopping hangovers and we looked like warm, mushy shit. Our heads were all down, our shoulders had fallen, we were slumping and shit... just a mess. My head felt like the hamsters had jumped off the wheel, installed mini-Bose speakers and were addicted to house music. My shit was throbbing. I was having trouble trying to see at all. Man, I was fucked up.

Somehow we managed to drag ourselves back to the President's house to meet with them. In our sluggish stupor, we still thought we would see some parts of the campus. It didn't really work like that.

The 'rents were ready to go. They had gotten their fill, received the answers they wanted and didn't want to be exhausted going back to work on Monday. Yes, it was only Saturday afternoon but dude was driving back. With his navigating skills, we might not have gotten back to St. Louis until Tuesday afternoon. Just sayin'.

So, our tour wound up being brief as hell. We got right back into the van to leave when we connected with them. The Knoxville College campus was like a toddler's drawing of a bull. Make a circle then place a 'C' on top of it and that's the map of the school. You get on and off campus through the 'C' and all of the buildings align the circular portion. This made touring awfully damned brief.

So, that's how it went – we got a brief ass tour. The geographical-ly-challenged dad drove us around the hoop once. While we were rolling, the parents would shout out the buildings they recognized.

"This building right here is the library,."
"That's the administration office."
"That building over there is called the student center."
"You know, that auditorium was pretty nice."
"Alright, it's time to hit the road. Let's go."

That's how it went. We didn't see much of the campus. Hell, I couldn't tell you a damned thing about the school. I didn't meet a bunch of people, nor did we kick it with a lot of honeys in those couple hours. Still, I had a fucking blast.

On the first, terribly brief impression, KC looked majestic. We had arrived at night so my views weren't the best. I could remember the President's house, though, and it was fresh. When we left it was daylight but I was still under the influence. Like a mutha fucka! So, the impact of all those buildings I had never seen before loomed larger than how they looked aesthetically. The fact that it was in another state and I had access to it was huge for me, too.

I had been totally engulfed by the excursion. Visiting that school felt like an out-of-body experience. My decision to go or not wasn't difficult at all. Actually, it was made damned simple because it boiled down to very few factors. It was a college, I'd have a scholarship to play football, my dude Big Lou was there and it was far from home. That was a low ass bar but it was enough for me. The whole post office worth of mail at the house was rendered moot. I was sold: I was going to KC.

Back in the Lou, things were going splendidly for me in Kowrie. I continued taking leadership tests and excelling in the organization. More responsibilities were afforded me and I performed them with the pride they instilled in me. The better I did with those even more responsibilities followed.

There are three tiers of development in the organization and I had achieved two of them. There was a final wilderness test for both D Smooth and I in the summer. We had to ace it to achieve the final level. I was ready for that so I knew the summer would be dope. Unfortunately, that wasn't going to arrive without some measure of pain.

Basketball season was over and I was wrapping up my high school career. I was feeling good as hell and had a lot of time on my hands. So

I decided to get in some crazy shit. My ass got cast in a Kowrie Group stage play. The name of the play was 'El Hajj Malik El Shabazz'. It was obviously about the life and times of brother Malcolm and it was a wonderful production, just... marvelous! I was blown away that I could be in a production about one of the elders, particularly Malcolm, so I hopped on it. Both D Smooth and I rocked the thing and it was fun as hell. Better than just being fun, it was powerful.

Well, it was fun as hell until it wasn't. The play was a Kowrie production, it wasn't from school. That meant it also wasn't performed or rehearsed in school. We rehearsed at night and on the weekends at a church. We were only scheduled to perform on the weekends, as well. All of that was cool, everything was all good.

The original plan was for it to run for five shows over the course of a single weekend. We would perform once on Friday night, two shows on Saturday, a show on Sunday then another on Monday night. They were all going to take place on the same church stage. That was the plan: rock the production one weekend and wrap.

There's a bit of depth to this that you need to understand in order to appreciate the scope of the situation. This stage play summed up the entirety of Malcolm's life. What did that mean? Well, I already told you it was powerful, you can believe that. It also meant that the production was a marathon! It was a little more than 3 hours long. We had an intermission in the middle and everything. We put a lot of work into it and were really stoked to set it off for an audience. I mean, this was the life of Malcolm X we're talking about. This play was everything.

We put on one hell of a show! The first week went off so well that we got invited by another church to do it at their venue another week. We set that up and nailed it to the tune of yet another invitation. Two encore presentations in, we got invited by some ultra-liberal white people to rock a bigger performance on a bigger stage: the COCA theatre.

The Center of Contemporary Arts was a massive venue. It took the show beyond our target audience and made it a much larger message than the level on which we were previously sharing it. I won't talk about us being tired from all the performing and venue shifting for rehearsals and performances. Tired, schmired. Nobody cared about all that or mentioned it. We were Kowrie Group men and women, the work is the work. We handled that.

Being tired would have been cool if it was my challenge. It wasn't. I told y'all, it was the end of the school year, my senior school year. We had prom, graduation, senior functions and all manner of things were going on. In particular, my high school graduation was happening on the Saturday that we got scheduled at the COCA stage. My classmates had planned a senior trip to Six Flags afterward and I was going. This is my graduation we're talking about. I can't miss either of those things – the ceremony or the celebration. I earned all of that, man. That was huge stuff for my high school career.

In case I hadn't highlighted it before, the 'Group did NOT put a lot of stock into all that school stuff. Your little celebrations and events and stuff were precisely that to them – little. The mission was the mission, there was no compromising.

Drama.

I talked to our leadership and told them the additional shows would compromise me and I would need to miss that Saturday's show at the COCA. That went over like I had said I wanted to see aliens play badminton.

> "Yeah, I have a senior trip to Six Flags that morning, after my graduation ceremony. I won't be able to make it." I said.

"Young brother, the struggle goes on. We have this production to do on Saturday. We need you to be there." One of our leaders responded.

The gravity of what I was saying didn't reach him at all. I might as well have said, 'it's cold in the winter'. His response was the equivalent of, 'put on an extra pair of socks. See you at the show.'

Mind you, this wasn't the first date for the show. We're not even talking about the second or third weekend of the production. This was encore number three meaning it was our fourth time doing it. It was the fourth weekend! None of the last three were planned or projected on our calendar. Even crazier, it carried on so long that we had actual staff and cast changes. Everybody wasn't flexible enough to continue extending their commitments as the production droned on.

…AND, damn it, this is a one-time situation for me! In life! I would never be in high school again. There would not be another senior trip for me. This was a life milestone, man! My graduation and the celebration for it only goes down one time. Ever. I had saved up the money to go. I had bought some fresh gear to hang out. Hell, I even had a honey excited to go with me and everything. I'm trying to make a story out of some shit, log some memories, do something I regret (and/or brag about) for the rest of my life. Y'know? This is a no-brainer, it was not a negotiable situation.

Our leadership thought the same thing. They had no tolerance for absence or failure. If I was trying to deliver a baby they would be like, "there's doctors for that. Get your butt to the meeting/function/bookstore." Whatever the need of the Organization, that was the priority. There was no compromise with those guys. No wavering.

I respectfully drew out my argument in minute detail. My passion was apparent, my need was more than reasonable and we're still talking about things I've earned with my hard work. I implored him to grasp the impact of the moment: the opposing ends were a) a fourth iteration of a production versus b) a milestone lifetime achievement. This point didn't appear to penetrate with our leadership at all.

> "That's really great, brother. Our call time is 2:00. We need you to be there promptly."

I'm not even sure we were in the same conversation.

But I was beyond frustrated! I couldn't have been the only person who could do the role. They had replaced other people in the production, both on stage and behind the scenes. Didn't somebody have a little brother somewhere? Wasn't there a nephew out there who wasn't doing anything who could be an understudy? Couldn't somebody's little cousin step in? We were all Black people, we know how to make do with what we have. For one night they wouldn't have me - shit, 'make do'!

Well, sometimes you just gotta do what the fuck you're going to do. Asking for forgiveness and not permission was a powerful lesson for me. Actually, it's what landed me in the 'Group in the first place. It was the perfect time for another one of those.

I went to my graduation and rolled with my classmates to Six Flags. I had myself a good ass time! We all wore our caps to show off our graduating class. There were more grads at the park doing the same thing, so it was live as hell. Six Flags was a big ass post-high school party that day.

For a moment, on the drive to the park, I thought about how they would make out on the play. I hoped they could get it done and everything would work out. But the minute we got to the amusement park that was over. Not one thought of that shit was in my head while we were rocketing on roller coasters or eating big ass corn dogs. It was all fun and games at that point. Hell, I won a big ass stuffed animal and everything. That was a day for the record books.

Then it was time to face the music. The next day, I went to the venue for the show. I didn't say I couldn't make Sunday and I had no reason to miss it. So, I went. The leadership was not happy with me. That's putting it super mildly. Like 'the Grand Canyon is just a whole in the ground' -sized understatement.

"Young brother Busara, you let down a lot of people yesterday. That was real selfish, brother."

(Me?! I was selfish?!)

They leaned into me and I took it. Those were my elders. You didn't do any arguing or going back and forth. None of that was acceptable. Respect them, let them have their say and deal with it. That's how it worked. We rocked that show that Sunday and the conversation wasn't revisited. That's also the power of respect. They said what they said, I listened and we moved on.

I'm telling y'all though, I was certain I made a good choice. The Sunday show proved it. That stage play, in all of its empowerment and impact, was a repetitive thing. My senior celebrations weren't. I'm not entirely certain it was the right choice, that is debatable. But it was a good choice. And we moved on.

That was my penultimate disagreement with Simba. There would be one more. It was much larger.

Much.

Once I was out of high school I was busy preparing for the next level. You know I had plans to play 'ball so I began working out. I spent the whole summer working to maximize my body. I knew it as mandatory that I be ready to compete on the college level.

If you recall, I lived a couple blocks from the V and their field was perfect for the training I would have to do. They were our rivals but I wasn't in high school any more so that didn't matter. No one was there over the summer anyways. I thought it incredibly unreasonable to try to travel to McKinley just to stay in shape. So, I ran over to Vashon every day and did my thing on their field.

One Monday, I trotted up the stairs into the field area and the whole Vashon football team was there. They had started their summer practices and I was rolling into it like I belonged there. I saw their head coach's eyes bulge. There was visible muscular strain, I thought he might need medical assistance.

He rolled up on me.

"You play ball, son?" He said.

"Yeah," I responded. It was the truth.

"What size helmet do you wear?"

That was a really weird first question to me. Maybe he was saying I had a big ass head and wanted to get in front of ordering a helmet for the season. Honestly, I have no idea. But, that's the only question he asked me.

After that, he had me doing their workouts with them and running drills with the team. He didn't ask if I was going to play with them, if I was going to attend Vashon the following year or if I was even a high school student. He saw a big assed kid and thought he had hit the lottery. So, he wasn't going to stare a gift horse in the mouth. He rolled with it.

Shit, I needed to work out – I was doing it anyways. Having someone push me and some competition to work with would get me right, help keep my edge. There could be no better motivation than being able to blow up kids from my rival high school. That was the best part of the deal, actually. So, I rolled with the coach.

He wasn't asking shit. I wasn't saying shit.

I ran with them long enough to get issued some pads and start hitting. I enjoyed the hell out of putting the wood on those boys. I was wrong as hell for doing it and that probably made it feel better. Unfortunately for me, it didn't last long.

We had our wilderness camp for Kowrie shortly afterwards. I straight bailed on the team and went to do my thing.

I can't walk you through the minutia of any Kowrie Group camp. Hell, I'm not comfortable telling you any more of the general principles, either. What I will tell you is we were thoroughly tested. We were tired, nah, we were exhausted. There were times we were hungry or thirsty and completely worn down. We made secure shelters and foraged for whatever we were going to consume. It was a grueling experience that demanded more than the strength of your backside but the fortitude of your spirit.I conquered that shit! My dude D Smooth worked through it, too. We were the youngest Kowrie duo to take that level of test and we both passed it perfectly. By doing so we earned ourselves a distinction never given at our ages before. D Smooth and I were Wapinguzi.

Wapinguzi means revolutionary. This is further defined as 'one who makes change'. It's the highest rank you could achieve in The Kowrie Group. D Smooth and I did it at ages 18 and 17, respectively. It was a historic day on all counts and pride was in bountiful abundance. It is a spectacularly high honor and our whole Kowrie family celebrated this achievement as if it was their own. We were put in the Circle and shared in the joy of a proud village.

It was only a few weeks later when we were again in the Circle. D Smooth and I were preparing to leave the fold. We were both heading to Knoxville College to begin our journey to mastery. D Smooth was my first true brother in the 'Group and we stayed connected like that from the beginning. We became Wapinguzi together and were going to tackle college together, too. We were stoked about making an impact in college. And we were carrying the village on our backs. It was such a radiant moment of pride. The Circle was the way our Kowrie family was sending us off.

I committed to being a master in business, that path had been the most consistent reality in my world. The MYEP experience had emphatically accentuated the point. Entrepreneurism is a Dizzy family trait and I had been both (a Dizzy and a business builder) my whole life. This was clear to me. I was going to take my talents to Knoxville so I could further build the skills I'd need to bring business craft mastery back to the village. Or, at least, it would be the beginning of that path.

So, the Circle. This is a premise steeped in African tradition. It is as technically sound as it is symbolic for our people. A circle has no beginning and no end. Every part of it is as important as the other. It is the perfect symbol for equality. For unity. It represents completion: it is whole and without further need. Lastly, everything within it is protected by the solidarity of its circumference. Its most profound statement is that it represents one. One family. One village. One people.

One.

Our Circle was all those things. The entire Kowrie Group family built the Circle and placed us within it. Each person took time to reflect and share with us what they individually had for us. There is no activity more connecting than sharing our Circle together. They showered us with love and wished us well on our journey.

If you ever receive the honor of the Circle you can only leave it with your soul full. While you are surrounded by your family, you are encased in a bond that permeates time and space. Even the people who speak to you share from a protected space because everyone in the Circle is connected to everyone there. It is an embrace bigger than the reach of any arms and it is love more personal than your greatest imagining. For all of us present, it is an intimate intensity that invokes the ancestors.

I can't, no, I won't tell you the process of how our circle is created. You have to earn that. Sharing the impact of it, though, is a point of pride. And, in my humble opinion, a standard bearer of unity for our people. It would be beautiful if all of us could share in such a support system. Quietly, I think it is the way life should be done. We should all live empowered by the strength of those around us. Together we are more than the sum of our parts. Together we can do everything!

The Kowrie Group is an ideal proof of this concept. Of course, I might be a bit biased, sue me. I just know I'll be forever thankful that I was curious enough, that the ancestors reached out to me on that first day I saw, heard and felt the South African Gum Boot Dance. I knew then that it was for me. Every experience I had with the organization confirmed it. I am also thankful that whatever bravery it awakened in me took me to it. It is a testament to regarding fear as the alert system it is, then taking the steps you see necessary anyways. Fear would never be a decider for me again. That was over.

Alright, I'm off my soap box. Talking about this moment in time is emotional for me. I was leaving my trusted nest of support. I didn't see it like that at the time but I felt it. It truly was a boy-to-man moment. Everything that was to come in my life would be different from all that I had known before. It was a hallmark for my life, talking about it is powerful enough to grip me at my core.

I was more than glad to move on from Ma, though. Don't get me wrong, I loved her through and through. I told you long ago, that's my girl! She just represented authority. Control. I was more than ready to shed those things for my life. I had to get out of the position of a child. I had to be free of the obligation of answering to a human being for my choices. No man can truly be a man under the thumb of a woman or anyone else. I had to be accountable to me. That was a large factor in my choice to leave the state going to school. I wanted that room to breathe. It was time for that.

Likewise, Ma wasn't the one to take me to school. Kowrie did! They offered to give both D Smooth and I our last send off. Start our college careers off with the force of the village behind us. They got hold of a van then packed our things and a few members in it. I'm telling y'all, the Kowrie Group was everything.

That ride to Knoxville took long as hell. I mean, we didn't have any navigation issues or anything but my anticipation was on 1000. The transition was real! I was leaving everything I knew; Ma, my little sister Lori, the Kowrie family, my football team, the basketball squad, my fellas from the 'hood, hell, the city of St. Louis – I was leaving it all! Shit was serious.

All in a moment it became clear to me: I was scared. Coming to that realization straightened me out. My fear was telling me that shit was serious, pay attention. Well, I was duly alerted...... it was go time.

Oh, one more thing: I never went back to the V. Once I went to camp with the 'Group that was over. I wasn't going to work out with them again and, obviously, I had no love for them. So, I simply didn't go back. The gear? Well, nobody at my house would use it (neither Ma nor Lori played football - yeah, I'm being a smart ass). So, I took it to KC with me. I figured they weren't really gonna miss it. And, I might wind up being able to use it at school for something. Who knows?

Yeah, it was wrong. So? It was the V, I ain't have no love for them.

CHAPTER 21

WHERE AM I?

I was hyped to make it back to Knoxville College. After the summer I had the year before I knew this would be sensational. The SLU dorm rooms were cool and I was inspired to go to college from that alone. But I had recently seen the President's house at KC, it was plush. Damned near regal. Add that to the way we kicked it when I visited and I was convinced that the campus life had to be banging.

We had left from St. Louis at the pinnacle of sunrise so we arrived in the early afternoon. We laid eyes on the Knoxville College campus squarely in the middle of day. It was one of the first times in my life that I was sober but wished I was drunk. I wished that what I saw wasn't real. I had good reason to expect better but those expectations were dashed by daylight and anyone's half-decent eyesight.

When we arrived at Knoxville College I felt right at home. Nah, that was not a fucking good thing. My home was the projects. This was college so, to my mind, it should be vastly different. I left home to escape any and all of its entrapments. I was looking for, and expected, new horizons. I wasn't immediately angry about it. In fact, I found a degree of comfort in the familiarity of the surroundings. Comfort, though, is a hallmark of stagnation. That was not acceptable in my world.

The nagging reality for me was, one of my young shards of wisdom was sticking me in my side. I knew if you wanted to achieve something new, you had to do things you hadn't done. You had to go places you hadn't gone. The 'same' wasn't going to get me where I wanted to go. A university-level experience, going to college should be a world of epiphanies. It should be a tempest of fascinating newness that overwhelms the senses. I expected my life to be awash in premier exposures that would take concerted measure to process. I expected my collegiate arrival to blow me away with fascinating horizons.

Instead, this place looked and felt like the next government project in my life series. It was old and decrepit. Many of the buildings looked like they were one bad winter away from crumbling to the ground. When we rounded the hill that put us on campus I was damned near in shock. Nothing about how I recalled Knoxville College was how it looked.

Actually, in front of the school was a government project complex. You had to pass it every time you entered or left the campus. The caliber of architecture implied that it could have been a part of the school. They had the same lackluster, indigent look. It might not have been a bad thing if they were at least an actual part of the school. Hell, it would've made for a bigger campus. But, alas, they weren't. They just helped KC look like dirt cheap real estate. Again, I wasn't livid as I processed this information. It simply wasn't inspiring.

Until I got to my room, then I was fucking pissed! Man, it was an absolute hovel. A despicable, dirty 'I'm not spending a second in this bitch without cleaning everything twice' fucking mess. There were cockroaches in our shit, dawg. Fucking cockroaches.

And I'm not talking about those cute little things that look like almonds with legs. I mean some fucking body created an experimental growth serum, let some Texan cockies practice beginner-on-back swimming techniques in it then their mutates flew to Knoxville for the cooler climate. 'Flew' is what one of those fuckers did to my face: it flew right at me! Those shits sounded like... you ever attach a playing card to the frame of your bike to make the tire spokes flap loudly as hell? That shit! That's what they sounded like while they were flying. Scared the shit out of me! They were about 3 inches long and looked like miniature birds with armor on. These were fucking bat roaches!

IN OUR ROOMS!

I let one of them land then tried to stomp on it to kill it. That mutha fucka threw me out the room - picked me up and threw me out. I ain't bullshittin'! Okay, yes I am. This ain't a damned cartoon, but they were big as hell. They had my flesh crawling and the whole nine. Just nasty, y'all. Nasty as fuck. I was pissed!

So, our last chore with the elders was going to the store for cleaning supplies and bug spray. Once we said goodbye to them, we spent that first day and night cleaning until lemon scented Lysol was singeing our nostrils. It was lemon everything everywhere when we were done. We ate pizza for dinner that night and even that tasted like lemons, y'hurr me? It was a hygiene marathon because we had to clean two rooms, D Smooth's and mine.

We weren't just in different rooms, we were at separate dorms. I was staying with the football team who had their own dorm. D Smooth stayed in one of the other buildings. We had arrived early for football camp, in true Kowrie form. Once we got squared away, we were able to look around a bit.

There were very few people on campus. Basically, it was us, a few holdouts from the summer sessions and the band. The band was there trying to put it down already. We watched them for a couple days because we didn't have shit else to do. And, neither of us had ever watched a band rehearsing before. We could tell they hadn't quite gotten it together but they were working it out. It was enjoyable none-the-less.

Football camp started a few days later. It was some 'good ole boy'-type bullshit right out the gate. See, the coach was a Texas dude who was very particular about people who came from Prairie View. There was a whole team worth of them: the players and the bulk of the coaching staff were Texans. It was evident they had set up some form of pipeline with a high school or two from that city. Whatever it was, they had who they were going to play and they weren't flexible about it.

They started camp by making us do strenuous conditioning and standard preparation drills while those assholes were running plays. We were sweating our asses off running in circles while they practiced blocking schemes and running halfback tosses. It was like there were two separate teams. That was just blatantly disrespectful. To make it worse, the coaching staff singled us out and referred to us as 'the boys from up north'. They gave us no love and left us out of every play rotation. It was the oddest shit. It felt like we were being hazed by the coaches.

Big Lou showed up the weekend just before camp started. There were a few of us from St. Louis who were 'the boys from up north' they referred to. Lou figured if they were going to single us out, we were going to stick together and make it official. So, we clicked up and did everything as a pack. Before long we all said fuck them and their program. We quit the squad a few weeks in and moved out of the football dorms almost a week before school started.

You already know my Kowrie background. That exclusion-type team management was straight up oppressive. The football team had created a system where we weren't seen as or treated equally. Fuck that! Any type of oppression or disempowerment from any source just wasn't going to fly with me. That included our own people. I also uniquely understood how we had been programmed for such failure as a people. That was worse than any outside group doing damage to us. It was unacceptable in my book.

Seeing this as my introduction to a Black College campus was incredibly disconcerting. This particular shit, referring to us by a group name and keeping us out of the loop, felt personal as hell. They were trying to play us like Rudolph and I wasn't for that Christmas shit. Fuck them and their reindeer games.

To make it worse, Big Lou told us about the bullshit they try to do to freshmen. Some shit about sneaking in your room while you sleep, holding you down and spraying shaving cream in your ass or some crazy shit like that. Stripping guys of their manhood and their dignity to have some perverse, homosexual-type of laugh.

Nah. Fuck nah. Hell fuck nah!

Far as I'm concerned, they were raping mutha fuckas. As a damned hazing prank!

Dawg, fuck! That!

Them mutha fuckas were never going to get ahold of my ass while I was sleeping. You can forget that shit. I don't have to be the toughest guy on earth to be furious or vengeful. Believe, every mutha fucka that would ever lay a finger on me was going to get it. I would have caught each one of them and sent them to the hospital, at least. I would never be violated like that!

It took everything in me not to start some shit; some type of protest or file a complaint with the dean or something. Or, just start whipping dudes asses for being that foul, y'know? But, I wasn't there for football anyways. It was my way in and that was it. So, when we banded together to walk out of that bitch it wasn't even a letdown. I never looked back.

But that was strike two on the school. And classes hadn't started yet. Not the best beginning.

D Smooth got a roommate less than a week after we had arrived so I couldn't move in with him. Instead, I shifted to the Brandon dorm with my guy, Roostah. Y'all know we go way back, I thought it would be fun. I started preparing to schedule classes and attend my first semester of college. Meanwhile the campus was filling up. The dorm was getting full, ladies were rolling around the campus – it started to look like more of what I imagined.

Roostah and I wound up in a beautiful little place. I had that scholarship money from the MYEP competition and decided to use it. We went out and grabbed a piece of carpet. We put a pair of huge speakers in the room. We connected them to a component set, one of those old five or six tier music cabinets that looked way more fascinating than it was. It had a 5-disc CD changer, when CD's were a new technology. So, we had the new hot joint and had to let everybody know it. We damned near blasted out the windows at Brandon Hall. I loved it. Our room was fresh as hell and we got super comfortable in it.

When more people started showing up, I decided I had to start making moves. Ma had sent me to school with more than a few things to make my life easier. One of them was an industrial-sized bag of popcorn seeds. The bag was about 2½ maybe 3 feet off the ground. I swear it had to be twenty-five pounds worth of seeds. She also sent me with a hot plate. I'm a hustler, I went to work and got busy.

I went to a local grocery store, Lion Foods I believe, and bought a bunch of paper bags. I'd make the popcorn in the hot plate, put butter and salt in the plate before it stopped popping then dump it off in a big paper bag. I made little bags off of that and sold those jokers for $1 apiece. After a while I got sweet popping that corn off that plate. As fast as I could make a batch and bag it, they were walking out the door. Things were rolling so well that I got a little saucy with it and started adding flavors. (Regular buttered, Lawry's seasoned, hot sauce flavored, etc.). Man, business was booming.

You'd be surprised how hungry kids got in the evenings and just wanted something they could easily access. One of the best things about popcorn is that it advertises for itself. People can't ignore that smell, man. I would get that hot plate going, the smell would run through the dorm and my room would get full as hell with customers in no time. So, business was popping (believe it or not, that pun was unintended. I'm not that corny. Damn it, I'll stop). I sold out as fast as I could pop it all. Then I reupped on the seeds and kept that hustle going for a few weeks.

Let me tell you about my first real fight at KC. Fucking around with Roostah, I put myself into something I instantly regretted. Something had happened with him where I showed up outside one of our dorms and he was standing there crying. I was befuddled as hell and instantly alerted. So, I start asking questions.

"What's up, dawg? What's going on?"

He started throwing out a word salad, something about a guy named Shady.

"Shady, man. That mutha fucka Shady tripping, man! Rubble, rubble, rubble…"

I don't know what his ass was talking about.

Big Lou and Donny Don showed up right after me. I was trying to understand what he was saying but I didn't really care, I was just going to handle it.

I need you to understand something in order for you to aptly appreciate this scenario. See, the city of St. Louis functioned like one family on campus. It's a thing that Big Lou started when he got to KC the year before me and it became the standard. St. Louis stuck together, no questions. Well, Big Lou showed me how committed he was to that when he had beat up dudes three times on my behalf when I arrived to KC because 'St. Louis took care of St. Louis'. So, I understood exactly how real that was.

I looked at Roostah's situation as 'my turn'. I had been in 'I wish a mutha fucka would'–mode for a good minute. "Somebody say something bad about St. Louis, Imma tear they ass up". That was my foolish daily disposition. I was walking around committed to a confrontation that hadn't even happened yet. That brand of stupid shit usually doesn't work out.

With Roostah's situation, I figured it was time for me to step up for somebody. He was crying and shit, I figured something had gone sideways or someone had did him really wrong. So, I was hot! I didn't know why they were in an argument, I didn't know what it was about, if Roostah was wrong... nothing. It was just time for me to be the guardian. I was amped.

What I didn't know was that's just Roostah's angry response. He cried when he was mad. That was his crazy, emotional-ass thing. Big Lou knew it but I hadn't experienced that with him before. So, Big Lou was much less sympathetic than me.

> "Alright, man. We'll kick the mutha fucka's ass man. Cut out
> all that crying and shit." Big Lou said.

If I wasn't busy trying to be hostile, I probably would've laughed my ass off. Why the fuck was that 18 year old dude boo-hooing, man? His ass was acting like Arsenio on 'Harlem Nights', shooting a 12-guage with Niagara Falls running down his face. That shit was crazy. It didn't hit me as funny, though, 'cause I was too set on my stupidity mission.

Even crazier: Big Lou knew Roostah cried when he got mad because they boxed together! This mutha fucka Roostah was a really solid boxer. He could've handled himself without a problem. So, whatever reason he decided not to make a fight out of it should have been good enough for me. It wasn't.

So, Roostah, Donny Don, Big Lou and I walked down to Shady's dorm. I started yelling halfway up the Hoop. (That's what we called the circular road on campus).

"SHADY! HEY SHADY! IS THERE SOME MUTHA FUCKA AROUND HERE NAMED SHADY?"

Yeah, that's right. I didn't even know the dude he was talking about. I don't think I had seen him and I certainly didn't know anything about him.

A scouting report would have been really nice but I didn't have that at the time. Shady was an Alabaman Kappa. A better description would be that he was *the* Kappa. See, the year before he was the only person on his pledging line.

Just him.

So, the whole fraternity took out their hazing rituals on that guy. He got it for the whole line that they didn't have. You know what I'm sayin'? They beat his ass something brutal the entire process but that dude stood up and surpassed the beatings. You can feel free to understand that to mean that Shady was nobody's punk because that's exactly what it meant. Thusly, he got respect on the Yard like he was the Chosen One. Shady was a made man.

So, as my unawares-of-whom-I'm-fucking-with-self rolled up to the dorm, Shady walks out.

"Who out here yelling my damn name?"

I didn't say a word. I walked right up to him and put both of my hands on his chest. I shoved him so hard he flew backwards about 12 feet. I'm not a little dude, it was basically a two-handed punch.

Nobody told him that. He didn't fall because he caught his balance then sprinted towards me, fists flying. It was the strangest of events. I fought him like I was fighting one guy but he fought me like he was fighting ten. Dude was fucking relentless.

And those fists were hard!

Now, we were fair fighters, the guys from St. Louis, that is. We didn't jump people in one-on-one fights. We let it play out. You win some and you lose some, that's what life is. Now, if you go to grabbing weapons and stuff then all bets are off. But, as a rule, we let fair fights happen.

That was unfortunate for me. If you had put me under oath I would have told you seven weightlifters were accosting me with dumbbells. The way that dude was fighting didn't feel fair to me at all. Once I took enough lumps, all the guys standing around broke it up and pulled us apart. As they were walking the opposite direction with Shady, he was talking shit over one of their shoulders.

"He don't want no more. He don't want no more of this!"

He was damned right! Like I said, those fists were harder than a mutha fucka! I don't know if I won or lost the fight but I was more than good on bypassing round two. That didn't stop me from talking shit while they were pulling me back.

"Fuck him, man! I'll whup his mutha fuckin' ass! Let him go! Let him go!"

But I didn't once tell the guys holding me to let me go and I wasn't trying to get away, either. Shid! That man was a machine. I wasn't about to put another quarter into that dude.

My first college fight taught me to be careful of what I wish for, particularly when it's stupid, because I might get it.

As the school filled with the student body it became more intriguing. There were people from all over the country. Detroit, Milwaukee, New York, Dallas, Los Angeles, Baton Rouge, Atlanta, Miami, Baltimore... the Yard was a melting pot of the country. It was surprising that this miniature school had such a broad diversity. Turns out, that's a four-year institution thing. You can meet people from all over the planet and learn about the world on a single college campus. KC was no exception, there were people from everywhere. So, I advise everyone to go to college somewhere, if you get a chance.

The student body mix at Knoxville College was most surprising to me because the campus was super small. The description I gave you earlier was accurate as hell, the entire campus was like a toddler's drawing of a bull. I'm certain there were less than 20 total buildings for the whole school, and eight of those were the dorms (one of those was for the staff). When I came to understand the full breadth, or the limit, of its physical size, I was worse than underwhelmed. I was disappointed.

My discontent was really getting to me. I was thinking about bailing on the school. Roostah and I were in the room one day and I told him about it.

"Man, this place is whack. I might just go home." I said.
"Nah, man. This place is cool. You just have to spread your wings a little bit. I like it!" Roostah shot back.

I'm sure he didn't even see his pun. Y'know, a dude named Roostah... spreading his... you get it.

"It's not working for me," I offered. "It's just, all of it is just... small."

"Well... yeah. But think of it this way: if you can't make it in this small ass place, you can't make it anywhere."

Roostah wasn't the most sage cat in the world but he hit me with one that day. He was likely incorrect, I would've thrived in a challenging setting – that was my thing. So, yeah I could definitely make it in a bigger setting. That still didn't mean I should cave to the little one. Fortunately, I wasn't really ready to pull the trigger right away. Everything about the little campus wasn't bad. I figured I'd at least stick it out for one year. See what happens.

We all know there's a big taste of chocolate in a little Hershey's Kiss, right? That was KC. It was small and it wasn't the most plush of schools. Shit, not much about the institution was remotely impressive. But once the Yard got full, it was live! There was a vast collection of great minds gathered there. The student body was somewhere near the 1,000 mark but it often seemed like five times that amount.

The best thing about KC is it was a true HBCU. In my experience, most of them function as extended families. There's a love and sense of community that you typically don't find at other institutions of higher learning. It's a place where intelligent young Black students persevere and conquer the challenge of higher education.

Together.

That was the richness of the school. All of those people I met from everywhere all worked together. School spirit groups helped (football, band, basketball, cheerleading, etc.) but they weren't the limit. The school was short on many things. Hell, there was only one cafeteria (The 'Caf) and it was closed by 6:00. Young people definitely get hungry after that and stay up late as hell. We had to stick together to get through tough times. It made us incredibly resourceful and uniquely sociable. I could easily understand why our high school coach had such a strong connection with KC. I was glad as hell Roostah talked me into giving it a chance.

My family wasn't poor but we weren't rich. Hell, my whole neighborhood was entrenched in the struggle. We knew how to make 'too little' last as long as we needed to. So, like I said earlier, I felt right at home in the KC challenges. My whole life had prepared me for them.

Bringing all of that full circle, that's how I got my hustle on selling the 'corn. I knew I would have to keep money in my pocket because scarcity was real. I mean, there's never a bad time to have money, of course. But the cafeteria schedule at school made nourishment an outside-the-curriculum test. Getting money was the easy answer – both to supply a need to the student body and cover my own grub. So, I did what I was used to.

I hustled.

CHAPTER 22

HUSTLE LESSONS

The good part about my side groove was casually meeting people. That was easily the best part of KC for me, the people. I got cool with a lot of dudes, met a lot of honeys, and had a more broad social involvement just by slanging popcorn. I hadn't planned for it but selling 'corn was a magnificent acclimating tool for me. There was a steady stream of people that came through my room and I kept money in my pocket. Worked for me.

Part of what was missing for me at school, though, was my Afrocentric habit. Man, Kowrie was life! I was either involved with the Organization around the clock or led by its teachings in my efforts. I had functioned with The Kowrie Group as a daily cog in my life for the better part of five years. That was better than a whole fourth of my decision-making life. Not having it in my world was way different. So, I naturally looked for a substitute.

I pseudo-organically ran into an older brother named Umoja. His name alone said he was speaking my language. Umoja means 'unity' and it's one of the 7 Principles, an element of the Kwanzaa celebration. All of that was in my consciousness neighborhood.

The brother was from Knoxville and he lived near the campus. I saw him a few times eating in the 'Caf. He rolled in wearing a dashiki and I was like, "straight up? It's a brother in Knoxville rocking African flavor. I gotta meet him." When I saw him, I easily gravitated toward him. Everybody wants to be in the company of likeminded individuals, that's what I was on. The brother taught me some things I didn't know. I schooled him on some of the wisdom I got from the 'Group and it was cool. We formed a bond on mutual respect and hung out for a while. I definitely grew because of it.

And it was school, after all. I was there to learn, that wasn't an exclusively scholastic or academic principle. So, I took in as much as I could from my interactions. I became somewhat of a social scientist, experimenting my way through scores of different people, cultural norms, religions and equal rights groups. That could have been a college course in itself. My eyes were wide open and I was taking it all in.

There were cats from the east coast who were 5 Percenters. That was crazy intriguing, I tried to dig into that a little bit. I learned a good deal about the Muslim faith from actual Muslims. Those brothers confirmed a few things for me and changed my mind about some others. I was really thankful for that experience. There was a Masonic group, basically from Alabama, rocking paraphernalia on jewelry, clothes, license plates – you name it. And the GD's from Chi Town, they had their own formalized system of justice and order. I was gladly bombarded by whole worlds of life that I had little or no previous exposure to. It was like I had gone to an education mall or something, everywhere I looked was a retail store of different mental processes. That shit was dope! I was glad as hell to be there for that.

I was still homesick, though. Not because I missed St. Louis so much, but the African-cultured and charactered surroundings of the Kowrie world were definitely missed. So, D Smooth and I held Kiswahili classes in his room. We even had a brother or two studying with us and it was tight. The 'Group had built something within us that wasn't easy to ignore. We did what we could to keep it breathing.

Eventually, I stuck some actual classes into my collegiate experience. I mean, you can't do schooling without classes, right? My fall freshman semester was a full schedule with six courses – I carried 18 credits. The plan was to dive in early and make a huge dent on my requirements to make my latter years easier. The same way I handled high school. I was going to hit it hard those first three years. Most of my schedule was core classes but I managed to have a business course or two, ideally, to keep me inspired.

I anticipated a definitive leap in scholastic challenge. When I left middle school, I entered high school uber confident. The work level was different, though, and it came with a bit of demand that made me adjust. It taught me to be humble and to always expect challenges to come my way. My logic said that if jumping from middle school to high school smacked me in the face, then college would hit me with a car.

Honestly, because of that, I was a bit intimidated by it. Yeah, my high school beginnings were a bit rough but by the time I graduated I could nail grades in my sleep. So, I wasn't as confident that I was prepared for a new challenge in curriculum. I was sweating it until we started our third week of classes.

Why the third week? Well, the first two were snooze fests. I attributed that to all of the adjustments being made. I saw kids go in and out of classes, dropping and adding. People showing up to the school during the first week. Stuff like that made me think the professors were going easy on us. But by the third week, I knew all of that was over. It was just what school was.

And school at KC was shit to me early in the semester! There wasn't a challenge to be had. I mean, they were so easy at the start that I went to the registrar's office to validate that they weren't remedial classes. They tried to assure me that I, both, had the right schedule and that they would get progressively tough. They made a point to say few students have ever called my calculus class, with the professor I took, a cake walk. Shit, as far as I was concerned, that's just what their mouths were saying. At the time I went in that office, none of my courses in that first semester were as difficult as my hardest high school classes. Not one! This was a major problem for me.

No, I wasn't a glutton for punishment. I didn't look to suffer from a cumbersome scholastic life. However, I was principled. It was clear to me that progress had a price. I was looking to be a master of industry. A master! As I had no clue what that would take in college, I sought the schooling to imbue me with the necessary tools. If there was no challenge for me then how could I grow? The more the weeks carried on the more I became disenchanted because such a challenge didn't present itself.

That was strike three.

Despite all of that, college living was pretty cool. I got a taste of the Greek life and almost got caught up in it. There was a business fraternity that I decided to check out. I attended one of their smokers to see what they were all about. (Oh, a 'smoker' is an interest meeting where prospective pledges go to investigate a fraternity or sorority. It also alerts those organizations to interested students). It was probably never a real chance for me because I knew Greek organizations were imposters. Their origins are based in and borrow from African traditions. That precluded me being serious about joining. Still, I was young. Getting in the mix to see what I could see is what college life was all about.

Our knowledge of African history didn't prevent D Smooth from digging in. He became less and less available for hanging out. Before long, he let me know he was interested in joining one of the fraternities. I didn't know if he was actually pledging or going through the motions but he was up to something. That was cool, he was finding his own way.

I got to know a lot of people on the Yard. Big Lou had made it a thing to be from the Lou, we all rolled together. That created a comfortable social atmosphere for all of us. Still, I kicked it in the dorm sometimes. We'd set up card games and do some drinking and shit. For a while I leveraged that to sell popcorn. I had backed off once classes got started then rekindled it when I saw the classes were Magoo as hell. When studying didn't need to happen, making money made the time go by constructively.

The band helped to make it feel like a true Black college experience. They weren't the biggest band, they weren't the best I'd seen either. But they helped make it hype on the Yard. One of their field shows was crazy as hell. They had a freshman on the cymbals who was out there twirling his ass off. The sun reflected on them while he was spinning them so they were blindingly bright. That made it even better. But this dude went on his own mission with them and clowned for the whole school.

It looked like he either dropped one or it came off the strap he was holding. When the one cymbal hit the ground I thought it would be crazy embarrassing for them. But nah! Dude got on the ground with both cymbals and walked like a dog to the beat. The stands went crazy! I guarantee you he didn't do it on purpose, I don't think anybody watching thought that he did. But it was live anyways. That shit had the whole audience buzzing for the rest of the game.

I wound up meeting that cymbal player after the game. He was a dude from Detroit who they called B-Dub. He was a seriously cryptic dude. I asked what happened on the field and he completely acted like he didn't know what I was talking about. I pressed but he never even copped to something special happening. He wasn't an asshole with it, but he had a shitty smirk the whole time. I laughed my ass off. Once I got to know him it quickly became clear that he was like that with everything.

Stuff like that made the campus crazy enjoyable. The disappointment was still real, though. I wanted so much out of school. When you consider the value of effort versus reward, I was prepared to do nosebleed-level studying. Instead, the bulk of my time was spent hanging out just to stay engaged on campus. The workload was light and laughable. I questioned if a local community college might have served me better. That comparison out of desperation was not a win.

It vexed me to the point that I was pondering my next move. It was clear to me that a Knoxville College education WOULD NOT empower me to be a master of business. I wasn't sure it could help me on the path at all, actually. The impact it made on me was wanting. It was evident that something different must be done to improve my odds of success and I was open to solutions. Until such an alternate path was revealed, I would maintain the status quo to keep my options open.

All the while, I saw less and less of Roostah. We wound up running in different circles. That's how life goes, no sweat. I didn't spend a lot of time in the room. For the most part, he would be there more than me. Every now and then a couple people came by to holler at him. So, there was some really light foot traffic coming through from time to time. It was cool with me, I wasn't trying to regulate his life like he wasn't trying to run mine.

Roostah also left campus a lot. He was getting a lot more familiar with Knoxville than I was. The sparing times I would see him, he was always fresh. One day he rolled up on campus in a car he bought. He was making a life in the city and making stuff happen. I thought it was cool. When he came through we would go eat something somewhere or buy some grub for the room. I'd ask what he was up to and he would say he was working, that's why he had loot. Made sense to me, hustling is what we came from. So, I didn't even trip.

For Thanksgiving break, Roostah took us home in his car. It was four of us packed in the ride. He didn't drive, though, not at all. He had just started smoking weed since we had arrived in Knoxville. You could tell he was green at it because of how he handled it. He spent the whole ride, the entire distance from Knoxville to St. Louis, smoking weed. That's why I said it was packed in the car: it was four of us in the seats but the air was crammed with smoke. He had rolled a gang of joints and just kept lighting them. The next joint he smoked was always lit by the last one he had blazed. He was acting like he needed to make up for lost time or some shit, or like he had a quota he needed to hit. Just chain smoking his ass off.

None of the rest of us in the car smoked but it was his car. We couldn't tell him not to light up in his own shit. It was smokey as fuck in there. I'm certain it was filtering out of the seals of the windows into traffic. Fortunately, it was cold as hell in December so it probably just looked like cold air from the outside. If we got pulled over, though, all of us would've gotten locked up. Period. He was high as fuck by the time we got home. The rest of us were just a little high. The difference was we weren't happy about it.

We were at home for a week. Ma talked to me with another level of pride because her son was a college man. That felt really cool. I was happy to spend some time with my little sister, too. I had missed her. Reconnecting with the Kowrie Group was dope, man. I needed the boost. Fortunately, I was able to attend two meetings because we were there a whole week. The meetings were reinvigorating as hell.

Other those things, I was really ready to leave the crib. There was nothing there for me to hang around for. The bulk of my fellas were all at the same school with me. Ma had her usually busy schedule so she wasn't very available. And the streets were never welcoming. I wasn't trying to be hanging out in those too much. Also, I had gotten used to the collegiate world. When it was time to leave I was ready as hell to go back.

I wouldn't say I was stoked when we got back to KC but I felt… comfortable. The school, my dorm room had become my dominion so I was good being in that space. Still, I wasn't satisfied being there because I was certain it wouldn't supply what I needed. It was clear I would have to make some moves. I just didn't know what they were.

Yet.

One night a few days later, I was in the room by myself actually working on an assignment. It was in the middle of the week and I had a paper due. I looked up at the clock and saw it was only 9:00 but I was tired as fuck. I told myself, out loud, that the paper was going to get finished before I went to sleep.

(Alright, bruh. You gone finish this paper first then fall out. I'm not waking up early to do this shit.)

KNOCK! KNOCK! KNOCK!
Somebody knocked on the door and I got up to get it. A weird guy, he looked a few years older than me, was standing in the doorway.

"Hey, what's happenin'? Uh, is Roostah around?" he asked.
"Nah, he ain't here."

I had already shifted my weight to close the door. He continued.

"I don't know if he told you or not but I'm here to pick up something from him."
"Nah, he didn't." I said almost irritated.

"Aw man, damn. I was really looking to get that." He was cool about it but he seemed a bit anxious.
"Well, I can't help you with that. He ain't in here." I said.

I could see in his face that he had switched a gear. Whatever he was thinking made him perk up. Dude was as cool as the other side of the pillow and smiling. Absolutely undeterred.

"Oh, uh, that's cool. I know where it is." He said with all confidence. "Look in that bottom drawer, in the back left corner and hand me one of them bags."

"What?" I was tripping.

"Yeah, just open that drawer. You'll see."

I didn't really know what to do. So, I shrugged my shoulders, opened the drawer and checked the corner. Sure enough, there were several zipped baggies with white powder in them.

The dude was holding a one hundred dollar bill in his hand when I turned around.

"They usually cost $80 but I don't have change. And this is so you know I'm on the up and up."

He thought for a minute, "unless you got change."

I was so slow on the uptake that I didn't try to answer him. Ultimately, I leaned my head as if to say, "mutha fucka do I look like I got change."

He caught my drift.

"Nah, man, its' good. You can keep the change. Go'on, take it." He continued.

Again, I was a bit lost but it seemed like a good deal to me. I took the money and handed him the pack.

"Thanks, man. Just give that to Roostah when he gets back. Now, I may be back so don't trip. In fact, you be here?" he said.

"Uh, yeah. I'll be here." I mumbled.

"Cool. Thanks, man."

He left and I stood there… breathing. I didn't entirely know what that was all about, it happened so damned fast. But it was clear to me that I just did a drug deal. It took seconds but I had $100 in my hand. What the fuck was really going on?

Then it made sense. Roostah was working alright… drugs! That's why he wasn't around and why he was always fresh. He had money every time I saw him, too. AND this mutha fucka had rolled up here in a car! My dude had got in the drug game.

Mutha fucka.

I tried to wrap my head around it a little bit. Then I moved on and went back to work on my assignment.

KNOCK! KNOCK! KNOCK!

The guy had returned. About 20 minutes had passed.

"Hey, wassup?" I said.

"Told you I'd be back. We good?" He asked.

"Uh, yeah." I replied on reflex.

Suddenly, I got nervous. I didn't want anybody to see him outside the door.

"C'mon in, dawg." I said.

I closed the door behind him pretty rapidly but not loudly. I grabbed the pack, swapped it with another $100 bill and dude bounced.

I put the money together in that drawer, closed it and sat there staring at the drawer for a minute.

(I just got $200 in 20 minutes! This shit is crazy. This is wild then a mutha fucka).

I tried to get back to my assignment but I was half doing it. I just kept thinking about how lucrative that had to be. The powder that guy got from me was miniscule. I wondered how much it cost. It was a relatively small amount, it couldn't be too expensive at a bulk price. Then, how much was the profit from each pack? Where did he get the product from? Who packaged it up? How did he know who to sell it to? How did he avoid the police?

...a whole avalanche of thoughts ran through my head in hyper speed.

(I mean, how did he market it? Was his customer base small? How did he increase it? Which customers could he trust? Did he have police connections? Was anybody looking out for him?)

That last one stopped me in thought. This was my dude from the 'Lou. We out here in country ass Knoxville and we've only been here a few months. How did he get connected? Who is he talking to? Who is he running with? Can he trust those people?

...and... and... AND... this shit is in my room! How long has it been here? If the cops come through here they would get my ass, too! I probably better get my act together and figure out what the fuck is going on.

KNOCK! KNOCK! KNOCK!

(FUCK!!! That better not be the police! This is some bullshit. I just learned about this stuff, they can't pin me with this, man. What if dude was a cop…)

KNOCK! KNOCK! KNOCK!

"Hey dude, you still here?"

It was the guy who had already come to the spot twice. I could tell that was his voice.

(Shit, I can't stay trapped in the room. Ain't no other way out. I could stay quiet…)

KNOCK! KNOCK! KNOCK!

"Hey, man. You good? You still here?"

I sat quiet for another few seconds.

(You know what, fuck it.)

I opened the door and the guy stood there alone again. Smiling.

"Shit, I thought you left on me. You good?"
"Yeah, I'm… I'm good." I said.
"That's cool, that's cool. But are you good?"

He leaned a bit to look past me, eyeing the drawer.

"Oh, yeah. Yeah. Let me handle that. C'mon in, make sure you close the door."

There were two packs still left. I handed him one of them and he handed me another $100 bill.

"Thanks, man. I'll see you around."

He said that as he turned and walked out the door. Of course, I told him the same then closed the door behind him.

I walked over to the drawer. This time I didn't put the money in. I pulled the other money out. Then I sat on my bed with three $100 bills in my hands. Tripping.

I looked up at the clock and it read 10:06. In one hour I made $300! I hadn't made a total of $300 with that popcorn since I had arrived on campus. It took approximately 66 minutes to make 300 dollars. That's $100 every 22 minutes. That math was blowing my mind.

I was doing something wrong.

CHAPTER 23

THE PREAMBLE

Some shit was going down that I needed to be in on! If industry was my thing, and business was my thing, hell, if *money* was my thing then I *had* to get in on the change they were making. To that point in my life, that $300 was the most cash I had in my hand at one time. And it was all earned in an hour!

Now, you know my first job gave me a $700 check, but Ma deposited that. I earned the summer entrepreneurship scholarship check that was a few thousand but it was, again, a check. Actually, it was a big ass carboard banner first then a plain paper check that got deposited. What happened in my dorm room was cold cash earned as an entrepreneur. Illegality was a moot undertone. I had already been sold on the notion that the school and its lackluster and non-compelling programs were not going to give me what I was looking for. I felt that somewhere deep. Having those dollar bills in my hand profoundly resonated with me. Its impact was obvious and immediate.

My charge was to become a master of my trade, of my craft, to *own* my dominion. Knoxville College seemed like it would do the bare minimum in helping me achieve my conquest goals. I had to have another outlet to substantiate my committed level of impact. Selling drugs seemed like it could do that.

Still, I was challenged by my moral compass. Everything I knew said selling drugs was wrong. Not illegal, wrong. 'Illegal' is about government access. 'Illegal' is about whether or not the feds are getting their cut. I wasn't at all concerned with that. I had every disrespect for the law and their imposed system of governance that kept us impoverished. They weren't my issue.

Nah, my challenge was about the people I would serve. I had spent the bulk of my life learning what it is to be Black and how that is synonymous with community. My purpose in being in school was to empower my community. My commitment to become a master of commerce was about building the Black village. I couldn't have more of an Afro-centric, Black American focus. I existed to be my brother's keeper. I was all in for my people.

Drugs murder communities, though. Every idiot knows that. That made selling drugs the antithesis to my purpose. If I began working product, I would be that murderer. That was tough as hell to swallow, shit, it was tough to say. The questions are, if I didn't do it would they still get their fix? Would someone else sell it to them? Yeah. Definitely. So, if I abstained would I actually be helping? No. Not really.

Shit, Roostah and whomever he was working for were proof of that. They weren't about to stop what they were doing and I'm certain they already had competition. Speaking of which, I was already taking a risk! Roostah had that stuff in my room. If the cops ran up in there I already had exposure. Particularly once I knew about it.

I was already taking a foolish risk, whether that was my intention or not. It was worse with the money passing by around me. Shouldn't I have benefitted from it? Shouldn't I have made some paper? Doesn't that make all the sense?

And, what would I have done with the proceeds? Where would I have put the profits? Those are also incredibly pertinent factors. If I built an empire and used that money to support... Kowrie and to... create another legitimate business that hired our people then it's more than 'not wrong'. It would be smart.

Suddenly it hit me that I was sitting in a college dorm room having these thoughts.

In college.

There are all kinds of people who never made it to college. Many wanted to but couldn't either afford it or make the grades. Hell, the college I attended was created because Black people didn't always have the opportunity to go to schools. Qualification had nothing to do with that: they weren't allowed because they were Black people! This school exists for me and people like me to give them opportunities to do better than what I could do back on the streets at home.

Yet, there I sat in a great state of preponderance. At a historically Black college.

(Do I press this 'reading books and turning in assignments thing' or make money right now? The same way I could do it if I just stayed at home on the streets.)

That stifled my thought. "...same way I could... at home on the streets". 'At home on the streets' stung a little bit. I began thinking about it literally.

(Could I sell drugs in my neighborhood? Would I be alright with ·
that? Is this any different?)

Then, the clincher,

(What if Ma knew? How would she feel? Would I try to justify it to her, would I be ashamed or would I stand proudly?)

It wasn't about Ma and what she thought that decided it for me. Of course, I love my momma. I respected her like few other human beings who ever lived. But it's my own conscience I had to reconcile with. Ma was my truest compass of that. If I couldn't even think about standing tall and telling my mother what I did, even making $300 an hour, then I had no business doing it. Dignity doesn't allow me to make choices I'd be ashamed of.

Alright.

I made the decision that night not to move forward with it. My mirror matters to me. If I couldn't stare myself in the eyes and smile back at the reflection then it would mean that I was living wrong. Not being able to proudly tell Ma what I did to make money was the same principle. I decided to take a pass.

As for Roostah and his stash at the room, I started by avoiding the room more. I figured that I could easily make a case that it wasn't mine, if it came to that.

Quick disclaimer: when I gave him that $300 he thanked me for handing it for him. He confirmed it was for three packs then he tossed me $40. The fiend, or whoever he was, told me the truth. They were normally $80 apiece. Roostah made an extra $20 and I made $40 in an hour. In 1988. Just for being where I was, in my room. So, for an hour, I had technically been a drug dealer. That was some bullshit.

All that aside, I wasn't in business with him and that would fly because it was true. Or, at least, I could convincingly say it because it was true – I didn't work for or with him. It would be easy, and possibly convincing, to say that I didn't know about it, if it came to that. We only had a week or two until the new semester, I'd just switch roommates then.

That way, he'd still be my dog and not take the change personally. Then I could be clear of the risk. No sweat. I could make it a few weeks and be done with it.

This is what my naivete told me.

With more than a little effort, I shifted my mental focus. I finished out my first college semester with two things on my mind: 1) nailing my grades and 2) nailing some ass. I was not trying to win the Dusty Dick Award. Man, listen: I had changed my perspective on sex a bit. I was no longer a virgin because I had handled that in my junior year. (I didn't want to take y'all through that detail but it happened). So, I wasn't exactly interested in abstaining but I hadn't reached hoe status, either. I was in a... sort of a midway point where I was sexually active but not overly so.

At KC, I hadn't yet been active at all! My crew was making a big deal out of it, of course. That's what it was to be a collegiate man in a crew of young men. We talked shit about sex, dawg, that's just how it was. And, my fellas were clowning me because I was one of very few who hadn't yet connected with a lady. When that changed it wasn't exactly a banner I wanted to wave. It wasn't because I was on my gentlemanly manners, either. There was one huge reason, though.

So, I got chosen. I wasn't a small guy at the time so I didn't really fancy small women. That didn't mean I was particular about huge women, either. Turns out, that didn't really matter. Well, it just didn't turn out that way.

The young lady who chose me was around 6'2" or 6'3". Man, if she told me she was Shaquille O'Neal's twin sister I would have believed her straight out. I would have also believed that she was the older twin with the lion's share of the genes. Just sayin', she was NOT a little lady.

Our entanglement was... eventful as hell. We connected in her little bitty dorm room. It's not like I had endless hosting options – I didn't. It was either her or my dorm room, I picked hers. Quietly, I wanted to be able to bounce if things went south. That's much better than having to kick her out, y'know? Just being real. So, her room it was.

The dorm rooms had twin-sized bunks and, like I said, I wasn't a small dude. The two of us just trying to fit in that bed was like forcing four armadillos to wrestle in a hamster wheel. There really wasn't a lot of room to work with. AND the walls in those rooms was paper thin without much insulation. You could damned near hear your next door neighbor's farts.

That didn't slow her down... any. She apparently didn't give two shakes of a rat's ass about making noise, being heard or getting caught. From the rip, she was straight hollering as if we were in a soundproof booth. Back then, we would say protected sex was 'practice' for baby making. Shit, she sounded like she was practicing a literal baby delivery. She was making all kinds of damned noise. I wasn't sure if she was enjoying herself or having hip problems. I ain't bullshittin'.

Then she made it graphically clear when she threw her fluffy legs up over my shoulders. Nope, no problems. No problems with those hips, at all! In fact, she was crazy limber - especially for such a big girl. I guess it got good to her because she decided to completely cut loose. She went to work with her legs on my shoulders like a gymnast in an Olympic qualifier. She was having a good ass time!

Man, it felt like I was holding up a pair of telephone poles. Those legs were heavier than a mutha fucka! Then she got in a zone: she yanked me down, with her legs, and plopped my head squarely into her stomach.

And that was the beginning of the end. When both of my heads were swimming in shallow pools it was time to call it. She laughed about having my head nestled in her stomach. Straight up? I laughed hoping that meant it was over. I eased backwards, half chuckling, and started pulling myself together. When it was over I didn't know if I should kiss her, give her a high five or put up a score card. She had performed her ass off. I was straight up impressed, y'hurr me?

On my way back to the dorm, I laughed myself across the entire field. Dawg, I was sore like I had just ridden a wooden roller coaster. Man, you know those mutha fuckas beat you up. Your ribs, your hips… it just turns you into a boxing heavy bag. Apparently, while I was trying to rock her world, she was going Rocky Balboa on mine. Maybe more like Clubber Lang talking 'bout, "I got a lotta mo'! A lotta mo'!" That shit was funny as hell.

Now, I'm not a total ass. I don't want to cast aspersions on the sister (well, I guess it's possibly a bit too late for that). It's not my idea to disrespect her. Quietly, we all know kiss-and-tells are disrespectful by their very nature. In my defense, there's no other way I could really put y'all up on game about a sexual exploit without some degree of being foul. So, my bad.

That said, the young lady was a beautiful person. I mean that. And not in the way that people say your baby is 'precious' because they don't want to say its ugly, either. Nah, straight up, she was a beautiful person. And she was super chilled. Good people. A little aggressive, for sure, but she had a tender character. Please forgive me for coloring her a bit harshly. However, it is a graphic memory so it was best shared with a degree of visual description. You were actually spared some of the more, uh, *colorful* details. Believe me, it's better that way. It was a weird thought to me, but, when we finished I was just glad it was over.

That was also pretty awkward. I mean, how many dudes want sex to be over? It wasn't an emotion that had ever returned to my sex life, you can believe that.

Best part about it? I was no longer a Dusty Dick award contender. It was the first time I was working to NOT earn the number one spot. That was pretty hilarious. It's not like it had any importance of any sort. It was just one of those stupid ass things fellas do. We got swept away with menial shit sometimes. We were young, man. Fuck it.

I could have spared you that whole story, right? But this is about my college life: it wouldn't be real without sex. Whether you had sex in college or not, it was definitely happening. A whole lot of it! I had to put y'all up on a little of the business just to keep it authentic. But, that's the only dose you get. For now, anyways.

Well, a few weeks later it was time for Christmas break. I had demolished my classes so I was putting my first college semester in the win column. I wasn't happy or, more accurately, content with what the school offered. But, everything that needed to be handled was well under control.

Fortunately, the classes got better, which is to say they became more challenging. The word I got from the registrar was on point. That calculus was a mutha fucka! Ultimately, I zoned in and knocked those out, too. That made me feel a little more positively about my choices and my odds of getting what I needed from the institution. It seemed like I was putting myself in a better position to succeed. It still wasn't optimum but I was taking steps in the right direction.

Everybody was busy sorting out their transportation home. I got connected with a few brothers who were going to St. Louis a little late. One of them worked off campus and wanted to put a few days in, after the break started, before heading to the crib. No sweat, I wasn't in a hurry.

One morning after campus had essentially cleared out, I was chilling in the room alone. It was a bullshit day for me so, I got up late and got a shower. When I got back to the room, Roostah walked in the door behind me. He was carrying an all-black duffle bag. I didn't know what was in it but it looked kind of full and a little heavy. It was one of those really long duffel bags, it might have been about four feet. He could've been smuggling a pair of midget prostitutes in it and they both could've comfortably enjoyed the ride. It was a big ass bag. I thought he was preparing to leave school for the winter break or something.

He was with this huge, NFL football player-looking dude who walked in behind him. The guy was a big ass 3-steak-sandwich-eating mutha fucka. And I mean he eats one sandwich with three steaks in it. But he wasn't fat, just… thick. He was a huge man.

The huge dude was dressed, though. He was fresh from the Jordan hat on his head all the way to the fresh-out-of-the-box-this-morning Jordans on his feet. He had a gold watch, matching herringbone necklace and bracelet, rangs (not rings) on both hands… the whole nine. This guy dripped of money.

By the time I half-realized I was staring at the mutha fucka, Roostah introduced us.

"Hey, Busara. Wassup?" Roostah said.

"Wassup, dawg?" we exchanged dap.

"This my man, Skins. He a Knoxville mutha fucka but he alright." We all laugh.

"Ain't that about a bitch," Skins said laughing. "What's up big fella?" He reached his hand out.

I shook it, "what up?"

"Hey man, we got some shit we gotta do for a minute. Might take about an hour or two. You good?" Roostah asked.

"Yeah, I'm good. It ain't shit." I responded.

"Straight. It'll be a couple mutha fuckas rolling through in a minute. We waiting on them right now."

"What's up?"

When I asked, it had just fallen out. I didn't think about it first. Skins spoke up.

"Aw, it's just a little business. It'll be done and over with before you know it."

"Aight. Y'all need me to leave?"

They looked at each other then gave the universal 'I don't give a fuck' sign to each other.

"Nah, not really. You cool" Roostah said.

"I ain't the kind of dude that would put you out your own house, big man. That would be rude as hell." Skins said.

The two of them sorta chuckled. I just gave the 'aight' kind of head nod.

Now, I was curious. Neither of them had said much but that meant to me that it was going to be some big shit. Something was up! I wasn't comfortable just sitting there in their faces, though. I don't know, something about the moment just made me want to take a breather. So, I did.

"Hey man, I'm going to grab a Coke. Y'all want something?" I asked them.

"Shit yeah," said Skins.

He reached in his pocket and pulled out a fat ass knot (a massive wad of money). It looked like he had wrapped a softball in green construction paper. He ripped a twenty dollar bill out of the middle of it and handed it to me.

"I'll pay for yours just grab me one, too. You want something, Roo?"

"Yeah, I'll take one." Roostah said.

"Aight, just grab a twelve pack or something. And a bag or chips or two. That'll be tight. Thanks, bruh."

That made me feel like the errand boy, I didn't like that shit. I didn't like it at all. I mean, I asked the mutha fucka and he just capitalized on it. But something about it just rubbed me wrong. And it stuck with me.

I bailed, though. I rolled up to the store, grabbed the stuff and walked back.

As I was walking towards the dorm, musical bass started shaking through my chest. I looked for the sound and it was pulsating from a red Chevy Blazer rolling up onto the Yard. It had huge chrome spinning rims and obviously some fat ass woofers in it somewhere. It was rattling the buildings it passed, the windows were vibrating and everything. I got near the dorm as they pulled into the parking lot. I figured, rightly, it had to be the cats they were waiting for.

There stopped being a doubt in my mind that minute. It was a drug deal about to take place. The dudes in that truck, shit, the truck itself, had 'drug dealer' written all over it. Hell, everybody knew the Blazer was 'the official car of drug dealers everywhere'. Personally, I thought these dudes clearly weren't the sharpest knives in the cutting block. Why you gotta tell the world what you do? Like, super stereotypical everything. They were either marketing for drug dealer groupies or they wanted to get caught. That shit was way less than brilliant. I found myself making mental notes.

I walked to my room and passed Roostah on his way down the stairs. He was going to grab the dudes from outside. I rolled into the room and it was just Skins and me for a minute.

"How you like school, big man?" he asked.

"It's Busara, bruh. And it's cool. The honeys are alright."

He chuckled at that.

"My bad, Busara. Respect." He continued, "yeah, I like the
honeys here, too. I went to UT. It's way better here though,
more Black women. I love KC."

He was quite a few years older than us so the 'school honey' comparison seemed a little off. Like, he shouldn't be round here messing with
young girls or something. My Wapinguzi leadership vibe put me in an
awkward space of protection for our sisters. So, him talking about preying
on Black women students just didn't rub me right. It was another unset-
tling alarm bell about the dude.

Before we could get more uncomfortable in that uncomfortable
ass conversation, Roostah returned with two guys. One of them had a
Superfriends backpack on his shoulder. Both of them had cell phones.
Actually, I should call them cellular phones. They were too big to abbrevi-
ate. That's not a diss, though. At the time, only doctors, lawyers and drug
dealers had them - and not all the doctors.

They came in and dap was exchanged all around.

"Did y'all take the scenic route? Or did you eat some bad
Waffle House and take a pit stop?" Skins joked.
"Naw, Shawty. You know dem freeways in A'lanna be futt'd
up. It took forevah to get otta 'dere. Shoulda took a helacopta."
One of the guys said.

Everybody laughed. Except for me. I was too busy wondering if they
had that kind of money.

Now, I had been in school for almost four months. I met a lot of
people from Atlanta, very few of them were as, uh, dialectically colorful

as the pair of cats in my room. Those two mutha fuckas were as country as a banjo sandwich.

> "I don't know why you don't own one already. Money ain't nothing to a baller." Skins said.
> "You got me awl da way futt'd up, playa. They cain't haav my munny lite 'dat. I'm too bizzy out heuh gettin' paid, y'hurd?" The bumpkin said.
> "I don't know, bruh. Only true ballers show up in the spot with Zan and Jana on they back." Skins said, fighting a boisterous laugh that he immediately let out after.

All of us cracked up laughing. That's when I got unexpectedly blinded. I had no idea what glimmer of sun was accosting my corneas but I literally put my hand in front of my face to stop the sunspots from forming.

One of them Atlanta guys had full gold fronts. That's all I'm going to say about that. I'll let y'all deal with it as you see fit.

> "I daught (thought) we was on a skoo (school) kampis but it luutliik (looks like) we dunn rowed into a cummedy klub. You gat jotes (jokes) an' shiet!"

I'm gone call dude Jedidiah. They never said their names but it just sounds like it fit. He said his piece with half a grin but I wasn't sure he was pleased with being clowned.

The first bumpkin threw some more sounds out. Okay, I should call them words because I know that's what he intended.

"Luut mane, we gat dis heuh baatpaat (backpack) so we kan fit in wit' da' skoo. We trynna be lo kee ott heunh."

I didn't understand everything he said but I got the gist. And I was flabbergasted! These mutha fuckas rolled up on campus with chrome-glimmering spinning rims on a truck that sounded like a whole concert was happening in their backseat. It would've made all the sense in the world if a crew of recording artists climbed out when they stopped, so they could go to the bathroom. After all, it belonged to that pair of clowns, it could have definitely been a clown car.

And, they could've booked the group with their military SAT-phones. They were just one step above the huge ass bag, if you remember those. When they weren't calling people with the apparatus they were working out with them. They looked heavy as hell. The minutes probably cost like $6.75 each.

The drug dealers individually looked like they barely survived the set of 'I'm Gonna Git You Sucka' where they both would've suffered from OG'ing (dying from wearing too much gold). Including one of their mouths being decked out like it could've prevented the Californian gold rush. And their idea of being "low key" was their product being transported in an old, overfilled until it looked like it would burst, Saturday morning cartoon backpack – on a college campus?

Everything they did, and I mean everything, screamed that they were drug dealers. I figured it would eventually be fatal for them that they obviously didn't see how dramatically perspicuous they were. The minute I had that thought it astounded me that they hadn't already been caught. It couldn't have been too far off.

Skins kept the deal going.

"I'm with that. Let's make this happen so we can all slide out of here like grad students, smiling about the paper we earned."

They agreed, everybody got focused and the room fell quiet as they went to work.

Roostah cleared off his desk. I took his cue and cleared everything off of mine, just in case. Then he reached into the top shelf in his closet and pulled out a triple beam scale. My eyes got big as hell, I didn't know he had that!

My guy, Roostah, had been crazy low key with me about what he had been doing. I lived in the room with him but was almost completely in the dark about his work. He knew the kind of straight arrow my life had followed so it makes sense he didn't try to recruit me. He had every reason to suspect I wouldn't ride, anyways. So, maybe Roostah was protecting me so I would have plausible deniability. Admittedly, that's some generous logic. I'm most inclined to think he was just being discreet. Either way, it was smart. I logged that train of thought as valuable.

That made me question why I was in on *that* meeting. I certainly wasn't an original part of that plan. Maybe they thought I would be gone from school when they set the appointment. It was clear that he trusted me as a person, or at least, that meeting was good reason to think he did. So, once I wound up staying extra days he just rolled with it. That makes sense to me, we'll call it that.

Roostah and my relationship was in a different stratosphere once we entered that meeting.

While Roostah broke out the scale, the Country Cuzzins whipped their backpack onto the other desk. They opened it and showed they had brought three tightly wrapped white bricks into the room. Each one of those 'bricks' was a key(kilo) of cocaine. That backpack worked like an actual clown car because they pulled a lot of shit out of it.

They had a money counting machine in there, too. They put it next to the cocaine on the table. And I saw they left a burner (a gun) in the bottom of it. From what I could tell it was a nickel-plated 9 mm Beretta. It was awfully bright in that bag. They didn't pull it out, I guess they didn't want to make the situation more tense than it was. One of the two of them already had a burner in the small of his back, so they were ready regardless. They might have had a DC backpack but they didn't plan on throwing Batarangs at mutha fuckas if shit went sideways. Y'know what I'm sayin'?

In response to their unveiling, Skins put their massive duffel bag on my bed. He unzipped it to reveal money in a large collection of bundled dollar bills. It was a whole lot of fucking money! I knew the bag had a specific capacity but it seemed like an endless ocean of dollars to me. Floating in that lucrative sea was what I would come to understand was an UZI submachine gun. Neither one of the crews flinched from seeing the weapons but both sides saw them. Preparing for gun play was, apparently, just how business got done.

The guns weren't as impressive to me as all that fucking money. That was a ridiculous bunch of dollar bills, man. I did everything not to fawn over the shit like I had never seen money before. Except,

I HAD NEVER SEEN THAT MUCH CASH MONEY BEFORE. NEVER!

When they got done with their exchange, they traded two kilos of cocaine for $50,000. They worked out a deal to front the extra kilo to Skins and his team. (A 'front' is when the product is loaned out and the payment comes later. Usually, it's more expensive that way). The bumpkins said that kilo was supposed to go to some other cats but that deal fell through. The guys didn't want to roll back into Atlanta with that amount of money and product on them. When they worked it out, everybody was happy with it.

I wasn't happy. Not even a little bit. I was in shellshock. Who the fuck has that kind of money? Cash money? And how the fuck was I in that room with all of that?!

And those Atlanta guys... everything about the way they handled themselves convinced me that I could clearly do better than them. With half my body in a prison cell I could have done better than those guys. Yet, they walked in with Gleek on their backs and walked out a few hours later with 50 large. AND more money owed to them! They made it clear that $300 an hour was damned near poverty!

The Skins dude didn't exactly seem like a rocket scientist, either. To be fair, he clearly had some sort of cerebral ability because he was charming. You gotta have some levels of intelligence to pull off panache. I watched him do that in real time and I could tell it was a part of his managerial brio. He could get people to do things. At a bare minimum, he was emotionally intelligent. That was worth plenty.

Still, I didn't know the game at all but it was clear to me that it would be easy to trump all those guys. Just watching them and their exchange, I knew I could devise systems that would far supersede them and what they were doing. I didn't grasp it all but some things are fundamental and/or universal. Like, not everyone plays an instrument but you can visibly hear when the one trumpet guy plays the wrong note in the band. The right thing isn't always easy to grasp but the wrong thing usually pronounces itself. The Georgians had a portable PA system to help them pronounce their asses off wherever they went.

But they weren't 'all' dumb. The Georgians, I mean. It even took me a second to catch on, those mutha fuckas didn't have a 'deal go south'. That was bullshit. Selling three keys was their plan from the start. Why drive 400 miles to sell two keys when you can get off three? I mean, $74,000 is a better number than $50,000 every day of the week. (They gave him a discount for taking it). They not only made more money in the deal but they had a dude with influence, in another town, in their debt.

Holy shit! Even more bold was their (inadvertent or intentional) maneuver to commit their 'client'. There was no better way to ensure consumer loyalty than to have them pre-purchase product. That would keep Skins from finding another supplier and ensure they could keep profiting off of him. That was low key brilliant. And they did it all with the appearance of needing help yet without compromising themselves. In fact, they were the ones applying the pressure to get the deal done with the extra key.

Quietly, that was the most intelligent thing in the whole exchange. And I thought they were, basically, a pair of bricks with car keys. But that move took a bit of vision and savvy. They had taught me two lessons: learn how to leverage your assets to maximize your gain and never underestimate anybody in the business. It's a cutthroat industry, you'll be out here bleeding from the neck and thanking the fuckers who cut you. Straight up.

Watching their bartering taught me something else: the drug game is filled with addicts. I wasn't incredibly familiar with the drug world but there are a few things I understood. The dependency of dope fiends compromised them immensely, especially for their next 'hit' (dose of drugs). Because of their fiending, they often accepted less than they were worth or gave away items of great value for very little.

The way their bargaining conversation progressed I saw that Skins' greed had compromised him. His greed, his desire to have more product to sell was an addiction and it put him in a position of debt. The Georgians had leveraged his 'craving for more' against him, just like the dope fiends.

Still, they had an addiction, too. The Bumpkins wanted to make a deal. They had a plan for it that included a calculated risk, sure. Still, they accepted less than they were asking because they were addicted to that money, to their greed, to their need to win in the game. That is their 'fix', also like dope fiends.

Everybody left my room when they got done. They all knew it was best if they didn't leave together, so they didn't. I stayed there as they all left at separate times, then watched out my window as they each rolled off campus. I knew I could do what they did and be better at it. I would certainly, then, be more profitable than them if I worked my vision.

Then it hit me: that exchange, those experiences happened on a college campus. Listen y'all, I grew up in the projects of St. Louis. I had never pondered being a drug dealer in the worst of our times. Shit, I had never seen drugs, well, cocaine with my own eyes before, much less holding any in my hands. For 17 years of my life I had, basically, no narcotics exposure at all. But, there I was, 400 miles away in college, where I both witnessed and was party to $50,300 in drug transactions in just over 3 hours. In school! Talk about a fucking education, Knoxville College was the birthplace of an extreme evolution.

I left the Yard heading for home two days later, committed to building a better mouse trap. During that ride I knew two things would be true about my plan.

Comic book characters wouldn't be involved.

Neither would Skins.

CHAPTER 24

THE VISION

My return to the neighborhood was a little bit different. Ma had been dating a gentleman for quite some time. While I was gone to college they had gotten married and she moved out of the Peabody's to move in with him. They didn't live anywhere near the neighborhood. That was really cool, I was glad for her. I just wanted her to have some happiness.

So, I stayed at my Granny's house for the winter break. Other than seeing my family, my only concern was my access to Kowrie meetings while I was in town. Mama's crib was quite a bit closer to St. Stephens than Ma's new place and Mama's my girl, too. So, chilling at her house made sense.

It was time for me to get in the lab and get focused. Any spot that I could have solace, where I could just sit and let my thoughts create pathways to solutions, was considered 'the lab'. If there was ever a time I had to collect my thoughts, this was it.

There were no misunderstandings, I was about to get in some real shit. It wasn't like trying to create a landscaping job. This wasn't sneaking out of the house to go to a clandestine meeting. It was much more crucial than designing a clever business plan for a contest. This was risky shit with a lot of moving parts: death, jail and mortal wounds were probable, not just possible. Those are consequences of war and that's precisely what the drug trade was – war. It was emphatically clear to me that success demanded a plan, it's how I had lived my life to that point. So, I sat my ass down at Mama's house and made one.

Before writing out my plan, there was a lot of information I would need to acquire. I wasn't entirely clueless but the drug world wasn't remotely my thing. I didn't have a lick of experience, unless you would count that one hour of sales and the couple hours of observation. Nah, I was bereft of a whole world of knowledge that was mandatory in order for me to thrive. And survive. That's what having friends is for, especially rugged ones.

The day after arriving in town, I went looking for Big Lou. Rolling through the Webbes, I searched his usual spots but he wasn't around. Just as I was getting ready to give up for the day, his brother showed up.

I hadn't told you a lot about Big Lou's brother because, frankly, there wasn't a lot for me to tell. He spent most of my formative years in prison. I was a junior in high school when he got out. He was the main breadwinner for their family when he went in. Most of his providing took place through illegal means, that's what landed him in prison.

They lost their mom when they were, like, 5 and 9 or 6 and 10 years old. Something like that. They moved in with their grandmother and had to work immediately to provide. The only work they could find at such young ages landed them in the hustle lane. They've been there, on one level or another, their whole lives.

Both of those brothers were true family men. It's the way they operated, too. They not only worked in tandem to provide for the family but they hung out with each other. And they were very inclusive, they looked out for anybody in their circle.

His brother saw me leaving from their building and hollered at me.

"What's up, little man? You not so little no more, huh?"
He said.

We both laughed.

"Nah. I passed up 'little' a whole bunch of meals ago."

We laughed again.

"You good?" Big Lou's brother asked.
"Yeah, I'm just looking for Lou."
"You wouldn't find him around here. He's out making paper for winter break." He said.

It was a life habit for them to just make money. It never stopped because they're both used to taking care of their family. Even school breaks were no exception.

"Word," I responded. "Actually, I was kinda going to ask him something about the game. I need some help."
"Dawg, wassup?" He asked.
"Well…"

His brother was the business. Period. Everybody knew he was the real deal and he got all the respect. When he got out of jail, at 17, he hit the streets. He was a devout provider so he made paper, it's just what he did. I knew every word he would have to say would be worth hearing.

I told him about my plan to build a business selling cocaine at school. He asked intelligent, pertinent questions and listened intently. I never would have guessed he'd be so attentive to detail and so patient with everything about my disposition. What I did know is that he would have a lot to say about it, whether he would say it to me or not was the only question. I thought we were cool but listening to him talk at length was proof. I never heard or saw him do a lot of talking. This particular conversation was a major exception.

He put me up on game and didn't hold back a thing. Much of what he said comported with what I knew about general business principles, just translated to a street platform. That gave him a different level of credibility with me. It was apparent to me that he knew what he was talking about.

Then, of course, there were street items that didn't translate. Despite the fact that the game was totally illegal, it came with a whole lot of rules. The more rules you ran your operation with, he said, the more successful you were likely to be. You would need a system to measure your successes and failures so you would know where to tweak it to get the results you wanted. As long as those rules were good ones and ones you made up for your operation, he said.

Then again, some rules and consistencies would get you pinched (get you caught), at least that's the way he put it. He told me that anything that makes you predictable will get you fucked up. Staying off radar and keeping your systems out of sight is the safest way to work. The best thing you could do for yourself, he said, was look like you weren't a drug dealer.

He also said that really solid systems can make you consistent, predictable and, ultimately, assed out. The trick is to be smart enough to know which rules were which. Any rules from somebody else were completely out of the question.

"It's a lonely game, Busara. Trust nobody."

There was one thing in particular that he said that really stood out. The second he said it to me I took it to heart. It was going to be my toughest test. The information was grave but he talked about it like we were having a gym shoe preference conversation.

"The biggest truth about an illegal game is it ain't no rules. 'Do what the fuck you want' is how it works. And everybody is in it for money, that makes mutha fuckas dangerous."

He paused for effect.

"So, when you start moving product and your game is bangin', it means, more than likely, you selling to someone else's clientele. You taking food off somebody else's plate and they don't have rules to let you keep doing that. We not talking Walmart and Target, here. "Fair market share" or "sharing customers" don't exist in the game. They gotta be *your* dope fiends or theirs. So, sooner or later, you gotta take out your competition. Or they will handle you."

He looked me dead in the eyes.

"Listen to what I'm telling you. It's not a 'let them swing first' type of thing. They makin' money, you tryin' to make *their* money. Right now, they don't know you're on your way in but you already know they're in your way. You know what's gotta happen, so get the drop on they ass and get it done. Period. Take them out, take their soldiers, change your prices then start moving weight. Handle that immediately to make sure you're first: when you do it right, there ain't no second."

That last word was everything. As often as people call it 'the drug game', it is declaredly not a game at all. It's either prosperity or death. That's what the business is. Anything else means you're doing it wrong. Big Lou's brother was emphatic that I learned that truth.

He wasn't done.

"If you ain't prepared to end mutha fuckas, keep yo' ass in school, Busara." He punctuated.

I was thankful that I ran into him and that he put me up on game. It was exactly the 'pep talk' I needed.

I went back to Mama's house and got busy. My plan was fashioned with all that I had learned about general business practice and drug dealers. I put all my street hustling, college semester and MYEP lessons to full use. The words of Big Lou's brother weighed heavily on my calculations. Everything he said became foundational to my plan: eliminate the enemy on every level. Because of that direction, one of the line items of my plan was going to be murder.

I sat down and tried to lay out everything I could foresee. First, I wrote down all the things Big Lou's brother said. I knew much of it would be key and I didn't want to forget one word. I borrowed some of the business tenets learned from the entrepreneurs the previous summer. Sound business practices work in every business setting. I didn't see this business as being an exception. Hell, it could even prove to be more of a pertinent workspace for those practices.

My first semester business classes were still fresh in my mind. There were several techniques that could be applied from them, so they went into the plan. Then I utilized elements of the ridiculous situation that had just unfolded before my eyes at KC. There were lessons all over the place and I tried to take every one of them in.

Lastly, I added some of the Kowrie responsibility principles. Again, principles can be applied to benefit you in any situation. My lessons to that point in life were flexibly taught to me so I could make use of them as I saw fit. This situation would require every asset I could summon and every lesson that could be applied. After all that was exhausted, I also recognized the need to just wing some shit was certainly arise. I was mentally prepared for that. Or, at least I thought so.

Several items stuck out in the plan that I thought should be shared with you. First, the guys from Atlanta could not have been more extravagant if they tried. Had I seen them anywhere I would have immediately known their 'profession'. Straight up. That struck me as rank idiocy. Conversely, Roostah's incognito approach was shocking and very effective with me, his roommate.

So, rule one was frugality. My plan was founded on the exit strategy: stack and go. My team was going to keep a tight leash on money and stack it. That was as much about empowerment as it was safety. I planned to make money to have money, not necessarily to spend it. My ultimate goal was to take the revenue I raised and fund legitimate businesses. It is what I've fashioned my whole life to achieve. There was never a vision to become a drug dealer. That thought was… degrading to me. That was vastly too far beneath my self-image and I expected a great deal more from my life. No, the drug world couldn't be my endgame.

This business would be temporary, that was the vision. It had to be treated like a tool, not the goal. I was a college student and that was going to continue. This was merely going to be a way for me to 'work through school'. I just had to stay cognizant of the fact that the job hazards of my chosen field were a mutha fucka.

Keeping a low profile was mandatory. I knew the lay of Knoxville College and which dorms had direct access off-campus. I imagined the bulk of our clientele coming from the locals so we needed easy access to the public. I chose Brandon Hall because you could see the exit fence and the public street from a dorm room window. That's where I would need to live.

I had already planned to leave the room Roostah was in. But that meant I would need a new roommate that I could trust with the caper. That was how I chose D Smooth. He would have my back and I could operate without worry if he was with me.

Having a weapon on campus would probably be risky. I wouldn't immediately look for one but if, for some reasons, I moved off the Yard then I would definitely acquire a gun. The Yard provided a weird degree, albeit a small measure, of safety. Living off-campus would guarantee none. I would have to be prepared.

I immediately scratched out that last note. I would need a gun from the beginning.

That Skins dude had to go!

I had learned enough from dealing with Roostah to know that Skins was the veritable kingpin in Knoxville. I thought Big Lou's brother was right because it was inescapable: I was gunning for his business. Since I was going that far then I would have to gun for him. Straight up. I thought it was gruesome but that was the business I was getting in. Not getting grimy would likely cost me my life, and I liked living.

Yeah, that mutha fucka Carl Koffy was going to get done! I wrote that shit down to convince myself that I was committed to it.

One more thing that I wrote down was to be flexible and adapt. There were things that were going to happen that I certainly couldn't foresee. Shit, I didn't even know the lay of the city or what it was really like out there. It made sense that I needed to keep my mind active and stay vigilant of necessary adjustments.

Preparing an exit strategy for when the endgame arrived was a must. I wrote to be cognizant of what was going on around me and to know when to get out. Whenever it spelled itself out I would have to read it and adhere to it. Right then! Not doing that would definitely cost me everything. I felt that somewhere deep. I made a promise to myself to learn that limit and quit the moment it showed up.

The last thing I wrote was:

Get out alive!

There was no one with me when I wrote out my guide. Secretly planning to operate inconspicuously was actually comfortable for me. It is my whole background in the Kowrie Group. Maximize the vision to define the mission then execute with stealthy precision. That perfectly summed up the impression the Organization had on me. Be purposeful, be effective and be quiet while you do it. I literally sat with my pen and pad and allowed that theme to guide my every word.

I diagrammed my plan to the most minute of foreseeable detail. My operation would have to be built slowly and move in phases. Once I wrote it all out, I double and triple checked it. "Measure twice, cut once" was a Kowrie habit, I was thankful I had it. The application of Kowrie lessons and principles to this plan gave me a renewed appreciation for my training.

Speaking of the Organization, I clearly owed a debt of commitment to the Kowrie Group. There was no way I could have had those milestones of achievement to that point if they weren't one of my major influences. Once I officially earned the title of a revolutionary, I committed to the principle of Nia with my prosperity. (The textbook definition of Nia is to make our collective vocation the building and developing of our community in order to restore our people to their traditional greatness). My oath was real and one of my life goals was to ensure that Kowrie thrived. They always believed in me and supported me in my efforts. (Well, in all the efforts that didn't clash with my responsibilities, I should say). Hell, they delivered D Smooth and I to college in Tennessee. I had to tell them my newly chosen path and it had to take place in a direct conversation. It was the right thing to do.

While it is true that the Kowrie Group was founded on anti-establishment sentiment, I knew drug dealing would be a problem with the leadership. Not because it was illegal, but because it was destructive in nature. No mentally-wholistic or righteously-built system would approve of drug dealing. It mauls lives and destroys whole communities. Selling cocaine was against the nature of everything Kowrie stood for. My last test for doing this thing was talking to them about it.

The best way to confront something you dreaded was to do it immediately. I learned that at a very young age. The Kowrie Group had helped form my manhood. Because of that, I had a challenge with shame for my chosen path versus standing in my own authority. For me to be right in my soul, I had to challenge this discomfort directly. So, I went to the first Kowrie meeting I could attend so it could be handled.

We had arrived in town on a late Friday night. I worked on the plan all weekend, to include my 'interview' with Big Lou's brother. Come that Tuesday, I was confidently committed when I walked into St. Stephens.

Of course I was there early, everyone was. I had hooked up with D Smooth and we went in together. Reconnecting with everyone was awesome. I found out my young brothers and sisters were doing well and the Organization was thriving. There were even a few new faces that seemed eager to get the meeting going. It was magnificent to see.

The meeting began with the usual procession. When we arrived to the news report segment the elders took another direction. After we got in the Circle, Mwalimu turned to D Smooth and me.

> "Let's welcome back the two youngest Kowrie Group members who ever became Wapinguzi: brother D Smooth and brother Busara. Give them some love, y'all."

You would have thought we were recording artists or movie celebrities. The reply was thunderous because the love was real.

> "It's really great to see you brothers back in the Circle. Tell us a little bit about your college experiences so far." Mwalimu said. "Please share with us your major and your vision of how you can further empower the village."

D Smooth and I looked at one another and I deferred to him. He was the senior of us, after all. He stood up to address everyone.

> "Habari gani, family," D Smooth started. Everyone appeared to respond.
> "Nzuri!"
> D Smooth continued.
> "So far, college has been really cool. I'm majoring in Chemistry; I will become a professor at an HBCU to educate our people and help build their lives. So far, I'm well on my way. I had a 3.6 this semester and I plan on doing better when I return."

Everyone cheered him on.

> "The social life is cool. I've learned a few things about organizations and people from different places. Living in the dorm is different but it's really cool." D Smooth said.

One of the young guys yelled out.

> "I heard it was crazy honeys at school!"

There was a smattering of laughter. Both D Smooth and I chuckled a bit.

> "Well, yeah. Historically Black Colleges are known for housing some of the most beautiful women on the planet. We are talking about our Black sisters, here. My school is no exception. There were, are, beautiful women all over the campus. But that's not my focus right now, young brother. I have a career to build and empowerment to accrue. Once I've done that, or at least when I'm well on my path, I can afford to focus on a young Black queen to build my life and family with. My true goal is making certain I'm an asset to our people. I don't want to distract myself and get sidetracked."

D Smooth said all of that shit with a straight face, too. Man, that mutha fucka knew he had been on some hoes. The second week we were on campus he already had women in his room. The word for woman in that sentence was intentionally plural.

But he did the right thing. Telling the young fellas where their heads needed to be is certainly what we should have done. They'll handle the other parts on their own. You certainly don't want to be in the middle of those other parts, anyways.

Mwalimu was beaming.

> "Spoken like a true revolutionary. Thanks for sharing brother D Smooth, it's great to see you back in the building. We know you are well on your way to marvelous things. Welcome home, young brother."

"Thank you, Kadamu." D Smooth said magnanimously.

D Smooth took his seat next to me. Mwalimu shifted his focus.

"And it's really good to see you here, young brother Busara. How about you? What's your area of focus and how was your first collegiate semester."

I stood up to address the Circle.

"Thank you, Kadamu. I appreciate all of you receiving us with open arms. It's really great to see all the new faces. You young guys made the right choice. You're in the company of a powerful family. I'm only a freshman in college right now but I've never made a better choice than coming to these meetings. I continue to be thankful for everything I've learned here."

I took a glance around the room and saw all the guys had smiles on their faces. Except Mwalimu. He felt something, I could tell. He was right.

I continued.

"It is my commitment here, to our people, that has chosen my path. I went to Knoxville College to begin my journey as a master of industry. I'm a business management major. My entire goal is to further empower our people by enhancing our fiscal strength. My college experience has been... a journey. I was a bit disappointed at first but I adjusted a bit and it got better. Then I learned something."

I took a breath and looked directly into all the eyes I could see. When I relocated Mwalimu I finished.

"I learned I could be empowered right now. That I could help my people right now. That I could earn vast sums of money right now. So, that's what I'm going to do. I'm going to sell drugs while I go to school."

The entire room got dark with confusion. Every pair of eyes tightened or bucked in shock. However, not a sound was made. That is, until Mwalimu spoke.

"Are you serious? You left here as the single youngest official revolutionary ever just to… become a drug dealer in college?" Mwalimu cried.

When Kadamu addressed me directly, I immediately moved to angulia (the position of attention). It was a mix of my habit from the training and to make a point for the young people there. You always respect your elders, there is no exception.

"Appreciating what's been said and if I understand everything correctly, that is not why I went, Kadamu. My direction is an assessment I've made in observing the situation once I arrived and recognized a demand. It's one of the business principles I've been taught. 'Identify a need then supply it.' That's exactly my plan." I responded.

My formatted response was the same as speaking from angulia. It was equal parts habit and reinforcement for the young warriors present.

"And that's why you think it's okay to sell that poison to our people? Because it will fill a need?" Mwalimu asked.

"Appreciating what's been said and if I understand everything correctly, that's not why I think it's okay. I just don't think of it as a matter of being okay or not. It's a business decision. And those aren't our people, Kadamu. We're talking about people in Knoxville, TN." I defended.

"Young brother. You were emphatically taught that both sides of the equator, from the center of the Congo, around the entire planet and back again, all brothers and sisters are ours. There is no distinction due to location. It's one of the many ways the white man divides us. We cannot allow that." Mwalimu exclaimed.

"Appreciating what's been said and if I understand everything correctly, I believe everything you said to be true. However, there is a supply and demand that will not cease just because I don't participate. I've seen the market, I've made a plan and I will succeed. Once I'm fiduciarily empowered, I can help those same brothers and sisters and more. When my plans are executed, I will operate from a position of abundance. I can't do that from where I currently stand." I again defended.

Mwalimu wasn't pleased with what I said but a smirk crossed his face. I think he thought he had an angle to dissuade me.

He first addressed everyone then focused on me.

"You see, young brothers and sisters? This is why we have a guideline against abundance. Many a man has fallen from greed." Mwalimu preached.

"Appreciating what's been said and if I understand everything correctly, this is the one area I don't agree with the teachings. Abundance is the power that puts us in position to counter

381

and conquer our enemies. They're built on money and power, not principle. They will never join us in a battle of principle or character. It's not where they operate. So, we need money to fight on the battlefield they occupy. I will make sure we have some."

"Young brother Busara, you've made a few good points. I can admit that. But you don't have to be the brother out there supplying that poison to our people! That's not necessary." Mwalimu pleaded.

"Appreciating what's been said and if I understand everything correctly, that's also a true point Kadamu. But it will get done regardless, whether I'm helping our people benefit from it or not. It's better that I do it and redirect the resources for the good of our people than the fools I observed with no direction or sense of community at all."

Mwalimu was clearly frustrated. It looked like he had leveraged his last point of argument and got stuck.

He looked to D Smooth.

"You in this, too?" He asked him.

"Hapana! No, sir." D Smooth replied flatly.

I had not yet conversed with him to include him but it was my plan. He just didn't know at that point.

"So, you're certain this is what you're going to do?" Mwalimu asked me.

"Yes, sir. I feel it's where I need to be right now." I stood firmly saying it.

Omni was in the building. He stepped forward.

"Everybody stay here." He said.

He gestured to the rest of the elders present and they all left the room. There were about six elders in the building that day.

We all did as he instructed: no one left the room. Because it was the elder Omni who spoke, few of us in the room even shuffled a bit while they were gone. I told you, that brother made an impression that was not to be trifled with.

D Smooth looked at me in awe.

"I can't believe you told them all of that like that." D Smooth said.

"Being a man is not about hiding stuff, brother. I'm done with anything like that. That's why I came here, to stand on my own two. If I couldn't tell them directly then I have no business doing what I do." I replied.

"True that. Respect." He responded.

The elders returned to the Circle led by Mwalimu. He waited to make sure every eye was focused on his words then he began.

"While this is not the path we want you to take, we respect your choice as a man. This room is family and nothing we've shared in here will leave this room. Everyone here understands that."

It wasn't a question and wasn't intended to be. He looked around the room to make certain it landed.

When they were certain it had sank in, Omni continued.

> "You will not go forward with our blessing but with our guidance. We have consulted the ancestors and they have revealed some things to us. When you make this choice there are several perils that will befall you. You will be shot three times if you do not abate. The first time it will be by a man wearing a red shirt. The shooting is going to put you in a wheelchair. You will recover from it and it won't stop you. The second time you will be shot by a slender man wearing white gloves. You will survive this shooting, too, but it will leave you paralyzed. If you continue beyond that you will be shot a third time… and it will kill you."

Even though the room was already silent, it appeared to become coldly so after Omni spoke. It was like a dark cloud had invaded the space and touched each of us. His words hit the room with an indescribable finality. None of us knew how the elders could foresee what they said.

The Group believed them.

Mwalimu took the mantle.

> "The ancestors have given us this word for you, Busara. How you decide rests with you, Black man. You're family so we've done our part, we won't do more. We're not happy about your choices but we're glad to see you here. And we still wish you prosperity and clarity in all you do."

He let that sink in then he moved forward with the news reports.

The Organization was unflappable. I had clearly disrupted their flow with my news but nothing disrupts what they do. The program is the program. They continued from there as they normally would.

I left the meeting inspired. No, I hadn't received good news. But, I felt more confident that I respectfully withstood their objections and was assured in my direction because of it. They even gave me a word to move forward on. So amidst the disturbing news, I walked out of there with more than I arrived with.

Now, I respected the elders. I honored their ways and I had every trust and confidence in them. However, when they said I would be shot, it... didn't land with me. I'm sure it was mostly because I was young. We all have that sense of invincibility, that we're somehow immortal, until we get old enough to feel ancillary pains. Enough damage to you in life, and watching others lose their lives, will either teach you that you're not indestructible. Sometimes, foolishly, those things will convince you that you are. Not enough had happened in my life to reveal my mortality to me so I was still in 'indestructible' mode. I just didn't fear any threats to my life.

The other thing was: how could they see the future? How could they take a quick break from a meeting and come back to tell my fate? Before it happens! That's just hard to believe altogether. I think we were all caught up in it because they were our trusted elders. They wouldn't pull our legs or tell us something to trick us. There was too much respect in the foundation of the 'Group for all of that to happen.

Still, when they said it they spoke with conviction and clarity. And detail! Dude in a red shirt? Slim guy with white gloves? Wheelchair? It came across as fact. It was crazy impactful. And it was a lot to digest.

Arriving back at Mama's, I went straight to my plan. I wrote down the details they described to me. I was confident that I would be fine but their words stuck out to me enough to make sure they got put into my records. I went over my details and made notes and adjustments. It was time to set it in motion.

When I got to the words 'get out alive' it took on a new meaning. What they revealed to me made those words ring true. I made a pact with myself that I would look for the signs they warned me of and decide accordingly. Staying alive was an easy priority.

My plan didn't include every single step I would take but it covered foundational approaches. Working with Roostah was out. That would have run counter to my blueprint. After watching how they operated, I knew there would be a 'seniority' issue. I wasn't for that. I was born as an entrepreneur, working for someone wasn't for me. I had to build my own empire. So, nah, I wasn't going to ride with Roostah on this. He was still my guy but this was business. I had to do me.

I couldn't operate in that massive foreign space by myself, that was for sure. I was going to need some human assets. Automatically, I put D Smooth in because he was my Kowrie Group brother and my guy all around. He saw me stand up to the elders, he even commented on it. It made sense that he would ride with me. D Smooth was essential to my plan in order to help keep the op low-key. But the true source who was necessary to get it done was Big Lou. Having him in the mix was an automatic win, if he was down.

Trust me, I'm not overselling him. Anyone who knows Big Lou would vouch for him the same way. He was a fierce, ferocious competitor but, still, if he was eating good then *we* were eating good. I've known few people more considerate than him. He possessed a temperament, a level-headedness and a working wisdom that were essential aspects for achieving my goals.

Still, he was like a twisted reality of a 'gentle giant' and a brawler. This is only possible because he was a huge dude. And I don't mean freakishly huge but substantially bulky. If you did a genetic cocktail of Groot and Drax you'd get Big Lou. He was just a monster of a man in stature.

And sometimes he was just a monster. He made the phrase 'Big Jack' popular with us in the 'Lou. A Big Jack can only happen when you get in an altercation with someone wearing a hat. If you can hit them, knock them out with one punch and catch their hat before it hits the ground – then you have performed a Big Jack. Think about that. Not only was he capable of such a thing but he did it so regularly that somebody gave it a name. Personally, I will pass on fucking with a dude who has a named knockout blow.

On the other hand, he treated everyone close to him like family. He wouldn't wait for you to ask for what he had if you didn't have any. Oddly, this did not make him a walking conundrum. Nah. He was just a good dude who wasn't about any of the bullshit.

Without a doubt, he is one of the most solid natural born leaders I've ever met. Out of everyone I knew, especially within my Knoxville options, Lou had the experience and the street savvy to make it work. How he got it, his specific collection of skills, is more than compelling.

You know what? Instead of me trying to sell him to you, he can tell you himself.

CHAPTER 25

MEET BIG LOU

Busara told y'all about one part of the projects in the 'Lou. The soft side. His 'hood was straight up like a village, they did generally look out for each other. I mean, they definitely had the cutthroat life, too, but that was only like a portion of their days. Chaos really waited until night time over there to truly cut loose. Otherwise it was essentially the Black version of Mayberry with much grumpier tenants. We just called them soft.

Well, that's what the Peabody's were like compared to the Webbes. For starters, the Peabody projects only had about 3 floors. The Webbes were as tall as 11 stories in the sky. And I'm telling you, life in those towers wasn't no joke! It may surprise you, but, how the structures were built had everything to do with how they affected our people. Our local government stuck us in there for a reason and it was as American as baseball and apple pie.

That reason was fucking over Black people.

Before they built our projects (the Webbes), the government conducted a lab experiment series in 1950's called the Behavioural Sink or the Mouse Utopia Experiment. (4) The focus of the experiment was to study the effects of overpopulation. They stuck a group of 8 mice, 4 males and 4 females, in a living environment built for 3000. The mice were contained in a limited space but supplied with unlimited resources. The controls of the experiment allowed them to run free. Disease was

monitored and removed. Predators were kept away so there was no repro-
ductive interference. They were allowed to freely mate and multiply their
numbers.

The results? After a few generations of norm building, all of the
succeeding generations of mice defied those systems. They multiplied like
crazy, ballooning to about 2200 before, basically, losing their shit. They
eventually became pack-like and territorial. Shortly afterwards, the entire
environment was generally hostile and combative with no harmony within
the structure. Pandemonium and hostility festered eroding any semblance
of structure. Ultimately, the entire mouse population died. The test was
run repeatedly to learn if there were any consistencies in the results. It
failed the exact same way every time.

So, what did they learn? What was the point? Limited living space
was a fundamental way to destroy a community. The room to operate and
thrive is an essential factor for a productive, peaceful society with any
social creature. Including humans. They noted that, as the time progressed
with the mice in limited space, some of them began to train new generations in destructive habits. This became a trend. The conclusion is that
limiting living space in a densely populated area will consistently and
perpetually have derogatory consequences.

With this information in hand, the government built these exact
living conditions for human beings on the lower-north side and the south
side of the 'Lou.(5) Middle-income whites were leaving the city in droves
because quality housing was scarce. The problem the government had with
that is their homes were being filled by low-income families. At the same
time, the slums were growing. The city government decided that building
high-density community towers would do just the trick. Jam a bunch of
people together in a small space and save the city. Awesome vision.

Nah. That shit was just fucked up.

It began with the Pruitt-Igoe Projects in the late '50's. (5) They consisted of 33 towers that were all 11 stories high. Life was so fucked up then that they were openly planned for segregation; the Pruitts were for Black people, the Igoes for whites. Separate, so they could be unequal, is America. So, the plan for this was the same shit. It's foul but nobody was surprised. Hell, nobody even protested it.

Then they built the Darst-Webbe and Vaughn projects. The entire collection of them was an attempt to get middle-income whites to return to the city with affordable housing. It was supposed to be built with the most contemporary of technologies to elevate the standard of living. At least, that's the press notes they released.

Despite their best efforts, including blatant segregation, the middle-class whites didn't return. Only low income families moved in, largely from the Black population. It became an almost strictly Black housing development in a really brief span of time. This flux in their plans devolved into criminal negligence on their part.

At first, the high-rise projects were lovely. The architect who designed them was even widely lauded for the design. However, the structures were widely criticized for their price. Construction for the massive project came with an exorbitant price tag. Still, it was a failure from the start. They were aesthetically pleasing on the outside but they weren't built with the living perks the government promised. Budgeting was a mess and the mismanagement of the funding resulted in a huge focus on some areas while leaving others unaccounted for or woefully inept.

This is where the viciously heinous intent of the white people was obviously aimed at our demise. In the Mouse Utopia Experiment, it was a bountiful space built for 3000 mice that didn't make it past a population of 2200. Once the middle-income whites passed on it, the Black people of the 'Lou were eventually crammed together in much greater proportional numbers than the mice but weren't provided with the abundance the rodents received. Nah, it was much worse than simply 'not providing', they were robbed of actual necessities.

After building these towering domiciles, the government completely welched on providing very basic services to the community. Smackdab in the middle of the sweltering-summered Midwest, the A/C units didn't work in the skyscrapers. Quick physics note: heat rises. Do you know what kind of 'hot' those mutha fuckas could be? So, you have a bunch of Black people under the stress of poverty that are hot and irritable every day. That's not exactly a recipe for success, no matter the race of people.

Then, in these heavily populated skyscrapers, the heating systems failed regularly in the frigid winter. Not having heat was a dire crisis during the extensive colder Missouri months. Even the elevators broke down often. This forced the disgruntled masses to travel, in close proximity, up and down crowded stairwells for nine, ten and eleven stories on a daily basis.

Now, there's a true nugget of complete and utter failure: the fucking elevators. Their 'brilliant' design did not include an ability for the human transport to service every floor. There was some shitty thought that such an elevator would cause 'rider congestion' that would make life in the tall tower more uncomfortable. So, they programmed them to only open on every third floor, requiring people to walk the stairwells for all of the levels between stops. Apparently, they thought congested and non-temperature-controlled stairwells, with people uncomfortably forced to trudge them, would be more desirable. I would love to meet the mutha fucka who thought this was smart.

Unfortunately, the design was so bogus that it often failed completely, causing the tenants to walk up and down the entire building. The trash services also weren't maintained so the place became ridiculously rank and disgustingly unsanitary. It seemed like they were literally trying to make us live with mice.

It may sound like hyperbole but that shit is real. After being vacated for frozen pipes, one of the buildings was left vacant for two years. True, it provided a space for desperate homeless people – not because they trying to do them any favors, mind you. But do you know what else was going to exist in that space? Rodents. Rats were able to thrive without contest. Right in the middle of the projects.

So, you have droves of Black people living in poverty who are hot and sweaty or freezing and irritated, but you force them to walk up and down countless flights of stairs in a smelly building. Every day. They also had to deal with 'Ratatouille Towers' next door, with trash overflowing everywhere to draw them near and keep them thriving.

That's that bullshit.

There was no early plan for a dedicated local police service at all. Remember, the vision was to fill the projects with middle-class white people. So, there were no integrated police stations in the plan nor was there a design to have patrols for the community. That meant the police presence was sparing, at best. That was, of course, the plan because they treat white people differently. By the time it all came unglued, law enforcement was afraid to go in. Even when they were called for emergencies the cops wouldn't dare to enter the buildings. So, after sparking a powder keg, they left the people to fend for themselves.

They set us up for failure in a proven maze of death.

Remember the bit about the mice turning on themselves after several generations? Well, the Webbes were built in the 1950's. My siblings and I moved in them around 1974. Black people were quite a few generations into the Webbes before we arrived. Crammed into that space, just like the mice, our people had already turned on ourselves like a mutha fucka.

Now, maybe you're thinking there's no racial spite. Right? I mean, they built the first of these buildings for middle class white people, right? There's no way there's an intent to harm the Black population. It just went sour by... let's call it 'coincidence'. And maybe there was no link to the experiment and the housing. Maybe the government developers weren't aware of the government research that forecasted the inevitable catastrophes. Why not?

You'd have to then explain why the vicious failure of this system was repeated in metropolitan areas across the country. New York, Detroit, Chicago; what is the level of coincidence that these particular cities, high in Black population, all received similar government housing? Think a little further: how similar is the failure of their governmental regulatory systems? The trash, the architecture (with plumbing and temperature controls, etc.) and the police involvement – what do they have in common? Last thought; how similar are the outcomes of these projects? How similar are they one to another and to the Mouse Utopia Experiment?

Once you add up all of that, you get it. Either that or you're lying to yourself. These are not mistakes. It's the repercussion of a system that values some people and discounts others. A system designed to divide people and classify some as 'less than'. One that has created a class system, a caste system while snowing it's people into believing it doesn't exist.

We know it does. It's real than a mutha fucka.

We lived on the 9th floor, the top floor of our building. The Webbe buildings across the street had twelve floors. It was a big deal living up that high. There were no parks or playgrounds inside the building, I'm sure y'all know that. You had to go outside for that. So, I had to watch life happen from the ninth floor or go outside.

When you went outside you were going to have to fight. Straight up. There were some dudes hanging out just to get into shit with people. You had to face them and anybody else that came up with some bullshit. I refused to be stuck in the crib so I went out and fought all the time. It would've been cool if all we had to face were knuckleheads who wanted to fight. It wasn't.

As a kid, I've seen people take flight out of the Webbe windows on frequent occasion. Because they were thrown out. Yeah, it was a typical day for me to watch the process of murder get carried out. It was normal to leave the building and have to walk around a splattered body that found out, the hard way, they didn't have wings. I still have vivid images of brains disseminated across the walkway. I can still clearly see bodies with broken bones protruding through the skin.

We stayed in Olympic-level shape taking the damn stairs up and down the entire building when the elevators were broken - nine fucking floors each way! That sucked ass. But it was leagues better than waiting for the elevator doors to open to a dead body. Few things make your blood start pumping like looking at a fresh carcass, riddled with bullets, blood rapidly coloring the elevator floor. It's not a rare thing that the elevators were inoperable because they were cleaning out bodily remains. Between that and the shitty design, we got real familiar with the stairwells.

Living there was gruesome as fuck but we couldn't avoid the shit. Even when we played between the buildings we would have to jump over corpses just to play tag or hide and seek. It was traumatic as hell to deal with dead people all the time. But, like all things, repeated exposure creates the mundane. Seeing dead people was as regular as taking a shower at night. So, we just got used to it. That's a terrible thing to say about deceased human beings, an even worse life to live, but that was the Webbes for you. You dealt with foul shit and kept pushing. That's just what it was.

So, yeah, I grew up in the Webbes but I wasn't born there. We moved in there with our grandmother when I was 5 years old. She became our sole guardian and the hero of my life. How did we land there? Well, it was basically the hardest time of my life. There's no easy way to put it because it was a... devastating tragedy. Still, those words pale to the reality. There is no way to express it in a phrase that will address the gravity of it. I actually don't want to tell you about it because I don't want it to be real.

No kid would. Sadly, it is real. And undeniable. So... when I was 6 years old, my older brother and I...

...watched our mother commit suicide.

We never received any kind of official therapy. I mean, social services and shit like that exists, allegedly, to help people through stuff like that. Especially children. Right? But, again, the system we're in doesn't give a flying fuck about us. Basically we were told to get over it. No damned empathy or humanity at all! Dawg, you don't tell a 5 year old and a 9 year old to 'just get over' watching their mom...

So, we did what we were forced to do. We moved on. In fact, we relocated into the Webbes afterwards and experienced death steadily. Fortunately, we were guided by my Granny. She made sure we couldn't be easily broken by raising us to have steely hearts. We simply learned to cope with the loss of life and to keep moving. It kind of kept us unaffected by things. None of it compared with losing my mother, of course. That was...

I'm not going into any further detail than that. I don't need to. Everything you're thinking about how difficult it must have been means less than shit. Whatever you have in mind I GUARANTEE YOU the reality was worse. Incalculably worse.

So, we don't focus on it. We didn't focus on it then. Moving forward was the only remedy. We couldn't afford anything else anyways. There were four of us that moved in with my grandmother; my older brother, me and our younger twins. She lived in the Webbes because she couldn't afford to be somewhere else. Having the four of us there certainly wasn't a help. So, we struggled together. We hustled together. And we lived.

Together.

The stress of our situations affected us all differently. My little brother and sister, the twins, they had to grow up without ever getting to know their mother. That's a lot to deal with. Consequently, they were the baddest kids in the neighborhood! They got into and tore up shit all the time. It's like they would invent new ways to fuck up stuff. They were a straight pair of baby hellions, dawg.

They got their butts tore up daily! If it wasn't one of them it was both of them. They were always into something they had no business getting into at all. Granny lit them up for cutting up every day.

My older brother and I got toughened in the streets, dealing with the project life. The twins got tempered by Granny for being hardheaded as hell. You gotta respect their gangsta: getting their asses kicked didn't even slow them down. They weren't bad because they got away with doing shit. Both of them got caught for almost everything they did and they would get lit up for all of it. They didn't quit, though, and Granny didn't either. They respected Granny but nothing else. That's what kept their asses in trouble. They were some bad little jokers. For real.

My big brother? He went cold and laser-focused as manhood came early for him. When we arrived at my Granny's, he was the oldest male on deck. It made him become a provider at 9 years old by default. He had to make bread (money) for the family, by any and every means necessary. Nothing else mattered to him. He hustled on the street and brought money to the house.

It didn't stop him from being a nice guy, though. He was a caring provider. If he knew you, he would look out for you. The family credo is 'if I'm going to eat, we're all going to eat'. Granny definitely set the tone but my brother made the credo breathe every day. That's how he handled life.

Now, don't be foolish enough think that means he cared for every-body. He didn't. And he was ruthless. When my brother didn't know you then he didn't give a fuck to know you. If you had something he wanted or valued then he would have what you had, y'know what I mean? He unabashedly cared for all of us and proved it by putting us before everything. Himself, any other people, laws - you name it. We were first with him.

So, my brother fought with everything he had to provide for the family. The twins fought against everything and everybody. Meanwhile, our grandmother fought to take care of us. One minute she was an empty-nested grandparent and the next she had a house full. She had to deal with the life adjustment of losing her daughter by raising us. All of us had a lot to deal with.

We were truly blessed to have Granny. She taught us to have tough skin. She didn't really give us time to mourn either because, candidly, that wasn't going to do anything for us. We had to live, she was busy getting us on with that.

Granny ran her house like a military camp. She was a serious ass drill sergeant, straight up. We lived a tough life in a tough place so we were going to be tough, there were no options. She didn't afford us any.

And, part of the reason for that military comparison, Granny was a fervent believer in corporal punishment. If you got disrespectful she was going to draw blood. She had a backhand that was wicked as hell. It was fast and accurate. You'd catch one in your mouth before you finished a sentence. She was having none of that shit. My grandmother was an old school disciplinarian.

Real quick: so, Granny always made us do chores, right? Three things were always going to happen: we were going to be 1) clean, 2) responsible and we were going to 3) respect her and everything she said. At least, that's what we did if we didn't want to get lit up.

So, my chore was to take the trash out every night. Well, every day after boxing practice, we would go downstairs in the recreational center and we played basketball. Well, this particular day we played until the 'Rec closed. I walked home and got into the house hungry. Granny had left some food in the oven for me, she was dope like that. I warmed that up a little bit and grubbed.

You now know, and I definitely knew, that I was supposed to be taking the trash out. That's what I was responsible for handling, right? My Granny had a pet peeve about it and I was tasked to take care of it. Right? Well, by the time I got finished eating I didn't want to go to the first floor to throw away the trash. So, I called myself trying to be slick: I checked on Granny's room and saw that she was asleep. So I went to bed, too! I figured 'it'll be fine if I just take it down tomorrow'. I thought I was good, fell right to sleep.

THWACK! THWACK! THWACK! THWACK-THWACK-THWACK! SMACK!!!

At 2:00 am, I woke up with singeing pain travelling like lightning through my shoulder blades and my ass was on fire! My Granny had lit up my whole backside, in my sleep, with a broomstick. She was vicious as hell with that thing. I got hit more than just a few times, I'm sure it sounded like a damned drum solo.

"What's wrong, what's going on? What I do?" I screamed out.

I was panicked, aching and clueless. She caught me in full REM sleep. Was probably on sheep number sixty-something. I was in deep, you know what I'm sayin'? Have you ever awakened without any bearing on where you were? You try to focus on something you recognize but you still feel like you're in a foreign country in your dream at the same time? Yeah, I was doing that shit except my back was killing me! My eyes were rapidly scanning all over the room like I was looking for the whole group of people who had attacked me or something. I thought I would see the Baseball Furies from the Warriors movie, or some shit.

Granny was standing there pissed, holding that broom in her hand like a ninja fighting staff. The handle end was high in the sky, ready to strike again.

"Get your butt up and take that trash downstairs. Right now!"

The fire in her eyes was terrifying.

"Yes ma'am!" I said.

I ran out of my room, grabbed the trash and started speed walking towards the door. I had to go down all nine flights of stairs and all the way back up.

At 2:00 in the morning.

In some of the worst projects in all of St. Louis!

I hit those steps like Carl Lewis! I rounded those staircases so fast that I was half-way dizzy by the time I got to the first floor. I swear I was hyperventilating. When I got outside to the dumpsters, it was dark as fuck. And terrifying! I knew there were rats running 'round and shit. It was mad creepy.

Now, I was glad I hadn't crossed a dead body. That would've been trippy as hell in the dark. That's next-level-trauma type stuff. Not seeing one was cool but I didn't want to become one, either. So, I was trying to move my feet as fast as my heartbeat. All the way down and back up the stairs. Shit.

I was living with some serious levels of PTSD. No doubt. Dead bodies were frequent enough in my life to make me think about them even when I wasn't seeing them. So, that 'zero dark thirty' half-sleep sprint through the gauntlet felt more like an 'Indiana Jones' movie than it probably should have. That didn't stop it from being scary as shit.

Because of that, I wasn't about to walk all the way over to the dumpsters – fuck that! When I got close enough, I threw that bag in the general direction and ran my ass off. I didn't know if it made it in the dumpster or not. Before it landed, I had already turned around and was running my ass off again. Man, fuck that trash.

That was some of the scariest shit I ever did as a kid. In the wee hours, I had to survive the Temple of Doom *and* return to my broom-wielding, angry Granny. She was my real fear. Granny didn't play, dawg. She meant what she said and you weren't going to disrespect her, not in any form! It was crude as hell but effective than a mutha fucka. I was eight years old when that happened and I never tried to pull any shit like that again on my grandmother.

Granny was the cognoscente of hygiene and her house was going to be clean. Flat out! Dishes were always going to be washed after they were used and trash was going out every day. Every. Day. She didn't like it in the house. I found out, the hard way, how much she meant that. Believe me when I say it, that lesson was well learned.

My grandmother heaped responsibility on our shoulders, too. It was her theory that we could handle it so she made us handle it. It was also another way to keep us focused and engaged. She handed us responsibilities then held us accountable to her high expectations.

So, Granny wouldn't wake us up for school. Her philosophy was you knew what you had to do daily - do it. Period. If she had to wake you up it was going to be with her Bruce Lee broom handle skills. You were going to arrive at school with some knots on your head. Like I said, that lady wasn't playing.

She was an extraordinary and amazing woman, though. Our circumstances had no effect on her spirit. My granny was beautiful inside and out. She was always upbeat, I never saw her downtrodden. And she had a fantastic sense of humor. She kept us laughing in the house all the time. I definitely got my sense of humor from her. She was an inspirational blue print for many facets of my life.

CHAPTER 26

MULTI-TASKER

Everything that I value about myself came from my grandmother. That includes being incredibly well-mannered. She instilled that in all of us with her relentless 'taking no disrespect' thing. The opposite of that, of course, is respect and admiration. We certainly had an inexhaustible amount of that for Granny. My sister, my brothers and I were taught to have love for all our elders and we were always courteous. All of that is directly due to our grandmother's influence.

My mean streak came from Granny, too. I figure, If I'm gonna tell you the good stuff then I might as well tell it all. She had that unmistakable fire of fury inside of her. I'm sure it was a 'don't mistake my kindness for weakness' kind of self-preservation. She wouldn't pull the beast out wantonly, you had to earn that lashing. Whenever it welled up, though, you could virtually see it but you did NOT want to physically see it. It would be terribly ugly for you when you did.

I discovered my testy temper when I was really young. I had a full galaxy worth of innate issues boiling under the surface of my skin. It only took one idiot to show me how to channel it. Said idiot revealed himself in the second grade.

When we arrived in the Webbes, I went to Peabody Elementary School. The class bully tried to come for me on my first day. Surprise, surprise right? That's what bullies do. He had to try to put 'the new guy' in check in a hurry. The problem for him was that I wasn't *that* new guy. He didn't know I was uncheckable but he found out quick.

He tried to flex on me, running his mouth. I guess he thought he was going to embarrass and punk me, like he did them other kids. I stood up the minute he started flapping his gums. I didn't wait 'til the bell rang or after school or none of that shit. I walked over and hit him with a quick two-piece: BOP-BOP!

Dropped his ass.

That was the last time we needed to have that conversation. One of the kids in class was Donny Don. He was tripping on it. He saw me put the bully on his face and invited me to the ring. Donny Don was like,

> "You gotta go with us to the boxing center after school, dawg!"

I went to check it out and got hooked. It was a place where the hungry came and it was usually packed. If you arrived in the middle of the day it could take an hour before you got a rope. There were some real fucking boxers in that gym! Shit, the sparring sessions were usually better than the advertised fights! It was a helluva gym to be in and it kept me driven.

You've heard of Leon and Michael Spinks, right? They were the first pair of brothers to win gold medals in the Olympics. They are sons of St. Louis who worked out in my gym. There were 12 different weight classes to box in. Fighters from our gym won 7 or 8 Golden Gloves championships annually. Straight up, it was like a successful boxing factory. I was in a good ass gym.

I got into boxing and loved it. It was the perfect place to take out some aggressions, anger and anguish. You could just let it all go with the snap of your gloves. It was really therapeutic for me. I was able to sort out that mean streak Granny gave me and not land in a cell somewhere, too. In fact, sports became one of the ways I stayed focused on moving forward in life. They gave me balance.

But I always focused on family. That never changed. What did change about it, though, was my definition of family. Living in a cutthroat environment, when everything around you was fucked up, trust was limited. The people you did trust became family and y'all stuck together. You didn't count on anything or anyone else.

Granny, my brother and the twins were my first family. Everything about our struggle made us closer. We bonded together through our challenges. It certainly taught me the value of my personal circle. That became my personal mantra: my circle was my family. Nothing has ever been more important to me than taking care of my family.

This extended to the Webbes. My fellas that I ran with in the projects were my family, too. Hell, the bond was damned near the same: we went through all kinds of bullshit in the projects together, too! Donny Don was one of my first dudes in the Webbes. I rolled with him, Roostah and a few other cats kinda tough.

We played together, did our dirt together, went boxing and sometimes we hustled together. We had each other's back when anything went down. So, we didn't fuck with anybody else and they couldn't join the circle. If you weren't from the Webbes we thought you weren't shit. And we'd probably whip your ass or rob you. Maybe both.

Most of the times, I was the ringleader of the crew. Nah, I'm being modest. They always looked to me when we made decisions to do shit. Some of it could have been because I was a prototypical leader. I've been built kind of big my whole life, I was afraid of nothing (except Granny) and I had a right cross that put mutha fuckas down. I was wild, too, and that made shit fun. They never knew what we would get into when they were rolling with me. So, yeah, the crew was all about kicking it with me since I was low level crazy. But those weren't the reasons I led the posse.

I've always cared about everybody. Well, what I mean is, I looked out for everybody that was down with me. Taking care of my family at such a young age put me in a space where I had to always see more than myself. I had to be concerned with everybody's welfare. That's not a thing I could stop.

So, if you rolled with me, I looked out for you. All my fellas were like my little brothers. Anybody fucked with my brothers then they fucked with me. That's just how I operated. There was some inherent leadership in that disposition.

I used to love kicking it with the fellas but I never lost focus. Hustling was mandatory! Living in the Webbes meant you didn't have much, that's what produced some real hustlers. Like they say, necessity is the mother of invention. Or reinvention, because it certainly made my brother and me reinvent ourselves to make money.

My older brother and I were hustling basically the moment we moved there. I started out collecting cans and bottles to recycle them for change. It wasn't much but I was adding to a nearly empty pot – every bit helped.

Traversing our building could be cumbersome for the elderly – all that going 'up and down' was a lot. So, I would knock on elderly women's doors to see if they wanted me to shop at the store for them. I would introduce myself as my grandmother's grandson and they would give me the loot to shop for them. After a while, they started calling the house, putting orders in.

"Tell your grandson to come on down. I need him to go to the store for me."

This was killing two birds with one stone. Shopping for them, I made a little change and helped out the elderly at the same time. Worked out well for everybody involved.

When I was around 10 years old, I started shining shoes at the diamond. Baseball was, and is still, huge in St. Louis. People from all over the city continue to go out to support the 'Cards. The foot traffic was nuts on game days, there were crowds were all over the place. That made it easy: when you know where all the people will be then that's where you set up camp to make money. I would grab my kit and head to the park a couple hours before the game. I worked until all my supplies ran out or until everybody left the premises.

I'll tell you what I thought was a cool part of my grind: I built my own shoeshine box in school. I had an industrial arts class in the 6th grade and my first project helped me elevate my hustle game. The class itself was an indicator that the whole city was down for the grind, for real. Well, at least I can say that for our side of town. I was proud of my shoe box. It helped create a sense of ownership for me and added an element of legitimacy to what I was doing.

Making money was serious shit so I handled it like that all the time. I started my hustle with a brush, neutral polish, a t-shirt and a towel. Before long, I upgraded to brown, cordovan and black polish and added some edge dressing to my services. My shoeshine game was tight and I made significantly more bucks than my recycling and delivery hustles. Shoeshine money was real money.

I would take any loot I made straight to Granny. I told y'all, money was scarce and Granny and the twins had to eat. So, my brother and I made sure we looked out for the house first.

Speaking of we: my big brother had a grind, too. At some point he copped a pistol from somewhere and put it to work. There was a truck stop behind the White Castles in the neighborhood. He would go there and rob white boys so the family could eat. My brother never tried to rob any Black people, that I know about. That was his regular hustle, though. He and I had different paths and different means, for sure. But the focus was the same for both of us - providing. The paths mattered, though, and it wasn't long before we went completely different directions.

His path took him to jail. We all know that's how that shit works. He got caught breaking into houses and went to jail for almost 7 years. I was ten years old. That left me as the man of the house, basically. Between the two of us, we were keeping the family floating. Once he went to jail that changed my dynamic a lot.

Soon I graduated from shoe shining to ticket scalping. It was a quicker hustle and a much more lucrative effort to get money. Our household needed that. Fortunately, baseball has really long seasons. I was able to make money pretty steadily.

All the while, I stayed productive in school and I rocked sports to keep me sane. My gift in sports was that I hated to lose more than I loved winning. Most of the greatest athletes in sports history will tell you the same. If you want to be any kind of champion, you gotta hate losing. It's a different level of determination. This philosophy made me a fierce athlete.

I was a super solid baseball player. I was even better at football. Boxing was home, though. There was nothing like squaring off in the ring and chopping a dude down. Whenever I had the opportunity to get inside those ropes I would lace them up and get out there.

My whole focus in the ring was to brutalize guys foolish enough to get inside the ropes with me. I strategized, too. Of course I could box with a scheme, stick to a game plan and all that. But if I could put you down with one punch then you were out of there. You can bet your ass, I'm testing that chin the minute we square off.

I was always looking to put dudes away. I had a simple philosophy: leave no doubt. If the ref is picking a dude up off the canvas, the verdict is clear. I never wanted the decision to be in the judges' hands. I made the bout decisions by knocking mutha fuckas out.

And I had no problems taking a punch. That's a mandatory prereq-uisite to being a brute in the ring - you gotta have a strong chin. Likewise, there was a guy or two who really tried to give it to me.

Actually, a whole bunch of guys that got in the ropes thought they were bruisers. They didn't have skills, talent or decent training. What they did have was misguided confidence in their power and weak chins. Their whole plan was to brutalize somebody into submission early. That way they didn't have to box, they wouldn't need stamina and could win on raw strength.

Mike Tyson said it best, "everybody has a plan until they get hit." The difference between me and most of those guys is that I could take a punch. That's where I made my money: I'd take everything they could dish out just to get them close and overconfident. Then they would get to take a nap... when I knocked the snot out of them.

I was nasty in the ring. Straight up. I won more than a few city tour-naments and the neighborhood started calling me 'Champ'. Unfortunately, we didn't have championship belts in St. Louis back in the 70's and 80's or I would've been wearing a few. I would've made sure of it. It sucks that I didn't do any travelling, I would have loved to fight for some belts. This would've never worked for my schedule because I was always doing at least two sports year round. So, I couldn't afford to leave town like that. Taking care of my family also kept my focus on my local life.

My freshman year I went to the "V", Vashon High School. We had moved out of the Webbes that year and the V was the closest school to the new place. So, for the first time in my life, I wound up running with cats that weren't from the Webbes. Black Bruce, Boobie, Greyhouse and Mr.

Popular (y'all know him as Poppy) were my dogs at the V. All of us were freshmen so we settled into the school together. Those were my dudes, we hung pretty tight that year.

Other than hustling for my family, sports were the only constant I really had. Believe, I planned to put my mark on the school the minute I walked through their front door. I was psyched out: nobody was going to be in my league. The sport didn't matter, I was going to be that dude in everything I played.

You know the movie 'The Replacements'? "The football is like a one-man Cold to Clifford Franklin. Clifford Franklin the only man catching it, Clifford Franklin the only man coming down with it." (12) No shit, I bet you they wrote that line after watching my games. I'm the real life Clifford Franklin. I was a 6'2", 220 pound wide receiver. I snatched the ball out of the sky like I was mad at it. They couldn't do shit with me on the field.

Alright, they probably didn't write that movie line after me but they should've. I was flat out balling. The first season my stats were monstrous. Everybody knew I had a bright career ahead of me at the V.

Until I wasn't at the V. After one year away from them, we landed right back into the Webbes. This time we were on the 2nd floor, which was vastly better than the 9th floor, but it was the same shit. Life was straight up tight in the Webbes, it just was. It woke me up, though. I redoubled my hustle and recentered my focus.

My sophomore year was particularly tough. Since I had transferred from a conference school, I had to sit out a football season. I was salty as hell that I couldn't play ball but I dealt with that. I wasn't exactly happy about going back to the Webbes, either. It's already understood, my life didn't let me 'sit out' shit and 'happy' wasn't really a part of my math. So, I just got busy handling the transition.

With the extra time I had, I dug in on scalping tickets. Baseball plays until October, even further when we're in the playoffs. The tickets could have a high yield so I focused on keeping a steady flow of income there.

The next school year, I was able to play football. I met Coach Johns the year before and I guess I made the right impressions. It was my first year playing for him and he placed me directly on the varsity squad. I made sure the coach was glad as hell he put me on it. I went to work immediately.

First game? I had six receptions for 100 plus yards and a touchdown. Balling! I played like I was mad at the district for making me sit out a year. That Monday, my picture was on the front page of the Southside Journal. Everybody was talking about me. People were giving me love up and down the halls in school and everything. I was riding high as hell.

A brother's head was swollen! I was getting cocky as hell. My whole vibe shifted to, "I'm the man in this mutha fucka!" My coach peeped it and hollered at me. He told me,

> "Don't let this get to your head. That's what ruins careers, son. Stay focused and keep working. That's how you succeed in this game and in life. Keep working. Always keep working."

That man got nothing but respect from me. He became a real life mentor for me.

Now, Busara started at McKinley High the same year I did. He arrived as a freshman, though, and it was my sophomore year. I knew him but we weren't, like, super cool because I didn't roll with him then. Particularly not before high school. He wasn't from the Webbes. And, like I told y'all, we thought everybody else was soft. Shit, we used to beat dudes up from the Peabody and take their loot.

Real shit: the hottest fast food joint in the 'hood was White Castles. Everybody would buy them because they were open 24 hours and they were super cheap. You could get a meal with a drink for $3 and be good. Shit, if you had $2 you could get two burgers, some fries and still have change. Real cheap shit. That was on point for all of us because we didn't have a bunch of money anyways.

Well, White Castles was next door to the Webbes. Sadly for those Peabody mutha fuckas, they were on the other side of us from the restaurant. If they cut through the Webbes it would only take like ten minutes, they'd be right there. But they knew if they did that, the Webbes would cut through them and they might not make it at all. Best case scenario, they'd make it home broke with a bevy of lumps, burst lips and black eyes. We made them walk all the way around the projects, an extra twenty minutes or so, to get their food. And they had better have eaten it in the restaurant if they wanted to have any! Like I said, soft.

Once I joined the McKinley team, all of that changed with Busara. Playing ball is about sticking together and turning the odds in your favor with the team working as one.

Everything about that jibed with my life perspective. So, when Busara and I were on the same football team we became brothers. That's just how it was. It was cool because he was a thorough dude, anyways. He wasn't exactly 'Webbes hard' but he wasn't no punk. I looked out for him like a little brother and we rolled like that from then on.

As I told y'all, my football coach, Coach Johns, was one of my earliest male mentors. He was a good man. A whole bunch of things about him resonated with me. Just being a coach, he had disciplines and tenacity that I respected. He also saw me when I arrived at the school. I mean, he could tell what I was about and regarded me as a young leader. We hit it off right from the jump. Through the years, he put more than a few good words in my ear. That man was frequently throwing wisdom my way and I always listened.

Coach Johns was an alumnus of Knoxville College. It's a historically Black college in Knoxville, Tennessee. I had never heard of it before he told me about it. Hell, I hadn't heard of Knoxville either, quietly. I certainly didn't know shit about it. We had an awesome senior year on the field but I wasn't really prepared for the next level. I hadn't either committed to a school or made any plans.

After my senior year ended, I was working the streets. I stayed focused on looking out for the fam. My brother got out of jail that winter and he hit the streets, too. We tag teamed again to make sure our family was squared away. I didn't have plans to stay in the streets, that's not at all what I wanted to do. I just didn't have any other plans and I had learned to not pay a lot of attention to 'wants', either.

My mind was on money. So, I was basically resigned to skipping college. To me, that was just a place to go in to debt. We needed money. There was no way for us to afford tuition. So, I thought about going in the military or something. I just hadn't pulled the trigger on it.

Later that summer, Coach Johns called me up. He was on a mission. He said,

> "Hey, you gotta get outta these projects, man! I just got finished talking to the KC football coach. He said he'd put a scholarship together for you. I told him you would be on your way". He meant it.

Three days later, I was on a bus heading to Knoxville.
It was August, 1987.

CHAPTER 27
WORK STUDY

I didn't know a soul on the bus and that stayed real when I got to campus. I didn't know anybody. To make it worse, I had arrived for football camp: the campus was damned near empty. Football players, band members and cheerleaders were the only people at the school. It damned near felt like a ghost town most of the time.

There were only a few of us there so you really couldn't move around incognito. That made it really easy to meet people and really hard to avoid people, if you were trying to do that. You saw the same faces every single day.

Even though there were very few people on campus, things were already segregated. The old football heads rolled in one crew, the freshmen in another. The band members stuck to themselves and the cheerleaders were always guarded by their coaches. It was not a party.

I arrived a little late. The team had been there almost two weeks when I showed up. Things had already been set in motion so I went with the flow as much as I could. My roommate was also a freshman, he was from Texas. He was a cool cat, no drama or nothing like that.

I wound up rolling with the freshmen football players, obviously. It was cool, though. I didn't sweat rolling with the new cats on campus, shit, I was one of them. So, we stuck together. We ate together in the cafeteria and rolled as a unit after practice.

Old heads were big on trying to bully or haze the freshmen. They were always doing little shit, y'know? Trying to punk the fellas. I saw some sideways shit right off the rip and it had to stop. My code is universal: if you roll with me we're brothers. Brothers are family and nobody punks my family. So, I put an end to that shit real quick.

My first confrontation happened when I was standing with a crew of freshmen. One of the dudes from the offensive line walked over to us with a super shitty look on his face. I'm sure he thought he was mean mugging but he looked more like he ate some bad Mexican food and had a porcelain date coming. I was just about to laugh at him then he opened his stupid ass mouth.

"Wassup?"

Sounds like a harmless question, right? But dude's tone was disrespectful. And this mutha fucka had the nerve to do, like, a half-flinch at us. As if he was going to startle somebody. He didn't know he was asking for a time out. Dude had a baby chin. Looked like he never had a real fight in his life. I would've put his ass in a quick nap, no problem.

This is that shit you gotta check the minute it comes up. You can't let mutha fuckas come at you like he was trying to come at me. And I'm from the Webbes, he had me completely fucked up!

I stepped toward him, waiting for him to say some wrong shit.

"Bet' not a mutha fuckin' thing be up! What the fuck you mean, wassup?" I fired back at him.

He had me resorting to some old project-type shit. "School" didn't have a damned thing to do with where my mind was right then. If he was dumb enough to follow that up with the wrong shit, I was fully prepared

414

to ride that school-to-prison pipeline. Things on him were about to be broken - "things" as in plural! He had no idea who he was fucking with. Don't come at me with that bullshit.

He cocked his head back, startled by my moxie. He tried to play it off with a fake ass laugh.

"Heh-heh. I was just fuckin with y'all, man. Wassup?" He said.

I shot right back at him, "I'm a grown ass man. I ain't trying to be fucked with by no dude. You on some gay shit? Is this a school or prison?"

He stood there trying to figure out how to save face. I wasn't about to let him do that. He needed to smell that bullshit he was shoveling.

"And I don't know you, dawg. You ain't got to fucking talk to me at all, quietly. You can go on 'bout your fucking way." I added.

Another thing about the 'Lou; we weren't that kind of friendly. At home, people you don't know typically didn't talk to you. Normally that was 'fighting words' -type shit. Nobody says it's reasonable, that's just how it was at the crib. That mutha fucka was making me homesick.

Suffice it to say, dude went on his damned way. I had never been about taking anybody's shit but he pushed it to another level. My 'big brother' game became my way of life at school. I was going to stomp out every bit of bullshit I saw on the Yard from then on. Nobody with me was ever going to get punked when I was around. Period.

Turns out, bullshit was going to keep me busy. That following Saturday morning, we were walking to brunch at the Caf' (that's the cafeteria. There was only one on campus). Some upper classmen were standing on the porch of a dorm we passed. As soon as we went by them, one of them shouted out:

"That nigga from St. Louis think he tough."

I didn't take another step towards the 'Caf. I told the fellas I was with to 'hold up a minute'. Then I turned around.

At first, I would've just been content not letting them fuck with my fellas. But this mutha fucka made shit personal, tried to call *me* out. Well, that meant I had to go looking for a problem because I had every problem with anybody calling me out. That shit was not happening.

I started walking towards the biggest one in the group. In front of me was one of the team captains and a porch full of upperclassmen football players. I walked into the face of the biggest shit talker.

I walked up to him and put my hand in his face.

"Bitch ass nigga, I ain't tough but ain't none of you bitches gone fuck with me! Now what?"

I was mere inches from his nose. He replied quickly as hell.

"Aw, I ain't say it."
"Nigga, I thought so." I said.

He didn't say shit else. Neither did anybody else on the porch.
My freshmen crew started egging it on, instigating.

"OOOOH! Damn! Oh shit!"

All of that was bullshit. I told the freshmen,

"All y'all need to shut the hell up. If the upperclassmen woulda jumped me, all of y'all woulda just ran."

They all played ball, so they were in great shape. But they weren't about to fight nobody. There wasn't one real fighter in the freshman bunch. Those dudes were soft as hell and I'll tell you how I know.

The old heads had this shit they did called 'Greasing'. This was that bullshit, I'm telling you. They would get the RA's master key to get into the dorm rooms late at night. Some of them were RA's, so it wasn't hard for them to do. They would break in the rooms while freshmen were asleep - this is a whole bunch of mutha fuckas, now. A whole group of them. They would hold down freshmen and squeeze lotion into their underwear.

I'm going to run that back to make sure y'all understand: they illegally broke into a guy's room while he was sleeping. Pulled down his sheets. Held him in place. They put their hands on that dudes' drawls, while he was wearing them! Then squeezed or pumped lotion into them!

And that was... fun?

What in the actual fuck?!

First of all, who even thought of that gay ass shit? What did you have to be doing, what were you into that would make you think of violating another man like that? Second, why would you want to put your hands on another man's drawls? Ever! Particularly while he was wearing them! I know, sooner or later, *somebody* was touching another cat's dick. It's just the law of averages. You couldn't pay me to do no shit like that. Lastly, how in the hell do you do it so often that someone gave it a name? That was the gayest shit I had ever heard of any guys doing at that point in my life. And this was a bunch of football players.

This was a fucked up thing that they only did to freshmen, which would be all the cats I rolled with. So, naw! The dudes who watched me stand up to the upperclassmen weren't about to fight anybody or they would never have let that bullshit happen to them.

I wish one of them old head mutha fuckas would have come at me with that shit. When I found out about it, I stood at my door and yelled down the dorm hallways. I told 'em,

> "Let me tell you this: I'm leaving my door wide open. Every night! Y'all don't need the master key. Any one of y'all come in this mutha fucka you dying."

You 'best believe I meant just what the fuck I said. That was all they needed to know I wasn't for that bullshit. If they ever tried to fuck with my roommate they weren't gonna make it out of my room alive, either. That I know of, my roommate and I were the only freshman that didn't get greased that season. Not 'nan mutha fucka ever came in my room with that. I was having none of it. None. Pisses me off just thinking about it.

Around two weeks after I arrived at KC, a charter bus rolled up onto campus one evening. It had St. Louis written on its marquee. I was as happy as a runaway slave that found freedom. I was the only person on campus from St. Louis until then. I ran over to the bus to see what was up.

Who was the first person to get off? Black Bruce! Poppy was right behind him. There were a bunch of Vashon high school grads on the bus with them. I was happy as hell, the crib had arrived!

Out of all of them, I knew Black Bruce the best. We had more than a few classes together in the year I spent at the V. I didn't know Poppy, really, but I was familiar with him. I didn't have any classes with him and I only spent that one year at Vashon. But he was cool so everything was everything (it was fine). I helped them get their stuff off the bus but Poppy didn't want to move his luggage another inch.

A whole bunch of them got off the bus hot! Knoxville College was not remotely what they expected the higher education experience to be. All of the red clay dirt roads and the worn down campus was too much for them. Or not enough for them, all depending on how you wanna look at it. A huge mass of them said they wanted to go back home immediately. The bus they came on was returning to St. Louis in the morning. Most of the people that got off the bus said they were getting back on it to go home.

Including Black Bruce and Poppy. Poppy was much more vocal about it than Black Bruce but neither one of them was feeling it.

"This some bullshit hurr, dawg!" Poppy said.

"For real. Ain't we supposed to be at a fucking school?" Black Bruce threw out.

"That's what I'm sayin'. This shit hurr look like we landed in the projects with books, dawg." Poppy replied. He continued. "Look at them mutha fuckas right thurr."

He was pointing at the local projects in front of the school. They were a complex filled with two-story structures.

Poppy continued, "that's supposed to be our school neighbors, dawg? Ole country bumpkin-ass village huts and shit! That shit ova thurr look like Carr Square Village, dawg. They busted like a mutha fucka, man. Fuck this place, dawg, I'm going home."

"Well, y'all stuck here until the morning, bo-aah (boy). This same bus goes back tomorrow," I responded. "We need to get y'all shit out the street. We can put it in my room until then."

"Bo-aah, I'm getting out of this bitch in the morning, bo-aah." Poppy declared.

All of the luggage was off the bus and people were grabbing their things. Poppy caught the young bus driver walking back on to the bus.

"Excuse me, what time you leaving in the morning, dawg?" Poppy asked him.

"I'll be here at 6:00am and I'm leaving the campus at 7:00 sharp heading back to St. Louis." The bus driver said.

"Thank you. I'll see you then, dawg." Poppy said to the bus driver then turned around talking to Black Bruce. "We ain't got shit to do. Let's get fucked up, dawg."

We went to the dorm and carried their stuff to my room. Poppy immediately started talking about going to the store. So, we locked their stuff up in the room then headed out of the dorm.

When we walked out of the front door, we ran into one of the guys I knew from Detroit, Leon. He was standing on the porch smoking a cigarette.

"Dog, where y'all headed?" Leon asked.

"We headed to the store," I said.

"Yeah, dawg. If we gotta stay here we gone get fucked up tonight. I need some burrs(beers), y'know what I'm sayin'? Where the store at?" Said Poppy.

Another one of the football players spoke up.

"It's on the other side of the projects," he said.

"Man, don't go through those projects, dog." Said Leon. He was scared while he was talking, "them mutha fuckas is crazy. They be jumping people and shit."

I looked at him like he was crazy.

I said, "What projects?"

He said, "the ones at the bottom of the hill on the way to the store."

"Nigga, them ain't no projects!" I snapped back. "Our projects are eleven and twelve floors. Those are some mutha fuckin' townhouses."

Almost everybody on the porch laughed.

I continued, "them ain't no real projects, nigga. We going to the store. Mutha fucka, you want something?"

"I'm good, bruh. Thanks. Y'all be careful." Leon replied.

We walked through their projects to get to the store. We got what we needed and cut through the projects again to get back on campus. No issues. We made it back to the dorm and got full. Now 'full' refers to your liver being full and it means we were beyond inebriated. We got tore down, y'hear me?

We bought a lot of shit and drank all of it that night. They even scored some weed while we were in the projects! Now, I took my body too seriously for smoking of any kind. That's a boxing taboo and a lot of those disciplines were my life. So, I didn't smoke with them.

But I didn't try to stop them. They got high as hell. We popped open all the drinks we bought and we all got full! Now, because of my boxing background, I hadn't done a bunch of drinking before, either. So, it didn't take much for me to get sloppy. I definitely got sloppy. We all drank like fish and had a good ass time.

And we overdid it like a mutha fucka. LIT! (Incredibly drunk). We were completely lit! Not only did Black Bruce and Poppy miss the bus, by a lot, but we were late as hell for the placement tests that morning, too. Once they missed the bus they figured they were stuck. Might as well get some classes and be college students. So, with shitty hangovers, we ran up to the administration building and took those tests in the time we had left.

How did we do? They put all our asses in every remedial class they had. Introduction to Block Stacking 001 and all sorts of bullshit. We were getting credit for none of it. They gave us a schedule full of classes with about 2 credits total. If you had seen our first schedules you would've thought we were the dumbest cats in the school. Hell, maybe in town. We laughed hard as hell when we first saw them ourselves. Evidently, taking tests when you're hung over is a really bad idea. Duly noted.

Fortunately, it was standard for them to let you test out of those classes. After we went to one of the courses, where they were doing the equivalent to matching pictures of colors to pictures of fruit, we got the hell out of there. It felt like we were getting more dumb by the second in that classroom, I could literally feel my brain cells shriveling to nothing. We ran up out of that spot with fresh headaches and got real classes before the first week of school was over. I wound up taking Health 101 with Poppy.

Man, that health class was crazy. So, Poppy and I were on an assignment together. We were supposed to write a paper then present it in front of the class. Our whole posse was pretty studious, we were serious as hell about our grades. But not this health class. It was academically soft so we didn't really respect it.

We got to class on the due date of that paper and neither one of us had written shit. We were both sitting in class when it started and Poppy says,

"Dawg, I'm finna write this paper and shit."
I said, "alright. You write it then I'll get up there and read the mutha fucka."

Poppy did his part, finished the writing and gave the paper to me. I got in front of the class and started reading what he wrote. That is, I was trying to read it. He wrote it as fast as he could and that shit was crazy sloppy. After a few sentences in, I couldn't make out what was on the paper. So, I started freelancing.

When I looked up the whole class was staring at me with their mouths wide open. They looked like I just said I stabbed a sanctuary full of nuns or tossed six puppies out of a window for fun. I looked at Poppy and he was laughing his ass off. That didn't make it any better. I lost my bearing and I started half-laughing while I told the rest of whatever the fuck I made up.

I don't actually remember what I said because I couldn't have told you after that class period was over. I definitely had everybody's attention, though. Poppy and I both got a passing grade for it, too. So, as far as I'm concerned, it was a good ass speech. That's exactly why we didn't take that class seriously. Soft.

Let's get back to the beginning of the semester.

It appeared that a whole bunch of students didn't make it back to that bus in the morning. The campus was filled with people from St. Louis after that. Because of the way those football assholes were acting when I first got to the school, I huddled all the guys from St. Louis together in the 2nd floor foyer of Davis Hall.

I told them that we were going to stick together on campus. Never travel by yourself, always take somebody from the 'Lou with you wherever you go. I brought my Webbe mentality with me. We ate together, went to classes together, drank together, whatever. We all stayed close knit after that. You would always see ten to fifteen of us walking together or doing something. That became a known thing on the Yard, "them St. Louis mutha fuckas always together". Damned right!

This, wrongfully, earned us a gang designation. The Dean of Students had all guys from St. Louis classified as one gang. To my memory, it didn't include the girls from St. Louis. They had all the St. Louis dudes on their radar, though.

Except me. The Dean of Students was Dr. Smith. She was a Texan and she loved her some Lou (that's me). I couldn't do any wrong in her eyes. I had hit her with politeness and service right off the rip. Everything was downhill with her from there.

See, Dr. Smith was elderly. The first time I saw her she was trying to lift something she had no business. I immediately went to help her and it was on after that. I dropped by her office every day to check on her and just ask her if I could help her with something. She treated me like I was a virtual saint because of it. Dr. Smith loved me to death. The way I treated her wasn't even anything special to me. This was just a product of how I was raised.

I already told you about Granny's influence on my respectful upbringing. But there was another scary ass element, too. Even the real killers in the Webbes were incredibly respectful of the elderly. When they saw elderly women walking, they would take their hats off and greet them.

"How are you doing, Ms. Jones? Can I help you with something, Ms. Jones? Do you need any help with those bags?" And on and on.

You know, 'yes, ma'am', yes, sir,' and all of that were the standard. If they saw us doing anything different then they would slap the shit out of us. And you couldn't run upstairs and tell that because you'd get the shit slapped out of you again.

Nah, manners were a must in the Webbes. There were a bunch of general rules that governed how we were raised. Even with all those dead bodies and killing and all of that, respect for the elders never wavered.

That went for school, too. If they caught you out of school they would whip your ass.

"Nigga, get yo' ass in school."
"Nigga, this ain't for you. Curryo' (carry your) ass to school."

They wouldn't let us get away with doing wrong. The older guys made sure we were on the straight and narrow.

All of that was ingrained in me from the Webbes. It struck the right chord with Dr. Smith, so I flew completely under the radar the whole time. That wasn't by design, it just worked out like that.

For everybody else, though, she had it in for them. It sort of made sense but then again it truly didn't. Our crew was full of some wild ass jokers, including me. But we all had grades. All of us! Everybody that rolled with us had a 2.5 or better. We all went to class and we even studied together. When we got finished we usually got fucked up (inebriated) but we handled those books first. I was largely responsible for that whole vibe.

All of us St. Louis guys were basically the same age. A few cats were even older than me but they all looked to me as the big brother. After I called that meeting to get us all to stick together, it continued from there. My thing was: we were in a foreign place. I knew our strength was in our unity so I corralled us into one body. And I looked out for everybody. It became known that if you fucked with anybody from St. Louis 'Big Lou' was gone get you. That kept me designated as the 'big brother'.

In the spring, April 1988, Busara and Roostah came to visit with a couple other people. They arrived on a Friday night and we had a great time that whole weekend. Roostah was talking about returning for school while they were still in town. That made me think about bringing people to school.

Summer break in June, I went home on fire for school. I started recruiting as soon as I got back. KC was live as hell for me! While I was at the crib, I tried to get everybody I saw to go to KC.

Right in the middle of that summer, Poppy decided to fall through the crib to holler at me. Remember, we went to Vashon together when I lived on the North side for that one year. That's where he was from. Poppy told me he was coming through and I told him I would look out for him when he showed up. I started walking outside about the time I thought he would arrive. We stayed on the second floor, so it was a short walk.

Well, by the time I got close to walking out the door, Poppy already had a gun pointed at him. Donny Don was out there and heard Poppy say he was looking for Big Lou. Don didn't know him and just had my back outright.

Donny Don said,

"Mutha fucka, what you looking for 'Lou for?"

Right after that I gave Donny Don our whistle from a little ways behind them. We had a neighborhood whistle that we used, it was just our thing. Donny Don turned to see me and I told him,

"Hey Don, he cool. He with me."

Poppy told me he damn near fainted, man. He said that was the wildest shit he had ever faced. Nobody had pulled a gun directly on him before. After that, he and Donny Don got cool and our circle grew a little bit.

Once I settled in for the summer, I started looking around the crib. All the soft dudes, that I remembered seeing when I left, had a lot of paper (money). I was thinking,

> "My stomach touching my back out here and all these soft ass dudes got all this money? I should take they shit."

That wasn't my hustle, though. I had never been a stick-up kid so I wasn't about to start. But I was going to cash in on the new information.

After digging a bit, I found that the Crack game had exploded in St, Louis. I sat back and peeped the game for a bit. I figured out how guys were moving and decided I needed to get on before I got back to school. I found exactly who I had to connect with and I got on.

Quickly.

CHAPTER 28

HIGHER EDUCATION

Near the end of the summer in 1988, I bought a little Work. It was a few weeks before I went back to school. After watching how the streets were moving for a couple weeks, I figured out my angle: I was going to hustle for food stamps. I got a $100 rock of Crack and cut it up. Then I went for mine.

My whole aim was to be smart about it. Hanging out on the streets, becoming a corner boy trying to move product, wasn't the play for me. I couldn't afford to get caught out there, dawg. Selling wasn't my main thing and it wasn't going to be. Instead, I strategized by networking what I was looking for. Once I got the word out that people could exchange the Work for stamps, the clients started coming my way. When I got done moving it, my stash was worth a little more than $300 in food stamps.

It worked so smoothly that I reupped (purchased more product) and did it again. I bought $200 worth and flipped it for almost $700 in stamps. I gave half to Granny and took the rest to school with me.

The key importance there is I had figured out the game. I learned how to get some product then how to cut and package it for sale. Then I learned how to market it effectively. I had targeted my customers and found a high degree of success. Once that summer was over, though, it all got cut loose. I went back to school with those stamps and a fantastic attitude.

Poppy and I were joined at the hip that summer before I started slangin' (selling drugs). He caught a ride back to school with my older brother and me. My brother's hustle game was tight so he always had paper. He supported me the whole time I was in college because that's how our bond was. Y'all know the family credo. It applied to everybody who was rolling with us.

While we're on the road to Knoxville, he gave me some money in the front seat for that exact purpose. I guess Poppy didn't see it or wasn't paying attention.

Right after giving me the loot my brother asked Poppy,

"Hey man, you cool?"

Poppy said, "yeah, dawg. I'm cool."

"No you not! He was asking you if you needed some money, dawg." I told Poppy.

"Oh, okay. Well, naw. I'm not cool then. I'm broke than a mutha fucka, quietly."

My brother broke out about $500 or $600 in single bills. Then he handed them to Poppy and said,

"Hurr. You can have these."

When we left my brother, I started messing with Poppy.

"You need to share some of them damned ones with me, dawg." I said, half chuckling.

"What you mean, dawg?" Poppy said.

Poppy was laughing but he shoved the dollars deeper into his pockets. He was basically telling me 'go fish'.

"I'm sayin', you wouldn't have had nothing if I didn't tell you what's up. Can a brother get a finder's fee or something?" I teased.

We both started laughing.

"Dawg, you need to go on with all that, dawg. He gave you some loot, too. I know you good." Poppy countered.
"He did," I said. "But he gave me twenties and stuff. You got all them ones, man. You gone look like you a stripper if you keep all of them. Let me help you out."
"While you bullshittin'," Poppy said, "that was my last gig, mutha fucka…"

He started rolling his body as if he were working a stripper pole, shaking his money maker.

"The ladies love it, bay-bee (baby)! Don't be mad, dawg." Poppy yelled out.

We laughed our asses off. Then we took our first trip to Red Lobster.

My brother didn't know Poppy but that's just how my family was, though. Granny was one of the most generous and giving people I know. That's another one of the many influences she had on us. My brother shared with Poppy just because he was rolling with me. When you rolled with us the credo applied to you, too. That's why we both had some change in our pockets to kick off the school year.

So, this was the fall semester of my sophomore year. Busara, Donny Don, Jerry, Slick and a whole slew of people from St. Louis came to school as freshmen. Most of them went to KC because I was recruiting my ass off that summer. Jerry was one of those people. I knew him from his hustle back on the block in the Webbes. I told him about KC, that he could get out of the 'Lou and go to school on a dope campus. I was almost surprised he showed up. I was glad to see him there.

There were only a few people who came from St. Louis that year that I didn't personally know. When I saw all the people from the crib that fell through, I knew we were going to have another live ass school year.

Don't mistake the description 'live' as drama-free. There was plenty damned drama at Knoxville College. Shit, that campus moved like the Black teenage version of a telenovela. In fact, I remember Busara's personal introduction to KC. It was kinda funny, actually. It started off with a bit of curiosity then turned into an unnecessary conflict that I did all I could to make worse.

We were standing in the McCollough dorm foyer, chilling. I think it was the second day Busara got there. He had decided to play ball so he was in the football dorm with me, hollering at people. The door flung open and Huge Hugo's giant ass came walking through. He was called 'Huge' for a whole bunch of damned reasons. Most of those reasons were pounds.

Hugo was a massive, charcoal-skinned, ox-strong mutha fucka. His big ass belly was super junky and rotund, he could have easily been six months pregnant. His calves were straight out of the cartoons, they looked like Bluto's off of Popeye. He stood about 6'4" and weighed between 325 and 350 pounds. Huge Hugo was built like what a short bus would look like if it was painted an extremely dark brown and could stand upright. Just a big ole chocolate hunk of dumb.

Busara looked him up and down in awe like, "daaaaaamn!" His eyes were all big, probably from trying to fit this huge water buffalo-ass dude in his frame of sight. And it likely failed.

Problem is, Hugo was one of them bullying kind of assholes. So he tried to pull that shit on Busara. Hugo turned around and said,

"Nigga, what you looking at me for?" Trying to front on Busara.

I said, "you big old bitch ass nigga, he can look at you! Who the fuck you think you are, nigga? You ain't shit. What is you... some type of king or something? Mutha fuckas can't look at you?"

"Man, I ain't talking to you." He said.

"Bitch ass nigga, I'm talking to you," I said. "Now what?"

He responded, "aw man, ain't nobody said nothing to you."

"Nigga, this my little brother, nigga. You better not say another mutha fuckin' thang to him, neither. Mutha fucka!"

By then, the campus already knew about my hands. I put a few cats to sleep my first year when they came out of pocket (were disrespectful). In fact, I had to crush more than a couple cats my freshman year. KC was a small campus so word travelled fast as hell. Not fast enough for a few of those dudes in my freshman year but enough so that I didn't have any issues as a sophomore.

Its highly probable that he was thinking he didn't want to be the next dude I put to sleep. Now don't get me wrong, I don't profess to know what he was thinking because I didn't. What was vividly clear, though, was he didn't want any parts of me that day. Huge Hugo went about his damned business.

Busara was in awe again. He said to me,

"Damn! You talked to that big mutha fucka like that?"

I told him, "man, they better not fuck with anybody from St. Louis. And they know that!"

My habit of taking on bully-types came from my boxing philosophy. It doesn't matter how big you are: how strong is your chin? If you can land your wild ass punches (which dudes usually threw), I know I can take it. My right cross was wicked as hell and you can't take mine landing. If you could I would run but I never faced that. I never had to run in the ring or the street.

That's how Busara got broken into the campus. It wasn't a particularly notable semester. We did a bunch of drinking and fornicating. A whole bunch of people's daughters got "personal interviews", y'know what I'm saying. We had a wild ass time but don't get it twisted: classes were the standard. We handled those grades, of course. We definitely partied our asses off that for that fall session.

So, I arrived that semester with those food stamps from the hustle. Poppy and I had decided to be roommates and we ate awfully damned well for the first few weeks. We decked out our wardrobe and our room with the money my brother gave us. So, we were crazy comfortable in the dorm. After that money and those stamps ran out?

Starving.

The cafeteria on campus closed at 6:00. That was it. Anything else you wanted to eat for the night had to come out of your pocket. Our pockets went flat after those stamps and the money ran out.

I told my brother that we were struggling and he started sending money orders for $500 every two weeks.

One. Thousand. Dollars. Every. Month.

Man, we ate like fucking kings in Knoxville! We made Red Lobster our 'go to' spot. We went there every single day! We treated it like it was

Taco Bell or some shit. Sometimes we only got the cheddar bay biscuits or some shrimp or something but we were there daily. Eating like kings.

The mentality that came from our family credo never changed, it just shifted focus. At KC, the whole St. Louis crew was my family. If we were eating then everybody from the 'Lou was gonna eat. Poppy and I always kept food in the dorm room. If somebody was short on grub, we had 'em. Barbecues would pop off almost every weekend. We made sure there was always enough for everybody. When you rolled with us then you ate like us.

Knoxville College was supposed to be an alcohol-free campus. Shit! We took that literally, but a whole different direction. We threw keg parties all the time and didn't charge a mutha fucking thing. If that's what they meant by "alcohol free" then we nailed it. Man, we were cranking out cases of beer on Tuesdays and shit… we were wilder than a mutha fucka!

Alright, so I gotta confess: I turned a lot of good guys bad. There were only a handful of guys from the Webbes at school. We were used to a particular kind of living. Whole days filled with drinks and women and shit like that. The rest of the dudes from home were squares, like real 90 degree squares. Nobody was square after coming to KC. We removed all of that innocence. I was the key bad influence, can't even lie about it.

As college students, we often made our own rules. That's what the life is supposed to be like, right? It's the bridge between youth and adulthood. So, all the rules we made were partying rules! They were peppered with a modicum of responsibility, for sure, but debauchery was much more prevalent. And I was hugely responsible for all of it.

Near the end of the semester, I got a student refund check. After getting my bus ticket to get home I had a little more than $400 left. I took that money home with an intention to make it bigger.

Sure enough, I got home and Crack had completely blown the lid off the city. I decided to sit back and watch the activity, see where I could fit in. Dudes were making astronomical amounts of money and I knew I could run the game. So, I said, "fuck that! I'm going to get me some Work." I hit the streets to make my move.

My dogs introduced me to a Californian Crip. He wore blue everything all day every day, just like you would think. I took him $250 and he gave me a big Crack rock chunk. With some Work in hand, I put the hustle on ten(maximum).

I started putting that sweat equity in. Collegiate Christmas break lasted about 5 weeks. That was all I needed. I stayed out all night, working to move my product. I didn't take any breaks, didn't hang out, didn't even take a lunch. I was working.

By the next morning, I had sold out and took every penny I made to the Crip. He cut me a bigger chunk and I went right back out hustling. I sold out and was back the next morning, again. I did the same thing every day for a couple weeks.

Two weeks later I had $10,000. I took him that, too. He was like,

"Damn, Big Lou! This how you getting down?" he said.
"Shit yeah, man." I said. "Everybody going to the club and buying clothes and all that shit. Fuck that. That ain't me. I'm getting it."

He told me he would charge me $10k for a full bird (kilogram). I put that cash in his hand, took the bird, hit the streets and made $26,000 with it. I took that to him, too.

That time I got two birds from him. I flipped those and made $58k. That's when it was over. I had put in that musty-everything hustle: like I wasn't showering or changing clothes, none of that – just hustling. I had made $58,000 and it was time to go back to school. So, I quit and went back.

I took about $10,000 with me to school. I gave the rest to my little cousin so he could work it. That little mutha fucka started getting high and fucked over all of it. That's one of the three dealer pitfalls: (a) you start taking it, (b) you go to jail or (c) somebody ends you. My cousin was stupid, he picked (a) which always leads to (b) or (c). If you don't have discipline then you need to know the game ain't for you. It will swallow you whole and not give a fuck about you. That's why I picked (d) none of the above. My happy ass went back to school.

Right after I left St. Louis, the cops came out with a brand new drug task force. They launched a bunch of raids and tore the projects up looking for fools. They started bustin' everybody. Had I stayed, I would've gone into the (b) category, too. No doubt. Fortunately, I thoroughly understood myself and knew who I was. The collegiate campus had become my world and it's where I belonged. I was sure of that shit.

That Work life wasn't my limit and I was clear on that. There is no doubt I could do it, I was great at it actually. But everything you *can* do isn't something you *should* do. The test of the impoverished is to be smart enough to see that distinction and to be both wise and patient enough to make the right call. When you're starving it's hard to see beyond the next meal. That's why planning is essential.

When you have a plan then you can envision more than right now. Its very essence is the statement of more than 'right now'. A plan is a map to tomorrow which helps put your moments, your current situations into context. "If I can handle these things right now, if I conquer this stuff right now then seeing through my plan to fruition will land me at my destination." Having a plan helps you have that kind of patience. When you don't have a plan then 'right now' is everything. That sense of immediacy creates extraneous levels of stress and will most often put your life in compromising positions.

I won't lie to you, I didn't have a high level of planning. I didn't. What was obvious, though, was that college could take me to another plateau. Or, at least, that's what I thought. It was also crystal clear to me that I didn't want to have a career as a drug dealer, despite how lucrative it was when I tried my hand at it. That life had a limited value for me. I would only let it be a momentary means.

Most importantly for me, I had the discipline to end it when the time came. The money didn't have me like that, it didn't have a grip on me. There was never a doubt in my mind that the dope hustle was merely a short-term thing. I was a devout college student, I went back to school.

I made it back to the Yard for Spring 1989 and I wound up with Jerry as my roommate. Poppy was in the band dorm because he was murdering the drums. The drummers were live, dawg, that shit had the campus jumping! I was enjoying the hell out of campus life but I noticed it was moving differently.

I had peeped game again. There were fiends on campus and dudes were making money serving them the Work. It was funny to me: there I was again, watching soft mutha fuckas get paid. My hustling nature had a problem watching money getting made around me without capitalizing. So, I got busy.

My whole life had been about redefining terms. The word 'family' initially meant my Granny, brothers and sister. It became my Webbes brothers and then all of St. Louis in a foreign place. We redefined what 'alcohol-free' meant. In an extension of that, we also changed what 'full' meant. The next colloquialism on deck for my life was 'eating'. More accurately, the whole phrase 'we all eating'.

I knew my approach to the game had to change because the setting had changed. In the Lou, it was just me. I could hustle in the pockets and nooks-and-crannies of the neighborhood because it was mine. I knew every inch of the Webbes and the areas surrounding it. And, worse-case scenario, even if they weren't a part of my hustle, I had scores of people who had my back. Knoxville was not my city. Knoxville College wasn't my home. My support system was different.

It was clear to me that I needed to put together a team. The challenges I would face were plentiful. The school setting dictated an even more inconspicuous approach than what I was doing at home: operating on campus came with a higher risk. I also couldn't dedicate all my time to building and servicing the business because class would still be the priority. I could utilize some time to get the game flowing but not enough to sustain it by myself.

The guys I chose would have to be smart. Hustling skills would be pertinent, street smarts were essential and a business acumen was definitely mandatory. And they had to be dudes I could trust not to ruin the game and to stay low profile. So, I had to find some assets who could handle the level and type of operation I envisioned.

Then crazy shit happened. My little brother, Busara, came to holler at me while I was working through how I wanted to handle it. He was one of the most business-minded people I knew. He had that business contest stuff that he won the summer before where they decided to build a hotel because of him. That was dope. He was also a business major in college. We were tight on the football team and he was someone I could trust. I figured he'd be a solid asset to build this thing.

He asked if I was interested in making that money. Shit, I told him I was already planning on it. That was dope ass timing. We both agreed we would need a few guys to make it work but not more than a few because it needed to stay low key. We decided we would bring in one guy each.

The other cat I picked was Jerry. If you remember, Jerry was one of the guys I recruited from the Webbes. The dude was a side-hustle king back in the Lou. He stayed in the streets working to make loot. Selling yayo wasn't a part of Jerry's experience but he was non-stop effort. I knew, once I got him schooled right, he was going to hit it hard and get that paper flowing. We had to have one of those guys on the team.

Not to mention he was my roommate. That was just too close to keep him out. With Deans, campus security, haters, fiends, my competition and the cops all trying to get me, my roommate had to be in. Otherwise, those would be debilitating odds.

Busara's a loyal cat, so he brought D Smooth in with him. D Smooth was one of Busara's true dudes from the crib. They actually rode to school together, or some shit. D Smooth, Busara, Jerry and me - that made four of us. Our posse was set.

Busara got us all together for a meeting. I just hollered at them straight out,

"Y'all wanna make some money? There's some soft ass niggas on the Yard doing it right now. We can do this!"

We made a plan to chip in $250 each to buy our first sack, which was a full ounce.

After a few weeks, D Smooth said he was out because he couldn't come up with the money. Word was he was trying to pledge one of the fraternities, or something. I thought he just wasn't with it. Whatever, we adjusted: Busara, Jerry and me bought a half ounce to get started. We used the rest to take care of whatever supplies we would need.

Before they started riding with me, neither one of them had ever seen cocaine. They didn't know one thing about weight, packs, Crack, customers – nothing. I don't think Busara had even smoked weed before. These mutha fuckas couldn't have been more green if they grew out of the ground.

I had to teach them everything. I taught them how to weigh the powder. We broke out a triple beam scale and I showed them how to use *that.* I let them see what Crack was and how to rock it up. I was able to cook two ounces at a time and I taught them how to do that, too. They had to learn what amounts got sold at what price, how to package it – everything.

I found out quickly that I was rolling with the right brothers. Jerry and Busara were smart, quick studiés. And they were hungry! Busara was a wiz with that planning shit. He absorbed everything I showed him and the shit we were going through then he adjusted his blueprint on the fly. He was super sharp with it.

The minute we got our processes set, they got the operation cranking! They weren't the only ones new to Crack: the city of Knoxville had never seen it. We sold powder, too, but the effect of Crack took over the local users. They were running up to the back fence of the school like Hip Hop groupies after a concert.

And we had never left the campus! We only sold to students (when those refund checks hit it went crazy) or to locals that came to find us. It was strictly a college campus service. Fortunately for us, so much was happening on the Yard that we took full advantage of it and worked under the radar. The activity that we created blended in to everything that was already happening.

That's part of the reason we never went off-campus. Our active student body provided the perfect cover for the game to prosper. The locals at the back gate were a bit out of the normal loop but very little happened in wide open spaces because those didn't really exist. There were people everywhere on that campus. We had some older students who even made the older locals fit in. That was crazy as hell to me but it worked. Well, until you closely scrutinized those people, but that's another matter. Our operation ran incredibly smoothly and it was crazy lucrative.

How lucrative? We began the operation in January, 1989. We split our first $10,000 during Spring Break. The money began to snowball and by the end of the semester we had split $10,000 two more times. So, in 1989, three teenage college students (a sophomore and two freshmen) went from $750 and no assets to $30,000 in profits in five months. That's awfully damned lucrative. We were all eating!

In May, 1989, I started having conversations with my peers about their preparations to graduate. They were in my graduating class and it made me realize I was fucking up. My reason for being there was to get a degree, I needed to get on that shit.

As long as I was running the game I would need to stay present in it to fucking live. The drug game has ruthless competitors, relentless (clean and dirty) cops and opportunistic fiends all trying to fuck you, all the time. Sleeping on it, at all, can cost you everything - including your life. I decided that it was too expensive for me to simultaneously continue fucking with it and try to graduate.

While I was thinking about that, getting ready to make a move out of the game, I broke my foot. I'm in the middle of country ass Knoxville with a flat tire. My fellas were the bomb, they were my family so I was comfortable on campus. But I needed to be home to deal with a bum foot.

So, once again, I left the game. Right after we made that third split, I was out. Money never had me and that didn't change. It was time to make another shift away from it. I cut it loose and went to the crib.

Busara and Jerry got everything I could hook them up with: connections, skills and momentum. I let them know I was out and left them to do whatever they decided to do. They kept hustling. It's funny: Busara and I might have even got closer once I got out. He continued to holler at me while he learned to perfect his own system. Getting Busara involved was one of my best choices. The shit he started doing was dope!

I returned to KC to visit a few weeks into the following fall semester with a gang of St. Louis dudes. Man, we had a fucking blast! Saying this sounds crazy but, we bought 25 cases of beer every day we were there.

Every day! We set up camp under a tree on the Yard and invited anybody to come through and hang out. Our whole thought was, "anybody that wants to get bent (drunk), c'mon up! Let's drink, mutha fuckas, and have a good ass time". It was fun as hell.

We rocked the shit out of Knoxville. By the time we left, every mutha fucka that came with me had committed to going back. We wrapped up the weekend and bounced. The day we left town everything about the game changed for Busara and Jerry.

That morning, the Knoxville police department-version of ATF raided Busara's dorm room.

CHAPTER 29

ORGANIZING

So, Big Lou told you the gist of what we were doing and how it progressed. He could tell the story of our operation like he did because it wasn't that big of a deal to him. He had been in the game before we got our enterprise started so he wasn't out of his element.

Me? Shit! It was a brand new world. I was pressed to plan our next moves to make sure we succeeded while learning a bunch of shit on the fly. It was working, though. We didn't really have competition on the Yard. That afforded us the room to grow organically. That was a luxurious freedom to have while we were figuring it out.

Getting product was the first challenge. I certainly didn't have, or know how to look for, a source. But, like I said, Big Lou was clutch. He found a guy on campus from Detroit who was already working an angle. The dude had access to the product but he didn't want to distribute like we planned to. So, he became our supplier and it worked out for everybody. Once we connected with him, we were on.

Well, not immediately. After pooling our money to buy the Work, and with D Smooth dropping out making us each pay extra, we had very little budget left. However, there were mandatory assets that we had to acquire. We needed a triple beam scale, baggies and pagers, for starters. These were bare necessities. How did we get them? We were college students, we improvised.

The baggies were the easiest. We found a tobacco store not far away that sold all kinds of paraphernalia-type shit. Baggies were really inexpensive so we bought as much as we could. In fact, we negotiated a bulk deal to get the best bang for our buck. Our vision was to get all we would ever need from him the first time, we didn't plan to go back.

A local white guy owned the store and, frankly, we weren't going to trust him with repeat business. We didn't want to be seen making regular purchases anywhere because predictability gets you got. Right? He gave off the wrong vibes and our business was short on trust anyways. So, we found another resource shortly after. We tried to keep our visibility to a minimum in every way.

Part of the reason we thought to build an illegal business in this town is because it was insanely slow compared to where we were born. They were trusting and, that was beautiful but, it put them at a great disadvantage. What do I mean when I say that? There are loads of examples.

The gas stations piled cases of soda so high outside of their stores that clerks couldn't see what was happening outside. You could roll up at midnight or something, take rows of Dr. Pepper cases (or any other soda, of course), stack them in a trunk until it was full and they would have no idea that you pulled off with a chunk of their inventory. They weren't just piled high at the windows, either. It was all around the store. Practically giving it away to unsavory souls. I knew many of such unsavory souls at KC, straight up. Many!

The city was largely built on an honor system. So, 'dine and dash' happened frequently, too. This is when patrons would eat full meals then skirt out on the bill. I didn't personally do any of that but I was in the minority of the guys I knew. Gas stations were the same way. Dudes would fill up and roll out of the station. Camera coverage wasn't really a thing back then, police were rarely around and there was no way to trace a vehicle that pulled such a stunt. It should be of no surprise to you that I knew more than a few 'stuntmen'.

Some of our classmates had a boosting hustle, too. They would steal clothes from the fashion stores in the mall, or wherever, then sell them. The stores in town didn't have the advanced anti-theft tech and college students came from places around the country that did. So, preying on the Knoxvillian stores was easy work for them.

I knew guys on campus that dressed like platinum-record rappers without a quarter in their pockets. And I mean they were fresh! They wore crazy expensive Tommy Hilfiger, Nautica and Liz Claiborne clothing before many in school even knew what those brands were. There's no doubt those stores lost tens of thousands of dollars from shrinkage. The Yard was basically a fashion show because of it.

And, yeah, we were terrible for taking advantage of the city's kindness. They were trusting and decent. Those are traits that should be honored and cherished, for certain. It was terrific living in such an environment. We, however, were college students. The whole reason we were at school was to create a higher leverage on society. It's a sad thing that it would include illegal activity but that's college life across the country. We were all trying to figure out how to get ahead. For many of us, that had as few limits as we could get away with.

Listen, I'm a responsible man. The popularity of such delinquency does not excuse mine. That's not at all what I'm suggesting nor would I accept such logic on my behalf. My choices are mine. Period. I am saying, that an attempt to condemn us for being American would be incredibly hypocritical. This country is (not 'was', is) founded on getting over at the expense of others and continues to thrive because of it. That's all I'll say about that for now.

So, we got busy taking what was readily available. Our business was born of the ease in manipulating the system we lived in. That continued to be a theme in the city on multiple levels. As a matter of fact, how we worked our illegal business began with a multitude of local manipulations.

We had to finish acquiring our business necessities. As for the weighing scale, well, it was the first item acquired due to the naivete of the city. KC was a microcosm of that greenness.

For starters, our school was founded by the Presbyterian church so it was supposed to be non-co-ed. That was a riotous laugh. We ran circles around the guards and only fell just short of having orgies in the dorm rooms. (Actually, some cats I know basically did). Sexual activity in the school, in the dorms, was extremely high. Their security measures were flat out woefully inept.

So it was for the classrooms, as well. We knew there was a triple beam scale in the chemistry class and the windows aren't secured at night. The security patrols were also paltry. Straight up? There were never more than two or three guards on campus at once. Ever! So, one of us opened a window during class one day then returned that evening. We climbed in, did our do and climbed right back out.

Boom, triple beam scale.

Yes, that's definitely roguish, straight up. But, an illegal business fueled by illegal means is called consistency. That's just how we got down.

That was crazy anti-climactic though, right? You would think it might have taken some elaborate scheme or series of mad athletic feats to lift equipment from a collegiate classroom, right? Nope. This was truly indicative of how easy it was to go against rules, laws and norms in that town.

I actually only hit on highlights of the city to give you a broad picture of its innocence. However, the standing rule was if you were inclined to get over on the system in Knoxville then there were high odds that you would be successful. This created the enticement for us to exploit the situation.

Quintessential to our operational success was our ability to communicate. This is the end of the 80's we're talking about, cell phones were not readily available. The cellular phones that you could get were incredibly expensive and well outside our initial budget. Cell phone access to us would not have been tactically sound for our daily dynamic. They were still primitive and huge. Toting those around on campus, between classes or in the dorms would've been a signal to everyone what we were up to. They weren't at all suitable for our operation at the time.

But pay phones were damned near on every corner. They were also on every floor in the dorms. Our school was straight up bootleg, sad to say, so individual telephones in the rooms was a true rarity. It had to be done independent of the school and that was too expensive of a convenience for most. We settled for the pay phones in the hallways.

So, pagers were ideal for our operation. As college students, our time was largely ours to manipulate but we still attended classes. It was important for us to be able to hustle while controlling our availability. Pagers afforded us all the freedom and connectivity without the hassle, or expense, of cell phones.

Our modus operandi immediately became 'put our names on nothing'. That was one of our first rules. So, we paid one of our schoolmates to acquire pagers for us. The crazy thing about that is he didn't put them in his name, either! The dude filled out the application by spelling his name backwards and they still let him complete the process without ID for verification. He was able to get four pagers with monthly service subscriptions - all on a fake name.

Now, it's true that once he purchased the pagers, they could just end the service if the bill wasn't paid. That's not the point. The point is it was a typical standard operating procedure for Americans to identify themselves to begin any service contract. That's just how business was done in major metropolitan areas. Knoxville wasn't one of those areas.

So, we had a completely untraceable means of communicating to do our thing. Perfect.

Last bit on Knoxville, it was a beautiful place. It was nestled within the majestic Smoky Mountain range and fed by the rich Cumberland River. Sultry water banks and gorgeous mountain peaks were never more than a handful of minutes away from any point in the city. If you were on the right hill, there was lush foliage-laced peaks for as far as you could see. It was a picturesque setting to operate in.

The Knoxvillian public were throwbacks in their general sensibilities. They were widely welcoming, courteous and willingly helpful. Sadly, that wasn't just the delightful backdrop of our operations, it was the reason we began them. Much of what we were able to do hinged on the antiquated lifestyle of the small town. Our functional value for Knoxville was rooted in how we could benefit from it.

So, we had product, a scale, baggies and pagers all set up in a slow town. It was time to get paid! Our first customers were our most serious early tests. Once we got them everything else was downhill. Here's where sound marketing creates a profitable business.

We weighed our first batch a little on the heavy side. Each of the priced baggies had more in it than it should have. Our first priority was satisfied customers. Once we got them to come back, we could get them to bring others. So, we made our priced packages bigger than the competition. This gave our clients a motivating incentive. It cut down on our profits initially but it was a visionary move. It worked like a charm.

We also had better product than the competition. As part of our due diligence, we found out that the local cats were cutting (mixing with non-narcotic substances) their drugs with Lactaid. This was a way to create more sellable inventory with their drugs and make more money on their purchases. This practice, though, made their drugs have a weaker effect on the customers. We didn't do any cutting with the product we purchased. We knew this would make us hotter on the market.

One of the things I didn't quite realize at the beginning is that we had a secret weapon: Crack! Our enterprise had a dominating advantage over the Knoxville market once we introduced Crack to the city.

Yes, our crew was singularly responsible for bringing Crack into Knoxville, TN!

The city had never been exposed to it before us. Because of Big Lou's experience, we knew the level of addiction it would cause and how insanely profitable that would be. As soon as we purchased the product, he got busy creating our first batch.

Crack is a processed result of mixing powder cocaine with a small collection of chemicals. I won't take you through the minutia of creating it because it's not at all my intention to teach it to you.

In fact, I, in no way, advocate for the act of selling narcotics. Wanted to make certain that's clear.

But, Crack was the change agent for our operation so a little detail is in order. The gist of making it is, you have to bring water to a boil, mix the ingredients with the cocaine and the chemical reaction causes it to solidify. If you've ever seen the process it would be obvious to you that someone created it in a lab. It wasn't something a street dealer thought up then started experimenting with his stores of product (wasting it/wasting money) until they were successful. The reason why a street hustler wouldn't waste that kind of money is because there would be no reason to assume it would be more potent (diluting it with other random chemicals) unless you were a chemist who understood the human anatomy and the effects of a chemical mix. Nah, somebody made that shit in a lab, guaranteed.

That 'somebody' is the American government. Those white boys in office had it engineered to destroy our neighborhoods. The alleged 'war on drugs' was more like a war *with* drugs. The government devised a way to make drugs wildly addictive, destructive and easy to manufacture then unleashed them on our people.

THEN they unleashed the law on us to destroy our communities either by selling drugs to us or by imprisoning us for having them. It's no secret either: the government punished Black drug dealers and users alike. There was no empathy for our pains on any level. Expecting them to be humane with our plight is like asking a little white boy who tortures ants for fun to be sorry one of their legs fell off. Slaughterers have no remorse for the cruelty of their design.

Since it happens to be the tools of our empowerment in this story, I won't venture too deep into exposing its history. Yes, those mutha fuckas are guilty for trying to destroy our neighborhoods. Nothing absolves them of that. But, our experiences that I'm sharing with you revolve around leveraging their destructive design. I don't want to muddy the lines between our responsibility and their heinous intentions for us. I am the master of my choices. I own my shit.

My issue with becoming a proponent for the problem is documented. I even had to face my Kowrie elders to begin the venture in order to tame my soul about it. Yes, selling drugs to our people was foul shit. I knew that going in. My plan required me to grind for a period of time then begin legitimate ventures utilizing the revenue earned from it. The driving goal was for a benefit to my people. The onus was on me to never lose that vision. Until such a time, I would definitely be guilty of doing Satan's work. I know this sounds cheesy but, I felt it was a necessary evil for that moment. See, told you it would be cheesy.

I realize my position to criticize the government's measures is highly dubious. It's certainly hypocritical, no doubt. That changes nothing about the facts. They devised a way to drown our communities in misery. I decided to become a water broker by lifting the gates on the dam. Understood.

Getting back to creating the Crack. Jerry and I watched Big Lou put together the ingredients and go through the motions. After rocking it up, he taught us how to cut it. Then we were ready to hit the streets with our competition killer. We were certain Crack would be powerful in our customer acquisition but we also knew the town was used to powder. So, we kept half of our product untouched and bagged it in the way they were used to.

Our marketing plan for it was the oldest cliché in the drug game: the rock sells itself. We gave samples of the Crack away with powder purchases. Every sample came with an explanation of how to use it and, most importantly, a reminder that we were the only ones with it. We continued selling both products but it didn't take long before some customers came back strictly asking for Crack.

They returned more frequently for it, too. A quick lesson on Crack the drug: a pair of its major effects are 1) an incredibly euphoric high and 2) a very rapid de-escalation. The Crack high wore off superfast and compelled customers to return for more with incredible rapidity. This is what we introduced to the city that put us head and shoulders above the locals. Our business was booming in no time and we never left the campus to get it going.

To keep us from getting too hot we over utilized the 'put our names on nothing' policy. We highly encouraged our first few clients to bring back others or refer us to them. The lynchpin was turning our clients into a delivery service. They would collect the money from the customers they knew, then come purchase for the 'group' they represented. We would sell them work, they got their cut then passed on the leftovers to whoever they bought it for. They were more than glad to broker deals for the other customers. They likely kept money and trimmed some of the product for themselves but that wasn't our issue. They would also often smoke with the people they purchased for so they got sizeable perks for being middlemen.

They couldn't lose, well, outside of actually using the product. There was no winning in that. None.

The middlemen practice worked like magic for us. Selling to 'brokers' kept our local traffic down on the Yard. We were dealing with them through one of the back fences to stay out of sight. The more frequent that activity would have been the more obvious our deals would have become. Typically, those grown people didn't remotely look like college students so that would be bad business. Dealing with less people for more action considerably cut down on that. It allowed us to do a lot of business without a lot of visibility.

Lastly, it kept us off the radar of the competition. We stayed on campus and had the city brought to us. Not only could we stay covered by the school setting to keep cops off our asses, but the local drug dealers weren't coming to campus, either. This prevented all sorts of heat on our operation. We were able to keep going to class while stacking cash.

One of our early gifts was a guy named Larry Wayne. This seems awfully 'Forrest Gump' but the locals only called him by his full name, so we did too. Thing is, their accent made it sound like "Lare-wane" and it was all one word. We thought it was funny so we rolled with it.

Larewane was *the* agent. There were several others that helped us grow the business but none were like him. He was so integral to helping us spread the word and earn new customers you could damned near call him an employee. Beyond that, though, he put us up on the local scoop. He knew the cops and the local dope boys. It was a great mutual exchange: he got premium product with perks and he kept us in the loop of happenings off campus.

Now, Larewane was a high-functioning customer. He kept a steady job and was a relatively reasonable guy. His drug habit was just past recreational. He was definitely an addict but he handled it better than most we dealt with. Part of the reason we were able to steal him from the locals is because they treated him like shit.

The local crew close to us handled their customers with contempt and disrespect. We dealt with everybody like human beings. Larewane was a cool guy, he just liked to get high. Big Lou told you, we didn't condemn people we served. We were the nice guy drug dealers, we did business transactions with all kinds of jokes and good times, even. So, Larewane looked out for us because he got the hook-up and he liked us better. We were business men, we wanted every advantage in our favor. Being cool dudes was a real part of who we were and it worked to build our operation.

Having brokers like Larewane helped maximize our time. Instead of making 2, 3 or 5 deals often we just made one. And, we personally remained largely inconspicuous and unknown in town. We didn't want to be approached when we walked to the store and hung out off campus. Our focus was on maintaining low profiles. We had to stay 'college students'. The longer we could do that the more successful we knew we would be.

Our desire to remain hidden in plain sight caused us to be frugal. This also helped us stack our money. I had detailed the reasons for keeping a tight grip on money in my business plan. If we started balling in clothing or jewelry or if we had decked out our rooms it would become obvious that something was going on. So, we did none of that. We were misers with our every dime and we never splurged.

Instead, we constantly reinvested our money. We hustled, we saved, we bought more product and we hustled again. Rinse and repeat. Even people who were close to us didn't know we made money because we never showed off or showed any signs of it. Our team was banking thousands of dollars but we looked as broke as every other penniless student on campus.

That didn't make our exploits entirely invisible on the Yard, though. I mean, this was an institution full of intelligent young people. Someone was bound to take notice and take interest in what we were doing. Fortunately for us, it was people inclined to use our product.

To my surprise, there was quite an abundance of college students who did cocaine. Black college students who were cocaine users, that was weird to me. And, there was enough business on campus for it to be majorly profitable without massive exposure. There weren't many students that bought Crack from us. I think that would have crossed the line for me. But there was gangs of dudes, and women, who bought blow (cocaine in powder form). That market was seriously active.

By the time the school loan refund checks hit the student body for the spring semester, those who would be customers knew that they could hit us up. That became a boon for us. It provided us the kind of profit we wanted to see without making our operation much larger. It prevented the need to leave the campus in order to expand. Before long, we were sitting pretty in the dorms and profiting like we wanted. Everything was flowing.

You know it's difficult for good things to last long. We were smart and careful but we couldn't control everything – including our supply. Our business was booming! We were smooth in our transactions, the campus full of students provided a camouflage for our activity and everything was going swell. Too swell.

Then everything stopped cold. Our supplier on campus wasn't prepared for the kind of volume we were doing so he frequently went dry. That meant we went dry. We couldn't make any money without product to sell and the locals went back to their normal sources. Over the course of the semester that happened two or three times.

That was unacceptable.

A time or two, we came out of the shortages because Big Lou got product from home. We thought that was too risky to be a consistent source. It would have also put a demand on us to be a bigger operation and that wasn't the goal. At least, that wasn't the focus early.

So, we scrambled for a good minute looking for another local supplier while trying not to completely expose ourselves. We were committed to continue making money but it was essential we kept doing it quietly. That was a tough balance to effectively strike while you're looking for help. My search took me off campus.

Big Lou told you we split $10,000 three times over the course of a semester. The first time we did it, Jerry and I thought we needed some wheels. The 'stay low key' rules were always in effect so we didn't go big. Not at first. He and I decided we could ball a little without looking like it if we bought something on two wheels.

So, we went to a dealership and got a pair of Hondas. Seriously, we would have loved to grab some motorcycles. The whole planet agrees that they're straight up dope. But that would've been too much for both of us. Neither of us knew how to ride them and we weren't too interested in learning how right then. And they were a different kind of flexing statement. Motorcycles aren't incredibly expensive but they look like it. That would have been counterintuitive to our plans. Nah, we settled on grabbing a pair on Helix scooters.

Yes, a pair of grown ass college men riding Honda scooters. That was us.

They were fresh as hell, though! We rolled on campus with them for the first time like we had arrived with a whole motorcycle gang. It was just him and me - on scooters. We got mad love for rolling differently than everyone else. It also let us move around however we wanted. Shit, parking was never an issue. And, if we truly cared, it was a wise move for gas mileage.

Best of all, while we looked fresh as fuck rolling on them, having scooters wasn't doing too much. Simply owning them didn't tell anything about what we were doing. They could have easily been something we purchased strictly with school refund checks. They were also not the kind of vehicles anyone expected drug dealers to use as their main transportation. If they were one of many rides we purchased it would have definitely been excessive. But they were super smart choices as main rides. The longer we had them the more I liked it.

We purchased them with cash, of course. And we wrote fake names on the purchase orders. We weren't trying to reveal anything that wasn't mandatory. Cash makes the world run: when we handed them dollars bills, they wrote that shit up and shook our hands. They didn't ask any extra questions, we didn't offer any extra information. Truly, we were pretty damned consistent about staying off the radar.

The second time we split the money, though, I went out and got a car. Winter would come sooner or later and shit like rain happened. I had to get out of the elements. The guy who owned the car lot was a local guy, named Hawkley, with a bus load of businesses. While we worked towards a deal on the car he shared with me the whole laundry list of businesses he was into. He was a flat out hustler. We hit it off from the start.

I had broken up the car price into 3 payments. During the course of several casual conversations, he let me know he put work in on our arena, too. Hawkley was the "Skins of the east side", apparently. Since we had found ourselves in a pickle, I went to holler at him and we started doing business. He was like an anti-Skins guy in my perspective, that worked for me. I can't entirely explain why I had such a strong opposition to doing business with Skins but that's how it was. This car dealer dude was in direct competition with Skins, so he was more than glad to do business with us. It was a win-win situation.

Just so y'all know, he tried to sell me a fire-ass ride! He had a 1987 Buick Grand National. It was so clean it looked like somebody had just taken the wrapping plastic out of the interior. The rims were gleaming in the sunlight and it had a racing stripe on the nightmare black paint job. It was super sweet and he was offering me a fantastic deal on it. But it was a drug dealer special. Not the bargain he was offering me but the car itself. The minute I would have rolled up in that car I would have been obvious as hell. Just like the Atlanta cats. Not the plan. I picked a reliable looking hooptie instead.

I won't front, it was a 1982 Pontiac Grand Am. My girl was a straight muscle car with glass-packed dual exhaust pipes. When it was rolling those pipes would roar like a pair of lions. It was a little older so a lot of people would ask if the muffler was loose or something but that was the power of that engine... roaring. It was a little older and a little worn but, man, that thing could fly! It could easily pass everything on the street, except gas stations. It guzzled gas like it was cool. But that power made it feel like a racecar inside, even though it didn't look like I spent a lot on the outside. That's what I needed, something low key in some kind of way. I was explicitly trying to avoid any undue attention to my bankroll, y'know. I still thought the car was dope so everything was good.

I wasn't about to lose sight of the vision with my first vehicle purchase. I was tempted, I ain't gone lie. But, fortunately, my business discipline ruled the day. Money wasn't an issue, I could have afforded anything he had on the lot. My pockets made me feel like a baller, that was good enough for me. I got a car that didn't look like I could buy everything. That better suited my purposes.

With a new supplier, we blasted through the rest of the semester with ease. By the time summer break arrived, we had earned enough to split our third $10,000 stash. Our business venture had paid us extreme dividends in one school semester. We had $10k each in basically four months. We hadn't really faced many obstacles, we hadn't developed any heat on us and we were still pretty hush-hush all around – except with customers. We had actually earned a reputation that was really winning with our clientele. If we stayed smart, I figured, we could run the operation until we left the school. We found out quickly that it wasn't going to work like that.

When we split the money, Big Lou told us he was out. He was heading home for the summer and he was done working our Knoxville operation. I took a pass on returning to St. Louis. The system we had set up in Knoxville, the success we were having, the money we were making, was way more than enough for me to remain in town. So, both Jerry and I stayed to attend the summer session in school.

Part of our calculation was that the camouflage of campus was part of the recipe for success. We copped some more product with our portion of the money and continued working our system. It didn't make sense to us to let a good thing go to waste. Unfortunately for us, that didn't work out the way we figured, either.

It's funny; part of the reason I wasn't in a hurry to go back to St. Louis was because of the omnipresent effects of the street drug market at home. That's some incredible irony, isn't it? I was helping to create the drug-enriched environment that I was also trying to overcome. That's some rich shit.

Honestly though, aside from the Kowrie Group and visiting my family, St. Louis just didn't hold a lot for me at that time. And, as a practical matter, I'd rather deal with the situation that profits me than the one that wouldn't. I was a business man and Knoxville was where the business was for me. So, I stayed.

Our operation was doing exceedingly well. The money was flowing smoothly, that was obviously good, but it wasn't what gripped me. We were successful! We had put together a system out of thin air and it was killing the game. Our clientele list was extensive and continually growing, we had no heat on us and we had full pockets. We were winning and all of the winning had me. I got completely wrapped up in it. It became sort of a self-competition, I tried to top my success with every facet of the operation. That approach was working. I wasn't ready to give that up because the semester ended.

Jerry and I got some classes and stayed in a dorm room together. Living together made perfect sense. We didn't want to have to maneuver around different roommates who weren't in on the caper. Besides, we were stashing our money in our rooms with us. Having separate roommates would just be asking for trouble, on several levels. We fixed that, we thought, by staying together.

Then the world shifted on us.

During the semester, our drug traffic blended with all the activity on the Yard. Business was hiding in plain sight and it was cool. There were so many bodies moving around, so many working parts on the campus that our 'visitors' got lost in the shuffle. Walking to the back fence behind our dorm was barely a noticeable act. The clients we serviced made rapid exchanges with us and nobody was the wiser. Shit was smooth as a baby's ass.

In the summer session it immediately stuck out like a sore thumb. The foot traffic on campus wasn't remotely as heavy because attendance took a steep drop off. That's just what happened during summer school, less students attended classes. Mutha fuckas went home.

Knoxville College was a four-year institution with a student body mixed of every climb and place, every walk of life and a grand variation of ages. But it wasn't that grand. As I told you, our local clientele was generally people of a particular age. Those 'particular ages' were old as fuck compared to all of the summer session students. And they had a 'worn' look, y'know? They looked like life had given them some rough ass turns. Unlike the typical collegiate student, who usually looked financially broke but had an enduring optimism in the aura about them. Compared to that, our customers damned near looked dead. That was not working.

Clearly, the jig was up. We had to shift how we did things or we would certainly get busted.

This was the kind of change I told myself to look out for. It was time to make a plan B. The only option afforded us was obvious: we had to move the operation off the campus.

So, we found a nice apartment, a good distance away, and moved in.

CHAPTER 30

WELCOME TO KNOXVILLE

Jerry and I got an apartment together and began to settle in. Having a place out in town seemed like providence to me because I hadn't purchased my car long before we left campus. It was a mandatory tool when you lived out in town. The city's layout was expansive. Everything you needed was far away from everything else. The distance between our new spot and the 'hood was a real trek. That was the way we wanted it. They had city buses and all of that but my life couldn't afford that kind of timing inconvenience. So, fortunately, I was able to keep rolling without interruption because of my vehicle.

And we shed not one tear for leaving the campus. It wasn't the greatest to begin with. And I really didn't like that it reminded of the projects. The concern for that began to fade after getting settled in to the school but it never sat well with me. The students at the school were dope, they were my people. It was dope being with so many positive young Black minds. Other than that, as a physical matter, the campus was shit. I was glad as hell to bail out of those dusty ass dorms.

Living in town didn't affect my school life, either. Straight up? I didn't have a 'school life' in the summer. Yeah, I signed up for a full load of classes but that was just to get the loan refund check. I never had a plan to attend a class and I didn't. I rocked mad F's for the summer. At least, for college classes…

In real life, though, I had a 4.3 grade average. I was whipping ass, y'all. Our crib was the bomb! Especially by the time we got through with it. We spent a little bit of change to make it really comfortable for us. Still, we showed restraint. We allowed ourselves to do just enough to make it nicely livable. We were well versed in those frugality commitments that helped us stay under the radar to that point. None of us wore fat chains, gaudy watches or stayed in the most expensive fresh sneakers daily. I mean, even when we splurged with the scooters it didn't really look like it. That was a calculated risk. We were dead serious about being low key.

But this was my first crib ever! I was having that grown man moment when you realize you are completely the master of your own world. AND I was eighteen! The crib was off campus, no one knew us around there and we had the assumed privacy of public citizens. Shit! That crib was going to get decked out. We said fuck it and spent a little money.

Now, I have to keep it real: we were still relatively frugal. We had furniture and shit but it wasn't amazing. The only thing we really spent unnecessary money on was an octagonal fish tank. It was a big ass fish tank with a bunch of oscars and piranhas in it. It looked baller and gave the spot a little class at the same time. When women made it to the crib they were all impressed by the miniature aquarium at the house. We would even feed our fish so they could see them hunt the cheap goldfish and shit. It was cool.

That was us being spendthrifts. We bought fish. Yeah, we had a dope stereo and a nice TV but not much else. We knew our frugality was a great thing and it took a lot for us to commit to that level of discipline. That made it hard to break. We couldn't just toss it to the side freely and believe we'd stay safe.

Nah. We weren't that sloppy.

The operation demanded we stay low key to continue functioning with high profit. We both agreed that was the only way to maintain our activity levels. It's part of the reason we moved far away from the school. We chose to live a solid distance from where we worked to make certain those things stayed separate. We didn't want the people on campus, or our clients, to see how we lived or to know the location of our spot. The less we were seen outside of putting in work, the better.

Besides, peacocks were always the mutha fuckas who were actually broke. Those are cats trying to show some value they didn't actually have. We didn't need that. Our money was real, we didn't put a bunch of value in looking like it. Otherwise, we'd be those Atlanta cats, begging to be caught. That shit wasn't going to be us.

We didn't just relocate where we lived. That first Knoxville College summer session changed everything. Our entire business dynamic changed when we moved off campus. Almost every one of our clients on the Yard had left town for the summer. Those who were still in town didn't need to meet us on campus to get serviced. And, leaving the dorms changed our range of activity altogether. We had to become chameleons and adjust to our situations. This became a laundry list of shifts.

Even though we had previously remained on campus when we did our work, we knew the bulk of our clients came from a project complex and the surrounding area behind the school. That community was called Mechanicsville or, more fondly, "The 'Ville". Changing our 'service venue' meant we had to change our sales approach. Our clients could no longer freely come to us on the Yard because we weren't set up there. We had to make other arrangements.

Jerry and I posted up in the neighborhood but we kept our product back at home. When we started to run low on product, I would roll to the crib and grab more. It was a bit of a headache but precaution can't be cut short. Being smart and patient are synonymous with 'freedom' in the business. We couldn't keep it all with us, that wasn't smart. So, we only took a particular measure with us at a time and would make the run back to replenish our supply. Most times I would make it back before Jerry ran out. It was elaborate and risky and I didn't like it. I was constantly looking for another route.

We didn't have a room on campus so our access there was limited. It wasn't eliminated, though. Turns out that Big Lou's first roommate, Poppy, stayed for the summer. He and I had gotten cool after getting through the 'V-football-equipment' -thing. That was a low key tense but funny situation. I'll let him tell you about that. Anyways, when I found out he was still on the Yard, I hollered at him frequently.

Initially, we kept meeting clients on the Yard. We knew they would look for us there until we gave them another location. So, Jerry or I would roll up on campus and hang out for some hours. We started making sure all of our customers had our pager number so they could have off grid access to us. Whenever I took small breaks on campus I would hang out with Poppy.

He became useful, too. Let me explain why it was an operational procedure to keep our stash in a different location than the work site. That rule applied to the amounts (money and product) we kept on our person and where our stashes were kept. It was a different perspective on how to 'diversify our portfolio' but it was serious business with us. We separated our assets as much as possible on every level that we maintained them.

The business provided way more enemies than allies. We could get robbed by our clients – even though we treated them well they were drug addict clients, not friends. Another sales group/our rivals might get the drop on us and take our stuff at gunpoint. Lastly, the cops' literal job was to bust up what we were doing. The odds are, at some point, everyone making sales was going to face one of those things. These were merely the risks, and probabilities, of doing our business.

Prudence mandated that we function in such a way that we didn't lose everything should one of the aforementioned misfortunes happen to us. So, we never kept all of our stash in one place. That's just basic logic. It was the same with our money. We didn't keep it where we kept our product. Getting hit for it all at once would put us at an operational dead end. And it would just be stupid. That was unacceptable for us.

Our crib was on the opposite side of town from the campus. Trying to maintain storing the stock at the house while travelling back and forth was wildly inefficient.

So, after I while, I asked Poppy to hold product for me in his room while I went out and worked it. He said cool and I threw him some change just for letting it sit in his room. That was valuable to me so I showed it by compensating him. Two or three times a week I would scoop him up on the humble and we would go get something to eat somewhere. If I had delicious food out in town, sometimes I would drop him off some takeout. At KC, food was at a premium. That cafeteria situation with those limited hours was rough. So, he would hold my stash for me, I would toss him some loot and get him fed. It was a win-win situation.

So, we were out on the block, making the magic happen and we had a local 'stash house', per se. The only drawback there was: we were selling on the Knoxville streets.

Initially, I was really discontented with posting up in the wide-openness of the streets. There was no protection in the open air and everyone could see what you were up to. It was also a large divergence from the cover of the campus.

However, dudes that used to play dice at the 'Ledge would always say, "scared money don't make money". More than that, I refused to be led by fear. Everything you wanted to make happen in life, everything worth doing, would take effort. The things that you would cherish most in life were on the other side of your fear. You had to get out and do it. That 'doing it' would take me applying myself and getting out there. Only then would it be done. You understand? I was definitely scared but that wasn't my focal point. Success was! Once we got out there we knew we would figure out how to make it work.

So, we got out there.

There was a liquor store, a party store and a mom & pop restaurant that we would frequent from the campus. I told you the cafeteria shut down after 6:00 and teenagers ate like hogs. So, those hunger pangs struck harder than a mutha fucka every evening. That was super tough on students who didn't have cars or access to them. So, students would walk to those options all times of the day and night. Before I had a car I was doing it, too.

On those trips, I always noticed that there were a lot of locals around the area. Quite a few of those locals were some of the more 'impacted' customer types. You could see some of them completely strung out, trying to bum money from people or just dealing with their high while looking like space cadets. It looked like a good place to sew more seeds and get the clientele count up. I kicked it to Jerry and we agreed that would be our play.

Initially, it was kind of slow. Not a whole lot of activity brewed up in the first couple days. Things quickly caught fire after that. I told you, our product was a mutha fucka. We continued selling oversized packs of much more potent product and it made a freeway of activity in no time. The locals were instant fiends for it and our business multiplied accordingly.

Jerry and I took the loot from our 3-way split, along with both of our refund checks from the summer session, and used that to buy our stock. We had a nice stash to start the summer with and we thought it would last us for quite some time.

Fortunately for us, it didn't. The word spread, the fiends came and we were cranking in no time. From the beginning, it was just Jerry and me. We ran a lot of after-hour business through our pagers, and they stayed lit up. Otherwise, our customers caught us on the block and we served them that 'ooh-wee' that they couldn't get elsewhere. We had definitively carved out our own niche and business was booming.

Whenever we got down to a certain amount, one of us, usually me, would go get another pack from Poppy's room. That way we were never out of product while we were on-site. That worked pretty smoothly for us. We always had that Work when clients came to see us. Everybody knows that dependability was just good business. We decided to handle every facet of our work with a reserve from then out.

That's when we began to implement a phase of the system that would be long-standing. After running dry a few times with our first supplier, we created a reserve. Whenever we reached those stores we knew it was time to reup. That way, we would prevent having a mad scrambled to resupply while upsetting the flow of our sales.

This would be the same approach on the block when Jerry and I worked together. We would only keep a few single packets on our person. They were amounts that a drug addict would have, 2 or 3 hits max. This would keep our liability low if we were apprehended by the cops. We could argue in court that we were using and that's an entirely different infraction than being charged with distribution. So, we kept the bulk of the on-site product we were selling in an empty Weigel's fountain soda cup up against a building. (Weigel's is a brand of gas station/convenience stores).

This wasn't a special practice of ours. Actually, I would call that dope game 101. Your first objective was to never get caught. If you ever did get caught you would want to be apprehended with nothing at all – no product on your person and no weapons. If they did manage to get you with something then you would want that to be worth damned near nothing. A rock (Crack was cut into small chunks) or two could easily be explained away as consumption and that wasn't remotely as stiff a penalty as distribution.

These practices helped minimize charges so cats could preserve their freedom. That's how we would try to beat the system and prevent getting convicted of drug charges that would confine us behind bars for decades. Nobody was trying to waste all of their youth in a cage, man. Damn that! Preemptively minimizing risk was our attempt to achieve that wiggle room while still aggressively promoting our illegal operation. Pretty standard stuff for the business.

An incredibly fortuitous development made our invasion operation secure from our competitors. Oh, and believe, it was an absolute invasion! We were out in Knoxville as migrants from St. Louis, selling product that the locals could not provide. We barged in, set up camp and begun drastically outperforming them. Yes, we had invaded the shit out of their space! The way we began to command the market you could call it an outright siege.

Normally, I mean at home or other big cities, such an invasion would get someone killed. At the very least hospital visits were going to be involved. Initially, it was impossible to understand why that wasn't our immediate fate. I was certain there was a reason, though. There was.

Remember I told you that students went to those three area businesses frequently? And, remember when Big Lou told you there was a St. Louis rule in Knoxville where we all stuck together? Well, both of those things came together for us in a way that was difficult to see before it happened. But I was glad as fuck that it did.

There were more than a handful of guys from the Lou that stayed during the summer. For everything that we were, our posse was full of studious people. Most stayed in the summer to get ahead of their graduating schedule. Some just wanted to knock out tougher courses over the shorter semester. There were a couple dozen of us (St. Louis guys) at Knoxville College that summer. Because the campus was virtually empty, that gave us a much bigger presence on the Yard than normal. I think that made it even more of a thing to stick together because there wasn't much else to do.

You already know that people from the 'Lou were huge baseball fans. The whole city embraced the 'Cards (the St. Louis Cardinals) to the point that every game day was like a local holiday. When you walked around town in St. Louis, at any time of the year, you would see a veritable ocean of Cardinals hats with the famous 'StL' on the front. We loved baseball.

In Knoxville, that became a symbol of representation. In every group of guys from the crib, more of them wore those hats daily than those who didn't. As we coalesced on the Yard, it became even more of a thing. Unfortunately, it added to the misconception that we were a gang. The color didn't matter, the style didn't really matter either. We rocked the shit out of those St. Louis baseball caps. (Collectively, that is. I, personally, never got huge on wearing hats).

So, as these St. Louis guys travelled from campus to the stores I mentioned, they would pass us while we were handling business. They would stop every time, whether on the way or on their return. Oftentimes they would do both. They were just looking out, usually checking to see if we needed something from the store.

We had a concerted habit of looking out for each other, it was the St. Louis thing to do in Knoxville. It definitely applied to us while we were out there in the streets. I don't know what their visits looked like to onlookers but we were chilled. The guys would stand around with me for hours at a time, kicking it about bullshit while I was making money.

Even though we were all there for college, none of the people from the crib would trip that I was hustling. Shit, we were from the 'Lou! Whether you were a part of it or not, we were all used to the hustle. We'd seen it all around us for such a long time that the drug life didn't faze us. Part of the reason we were at college was to change that fate because we knew how real it was. So, none of them fronted on me for hustling.

I'm certain our business was every problem for the locals. They were easy to watch because they were never too far from the spots I stood. Even though I was making money in their area, they smiled or waved at me often. I thought that was crazy peculiar. Back in St. Louis we weren't friendly like that. We specifically weren't waving at mutha fuckas we didn't know. If you rolled into our projects like that, and nobody knew you, the last thing we would do was greet you kindly. Particularly if you came in our area with a hustle. That shit wouldn't fly.

In Knoxville, though, we were taking their customers but they never even looked like they wanted to approach us. That was really odd for everything I knew about the business. Our crew invaded their space, set up shop and got crazy busy. We had to be taking their customers, there's no other way to see it. Still, they were downright hospitable. It was clear that they wanted nothing to do with challenging us. At least that's how it started.

Business multiplied at a rapid rate, actually Jerry and I were getting overwhelmed. We weren't always there together at the same time. When it was just one of us, we would sometimes have customers standing by at a distance, waiting to get served after someone else. I got seriously concerned with having a waiting line. That, in my mind, was very bad business. It drew too much attention.

It got so bad (or good) that the fellas from the crib started offering to help. None of them wanted to put in serious time for real, they were all college students working towards a future career. But one or two stood around with me to make a little money and move on. So, I gave them $250 packs. The deal was they returned $200 to me and kept the rest. Those dudes would sell out their supply, toss me $200 and be on their way. Sometimes that took 2 or 3 hours, sometimes it took less than one. All depended on the day and if they got lucky.

I'd always been a stickler on dependability. Kowrie's systems had a whole lot to do with that. Being out of product was an especially offensive predicament, it was just bad business. When customers came through, I never wanted them to leave with money in hand. That was the worst business practice. So, when I was working the block by myself, I always looked out for when the 'Lou fellas would come through. If I was anywhere near low, I would give one of them my pack then go to Poppy's room to reup.

If the crew that came by didn't include one of the brothers I trusted like that, then it got handled a bit differently. I would ask them to tell Poppy to holler at me when they got back to the Yard. Poppy automatically knew that meant I was running low and would run a pack out to me.

I told you about the beauty and the naivete of the city. These things would be lying representations without addressing the entrenched racism. See, Knoxville is part of the old south, it's got the confederate love to prove it. The UT 'Volunteers', the lifeblood of the city, is an absolute homage to the confederacy. Some of the kindness and hospitality is also part of their whole 18th/19th century world. It is not the most modern town in any regard.

This is most visible in their segregation. Knoxville is a city of two sides: the east side and the west side. They are entirely different communities with wildly dissimilar constituencies. There are isolated pockets of Black people throughout the east side. Conversely, there's only a spattering of Black people in the western end of town. Like any racist town, the school systems are congruently imbalanced. That's a story for a different tale.

The area we operated in was definitely more western than it was eastern. It was a still a project-rich area and it was almost exclusively filled with Black people. The good thing was, its pseudo-western location placed it in the 'do not patrol heavily' zone. That was one of the largest symbols of a racist city – imbalanced policing.

My initial engagement of the city rarely saw a police presence. Their patrols were very occasional and they were not very invasive. In my experience, that's a respect we're not normally afforded by police, particularly in government project areas. Knowing why they were more respectful (because of the proximity to white Knoxville communities) pissed me the fuck off as a Black man. But, for the purposes of my business endeavors it couldn't have been more ideal.

There were a few specific cops who took interest in the area, though. The locals I served told me about a pair of plain clothes cops who would shake guys down then arrest them. They called them 'Starsky and Hutch', clearly they were white boys. These cops varied in height and one had blond hair, the other was brunette. Just like the TV duo.

The cops would appear out of nowhere, make the locals run their pockets then apprehend them if they found anything. Amazingly, Starsky and Hutch would still catch guys. The locals never adjusted: they didn't switch up how they did things or run when they saw them coming. They didn't even have a way to call them out when they were close by. They had a general police call but not one for the 'Hollywood' pair. That was about the dumbest shit I saw them do.

Well, one day, I was running low when the St. Louis posse came through on a daily store run. On their way back, I asked them to holler at Poppy for me. They told me they knew where he was and they would tell him to fall through.

Mere minutes after they got out of sight, I saw Starsky. Hutch was nowhere in sight but I figured he was around somewhere, too. Starsky was haranguing the local boys down the street about a block and a half away but I could plainly see him from where I stood. Then Hutch entered the scene from around a building. No sooner than I peeped him showing up, Hutch looked my way and started walking towards me.

I ran my ass off!

I could have easily hidden the rock or two that I had in my pocket but that wasn't enough for me. I didn't want him to see me or ID me. Prior to seeing that dude walking my way, I had no real functional fear of the cops. We had been working for almost 6 months with no police inter-action. I got comfortable. But watching him make a beeline for where I was standing scared me. All of my teachings and my life essence tells me nothing about me belongs in a cell. Seeing that cop walk my way brought all of that to bear and my physical response took over.

I ran like a mutha fucka.

I hit enough corners to satisfy my mind that I had lost him. I consciously stayed away from the KC direction altogether. Tipping off the cops to any of my assets was a no-no. This landed me on the opposite side of the campus. One of the students we knew from New York had a spot a few blocks away. I ran there and hit him up for a change of clothes.

I was pissed that the cop had scared me. Running from people wasn't what men did. That rubbed me wrong as hell. So, I refused to let the white boy run me off of my spot for long. I had more product to sell and the custos (customers) were going to keep looking for product. It was early in the month and they hadn't burned out their government checks yet. I was stubborn as hell, so, my work day was going to continue. I figured it would be wise for me to switch up my look before heading back over there.

The NY homie gave me a crazy ass fire red track suit. That shit was flooding like hell, the bottoms might have reached my ankles but I don't think they did. And it was tight as shit! If you looked at them from the right angle you would have sworn that they were a pair of leggings. He also passed me an incredibly lived-in grey fisherman's hat. I'm surprised that mutha fucka didn't have the hooks hanging in it. It looked like he had just come off of the lake and handed it to me. Then I snatched a pair of shades from off a dresser and immediately regretted it. It was a pair of green colored-frames with no lenses. Those frames didn't match shit! Covering my face made me feel like the disguise was complete, though. So, I threw all of that on and bailed from his crib, heading back to the block. I was a whole new human being leaving dude's house.

Walking back, I was upset with myself. I was pissed at me for running. Of course, no sane person wants to go to jail. But the reason why I took off is what angered me. It became clear to me that I was afraid of being imprisoned. That fear was different and it made me angry. Yeah, the cops have dominion over us when we're breaking laws. I gave that to them by hustling and so this mutha fucka had a power over me. I despised that idea. The whole notion of weakness, that someone else could rule my choices had me completely perturbed. I also hated that running revealed my guilt. It was an extremely frustrating walk back.

I carefully scrutinized the area while approaching my normal perch. There wasn't any suspicious movement or people or vehicles on the way or in the zone when I got there. Scanning the locals' activity, nothing seemed like it was out of order. They seemed to be on their normal level of relaxed. My assessment was that the cops had gotten their fill for the day and moved on. So, I pensively got back to work, keeping my eyes peeled for anything out of order.

A few minutes after I arrived, Poppy rolled up. He started talking to me as if I were a total stranger. The clothes I was wearing weren't familiar to him and they covered so much of me that he didn't recognize me at all. We kicked it for about five minutes before he figured out who I was. My own homie couldn't determine who I was when we were in full blown conversation! I'm gonna call that a successful ass disguise.

I was glad he arrived after me. If he walked up there with product for me and got pinched, I would have been pissed. That's not how you do people who look out for you. Fortunately, we were both good. I got what I needed, tossed him some loot and the hustle continued.

I had a dogged mentality about the hustle. It was unbreakable. When goals were set, I assumed they would be completed and my hustle matched that determination. That's how everything on the block got handled. I was relentless.

So, I was more than a little vexed when Jerry started slacking. It became a thing that I would leave the crib to go hustle and he wouldn't even show up for the day. That put me in a predicament to often hold down the block alone. It wasn't precisely new, both of us had to do that sometimes because there were only two of us. Shit happened. But this was different. This was turning into the assumption that I would be by myself. That had to be remedied.

One day, a brother from the crib fell through just to holler at me. Well, it was clear he wanted to talk to one of us, I just happened to be alone that day. It was a guy named Slick. He came by himself. Slick told me he had been checking out my operation and that he thought I was probably making good money. Slick said he wanted to be down.

I didn't hold him up at all. Business had picked up heavily and I was thinking about doing that exact thing – hiring somebody. The busyness of being a corner boy kept me working *in* the business. I wanted to work *on* the business. Help was definitely needed. It was more than prudent to put him on, it was timely.

Before adding Slick, we were a crew of bosses. Jerry, Big Lou and I were all equal partners. When Big Lou was a part of the operation, we all did what we could to put the work in equally. Losing Big Lou, and the change in our 'service venue', combined with our growing success demanded that we add some personnel. Then when Jerry started backing off, help was mandatory.

Slick was the soldier I needed. He was hungry, so he would come out and hit it every day. I started him out with $250 packs. Some days, he could go through two or three of those in a shift. The business was really moving and he was driven to keep it cranking.

Slick was my first actual employee. He got paid daily for the work he did. Jerry and I would cover our daily expenses but didn't receive personal payment, per se, until we split the dividends of our entire loads. In laymen's terms: when we sold a full bird, we split the profits of that 50/50. Then we would equally pitch in for the next batch.

Slick wasn't a part of that. He got paid to do shit and represented the next level of our operation. We were employers from that point on.

Here's the updated scoreboard: We made $30,000 in a 1989 school semester. We lost Big Lou, left campus for the summer session, got a crib off-campus and started working the streets. The locals couldn't like us there but they were no challenges to what we were doing. Cops were rarely present. Our customers not only began to be loyal but they were recruiting for us. Jerry started dropping off and I added our first employee because business was booming.

And we were running out of product.

Our business had taken flight. We were into our back-up supply long before we anticipated it. That was fine, though, selling product was everything we were trying to do. It was simply time to replenish the stash and build on what we were doing.

Y'all already know that was going to be a problem, right? Murphy's Law just has a way of showing up. This was that time.

Knoxville just was not a booming mecca of any sort. The bulk of major happenings in this city originated somewhere else and were brought here. That's a pretty far ranging reality. Knoxville isn't known for some type of commerce or creativity or cultural contribution. The only contemporary popularity associated with the city is the University of Tennessee. That's because of it's successful sports programs, mainly football, and those are incredibly dependent on national recruiting. The city hasn't made its mark on the country through its productivity of any sort. Or, at least, none that I knew about. Their only renowned claim is being volunteers for the confederacy. Fuckers.

The drug market was a model of the city's outside influences. The entire supply for Knoxville, no matter who was working it, came from out of state. When that didn't work out, for whatever reason, then they were simply dry. If you were a dope dealer, the only way to keep your business flowing was to either buy in bulk or have multitudes of connections.

Well, we found ourselves in a serious pickle. We were the amazing victims of success and we were in jeopardy of running dry. We had not yet established a huge multitude of options. My supplier from school wasn't in town and my new city guy was fresh out. I was in the unique and undesirable position of trying to find another source.

After searching however and wherever we could, the answer appeared closer to us than I wanted it to be. There was one guy running an outfit in town who was considered the kingpin in the city. I had begun our enterprise without allowing myself to consider him as an option. Ironically, his operation was the reason I thought we could be profitable in this market. I did everything I could to find a way around this resource. But, as we were rapidly running towards empty, I had to do what I had to do.

We needed to work with Skins.

So, I went looking for Roostah.

CHAPTER 31
PLANS CHANGE

Sometimes it takes a minute for things to dawn on you. As well as we were doing and as much as we were working, it hadn't occurred to me that we hadn't run into Skins or Roostah on the streets. Quietly, the word was Skins was the supplier for the locals down the street from me. Whether they were working with him or for him, I didn't know at the time. But I never saw neither him nor Roostah around. Nothing about them had ever come my way, either. There was a reason for it.

The students at KC saw Knoxville as small and slow. Basically, both of those things were true. However, it was still a city and it was very wide ranging. I told you about the segregation and a little about how it affected my operation. Well, there's another side to that story. The east side, to be exact.

There wasn't a lot of back and forth intercity travel with a lot of the locals. Whichever side of town they lived on is where they stayed and operated. Aside from their own family members, they typically didn't mess with people on the other side. Unfortunately, my clients were my main resources for finding people locally. When I came up empty with them I had to roll to the east side to find Roostah for myself. So, Jerry and Slick, mostly Slick, held down the fort for a few days while I looked for him.

Now, I'm certain the local boys I stared at every day could get in touch with both Roostah and Skins. There was no way they would help me with anything, though. Yeah, they smiled or waved daily but they weren't even the most remote of allies. That's just a preposterous notion. No matter how friendly the area was, I wasn't crazy enough to get it twisted. I wasn't going to approach those guys about shit. So, I headed east to find my dude.

Getting Slick on the team couldn't have come at a better time. It took me a minute to catch up with Roostah. My clients didn't know him because he operated on the other side of town. He might as well have been in another state as far as they were concerned. That left me with few leads.

I only realized my similarities to the locals when my search started. I didn't know shit about the east side either. Knoxville is not a gridded city. It is contoured by the Smoky Mountains, so it has twists and curves and bends. You could travel one street in one direction for a few miles and go every direction on the globe (east, west, north and south) before turning off. It took a few days for me to orient myself and figure out how things were positioned in proximity to other parts of town.

The hood is the hood, though. The signs aren't difficult to read when your eye has been trained to understand it all. There is a vibe, an energy in the hood that tells you what you need to know. You know the spots you don't want to be in the minute you see them. Those were exactly the spots I was looking in to find Roostah.

Accordingly, I found him in a dingy pool hall. It was the kind of spot that you knew you needed to be packing (toting a gun) to go in. That was no problem because I had a heater just for such an occasion. I was looking for a drug dealer in a foreign town in an unknown area. Everyone I dealt with, other than him once he was found, would be someone I didn't know. You can bet your ass the heat was riding with me.

There were a bunch of dudes standing outside the pool hall when I saw it. They were just posted up in general, standing around shooting the shit. They weren't particularly friendly looking and they were probably into grimy shit. Despite those looks, this was still Knoxville in 1989. When I walked up almost all of them greeted me some kind of way. I still love that about the city. It's a nice place, even for the cats doing dirt. Well, at least it was back then. It could be an entirely different beast now but that's a different discussion.

I walked in and saw him with a drink in his hand, smoking a joint. For the record, Roostah was a wiry dude. He would look like a featherweight boxer if he wasn't so tall. He was definitely welterweight because of it. Roostah liked the fact that he resembled Michael Irvin. I'm telling you, he could've been that dude's long-lost child. You could catch him doing the leg slide and spiking the ball for no damned reason, just because he looked like Irvin when he did it.

Roostah's skin was one shade into being dark and his face was... uneventful. He wasn't spectacularly ugly but he wasn't anybody's pretty boy. That didn't stop him from taking care of himself, though. He carried his brush religiously and was rewarded with a rolling sea of waves in his hair. That day, the bill of a fresh, brand new StL ballcap was hiding that feature.

Roostah was a high-energy, hyperactive guy. That was definitely a bad character trait addition for his particular brand of crazy. Even if he didn't know you he could smoke and joke with you and have a wild ass time just like you were best buds. Right up to the minute he shot you. He was a wild mutha fucka. That nickname was fitting as hell.

He was my dog, though. I was really glad to see him. Fortunately for me, he was glad to see me too.

"Heeeeeeelll naw! What's up, dawg? What the hell you doing here, boah?" Roostah yelled.

He had a massive smile on his face. He gave me dap that instantly turned into a hug.

"It's good to see you, bruh," I said while I smacked him on his shoulder.

"It's good to see you too, roomdog." He said that before we left the embrace. "Rolling up in here with heat and everything. Hell naw. Aight then. Wassup, bruh?"

He peeped the .357 in my waistband after the hug. When he saw the gun he took it as respect, that's just the way he's built.

I was looking for yo' ass, Roots." I said.

"Well, you fucking found me," he responded. Then he yelled out to anyone listening, "Ay! This my mutha fuckin' dog right here. My dude from waaaay back and my college room dawg. Get this man whatever he wanna drank. On me."

The pool hall had what they called a bar. It was so rinky-dink and busted that my assumption was they didn't have a liquor license. The available booze was still booze and mutha fuckas still drank it, license be damned.

"Mutha fuckin' Busara! What 'up, boah? What you up to?" He asked.

"Actually, I need to holler at you on some business."

He was taken aback.

"Okay. What kind of business?" he was quizzical.

"You got some where we can talk? Better yet, you got a minute? Take aride with me." I said.

"For you? Shit yeah. Let's ride!" He responded.

The pool hall was *his* spot on *his* side of town. The playing field needed to be more leveled for me to be comfortable. Flipping it to my court was just better positioning for the conversation. I was able to do that without any hassle.

We rolled out of the pool hall and jumped in my ride. When we got in the car my focus was on the conversation. I had no idea where I was driving and I didn't concern myself with it.

Roostah's energy was as high as always. He scanned the inside of the car and began rubbing the interior.

"Dawg, I like your ride, man. This is nice. What's going on with you, bruh, what you in to?" He asked.

"So, what? You catching up on lost time?" I jokingly said.

"What, dawg? What you mean?"

"You barely get in the car and you clowning me on the ride?" We laughed a bit.

"Nah, man. I didn't know you had a car. I was just vibing it. Don't be sensitive and shit, Boots." Roostah jabbed.

"Fuck you, man." I was still laughing.

"Straight up. It's loud but this shit is bangin'! I'm feeling it." He said.

"I appreciate that, Roots." I responded. "It's just a little something to keep me moving."

"Quietly, you need to get some of this paper then you wouldn't have to be sensitive about this dusty ass car. You can get something plush if you roll with me."

Perfect opening, so I cut to the chase.

"That's exactly what we need to rap about. I'm running an operation and we need some product. I know you can help me with that." I said.

"Wait... what? You slangin' yayo? Hell naw! Not you."

I nodded my head.

"Dawg, I been to one of them meetings, man. Remember? You was the mutha fucka keepin' *me* straight back in the day. How you out here slangin'? I know you trippin'." He said, half confused.

"I'm still about empowering my people. This paper is what's getting me there. I'm doing what I gotta do. One minute you telling me it's what I should do, next minute you giving me shit about it. Stop being sensitive, Roots. Can you help me out or what?"

He laughs.

"Fuck you, man. Hold up, you got a spot? Where is it?" He asked.

"Nah, not yet. For now, we working these streets in the 'Ville." I replied.

"Hell-the-fuck-naw! That's you?!"

He asked aloud and I nodded my head. Then he mumbled to himself.

["...mutha fucka. They *did* say something about St. Louis or some shit, nobody know what they country ass was sayin'... now it makes sense."]

He looked up and addressed me.

"Yeah, dawg. I heard about you but I didn't know it was *yo'* ass. That was *yo'* ass?! My mutha fuckin' nigga! ...it just fucks me up, man. Boots is in the fucking game... shit's crazy. But it ain't shit. I got you. No shit, Busara, I got you. Hell yeah!" He looked off towards the window. "...son of a bitch!"
"What's that about?" I asked.
"Nah, it's just... I woulda had you killed, man."

Didn't know where that was going but I needed to know. Immediately.

"What you mean?" I asked.
"Dawg, when they first told us about somebody putting in work in the 'Ville they asked what they should do. I ain't gone lie, boah, I straight told them to ice whoever it was. Get rid of the issue."
"Why didn't they?"
"Look, now, I didn't know it was you. It woulda been a whole different thang. Straight up, you like my brother, Boots. If I don't ride for you I can't ride for nobody. Mutha fuckas come for you they gotta come for me. I know you know that. I just didn't know it was you. It still fucks me up." He paused. "Anyways, Skins said naw."

"Why did he do that?" This was interesting to me. And important, I just had a feeling it would be.

"This is what I'm telling you. He said, 'don't go shooting up the block or some shit. Y'all will tear the whole neighborhood down. Ain't no telling who might get shot in that – kids, old people, some women. That ain't necessary. And, it'll bring the cops, they'd start getting in to shit and start shutting everything down.' He said the heat from that won't stop. He didn't believe it was worth all that drama. He was like, 'as long as they don't go after y'all or start no shit then let them make they little money.' It fucked me up. I ain't understand that," Roostah exclaimed.

It fucked me up, too. This Skins dude wasn't as stupid as he originally seemed to me. There was some visionary thought in that logic. And, there was some sense of community in it. All of that made me second-guess my assessment of him.

Roostah really struggled wrapping his head around me working. The way he tripped out on it made me remember my purpose. As much as that moved me, that moment wasn't the time to discuss it with him.

Unfortunately, no such time would ever come. In fact, if a person wasn't connected to my operation, or if we weren't strictly friends, then that conversation wasn't going to be had. I couldn't tell people in the field about my bigger heart, the liberation of African people. In the drug world it just sounded like weakness, a weakness that could be exploited. That would create problems and challenges for me that I didn't need. I made a pact with myself to keep that love for my people out of public speech.

Ultimately, I tried sharing it less. Not by what was spoken but by how I treated people. I made a concerted effort to remove emotion from my daily activities. I wasn't particularly mean but it definitely couldn't be coined as friendly. Developing a harder shell was necessary for the work we were doing, it's an expense of the business. So, I wound up offering less love to my people for a work that was killing my people so I could empower myself to help our people.

Yeah, as shitty and contradictory as that sounded it was perfectly accurate.

I kept driving and we hacked it up for a good minute. I talked about what kind of weight we would need and Roostah told me we would be good, they could take care of us. He let me know that the dudes in the 'Ville weren't their 'guys', per se, they just supplied them. Our competition had told them, erstwhile, that there were dozens of St. Louis dudes. They told him we were bringing more and more people into the city all the time. On any given day, they told him, it could be ten or twelve guys hustling. He was told we were a big ass St. Louis gang.

I was struggling to refrain from laughing at the information. Those country bumpkins thought everybody who stopped to holler at me, all of those college students… were working. Because of that, they had no idea where we began or ended. No idea how many of us were holding it down. That's why they weren't fucking with Jerry and me while we were out there: they didn't want the 'city of St. Louis' to come down on them. That fucked me up.

That, coupled with what Skins told them, kept them in check. I figured more than a small portion of that would become useful at some point – or create more problems.

He went on to tell me that it was no sweat for them (that meant it was no issue for Skins) how things went in the 'Ville. The truth was, if they were selling to both operations then they would win regardless. I knew it would work for Skins like gangbusters, and that wasn't my plan. I wasn't trying to make him more prosperous but I needed what I needed. I was good with Skins and Roostah making their money as long as I was making mine because of it. Win-wins are cool in my book, they usually keep things from going sideways.

Well, the arrangement with Skins would keep things from going sideways too soon, that is. Ugly shit was coming, though. I had planned for it.

Then Roostah and I started rapping about the fellas and catching up with each other. We touched on how things were in the 'Lou but neither of us really knew so it was a brief portion of the conversation.

Before I knew it, we were mere blocks from Mechanicsville. I was, apparently, on autopilot mentally and just rolled towards my stomping grounds. This suited Roostah just fine. In fact, it appeared I had done him a favor.

"So, I'll set it up for Saturday at 6. We can meet up at Callie's and handle it. That cool?"

"That'll work. That'll work." I responded.

"Yo, now I need to know if you got a minute. I need you to take me to this stop real quick."

"Yeah, that ain't shit. Where we going?"

"I need you to roll through the 'Ville for me. I gotta grab something." He said.

I agreed, we bent a few corners then rolled down Western Avenue. He had me turn off on College Street then we parked on the corner of Moses Ave. We were right behind KC but in the neighborhood.

"There that mutha fucka is!" Roostah said excitedly to himself. Then he looked at me.

"Dawg, you got that .357? Let me check it out for a minute,"

"What?" I was tripping.

"Yeah, Boots. Let me see your gat (gun), man." He said.

"You not about to shoot a mutha fucka, are you?" I asked.

"Nah, I don't think so. It won't take that." He paused. "It shouldn't."

Something about how he said it made me morbidly curious. I had half a thought that he would do something dirty with me but I didn't trip. What he didn't do a lot of was lie. If he did, he wouldn't have told me that he almost had us killed. He was just forthright like that. My inhibition was built on the life I was living at the time. Roostah was my dude at home but we weren't in St. Louis. In Knoxville, he worked for the competition. Regardless of how well we were acquainted, I had to factor that in. Letting my guard down was becoming tough to do.

When he said he regarded me as his brother, I believed him. Roostah had real family challenges, labeling me as family was no small thing. We were that kind of tight when we ran together as kids. He was my second choice for a roommate in college, only D Smooth would've come before him. We were definitely tight. It was damned near a certainty that he wouldn't do anything scandalous to me. I knew I was trippin', so, I gave it to him.

"Thanks, dawg." He said.

He got out of the car and trotted over to the guy he had spotted. There was a crowded basketball court on the opposite corner. Dudes were running a full court pick-up game and a group of people were dribbling on the sidelines while waiting. Roostah ran towards that group.

It was about 7:00 on a Knoxville summer evening. The sun was high in the sky and heading towards setting in the west. There was a scattered light cloud or two but it was bright and beautiful outside. The whole neighborhood was outside. There were kids running around, adults strolling on the sidewalks and elders sitting on porches. Somebody was watering a yard, a few teenagers were riding bikes, some girls were playing jump rope in the street - it was an incredibly active daytime scene. In legal terms, it was a witness-rich environment.

That didn't mean a damned thing to Roostah. He never tried to hide the gun, he had it in his hand the entire time. He ran with it down to his side while he approached the basketball courts.

"Hey Cal! Wassup?" Roostah yelled out as he was creeping towards him.

The guy looked like he wanted to run but Roostah was too close for that. There was fencing around the court but only at the two opposite angles from where Cal stood. The space between him and Roostah was wide open. So, he put on a sheepish plastic smile and responded.

"Hey, man. Wassup, Mad Dog. I was looking for you last week, man." The scared guy said.
"Oh yeah, was you? Then I don't know why you didn't find me 'cause I was in all my usual spots all week. That's some odd shit, right?"

Roostah said this while continuing to gain ground on the guy. Cal was itching to run but he just stood there, shifting his body weight side to side.

"But that means you got my money right now, then. Right?" Roostah said.

Roostah was a mere step or two from the guy. Cal threw his hands up in surrender. It didn't help.

"Nah, man. I was…"

POP!

Roostah, in full stride, smacked Cal on the side of his face with the pistol.

The sound was loud like a gunshot that pierced the evening air. He probably cracked the guy's skull on that first blow.

A low "oh shit" came out of the crowd. The basketball game behind Roostah and Cal stopped. The basketball dribbled to a stop on its own. All the guys stood still and eyed Roostah like they thought he would shoot everybody. The people who were standing close to Cal quickly backed away from the action, focused intensely on it the whole time.

Cal fell from the first hit. That didn't stop Roostah. He stood over him and hit him with every word he said until he finished.

"Don't! Play! With! Me! Bitch! Get! My! Money!"

He stood up and tried to make eye contact with everybody on the court. He pointed his gun at them as he looked around.

"Any one of you mutha fuckas got something to say?"
He scanned their faces.
"Huh?! Anybody? Say it now because if I hear you been talkin' shit about me I *will* be back here for yo' ass, too."

When none of them moved an inch, he decided he had made his point. He casually walked back to the car and opened the door. He yelled back over to the court,

"Now it's sixty!"

He looked around at the whole neighborhood before he got back in the car.

That shit made me crazy uncomfortable. The entire neighborhood had stopped what they were doing and started looking either at the guy on the ground or at us.

They were looking at my ride. That was too much for me.

"Hey man, get yo' ass in here!" I insisted.

He got in the car and acted like he had simply given the dude a high five. My whole aura screamed that I was pissed off to the highest level of pissivity (even more mad than Robin Harris).

While pulling off, I stared at him with disgust on my face.

He caught all of it.

"What's up? Why you trippin'?" He innocently responded.

"Everybody around here looking at us, Roostah. They looking at my car. You might have just killed that man."

"Dawg, that ain't shit. He'll be fine. He shouldn't be, though. Mutha fucka need to give me my money and shit like that wouldn't happen." Roostah said.

"You beat that man, with my gun, in front of all kinds of people."

"Oh yeah, you can have this back." He said. "Thanks, dawg. I appreciate it. You my dude for life."

He handed me the .357. I took the gun back and placed it under my seat. I was hot.

"Listen here, man, I operate around here. They will see me – frequently! My car for sure." I said.

"I know! I just did you a favor."

"How the fuck is that?" I was hostile when I asked.

"You think they trying to fuck with you when they know you'll do shit like that?" He said through a smirk.

Fuck. He definitely had a point. It wasn't the worst happening for the business we were in. But that mutha fucka crazy.

"Besides, it was principle, man. You can't let these mutha fuckas slide with your loot or everybody will try you." He said with conviction. "I ain't having that shit."

"What did he owe you, Roostah?"

"He was into me for $50, dawg. I just changed it to $60 just for the hassle." He said it like it was morally sound.

"Dog, you just pistol-whipped a man in broad daylight, in front of an entire village for $50?" I asked exasperated.

"Sixty dollars." He corrected.

"Roostah, you have no fucking sense, man."

"Having sense is overrated, dawg."

I believe he was actually trying to convince me when he said it. He definitely meant it.

I can't lie about it: that shit shook me. The bold lawlessness of it felt like the kind of thing that got retaliated against. I wasn't trying to be in a war of any kind. We weren't prepared for that.

One of the biggest lessons of a night full of them: the locals *assumed* we were ready for war! And, as fucked up as Roostah's actions were, they created a bit of insurance for me. When the locals would say 'them St. Louis mutha fuckas are crazy' they meant him. They attributed it to all of us, though. That, and the way they saw us stick together, put us in a power position. It was easy to recognize and I didn't plan on ruining that. That's why I made no mention of how big my crew was to Roostah. They weren't going to get any help from me that didn't make us prosper.

They were scared and I was going to leave it that way.

Who could blame them, though? If all people from St. Louis were like Roostah's crazy ass, and everybody from St. Louis on the Yard was down with me – would you have run at us? Hell naw. Me neither. That logic is part of their small town thinking, though. No group of people are all the same. That basis is where the logic failed. They were frozen in the stupidity of that fear. I was more than happy to pass their dumb asses some ice cubes.

Still, I went home that night feeling like shit. I really didn't want to fuck with Skins at all but my options were super slim. And, straight up, he hadn't done anything to set me off. My initial read on him was just real foul. Slangin' dope was not an industry where you threw a lot of 'benefits of the doubt' around.

In updating the scouting report, Skins actually had some sense. He might have even had some compassion. But he still just seemed… like a real snake to me. Snakes really don't have loyalty. They bite mutha fuckas when they're hungry and think you're small enough to eat. Straight up. From all I know that could be why that dude had that nickname. Fucking Skins, man. Really wasn't looking forward to working with that dude.

Discovering that he had some degree of decency in him was surprising. The man ran an empire, thinking he had no vision at all was probably just foolish on my part. I checked myself for not being a little more open, more patiently judicious in receiving initial information. Everything can't be what it seems at first glance. That's just not real, 'books and covers' and shit, y'know? Since those lessons had not yet cost me much I would say they were good lessons.

Then I realized I was trippin'. I was focusing on the wrong details. This dude was my one man hit list: what could be better than getting close to him? Big Lou's brother said I should take out my competition and take his soldiers. The best way to do that was to get access to what they do, get familiar with their soldiers. If I started working with Skins, I would get to see how his operation worked, learn his people and observe all his weaknesses then catch him slipping. The rest is history. The expression 'keep your friends close and your enemies closer' had found a real way to apply to my life. That's exactly what I needed to do.

I made the choice to get up close and personal with Skins in order to personally close his shit out. Sooner or later, it was going to come down to him or me. Everything pointed in that direction, according to my vision and tutelage. At the growth rate we had, it looked more like sooner. The inevitable was inbound on a speed train and it was of the essence that I positioned myself to make sure it rode over his ass. It was cold, it was vicious, shit, it was calculated and it was what had to happen.

Killing a Black man wasn't remotely ideal for me, just being perfectly honest. Shit, I never saw myself murdering anybody! It was tough to even think about doing it, much less making it a key focus of a plan. It's not at all what I wanted to do. Especially once I saw he wasn't a total mindless cretin. Killing a Black man with community consciousness went against everything I believed. That being true, getting killed *by* a Black man was much less desirable. That's the spot I was in. It was time to man up.

I was ready for that meeting.

Saturday came and I rolled into Callie's at about five minutes before 7:00. There were two guys rolling with me. Rolling into the den of iniquity alone wasn't my idea of smart. Besides, this was our initial meeting. A show or force made the right impression. That would obviously be important to create the situation I needed.

I anticipated waiting for Skins to arrive. That's not how it went. When we walked through the door, he and Roostah were seated in a corner. Another goon or two of his was also in the building. There were a few people there who worked at the spot and no one else.

Skins looked at me with a smile on his face like his best friend had just showed up.

> "What's goin' on, Busara? I thought you were going to be late, it would have told me a little about you. Just like you being on time does." Skins never broke his smile while talking.
> "A man who doesn't respect time is misguided and confused about the value of things."

(What was that shit, Busara? You Confucius now?)

I didn't like sounding like a Buddhist. It was corny and way out of left field for the moment but it was automatic for me from my Kowrie experiences. Couldn't do shit about it once it was said so I let it ride.

> "You *are* a smart mutha fucka! Roostah told me you were the smartest dude he knows. To me, that was saying I was stupid. I didn't even get mad about it, either." Both of them started laughing.

I wasn't about to let myself be that kind of comfortable.

"Let's handle this business." I said.

"Shit, let's do that. Roostah said... oh, yeah! You were in the room with us last December. That was you, wasn't it?" Skins asked.

"Yeah. We were roommates." I said, referring to Roostah.

"Riiiight. You saw all that money and decided you wanted some, huh? Roostah did say you were a smart mutha fucka. And now we're here. Okay, what can I do for you, Mr. Busara?" Skins offered. He then continued, "have a seat, get comfortable. You need a drink or something? I can have one of my butlers around here fetch you something." He laughed.

"Where your fucking butlers at? You got Benson running around and I don't know about it?" Roostah responded.

They both laughed more.

"I thought your name was Jeffrey, ain't that you? Is he your uncle? There is definitely a resemblance," Skins joked.

"Man, fuck you." Roostah was still laughing as he said it.

"Nah, Roostah is like a tall Black Tattoo and shit. 'It's da plane, boss. Da plane, da plane'." Skins mocked.

They both laughed hard as hell at that. I wasn't at all.

"Welcome to Fantasy Island, Mr. Busara. What can the Island do for you?"

He seemed like he was both dead serious and playing at the exact same time. His tone was just a hair off of being disrespectful and I didn't appreciate it. If he wasn't taking me seriously I would just find another option. It was a struggle being there in the first place.

"You know I'm here for real shit, right? I'm here to forge a relationship where we both make some real money. If you good with that then let's work out the details and make it happen. If you think I'm here to play, I'll just go somewhere else. It's that simple." I said.

"Naw, youngblood, it's cool. You ain't got to be a hard dog with me. We here for real, this conversation is for real. We can forge some shit, for real. Ain't nobody playing. What you need?" He said, still half-smiling.

"That depends on the prices I'm looking at. So, what are you offering?" I asked him.

From there, we deliberated our business positions with reason. He turned out to be an easy conversationalist. He tried to crack jokes a lot. Not being in that joking mode, it mostly came off to me that he was an asshole. I understood he was trying to keep things light, though. That's just not where I was. Business was not a joking matter and I didn't trust the mutha fucka. I wasn't about to let my guard down. Period.

Then the light came on for me about Skins. He had a southern charm and the jokes are part of it, for sure. But that 'country bumpkin show' was his veneer. He was playing the 'I'm a good ole boy from around the way' -thing while he was snatching candy from babies. My first assessment told me Skins was a snake, but it turns out he was more of a snake charmer. Most importantly, he was nobody's dummy. There was much more to the guy than my initial read on him.

I was a truth-seeker. The truth is a universal principle that transcends religion. When a new truth reveals itself it is my every effort to conform to that altered understanding. It's what the wise do. I wouldn't dare compare myself to the great El-Hajj Malik El-Shabazz, but I did learn from Malcolm X's example: finding new truths changes me. Honest revelations demand that. Once Skins was more vividly uncloaked to me, it demanded that I shift my perspective. I was amenable to that.

I was more than impressed in that first meeting. Skins had unveiled a cunning calculus, and a subtly omni-present wisdom. After all, this dude was in the power position he held for a reason. That revelation made me even more alert about what the endgame looked like for the two of us. It became clear that I had to proceed carefully in dealing with him.

We agreed on our first purchase amount and price and where to do the switch. It was going down the next day. When the terms were done, I stood up and reached out to shake his hand. He stayed seated and didn't shake.

"Alright, so… how bad you want this deal?" He asked.

I took my hand back.

"What?" I responded. Fuckery was afoot, for sure.
"I said, how bad do you want this deal? I don't just roll like 'we agree and you get what you want'. This my town. You want a deal, you gotta kiss the ring." He declared.

He lifted his hand up to show a fat ass professional championship ring on his finger. It was authentic from his sports career. I didn't give two fucks about his damned ring.

I simply repeated my disbelief.

"What?!"

Skins had a more serious expression on his face than he had at any other time in the meeting.

"You heard me. You want in, you wanna get what I got, you gotta kiss the ring. It ain't no other way. And you already know, I'm the only dude in town who run like I run. If you don't get it with me, you don't get it in Knoxville. So, you want it or not?"

He stuck his hand out like some bullshit on TV that he had seen somewhere. As if he had completely expected me to do that shit.

Fuck. Him.

"Man, I don't know what kind of bullshit you used to and I don't care. I ain't kissing a mutha fucking thing. Certainly not your dirty ass hand. I'm out. The fuck I look like?"

I moved my chair a bit and went to walk right out the fucking door. My guys caught the drift and they were heading out with me. I was pissed.

Man, y'all need to understand something before I move on. Skins was an intimidating, ole house-sized mutha fucka. Period. This dude had played major league sports and looked like he could 'check' me and all the guys who were with me against the ice rink wall at the same time, and leave two of us unconscious. Serious shit. And, at the inception of our venture, Big Lou had been the muscle but he was gone. Flexing had never been my role. I was *all* business, that was my pedigree. My strength would be sticking to what I knew. So, naw, I wasn't trying to test that behemoth. Hell naw! But it would have been bad business to let anyone run over me. That wasn't acceptable in any situation, WWF-wrestler-sized goon or not.

Skins and Roostah's ole silly asses started cracking up laughing. They got out of their seats and were cackling their heads off. I mean, they were hollering, breathing heavy, holding their stomachs, leaning on each other and everything. I swore I saw a tear fall out of Roostah's eye.

"Naw, naw, naw, youngblood. Don't leave." Skins called out between laughs, "I was just fucking with you, man. I wanted to see who you are. I can't be doing business with punk mutha fuckas. It appears to me that ain't you. We good." He punctuated it by putting his hand out.

I stopped walking but stared at it. I wasn't thinking about shaking it.

"C'mon, Busara. We good, bruh. I was just bullshitting."

So, this mutha fucka was a practical joker. That's never been my cup of tea and I didn't plan on drinking that shit that day, either.

"Look, I didn't come for games. Ain't no children in here. If you want to make this money, we can do it. You can save that playing shit for mutha fuckas who are with that. That ain't me, I'm not for the bullshit." I said firmly.

I wasn't disrespectful when I said it but I was definitely assertive. He had a few dudes in there that I could see, probably some I couldn't. I'm sure all of them had heaters. Roostah was my mans, and I believed that, but I didn't wanna test it. If things went sideways it would *only* be real ugly for us.

Regardless, he needed to know that I wasn't afraid of his big ass and I wasn't about to play games with him. At the same time, like I said before, my crew was not prepared for war. And, situationally, there was a unique logistical disadvantage for me and my guys in that restaurant. Still, I wasn't trying to deal with that bullshit he was throwing at me. Not in that situation or at any time in the future. Right then it was necessary to make that clear or that bullshit would've continued the entire relationship. You give a mutha fucka an inch of rope in this business and he'll find a way to hang you with it. That was a 'fuck no' for me. Every thread of that notion had to be torched.

"Nah, it's good. I joke a little to keep things interesting. You can't have a little laugh with me then I won't fuck with you. That's cool." He said.

He reached out to shake my hand. I looked at him sideways to measure him then I shook it. He gripped my hand for a second extra.

"Just don't fuck me over or disrespect me and we'll be cool. We can do this work, cool?"

He was trying to 'son' me. That shit wasn't working for me. I shook his hand harder.

"Don't fuck me over or disrespect me and we can make this money. Cool?"

He looked at me, analyzing my face for a few seconds. He was serious and kind of intense. It seemed like it took minutes.

Then he smiled and let loose a small chuckle.

"Yeah, that's cool, Busara. I like you, dog, you alright. We can do this."

I walked out of the gates of Hell to exit the building once my business was done with Beelzebub. No doubt, I had just made a deal with the Devil. I had the red ass hand to prove it. I didn't realize it while it was happening: he had gripped my hand like he was in a heavyweight arm wrestling championship. That mutha fucka. It was sore as hell.

My written plan called for me to permanently end Skins. Yet, I had just made a deal that would help keep him in business. He was automatically dubbed as my enemy the minute I decided to get into the dope game and his product was more expensive than any we had purchased to that point. This was the full embodiment of that same plan advising me to be flexible. It wasn't what I wanted to do, fuck *want*: I had *planned* to not work with Skins. But we were past that.

The deal got done and we were going to be able to continue rolling. Business was business and we were staying solvent by ensuring we had stock. I convinced myself that it was the only thing that mattered. That still didn't stop it from feeling like I had just sold my soul to Satan.

I wasn't shaken up about it, though, because the inflated cost of the raw materials through Skins would also increase the market value of the end product. This wasn't angels' work we were doing in the first place. The more my business developed, the more comfortable I got in the heat.

A couple of the bruhs from campus rode with me for the switch the next day. I didn't trust Skins and his crew but that wasn't a shocker. Trust wasn't part of the business. So, I needed somebody to cover my back. I also had to maintain appearances, they needed a sustained reason to think we were a mob. Moving as a crew had served a true purpose to that point, I was going to continue it.

The trade went off without a hitch and we were in business. After dropping off the product, my fellas stayed with me for a bit. I fed them and tossed them some loot for rolling with me.

The 1989 summer was the most transformative time of my life. It began with me as a college student who sold drugs on the side. It ended with me as a drug dealer who had college classes.

That criminally slanted trend would not only continue but intensify.

CHAPTER 32

BUSARA

The fall semester of 1989 was… different. I moved back on campus and enrolled for the semester. The fish tank was really the only thing that came with me to the dorms. My first outing as a tenant was short lived, I decided a keepsake was in order. The fish tank made our dorm room dope but it didn't leave a bunch of room to operate.

I still embraced the idea of trying to graduate, that 'sounded' great. Maintaining the façade of a student, though, was much more pertinent for business. Enrolling allowed me to cover both. So, I was back in the dorms, doing the student thing. Sorta.

The large bulk of us at KC from St. Louis still functioned like we were one family. We moved around on campus together and studied together, all of that. If you messed with one of us you had a problem with all of us. It was the same as Big Lou had led us to do, no different than my freshman year.

Except Lou didn't return.

That left us as a massive family, often perceived as a gang, without a leader. That was bound to change. I hadn't thought about it directly, I'm not certain anyone had. Because we weren't an actual gang, no one was looking to be 'led' and nobody really stepped up for the role. At least, not until one of us thought we needed one.

One day, I was in my dorm room and one of my homeboys, Cable, came in with his heart racing. He wasn't scared but he was upset when he ran into the room. It looked and felt like a fight was going to happen. He had that energy, y'know? He was breathing heavy and walking on his toes that made it seem like he was jumping up and down even though he wasn't. It's that 'I'm about to buck' energy. I had no idea about what was going on but I figured it was physical.

> "Hey Busara, man, I ain't start the shit and I'm trying to be cool." He said.
>
> "What up, Cable? What happened?" I asked.
>
> "Man, this mutha fucka ran up on me outside, dawg. Talkin' 'bout I'm trying to holler at his gal!"
>
> "Are you?" I thought I might as well ask.
>
> "Naw, dawg. I ain't did nothing wit' his gal. But that's between him and her, anyways! He need to keep his bidness in his own hause (house)."
>
> "True. Did you tell him that?" I asked.
>
> "Yeah, boah! I told him I ain't said nothin' to her. He ain't listening, man. He just keep trying to get at me."
>
> "Hold up, who is it again?" I had to make sure I knew who we were talking about.
>
> "It's Braxton. One of those M.O.P. dudes. That's why I been trying to be cool. But I ain't about to let this mutha fucka keep disrespecting me, dawg."

While attempting to process being in the position of making this decision, I tried to be reasonable with the information given to me. Off the rip, I believed he didn't do anything with the young lady. I mean, why would he lie to me? That's not how the college-male-world went. You tell your dudes when you kick it with women. Especially in this case. You definitely *aren't* going out of your way to keep it secret, unless she ugly. This young lady wasn't.

And the M.O.P. dudes were cool with us. Four or five of them were from the 'Lou, so we were tight with that crew. Hell, Big Lou's old roommate played with them. So, he basically made them like Canada, nobody fucked with those dudes really. We definitely didn't beef with them, it just wasn't like that. They were nice with that drumming shit, we were good on them.

But that dude Cable? He was nice with them hands and he liked throwin' 'em. I didn't know if Braxton could handle himself or not but Cable left no doubt. I had seen him whip some dudes that previously looked like they outclassed him. Tore they asses up! He would mess around and beat on Braxton until something broke on him and wouldn't think anything about it. I didn't want it to go down like that.

Cable was still a man, though. His dignity mattered. He couldn't keep letting the dude try to hound him like that and just be disrespected in front of everybody. That wasn't going to work, either.

"Okay. If he approach you again just let him know, man-to-man, you not trying to holler at his gal. If he disrespects you after that then he got it coming."
"This mutha fucka down stairs right now, dawg." He said.
"Well, I guess you let him know right now."

As I said that, we rolled out the room and headed outside. Sure enough, Braxton was still out there in front of the dorm, huffing and puffing. That man felt disrespected too, apparently, 'cause he wasn't about to be cool.

Cable did exactly like I told him.

"What the fuck, man!" Braxton shouted out. "Why you disrespecting me like that with my girl? That's some bullshit!"

"Look, dawg. I done told you ain't nobody tryin' to holla at yo' gal. Man-to-man, dawg, that's not what's happening." Cable said, as patiently as he could put it together.

"It better not be, mutha fucka. I'll kick yo mutha fuckin' ass, bitch!" Braxton countered.

"Dawg, I ain't did nothing wit' ya gal. You need to just go on with all that, man. I ain't about to be too many more bitches out here." Again, Cable showed restraint.

"I ain't going nowhere, mutha fucka. I'mma whoop yo ass, bitch!"

...and that's the phrase that got Braxton's ass whipped. Cable didn't say another word. He got to swinging and beating on Braxton like that dude had stolen from his momma or something. I jumped in and tried to pull him off but it wasn't working. Cable was pissed off something terrible and he wasn't trying to quit. A bunch of guys chilling at the dorm had to help me stop him.

The craziest part about it? Braxton's ass was still talking shit when he was half-dragged out of the fight. His lip was busted, he had those wild ass 'fighting eyes' and everything. His shirt was half torn off of him and he looked completely disheveled. That didn't stop Braxton from continuing to talk shit. You woulda sworn he won the fight if you didn't watch him get his clock cleaned. Whether he was on some bullshit or not, the dude had heart.

Cable didn't say anything once we pulled him back. He stood there while a couple fellas drug Braxton away from the scene. Amazingly, Braxton really acted like he didn't want to leave. Dude didn't shut the fuck up until long after he was out of sight.

The fight wasn't the point of that story. Something incredibly significant had taken place. I didn't ask for it, and, frankly, wasn't looking for it. But something had happened. It didn't stop there, either. Another fighting situation arose where somebody would have gotten injured, maybe even killed, if I gave the permission for it. It was a group of guys from the 'Lou who came to me about putting the hurt on somebody. I saw the blood in their eyes and knew the character of the guys who were asking. Nothing good was going to come out of it. I told them to squash it and they did. Both their asking and adhering to my direction, particularly because of whom they were, made it official.

I was leading the St. Louis family in Knoxville.

Candidly, I'm not certain if my Kowrie training is why I became the leader of my situations or if it simply had prepared me for inevitable fates. Either way, throughout my life leadership roles migrated my direction in all my involvements. This one wasn't as spontaneous as many others, of course. After all, I was literally the man with a plan to build an empire. The fact that it translated into leading a campus full of my homeboys, however, was an unforeseen repercussion.

It was also a side effect of the previous summer. The plan was to stay low key and under the radar with our sales. Things progressed so rapidly in those few months that I constantly adjusted on the fly. This put a significant strain on maintaining a low profile. I included my college homeboys in our sales because we had swiftly grown beyond my foresight. That made me thankful for the one item of the plan that was truly visionary - the commitment to adapting.

The way the summer flowed, most of the St. Louis guys not only knew about the operation but got paid a bit from it. They kept it mostly on the low so that it didn't become widely known. Still, basically all of the 'Lou at KC knew some work was getting done. All the fellas knew it came from me. That's what changed the texture of the way the St. Louis crew moved from then on. All of the guys who worked were getting paid by me, so they deferred to me. The rest of our peeps just followed suit.

When I returned to campus Jerry didn't come with me. He basically stopped holding down the block entirely. He got majorly caught up with his gal and stopped working as much. His packs would go to some of our St. Louis dudes and he backed away. Dope fiends also did runs for him. Jerry had them do his transactions in order to distance himself from deals. He turned into much more of a delegator than a dealer. Actually, he moved towards being reclusive. He and his gal would chill at the crib for hours on end, sometimes days. Jerry became much more focused on keeping his hands clean and all the moves he made were aimed at it.

That wasn't an ideal development for me personally. If I wasn't paying attention and hadn't already been working on a remedy for it, he could have really put me in a bad spot. Fortunately, I had been building a small group of soldiers to help me distribute. They allowed me to work on the business as much as working in the business. I was able to keep building our influence and customer base while we were selling.

Jerry staying in the apartment was fortuitous for the operation. We were still able to keep product off-site while putting in work locally. Jerry had stopped doing any corner boy work shortly after the semester started. Instead, he was talking about moving weight and trying to create a client base for that. He didn't make any real efforts to deliver on that vision or to create his own lane, though. It was all lip service.

So, Jerry just wound up sitting on product at the spot with his girl. My hustle was too strong to be that kind of patient. I continued moving the way we had with the temp-styled help I recruited. Even with a few part-time soldiers, losing Jerry in the field was still life-changing for me.

It put me on my own as the business owner.

Then a strange break came. Well, it was a break for the operation but I don't think Poppy would have exactly called it good fortune. Poppy got caught with a girl in his room and was kicked off campus. That was just how KC was with their Presbyterian-non-coed-thing. No matter how miserably they failed at it (and it was daily abject failure) they still tried to stick to it. So, Poppy got the boot.

Everything wasn't lost for him, though. He was able to continue attending classes he just couldn't stay in the dorms. Poppy had looked out for us, specifically me, all summer so it was only natural for us to return the favor. We set him up in my old room with Jerry.

Then it got really interesting. Jerry had stopped attending to his pager for sales. In fact, he would leave the pager at the crib and go do his thing. Well, Poppy knew where Jerry kept the stash. He would answer the pages and deliver product. Fiends beeped him leaving a code to indicate how much he should bring. Poppy wouldn't try to call the numbers, he just delivered. That pager became the work and Poppy kept the work flowing.

It got to the point where Poppy just kept the pager. Jerry wasn't trying to use it and Poppy was doing work. So, he had the customers use his personal code which was 57. That was his old football number. I guess some things never lose their sentimental value, right? It may have been a good omen because he was definitely winning with it.

Poppy didn't keep the money, though. He would leave it in Jerry's stash in place of the product he sold. The odd thing is, Poppy still wasn't officially working. He let me know when he made the sales and I tossed him some loot. Still, he never had his own sack. He continued attending classes and rocking life as a student.

That was a whole lot for him to do while not reaping the full benefits of working. It wasn't on purpose, but he wasn't even getting paid like the part-time workers. He wasn't calling me on it and I simply wasn't paying attention like that. Poppy was just extremely loyal as a person, and he and I weren't even that kind of tight! To that point, really, we were both from the 'Lou, we had homies in common and spent a year together in college. That was really it.

Our lack of extensive bonding had no bearing on how he handled things. Poppy never skimmed off the top of the money, never made side hustles and neither money nor product ever came up short. He just kept the hustle going. Don't let the illegality of the chore cloud the issue, Poppy was a really good dude. Eventually, I paid attention to it.

Because of his loyalty, I had run to his dorm room whenever shit went sideways. That's when you need somebody looking out for you the most, right? When shit gets hectic you always need that one person who's just down for you without questions. Poppy was that guy when he was on campus. For me, Poppy's room was like home base when you were playing tag. It didn't matter what was going on, the door was always open and he never asked shit. Always dependable.

So, when we first started in the Spring semester, we had a runner named Teddy Ray. Teddy Ray was another one of our Knoxvillian operatives. He was country as all get out and as smart as a whip. I really hadn't thought about it before but he was extremely similar to Larewane, even down to using both of his names all the time. They both had a first-name-basis relationship with the police. Now, that wasn't entirely rare. It was actually a Knoxville thing because the town was pretty small. Well, the Black communities were small. If they didn't know the cops as kids they knew them because the same cops patrolled the area.

Just like Larewane, Teddy Ray would give us the word on the street, let us know what was happening. He also put us down on the local lingo. Stuff like "BABYLON!", which meant the police were coming. Also like Larewane, Teddy Ray's activities afforded him some privileges. My crew treated him a little different because, in essence, he was working for me.

Teddy Ray got locked up for something. I believe he had violated parole or something but I don't exactly remember. We were cool enough, though, that his girl came to me to put money on his books. Now, he wasn't exactly my people, so, I wasn't about to go as far as bailing him out. But I didn't leave him hanging out to dry. I took her to the jailhouse and we gave him some change. I only dropped $20 or $30 but we knew it would be a big deal to him.

That was smart business for me, a bit of covering my ass, of course. He never knew details of anything I ever did but he knew the cops. If he wanted to sick them on me then he could drop a dime and we would have heat. I was just paying for 'insurance' to keep that from happening. He didn't threaten to do that or anything but I was investing in the insurance to make sure it didn't go there.

Well, when Jerry and I took his girl to the jailhouse the second time it was on her birthday. After putting the money on his books, she came out and dropped the report on us.

"It looks like Teddy gone be in there for a minute. So, today is my birthday. Which one of y'all gone hang out and celebrate with me today?" She asked.

Jerry immediately looked at me like 'I ain't doing it, bruh'. I didn't want to let the sister's face crack (embarrass her). So, I stepped out.

"I'll look out for you, sister."

In my mind, I was certain that nothing crazy was going to go down. That's because I didn't really know Knoxville women all that well. If I did I would have known 'something crazy' was her whole plan. So, some crazy shit went down… and so did she. I wasn't mad about it at all.

I knew her before Teddy Ray went in, so it wasn't extra that she felt comfortable coming to me. It was just a lot more comfortability going on than I bargained for. She was very decently attractive, by the way. When she made herself, uh, 'wholly' available it wasn't the worst of propositions. Again, we weren't tight – I wasn't anything you would call 'friends' with her or Teddy Ray. This was a customer we're talking about, I couldn't *let* it be too tight.

So, when his girl asked me for a 'birthday gift' while Teddy Ray was still locked up, I gave it to her. It may have been more to make the point that there was no sentimental alliance than anything else. I don't think she was a user but she was definitely trying to get used, if you know what I mean. Shit, I was still a young dude and we didn't turn down sex a lot. So, yeah, the simple fact of getting some booty definitely appealed to me.

Now, if Teddy Ray was one of my dudes that would have strictly been against the code. Sexing old girl wouldn't have been possible at all. You just don't do your homies' girls, y'know? But Teddy Ray? Man, nobody gave a fuck. Well, I guess I gave *one*. It was a night full of fucks given. To my recollection is was a good ass night, while you bullshittin'.

Just because we weren't actual friends, and that he was a customer, didn't make it any less dirty. I knew the guy, that should have been enough. I was on one, though. Living the drug dealer life, rolling with that moxie, I was going to do what the fuck I liked. Literally. I was going out of my way to draw a line. A very foul line. There was no way that Teddy Ray would appreciate that.

Not long after he got out, his girl told him about our tryst. That was some bullshit. I don't know if it was her intention to start some shit or something. Maybe they just had one of those weird open relationships where she 'opened' her legs whenever she wanted and he got pissed about it. I don't know, y'all, but it was weird as hell to me.

As you would easily imagine, he didn't appreciate that shit at all. Teddy Ray had asked me a few favors while he was locked up but fucking his girl wasn't included in the list. Actually, his gal got super friendly and became a repeat customer for my services. He was pissed about that, fuh sho! He felt straight up betrayed and that made sense. No man wants his gal to get ran through, period. But when it's by a dude you know that makes it a little extra stank. So, yeah, he was pretty miffed.

It actually turned ugly, well, even uglier than it started. I kept a .25 caliber automatic pistol on me at all times. Thing is, we had a practice of keeping our bullets separate from our weapons. We didn't want someone to ever get the drop on us and use our own shit against us. So, I normally kept my bullets in my pockets. When it was time to do something, I could easily load up. That was just how we played it.

One day, we were at her place. I emptied my pockets on the table (I was taking my pants off... you get it). Well, Teddy Ray came through while we were in the bedroom and dude had a key. He grabbed the bullets off the table and walked back outside to the bedroom window. He started tapping on the outside of the window with one of the bullets.

Tap. Tap. Tap.

He yelled through the glass,

"I know you wanna shoot me when you come outta thurr. Have a good time but you ain't gone be able to do it 'cause I got - ya bullets!"

That last part was said with the sassiness of a teenage girl – "ya' bullets". His voice was both country and nasal. He sounded like an intelligent evil cartoon villain.

Teddy Ray then threatened to call the police on me.

"I'm cawlin' (calling) Babylon onyeh (on you) ev'r time you
get down hurr on the block, too."

Like most bullshit, he kept escalating until it had to be something
real. This mutha fucka meant what he said. Teddy Ray literally went to
calling the police when he would see me around. It forced me to change
how I operated and created a real problem for me.

So, one time I was hanging on the block when he showed up. Teddy
Ray saw me and walked straight to a payphone. I was in a conversation
with a customer at the time and cut it short. I told them that Teddy Ray
was calling the police on me and I had to bail. The guy insisted, out loud,
that he wasn't going to do that.

"Teddy, you ain't gone call the police are you?" He yelled out.
"I shole am! I'm cawlin' Babylon ret naa (right now)!" Teddy
Ray yelled back.

It was something about hearing that screechy-ass, hollowed-out
country voice that pissed me off.

(Fuck this! I'm not running from this mutha fucka no more.)

I drove up the street to load my gun. There were only 3 or 4 bullets
in the car for my .25. I didn't have my .357 with me or it would have been
a different story. I drove back to the Callie's lot and unloaded on him while
he stood there at the payphone. I hit him three times...

POP! POP! POP!

I then rolled around to the other side of him, walked up to him and put the .25 right on top of his forehead. I squeezed the trigger but it didn't go off. He would have been dead if it would have fired.

I crouched down to him and looked him in his eyes while he was crying and yelling out in pain. My words came out as a heinous whisper.

"You lucky, mutha fucka. Keep my name out ya mouth!"

Then I sped outta there. I rolled up on the campus and parked behind Brandon Hall, on the opposite side of the Yard from Davis Hall. I walked across the campus to Poppy's room in Davis. He didn't keep his room locked, so I walked in with no problem and chilled there. Poppy was there and greeted me when I walked in.

I was calm as shit, standing in the window, looking out over the Yard. I wasn't making a sound. That freaked Poppy out.

"What's up, dawg? You alright?" He asked.
"Yeah."

When I spoke I was as calm as a morning slug.

"I just shot Teddy Ray."
"What??" Poppy replied.
"Yeah. I just shot him down at Callie's".
"Did you kill 'im?" Poppy asked.
"Naw. He alive. Just hurting."

I kept watching out the window and saw the police roll up on campus, three cars deep. They went straight behind Brandon Hall to my car. The cops hung around for a brief minute then rolled right back off the campus. I watched all of their activity from my perch in that Davis Hall window.

Poppy didn't believe what I told him because I was so casual.

"You really shot that man, for real, dawg?"

"Yeah, man. I shot him for real, boay. There go the police looking for me right there."

He looked out the window with me and saw the cop cars rolling around the Hoop.

"Damn, dawg. That's crazy! Lay low and shit. We'll figure something out." Poppy said.

"Shit, they leaving now. I ain't moving." I said.

"Yeah, just chill, bruh." Poppy continued, "we about to get something to eat. What you want?"

I had never shot *at* anyone before that day. We (Jerry and I) had done plenty shooting when we first got weapons. We wanted to make sure we could handle ourselves if the need arose. So, shooting at cans on a fence and exploding bottles became a thing for a while. But those were stationary targets, inanimate objects. That was all the practice I had before that point. Capping Teddy Ray was definitely the first time I had shot towards someone. Apparently we did something right because my shots were effective as hell – I didn't miss one! If you would have asked me how I would feel about shooting someone before it happened, I probably would have said it would have troubled me.

It didn't.

Poppy didn't appear to be troubled by it, either. He immediately focused on helping me out and did what he could to make sure I could make it through the bullshit I had created. Even when it was as grave as shooting somebody, he was automatically down. And he never asked for nothing. Shit, he barely asked questions about what was happening. He just looked out. Poppy was a loyal dude, man.

I had to learn that loyalty was just in his character. It's how he was built. Poppy exemplified the very ideal of the word 'brother'.

CHAPTER 33

DRAMA CLASSES

Back on campus, things were rolling like Michelin tires. Slick was my roommate and we kept making paper together. We returned to doing the drop-offs behind the school but we both continued our shifts on the block. The part-time soldiers would help hold down the corners and everything kept flowing. To top it all off, I got to enjoy all the trappings of a student-packed Black College campus. Everybody was making money and life was good.

Our business focus never strayed from growth and building. I borrowed from my entrepreneur studies to that point and tried to model us after the General Motors approach. They never took their eyes off of opportunities to grow. To be bigger than they were. Always looking to be one notch better. That was us.

We rotated workers and shifted their positions to find their best fits. Our team utilized pagers and hustled on the corners. We would catch the people walking up, the customers who were calling in and the ones on campus. I was even considering expanding to the other side of town. We were missing nothing! That summer was exceedingly productive and we kept building on it.

Consequently, our customer base had magnified exponentially and we were offloading product so fast you'd think we were giving it away. We only suffered one dry spell with Skins over the summer. That created the most spontaneous and unlikely alliance of my, to that point, short business career.

My dedication to keeping product in stock was intense and definitive. It was completely unacceptable to let customers look for us with money in their hands and walk away with it. That's the only way I viewed a supply shortage. We were letting money get away. We went to reup with Skins before our surplus ran out. He kept saying he would be dry for a while. No parts of that made me happy. I wasn't about to lay down and let it happen.

I put the word out that we needed product to a few dudes on the Yard. One of them came back with an option. A dude from Detroit was on campus for the summer, they called him 'Motown'. Apparently, he was working on the Yard and out in Knoxville, too. We didn't run the same circles so I hadn't heard of him before. I decided to meet him to see what he was about and to see if we could gain from knowing him.

Well, the word was that he was heading back to Detroit for some reason and wanted to offload the yayo he had before leaving. Everything about his operation sounded like competition to me. Still, the adage 'keep your enemies closer...' definitely applied. I needed to see for myself how much of a threat he was to our operation. If that also included keeping us afloat for a minute then that would be a bonus.

My guy set it up and we connected. Motown and I met at a local park completely off the beaten path. It wasn't close to anything associated with him or me. It was my idea to be off-campus, he picked the location.

When he drove up I was already parked. One of the part-timers rode with me, just as a show of force. Motown had arrived with one guy, as well. That was an amusing coincidence for me. We both got out of the cars alone. I swear it was like a scene out of a movie, or some shit, but we hadn't planned it. We walked up to each other at a set of monkey bars.

The brother walked up smiling like he didn't have a care in the world. For what I knew about Detroit cats, that was almost scary. Typically, they were the least friendly dudes I had ever met. This dude just didn't have any stress. It was apparent in that smile.

"What up, doe?" The standard greeting of a Detroiter.

"Wassup, man? I'm Busara."

"Motown." He replied.

We shook hands. It was formal for how handshakes usually go.

"So, I got this Work, what you wanna do, dog?" Motown said.

"Damn, you just come straight at me like that, huh? You don't even ask if I'm a pig or nothing?"

It was natural for me to test him. I didn't know him, I wanted to see where he was coming from.

"Mutha fucka, are you a pig?" His whole demeanor changed when he asked.

"Fuck naw! I'm just saying, you can never be too careful. We don't sell candy cigarettes out here."

"Dog, I know who you are, nigga. I been peeping your game on the Yard for a minute." He fired back at me.

"No shit?" I asked.

"No shit! I don't roll like you, not really trying to hit the Yard too hard. But you always have to know the climate, dog. You the main vein on campus, anybody trying to ride on the Yard gotta know that."

"Aight then. If you don't roll thick on campus where you make your money?"

He threw me off with his knowledge about our operation when I knew almost nothing about him. So, I went fishing to see if I could get even on some information.

"Mutha fucka, now you sound like a cop."
We both laughed. He continued.
"Nah, I hit the east side and put my work in. Walter P, Austin Homes, over there near Austin-East. I gotta always keep some change, dog. A brother can't be broke."

He had a way of connecting where I relaxed my guard without even trippin'. Not the best business practice, I know.

"There's paper to be made at KC, though. I ain't trying to convince you to be my competition or no shit like that. But why not move product there?" I inquired.
"It's too hot, dog. And I don't mean the cops and shit, because they not up there right now, but we in that cramped ass space. Too many eyes that can casually peep game. You never know who goes goody-two-shoes on yo' ass and drops a dime. Then 5-0 will be on yo' ass like it's cool. Then where can you go? I ain't fucking with that, dog. It's too close to where I eat. I'll let you have that."

He was right as hell. We launched on the Yard and blew up so I wasn't thinking about getting out of there. But he made a lot of sense. I stuck a pin in that thought because it might become pertinent.

Anyways, he was a cool ass dude. The situation was real: he needed to hop back to Detroit for the rest of the summer and didn't want to travel with product. He was trying to get rid of it quickly, I needed some inventory right then. Worked out perfectly.

I met him again that evening with the loot, he dropped the dope on me and we shook hands.

"Alright, dog. Now I know what you do and you know what I do. This don't have to turn into bullshit. I don't fuck with the Yard really and the 'Ville is you, too. I rock the east side. We don't have a reason to beef. If I need to look out, I'll do that. Where you at?" He asked intently.

"I'm with that. Bruh, you saved my ass with this. If you need something from me just holler at me." I offered.

"Word. You alright, dog. I'll holler," he said.

"Alright. Be good, bruh." I said.

"Flat out." He replied.

From my understanding, he left town that next day. Because of that meeting, my team kept rolling on the street with no down time. We were able to stack major paper and keep the ball rolling that whole summer.

My plan was put together with several facets of my business education. One of the more foundational tools of any successful business is the SWOT analysis. It's a common business acronym for strengths, weaknesses, opportunities and threats. When I drafted my plan, these elements were included but I hadn't organized them in such a disciplined way. If I did it would likely have had a larger threat analysis. Skins and the cops were really the extent of my list. It was way too short.

We were starving the local boys. Once our operation got into full swing, they just weren't making any money. By that third month of the summer, they were no longer in a greeting mood. That whole dynamic changed the minute it was evident we were clearly making more money than them. The local boys started straight mad-dogging us when we showed up. Shit was clearly evolving. It could have been foreseen but I hadn't given it much specific thought in planning.

Well, those local dudes were obviously coming unglued. Our reputation, and the obscurity of our numbers, was intimidating enough to keep them from fucking with us. So, they started fucking with customers.

One of their well-known clients had stopped patronizing them altogether and just came our way. They caught him on the street in their neighborhood and beat his legs with a bat. They explicitly told him to, "stop fucking with those St. Louis dudes". He went to the hospital, got casts and all of that. When he got back out on the streets, he came straight to us and told us what happened. And he still bought product from us. His injuries were the first vivid sign of the local boys' desperation.

Now, none of my crew tried to holler back at the local crew. We had no efforts or intentions to escalate things. And they didn't try to come at us, either, but they were definitely hostile. It was a volatile situation that, at that point, I knew would only worsen.

About a week after getting that product from Motown, the locals stopped posting up on the block. We just didn't see them standing around. My guess was that they had run dry. That kind of validated Skins telling me he was dry and that's why they were, too. We had no problem continuing to operate with them off the street. It was the optimal situation, actually.

A week or so after that, Skins sent me a page. He wanted to have a sit down. He actually invited me to a restaurant. That sounded like he wanted to butter me up about something. I figured it would be a good idea to find out what he was talking about.

Skins was super competitive. He was a professional athlete, after all. You only get to that level by being a fighter. He didn't like to lose at anything. It was particularly amusing that it included something as small as being on time. Whenever we had a meeting spot I would beat him to the rendezvous. This time, I walked in the restaurant and he was already waiting on me. That was obviously an extra effort because I had arrived 15 minutes early.

Skins was sporting his usual toothy grin.

"C'mon in, young blood. I know you hungry."

Somehow that was a joke for him and he laughed heartily.

"What's going on, Skins? What we into?" I asked.

I was trying to immediately get to the heart of the issue. He didn't bite.

"Right now I'm munching on this bread. I'm thinking about a steak. Whatever you want I got you. Here's a free tip in class for you, Boo Boo: you don't invite people out and let them pay. That ain't kosher. This is on me."

"Man, I told yo ass…"

"About 'Boo Boo'? Yeah, I know, man. I'm hardheaded. Ask my momma, she'll tell you." His smirk actually made me laugh about it.

"What's on your mind, Skins." I continued pressing.

"See? That's what I'm talking about. You are about that business! Always impressive, young Boo Boo. Always impressive."

He looks at me with a shit-eating grin for the nickname. I looked completely unamused while he took another bite of bread.

"I just decided I'm gonna ignore your old ass because you hardheaded and I don't play with other people's children. But you gone get one of them young dudes in the hood fucked up for trying to call me Boo Boo." I said.

"They gotta learn somehow. A good ass-whipping every now and then is good for the soul, Boo Boo. You gotta do what you gotta do." He said, barely containing his laughter.

"What yo' ass want, man?"

"Hey, respect your elders, young buck." He kept eating while simultaneously talking shit. It was almost skillful.

"First, thank you!" He said.

"For what?"

"The last shipment I had sold out faster than any I ever had that size before. You have been cranking! Money talks, your shit is yelling."

The context felt like an employee conversation and I wasn't feeling any of that. So, I ignored it.

"But the homies in the 'Ville been complaining to me."

"About what?" I needed to see where it was going.

"Whelp, your sales ran me out of product. That's not all bad – we selling. But it ran them out of product, too. They not selling right now. But you on the block, still cranking it out. They getting antsy about it."

"They not my concern." I returned quickly.

"Now, c'mon, Busara. You supposed to be smart. I know you're smarter than that."

"What's that supposed to mean?" I asked.

"They already salty that y'all are there. Then y'all getting more traffic, making more money. That's making them more than a little pissy. But you making money when they're not making any, that can turn that tense situation into some crazy shit. Nobody wants that. Right?"

"Look man, we making money. We not fucking with them and their ability to do the same. My crew just works a little harder and a lot smarter. So, shit rolls smoother for us." I firmly stated.

"Look, this is how this needs to go. When we take a break, we need y'all to take a break. That's how we keep this thing in control. Alright?" He tried to reason.

"You trying to control my money, man?" I asked.

"Naw, Black man. I'm just trying to keep the peace. Help me do that." He said. He let it sit for a minute.

"There's enough money for everybody. We don't want this shit to get ugly. So, when we take a break, y'all take a break. That'll fix everythang. Now, let's get some grub, Boo Boo. This is a good restaurant, young blood. I would eat up if I was you."

I heard what he was saying and some of the logic was sound. But Big Lou brother's words were echoing in my head,

"...thing about an illegal game is it ain't no rules. 'Do what the fuck you want' is how it works."

I didn't plan on letting somebody makes rules for me.

527

When got we finished eating, I gave him a pound and got up out of there. I went back to the block and we kept doing our thing. Even with him pulling my coattails about it, I wasn't giving the right degree of credence to the 'Threat' part of the SWOT analysis. It was more because I was young than because of greed. It was a bad look regardless.

One morning, a couple weeks later, I woke up in my dorm room with the street situation on my mind. I needed soldiers. The part-timers were cool but our level of business had changed and was continuing to grow. So, the organization size was due for a change, too. It was time to get somebody to roll with me permanently. I wasn't sure how to quietly recruit dudes who would be trustworthy in the situation. My network of Knoxville locals was still incredibly weak.

And the Black part of the city was filled with relatives. A lot of the people I ran into in town were cousins with somebody else I had met. Shit, I couldn't trust that any of them wouldn't be working against me. Nah, all my guys would have to come from school. It was a really tricky proposition. I had to approach Black college students about selling drugs. These particular students would likely be guys who largely had gone to school to escape the exact situation I was offering. It was something that would have to be marinated on (highly considered).

I was up early, in 'get it done' mode, and decided to just get my day going. I left the room and walked down to the showers. I was only wearing my underwear and a towel. The .25 caliber gun was in my draws. The bullets were kept in my toiletry bag, along with my deodorant and shit. I took that gun everywhere, and I do mean everywhere. All of the money and product, that got maneuvered or which was kept on my person, demanded protection. So, I stayed strapped, even in the shower.

I don't know about you but, a lot of my best ideas come out in the shower. There's something about the solace of being by yourself, maybe the soothing water… I don't know. What is consistent, though, is that I arrived at many solutions just by jumping in a hot steamy shower.

Zen-type shit wasn't going to happen that morning. About five minutes in, one of my 'Lou homies ran into the shower. He was totally about to lose his shit.

> "Yo' Boots! You gotta get outta this bitch, man! The cops rolled up on the Yard. Cars are pulling up to the dorm right now! Look out the window! You can see 'em now. You gotta get outta here!"

I grabbed my towel and wrapped it around me, left the heater on a bench and walked over to the window of the shower room and I could see the cars already parked. Sure enough, I got a glimpse of Starsky and Hutch walking their asses towards the front door.

(Mutha fucka! Now what?)

> "I see 'em. Thanks, bruh. Do me a favor, go to your room and stay there. Leave the door unlocked, though."
> "Why?" He said.
> "Man, trust me. Just do it."
> "Alright."

He ran off to his room. He stayed on the first floor.

I had to do some quick thinking. The showers are still the bomb because my brain was working, you hear me? There was no way I had to go with those mutha fuckas if I played my cards right. That dorm was filled with guys. If they didn't know what I looked like then they weren't getting me that day.

They caught me in the middle of showering so I still had soap on my body. I got back in the shower and rinsed real quick then toweled off and wrapped myself. By this time, I could hear the commotion through the hallways. It was obvious they were in the building and getting close.

Let me diagram the dorm for you. It was a four-level structure with three levels above ground. The basement was the laundry room. The main entrance was in the middle of the dorm. It had a sizeable staircase just next to the entrance but it only descended into the basement. There were entrances on both ends of the dorm with corresponding staircases for all-level access. The stairwells on either side released into every floor and to the outside on the first floor. The bathroom/shower room was located on the back right, or southeast, of the dorm's center point.

My room was on the right side of the second floor (if you're facing the building) so I made a few assumptions. Of course, the cops would have to walk up the steps. I assumed they didn't know that because KC didn't get a lot of police visits. So, my guess was they would stop and ask the dorm director some questions. That would give me a brief minute to operate. The quickest path to the room would be the right stairwell. I assumed they would use that. I also assumed they didn't know my face but had my room number, possibly. I worked with that.

They were going to my room. I wasn't. The best play for me was to 1) be seen going about my way, 2) be casual about it and 3) get away from the area. I took a brief moment to visualize how it would play out then it was time to make my move. They didn't sound like they were close to me. So, I thought I might beat them to the opposite stairwell, go down a flight to my lookout's room and put on some clothes to bail. Timing was key and that clock was ticking.

The shower stalls were separated from the rest of the bathroom by a tiled concrete wall. It had a wide ledge at the top of it. I placed the gun atop the rear portion of the wall, against the perpendicular wall of the room.

It was pseudo-hidden when I placed it there. I wrapped the towel around me and grabbed all my cleaning stuff then rolled out.

I walked out of the shower room... to an uber fail. The cops were already on the floor. And, they had taken the middle staircase! So, I walked out of the bathroom and turned right, directly into a few of them led by Starsky.

Thing was, on campus I was a student. The best thing for me to do was be a student getting ready to do student stuff. That's precisely how I played it.

I walked smoothly past about seven of them, holding my showering towel around me and a toiletry bag in my other hand, before one of the cops said anything to me. Of course the one who did was an absolute dick. Those were high odds, it wasn't remotely surprising.

"Hey, kid. What are you doing in the hallway?" The cop asked with a shitty attitude.

"I'm a student in my dorm. I live here. What are you doing in the hallway?" I shot back.

"Where you going?" He was even more shitty this time.

"To my room to put on some clothes. Where you going?" I responded with all the snark I could muster.

"None of your damned business. Get out of the hallway!" The asshole ordered.

"No problem." I did everything I could not to smile.

He waved at the cops behind him to let me pass. The only thing better than skating right past those bitches was getting an asshole to help me do it. I got to the opposite stairwell after all of the cops with them had come through. In total, there were a couple more than a dozen of them.

They really wanted my ass. I went down the stairs into my guy's room and closed the door.

The spotter gave me some tight ass clothes to put on. I had to free ball it because I wasn't about to wear dude's draws. I didn't have a fresh pair with me when I went into the shower. The clothes weren't close to perfect fits but they weren't county blues, either. So, I shut the fuck up and wore them. I told him I would throw him some loot to just chill at his spot. I didn't have any money on me at the moment but, of course, he knew I was good for it. It was dope that he had a VCR in his room with a few movies. We watched Beverly Hills Cops about six times. I was laughing off a planet full of nervousness while everything went to shit around me.

Meanwhile…

KNOCK! KNOCK! KNOCK!

"Knoxville Police Department! Open up!"

The lookout had gone to the room first. He woke up Slick and found out I was in the shower. Slick jumped out of bed, grabbed all the product in the room and set it outside on the window on a ledge. He had turned around to get my .357 to do the same with it when they burst through the door.

The Knoxville police put Slick face down in the middle of the room and arrested him. It was a good thing they caught him before he got to the gun. The cops could have easily seen that the wrong way and shot him. We were fortunate it didn't go down like that.

But there wasn't much else to be glad about. This was a whole combination of fucked up situations, especially for Slick. They found the gun and pinned it on him because he was the only guy there. The cops searched the entire room and found no drugs at all. But that wasn't something to celebrate either, they didn't stop inside the room. The cops continued searching vociferously because they were certain we had something. One of them was persistent enough to look out the window and find the pot of gold (or snow, I should say) out on the ledge. The cop reeled the drugs in with a stick. They charged Slick with possession with intent to distribute a controlled substance and for illegal possession of a firearm.

The drugs and the gun weren't the only things they found. The cops dug through all of our shit – all of it! They went through my drawers and found my written plan. The one where I literally wrote down that we would kill Skins. Yeah, *that* plan! I have no idea what the police would have done to me if they had found me there. I just know that the high probability is I would have become incredibly familiar with the inside of a prison system.

Then the violations began. These mutha fuckas searched almost every room on the floor. Yeah, they just wantonly barged into almost every dorm room on the floor. The cops didn't even know what I looked like, obviously, but they searched everyone's room on the floor anyways looking for... whatever they could possibly find. They looked for anything they could find on anyone. Those fuckas ransacked all of the student living spaces; flipped the beds over, pulled stuff out of their drawers and looked through all of their things. Like they were tossing jail cells or some shit. There was nothing legal about that. Straight up? That shit was infuriating.

So, they walked on our campus, a Black college campus, then proceeded to treat our students, almost an entire dorm floor full of students, like fucking prisoners. No respect. No privacy laws. No warrants. Just blatantly lawless disrespect.

One of the students was hot about it and went to the Dean's office. If it weren't for the Dean coming down to stop them, the cops probably would have gone through every room in the entire dorm. Lawlessly. The Dean was also angry about the level of disrespect and made them aware of their impropriety. They finally rounded up their entire mob and left the premises, Slick in tow.

It wasn't my plan to go to a different floor, it was just good fortune. The lookout who came to grab me happened to live on the first floor. So, I wasn't up there when all of that searching went down but I heard it and saw the aftermath. And I saw that they left the dorm more than two hours after they arrived. Through the lookout's window, I watched them take Slick out in handcuffs.

Now, the lookout wasn't an official sentry or some shit. He wasn't standing a post in the off chance some police or other infiltrators decided to invade the campus. It wasn't any shit like that. He was just one of the guys from the 'Lou who happened to be on the dorm's porch that morning. When he saw them rolling onto the Yard in a caravan, he darted to tell me about it.

This episode added a myriad of lessons and frustrations to what I already had. First, the Knoxville cops were a band of fools. How did they let me walk right past the whole lot of them when I was the reason they had arrived? One asshole damned near hi-fived me as I walked by half-naked. Somebody didn't do their homework. Then they disrespected a whole dorm of students because they felt like it. That's some shit that they would NOT have pulled at UT. Guaranteed.

Let me cop to the fact that I was the reason they came. My work drew the police task force to the campus. So, yeah I'm responsible for the derogatory attention. My culpability for their actions ends there, though.

Those fucking cops were responsible for their criminal disrespect. The cops didn't see us as equals so they treated us as less-than. Their incompetence had to become our collective suffering. It was the same shit that America always has been – cops dumping on Black people and we're blamed for their shittiness. They had confirmed everything I had previously thought about them. You could say I was irate about it but that just wouldn't be an adequate description. I was fucking pissed.

I waited a few hours after the cops left to escape my temporary hideout. My first move was going back to get my gun. It was still in the bathroom, exactly where I left it. But while I was waiting in the lookout's room, it was evident to me that some math needed to be done. The Knoxville drug task force walked straight to my dorm room looking for me and my product. There were all kinds of problems with that reality. How did that happen?

My customers, other than the college student clients, didn't know where my room was. That wasn't a street information item. Somehow, a student had to be involved in ratting me out. I mean, how impossible is it to guess which dorm room has product in it? The building was filled with rooms and there were six separate male dorms! They went straight to mine and that means someone talked.

Then I thought about what Motown had said and he was right as hell. There were over 100 students in just my dorm. There was somewhere near another thousand more students on campus. Any number of them could have seen or heard about our activity on the humble. Finding a leak on the Yard was going to be virtually impossible. Fortunately for me, that wasn't necessary for me to figure out my next move.

Being on campus was no longer tenable. That wasn't exactly rocket science at that point, right? There was no way we could continue operations with the school as a base. The exposure was just too broad and the campus had become hot. I had to bail. I would have arrived at that conclusion regardless, but Motown's words and demeanor had resonated with me. Living there *and* working there was a problem. That had to change.

I went to a hotel that afternoon. A few days later, one of the homegirls put her name on a spot for me and I moved right back out into Knoxville.

CHAPTER 34

BROTHERHOOD

My immediate agenda was to get clear of the flames. You wanna talk about a block getting hot (drug activity so voluminous that it drew the police)? The Yard was on fire so I had to stop, drop and roll with the quickness. Just because I could stand the heat didn't mean I wanted to go surfing in a frying pan. Surfing wasn't my damned thing! And, trying to brave through that situation would have just been plain stupid. My written plan had included knowing when to quit. I believed this to be a microcosm of that: it was time to move away from the campus.

I went into a hotel room that evening. Once I got off the Yard, and felt a degree of relief, I had to find out what happened. I did my best to analyze the situation without emotion. That approach had proven to provide my best fact-based answers and more efficiently direct me toward solutions.

Logic dictated that if it was someone at KC, a student with a moral compass and a commitment to do the right thing, I would never find them. Straight up. Motown was spot-on when he talked about that. I mean, sure, it was possible that they might have told someone that they had snitched and maybe that word would get out. But, aside from that kind of grapevine luck, there were too many students and those possibilities of a student snitch were vast. I couldn't expect much progress trying to pursue that line of information.

The search for a student snitch, in itself, could have been very compromising and extremely risky. If the wrong student heard that we were looking for an informant, well, even that could go all kinds of sideways. We could easily lose the support of those who knew what we were doing. They could then turn on us if they thought we were hunting students. Everything about that train of thought was a hornet's nest that would be unintelligent to shake a stick at.

Lastly, I was serious about my business and completely committed to succeeding. I had fully accepted whatever damage it would do to the community while I maintained a steadfast focus on my end goals. In my calculus, the collateral damage was merely an unfortunate element of the process. But, uninvolved Black college students weren't that kind of collateral for me. That was a bridge too damned far. So, a probable fruitless student informant search wasn't feasible for me.

That wasn't going to be my search route but you can bet your ass I was going to search. It was mandatory that I ensured my circle wasn't tainted. I had to make certain that particular people didn't have a hand in it. That was much more important than who did. If someone I was working with was in on it then I would be in jeopardy until they were removed from the situation. That knowledge was a much higher priority. So, I immediately went to holler at Skins.

It had only been a few weeks since Skins hit me with the "when we break, you break" speech. It was delivered out of at least a modicum of frustration in his tone. We kept selling like he hadn't said anything to me. I'm sure that had exacerbated his displeasure and the local boys had to be fuming. Maybe this was him trying to force me to quit. I needed to know, immediately, if that was real.

I called him and told him I needed to rap with him one on one. This wasn't the kind of conversation you had with an audience. Between the bluster and machismo of fronting for other people, it was difficult to see which fake thing was occurring if someone isn't being straight with you. Standing in front of his lackeys, he could start posturing to exert some type of false authority or lying because he's hiding the truth that he sent the cops my way. It can be difficult to discern which is which. Eliminating mental and emotional distractions would allow me to more vividly see through all of that. In my experience, it was better to deal with men of power on an eye level and without influences.

Skins agreed to meet at a park. I picked one on the northern end of the city. It was neither of our stomping grounds, I hadn't had a meeting there before and I was always cognizant of being a hard target. I was waiting in the parking lot when he arrived. The Kowrie Group made me a true believer in being early. Some habits you try to keep. We both arrived alone, and it felt Cloak and Dagger-ish but neither of us were trippin'. He knew full well the importance of keeping a low profile.

He walked up smiling like he had just hit the lottery.

"Wassup, Boo Boo?" He chuckled.

"Man, I told you about that 'playing' shit. Ain't nobody here for that, man." I sternly asserted.

"I got you, I got you. So, what's on your mind, Boo Boo? What's going on?"

Getting tied up in a trivial argument was a distraction that I didn't want to give in to. Not doing so would mean that I let him get away with that bullshit, I know. But there were much bigger fish to fry. So, I ignored his little shit as much as I could.

"That shit ain't cute, man. What you know about the cops coming for me?"

His face instantly went sour. It looked a lot more like anger than any other emotion.

"Shit! Not a damned thing. Are the cops coming for you? How you know that?" He asked intensely.

"I know because they raided my dorm room this morning."

"That's fucked up. You good?"

"Fuck naw, I'm not good! Did you have something to do with that?"

Beating around the bush wasn't my thing. Ma broke me of that as a kid. Becoming a man made me crazy thankful that she was *that* woman. This shit didn't need pussyfooting. I had to get straight to it.

"Fuck naw! Listen, let me tell you something. And I'm goin' to explain this once."

He got closer to me.

"I've feared damn near nothing in my life. Ever. This game can get you paid, dead or imprisoned. The only one that's a problem for me is a cage. Fuck. That. I ain't trying to be in a cell for nobody."

He paused for effect, completely locked into my eyes the whole time.

"Oh, I can get dirty, Busara. I'll have mutha fuckas off you or do it myself. Ain't no need to play stupid games. But I don't fuck around with the police, man. That ain't one of my angles.

That shit can only come back and bite you in the ass. My ass is going to stay unbitten, y'know what I'm sayin'? I don't belong behind no bars, Busara. I ain't trying to be there."

He paused again.

"I advise you to never play that game, either. The cops are not on your side in any way. Them mutha fuckas are bad for business, bruh."

He let that sink in.

"And, how the fuck will that help me? I'm banking with you! We making money like clockwork. But we doing that together. There are no pluses for me putting you in jail, man. Real shit? Having you in the cops hands compromises me. That's some bullshit. Speaking of which, how did you get out?" He asked
"They didn't get *me*. I walked right past them. Apparently, they didn't know my face."
"Well, that's a good thing. You don't want them mutha fuckas to know you. Who *did* they get?"
"How you know they got somebody?" That raised an alarm.
"You said it like you were the one they didn't get – not just that they didn't get you. What? You think I ain't paying attention?"
"Okay. You got that (which means you're right)."

I was half-embarrassed acknowledging his point. He paid more attention to how I talked than I did. The lesson for me was that I learned his strength. Skins was emotionally intelligent. He knew how to read people and empathize with them in order to manipulate them. His fine attunement to emotional waves is how he likely rode to the position he had in the city. Whenever I talked to him, he was reading my emotions to maximize his responses. I continued to watch him do that. It became my mission to stay concealed and not be readable.

He was right, too. I *did* say it like I was the *one* who escaped.

"Nigga, did they get somebody?" He insisted.

"Yeah. They got one of my guys with a heater and some work."

"He's out right now, right?" He sounded alarmed.

"I'm going to have somebody roll over there in the..."

He didn't let me finish.

"Nah, B.! You get his ass out of there right now! You never let your people sit in a jail. That's how you create snitches. Go get his ass! But have somebody else do it, don't you ever walk in there voluntarily. You want to avoid letting them see you at all costs. But get it done right now." He was dead serious.

"Aight, man. I'll handle that." I said.

I didn't literally start moving at that moment so he started for me. He turned and started walking and waved his hand like he wanted me to walk, too.

"Nah, I mean... right! Now! I'm not bullshitting. We done here. And, as long as we work together, you one of my people. You ever get grabbed by the cops, have somebody reach me. I'll get you out immediately! Pick somebody now and let 'em know how to reach me. One person, though. Don't give my shit to everybody. Just one mutha fucka, Boo Boo. And, make sure everybody in your crew knows what to do with you if they get caught up."

He was rushing back to his car to make me rush to mine.

"Never let them sit in jail, Busara. Never." He was emphatic in his insistence. "I'm glad you came straight to me, though. I told you, I like you, dude. You know how to do business. I appreciate that. Go get yo' boy, man!"

I got to a pay phone and called the young lady I was kicking it with at the time. She was waiting for me when I went to pick her up. I gave her the money to go in the precinct and bail out Slick. He was back on the street before 10:00 that night.

I was satisfied that Skins didn't snitch on us. He had valid points: I could drag his ass down with me. That he realized that degree of self-preservation was satisfactory. I made a few more moves to insulate myself and I was confident my circle wasn't the issue. Getting off the Yard would solve the immediate problem. If it rose again the possible causes would be more limited and give me better clarity on the leak. I moved from there extremely confident that I could handle the situation.

Because Poppy got kicked off the Yard, we needed another asset to stash some product whenever we were in the 'Ville. My new spot was also on the far west side of town, just like the first one. Transporting across town multiple times a day was out. So, getting a stash house was mandatory.

Poppy was one of the M.O.P. drumming cats I told y'all about. He was dope with that shit, too! As Big Lou's roommate, Poppy was most of the reason the drummers were like Canada.

Well, one of his running partners was also one of the drummers. The guy who was acting a fool with the cymbals on the field my first semester? It was that mutha fucka, B-Dub. Him and Poppy ran hard.

B-Dub's room was also in Davis Hall, which was the closest building to the performing arts center. It was largely known as the band dorm. That's where Poppy stayed before he moved off the Yard. It was adjacent to a back-cutting street next to the campus. So, it had easy walking access into the neighborhood – as opposed to a number of the dorms around the Hoop. He wound up holding Poppy's stash, or mine, and we would toss him some loot or feed him or something. He looked out so we looked out, that's how that went.

A few weeks later, a live ass weekend kicked off on the Yard. That wasn't an atypical happening but there was a home football game that week. Home games always put extra stank on the festivities. The whole campus was basically a massive party for any home game weekend.

We decided to kick back and hang out on the Yard for a bit, y'know, do some college shit. Poppy, Slick and I were in B-Dub's room chilling with him. Slick's girl came to holler at him about food. So, he took my car and they rolled to the Strip to get something to eat.

The 'Strip' is a college town thing. It's the spot, usually one main street, where all the businesses are. Everything you need to purchase (food, clothes, printing, nightclubs, laundromat, all of that) would be available on that street. This particular Strip ran through the heart of the UT campus but it was walking distance from KC. So, in essence, it was our Strip, too.

While Slick was gone, we decided to see how high we could get before he got back. I had a grip of weed that we all started rolling on a table. There had to be like 20 or 25 joints when we got done. Everybody grabbed one for themselves and we lit 'em up. We chain smoked them while we were waiting for Slick to return.

It seemed like he was gone a long ass time. But we were high as fuck, man. The only way we could measure the time was by how many joints we were able to burn through. We weren't tripping, really, except the munchies came calling. We got hungry as shit.

Oh, right – weed. I had started smoking out of excess and influence. My money was long because I wouldn't spend on bigger items. And, the dudes I was around smoked all the time. Shit, 'contact highs' were a frequent occurrence long before I even started blazing with them. Ultimately, I started keeping a small budget for recreation and it was rarely depleted. So, every blue moon I'd get a bag of weed so we could just kick it. This was one of those occasions.

Just before we got to the roaches of the third joints, we heard my car rolling back onto the Yard. It was a loud ass car and incredibly distinctive. Our wigs were super tight (we were very high) so we went to see if Slick had brought food back. Those munchies were calling, real shit. I grabbed what was left of the joints and put them in my jacket pocket.

It took us a minute to get out of the room, though. All three of us were high as hell and every distraction was good enough. We were cracking jokes and bullshitting for a good minute (a little while) before leaving out. Poppy took off down the stairs before I even made it out of the room. Ultimately, we all made it to the first floor.

When I got down there Poppy was already talking to the dorm director. Poppy was really tight with the older dorm director. That was kind of his thing - Poppy was always good with the old heads. It was natural for him to kick it with people who were our parents' ages. He was just an old soul and everybody knew it.

The dorm director was telling him that he had called security on Slick. They were arguing about some liquor that he had brought on campus and was drinking it out in the open. Slick had told him to fuck off. By the time the dorm director was finished telling us what was going on, the guard was outside talking to Slick.

We ran out there to see what was going on. B-Dub had to stop in the bathroom, so it was just Poppy and me checking it out. Some bullshit was going down, for sure, and Slick was our dude. We had to find out what was happening.

Poppy wound up leading the way over to the commotion. We stopped just behind Slick, Poppy was standing in front of me. Poppy was trying to tell Slick to just leave with us, not to even engage the guard but it was too late for that.

The guard was trying to get the liquor from Slick but that wasn't going to happen. Instead of handing it to him, Slick just put the bottle in his inside jacket pocket and that pissed the guard off.

"Hey man, give me the damned bottle." The guard ordered.

"Fuck you, man. Pay me for it and you can have it. Otherwise you ain't getting shit." Slick said.

"You know you can't have opened alcohol bottles on this campus," said the guard.

"Dawg, everybody on the Yard be drankin'. That rule ain't applied to nobody since I been here. You trippin'." Slick argued.

"Man, just give me the bottle. Or you can pour it out and go about your way. I'm fine with either one but you gotta do something."

"This is what I'm gone do. You can have this finger…"

Slick flipped the guard a bird in his face.

545

"That's all the fuck I'm giving you. I had to pay for this shit. It ain't free. I ain't pouring out a damned thang!"

That had to fuck with the security guard's ego or something because he took it to the next level. He got real hostile.

"You gone give me that bottle or I'm going to burst it in your pocket."
"Mutha fucka, you burst this bottle, I'm stilling (punching) you in your jaw!"

When Slick said that, he lifted his hands in the air and let the bottle show to give the guard a target.

The guard wasn't about to be outdone. He swung his baton and smacked Slick's jacket, squarely on the bottle! It didn't break the glass but it rang out like a submarine pinging for targets.

'POING'!

Slick immediately threw a haymaker at the guard's head and missed. The guard had ducked and clobbered Slick squarely in the head with his nightstick. Fucked his head up! It made a loud ass pop when he hit him. It sounded like somebody hit a baseball with an aluminum bat.

'POOK!'

Slick collapsed. It was like all of his muscles just gave up. He melted to the ground in a heap.

(Aw shit, we next!)

That thought was immediate and I wasn't waiting for it to happen. I reached over Slick while he was falling, and socked that fucking guard in the face. That's right, I socked him. He wasn't hit, punched or struck. I smote that mutha fucka in his dumb ass face.

Have you ever seen those NFL hit videos from back in the day where it's just clips of gruesome hits? You know, where Ronnie Lott from the 49ERS just eviscerates some poor wide receiver coming across the middle? Imagine that 209 lb. child-eating safety de-cleating some 172 lb. wiry wide receiver at full speed. Well, I channeled that level of energy into my fist and tried to completely knock that mutha fucka's head off.

The guard fell and hit his head on the curb. Poppy jumped right on him. While they were struggling on the ground, I picked up Slick. I started half-carrying him to my car. It was bad enough that he couldn't stand on his own power. But, watching blood seep from a gash on his head made me respond with urgency. I was going to drive him to the hospital and get him looked at right away.

Slick and I got to the car and I pulled off. I saw Poppy still tussling with the guard. I thought he would be fine, Poppy could definitely handle himself. My whole focus was on getting Slick some help.

While we were driving off the Yard, I saw my gas gauge was damned near empty. Instead of heading due south from the exit, I turned to go northwest to get to the nearest gas station. This made us drive around the outside of the campus and roll past the Davis Hall walking path on our way out.

I kept checking on Slick to see how he was doing. The bleeding from his head had begun to coagulate but I could still see it was kind of wet on his forehead. That's never a good look. He insisted he was fine, though.

"Hey, man. You alright?" I asked Slick.

More than anything else, I wanted to keep him talking. Head trauma ain't a game and I wanted to make sure Slick stayed awake. Going unconscious would be really bad juju.

"I'm straight, I'm straight. I just need a burr (beer)." Slick said.

"You sure? Imma be straight with you, bruh: you look pretty fucked up."

He laughed.

"Fuck you, Boots. I'm good, boah. Just get me a burr. I'll be tight."

He tried to shake it off. I wasn't entirely buying it.

"Alright. I'm grabbing some gas and I'll get you something there. Then we heading to the hospital."

"I don't need to go to no damned hospital, dawg!" He countered, "they'll start asking questions and shit. Nobody need all 'dat! Just get me something to drank and I'll be straight. I'm good."

"Alright. I got you." I said.

I wasn't going to argue with Slick, that would have helped nothing. The plan was the plan: I was getting gas off of Western Avenue and taking him to the hospital. Wasn't shit he could do about it.

Slick was right about the hospital asking questions. Quietly, that was why I decided to get gas first. It was a stall tactic for me to figure out how we could get him some help without that level of exposure. If I didn't come up with something on the way to the hospital then that's where we were going. I had to make sure he got taken care of.

When we got back up to that walking path, Poppy was waving me down. I pulled over and he jumped in. He was super excited and breathing heavy as hell.

"Dawg, that shit was crazy dawg! I tried to get it but I ain't get it 'dho (though)." Poppy said.

"You tried to get what?" I asked him.

"That gun, boah! I was trying to get that GLOC from that punk ass gawd (guard). I told y'all I was gone get it one day. His old wulliful (which means weak or gullible) ass, I said I was gone take it a long time ago, dawg."

"You got it from his bitch ass?" Slick asked him.

"Naw, dawg. Gotdammitme, his ass had some training from somewhere, boah. That mutha fucka pulled some ole WWF-type-ass moves on me, dawg. Next thing I know, this mutha fucka on top of me with his gun pointed at my face, boah! I was like gooooootdamn, dawg. This mutha fucka got me, dawg. What the fuck Imma do now?"

"Straight up?" I asked.

"Straight up, dawg. This mutha fucka had his gun pointed at my eye, boah. Point blank." Poppy responded.

"No shit? How you get here then?" Slick asked him.

"Gotdammitme, the daum (dorm) director saw the whole thang, boah. Y'all know we tight and shit. He told the punk ass gawd that I wasn't the one, he was trying to get him to go after yo' ass. He was like '*NO! NO! NO! Get off of 'im. That's not even the one that hit you. That's the wrong one, that's the wrong one! The one that hit you is goin' up the hill over thurr.*' The gawd gets off of me and then crouches on one knee in a shooting position, pointing his gun around, looking for y'all, boah." Poppy was still breathing hard while telling us the story.

"For real?" Slick asked.

"Dawg, he wanted to snipe y'all ass! That mutha fucka looked like he was an expert at Duck Hunt, y'hurrme? (you hear me) But he ain't see y'all. You had already got in the cauh (car) and started headin' off the Yawd (Yard). His eye was fucked up anyways, he couldn't see a damned thing. So, this mutha fucka takes off and starts running towards the front gate. I got up, gotdammitme, ran behind Davis and was gone go to a chick house in the projects, um, College Homes or something – call me a cab and get to the crib. Then I heard that Grand Am growling up the hill, boah. I ran out hurr to catch y'all asses. That shit was wild, dawg."

Poppy took a quick breath then shifted his focus to Slick.

"You aight Slick?"

"Yeah, Poppy. I'm good."

"I'on know, boah. Yo shit look like it's split to the white meat." Poppy told him.

"Naw, dawg. I'm cool, I'm cool. I just need a drank, I'll be straight." Slick answered.

"We gone take care of that right now," I told him as the Speedway came in to view just up the street.

We rolled into the station a few minutes later. I parked at the pump and got ready to go into the building.

"Just chill here, Slick. I'mma pay for this gas and grab you a brew. I'll be right back," I said.

"I'm chilling, Boots. I'm good."

Then I shifted to Poppy, "make sure he don't go to sleep, bruh."

"I got 'im, dawg. Go'on head," Poppy said.

I walked into the little convenience store half stressed out. Shit was ugly and I needed to get a grip on the situation. Slick seemed like he was stable but he still had to be taken care of. And a brew wasn't going to do that. That shit had no medicinal properties. Shit, the fact that he said it would help him meant his elevator wasn't going all the way to the top floor. You know what I'm saying?

(Fuck!)

Getting beer was a problem. I walked in the convenience station with plenty money but not my ID. My damned wallet was back in B-Dub's room. I wasn't old enough to purchase alcohol regardless but sometimes it worked to bluff 'em. Half the time they didn't even look at the date so I was still able to make purchases. But I didn't have an ID, I asked Poppy and he didn't have his, either. Slick was bleeding in the car and we needed to keep moving. I said fuck it, got the gas then we drove towards Nasty Jacks. 'Jacks never asked for ID.

We pulled out of the gas station and made it half a block.

"REEEOOOOOP!"

The cops had pulled in behind us and hit us with that loud ass single blurp, then put the flood lights and flashers on us. They pulled us over and walked up to our car. One car had pulled us over. By the time they got us out of the car there were six or more police cars and a paddy wagon. Then they got a little rough with us; banging us against the car, tossing us around and they hit us a few times.

"Y'all disrespecting the uniform!!!"

When they got through with their little workout, they put us in cuffs and tossed us in the paddy wagon. They saw that Slick was in pretty bad shape. Poppy had some bruising and stuff, too. So, they took us directly to the hospital. We were there for some hours.

Poppy and I were cracking jokes, singing different rap songs and shit. We hadn't completely lost our high so we were tripping. He was even fucking with me about the 'Boo-Boo' nickname shit. I told him if we weren't in handcuffs we would be trading fisticuffs. But everything was funny because we were high as hell.

There was a cop guarding us in the hospital the whole time and he kept trying to tell us to be quiet. That just made us be more belligerent. We were having a good ass time, sitting in cuffs in the hospital. The staff took care of Slick and Poppy then cleared us. 'Billy the Cop' then took all three of us and tossed us back into the paddy wagon. That was no chariot ride to the precinct.

In the paddy wagon, I paid more attention to Slick. He just looked like he was in pretty bad shape. He was up talking and responding to us but he was clearly not 100%. Poppy kept talking and singing and shit but I got more quiet the closer we got to the precinct. Those surroundings became every problem for me.

That paddy wagon was a rolling cage. I had never been in one before. They had us imprisoned like animals. Every one of the cops handling us was white. I felt that metal around my wrists, looked at my fellas bound the same way and it pissed me off. We had put ourselves in the spot where someone could take our freedom. This was everything I was mentored NOT to do, the exact situation I had no business in. Look here, man; I wasn't made for no fucking cages! Not only were we in a rolling cage but we were heading to a bigger one. Realizing all of that shit ruined the hell out of my high, I sobered up fast as fuck. I began to rein myself in to start strategizing.

Poppy noticed.

"Naw, dawg. Don't go quiet on me nah, man. We gotta pull through this shit."

I wasn't even listening to him. Instead, I was dealing with the situation we were in and counting off the charges we faced.

There was the .45 caliber handgun in my car, the one Teddy Ray had swiped the bullets at his girls' crib. That gun had the serial numbers filed off of it. Honestly, that was how it was purchased – I got it hot, of course. Nobody in my crew would've filed serial numbers off a gun but that didn't matter. When I got it, I wasn't thinking about what it could have been used for before me or who had it. I hadn't thought about any of that kind of shit. I was just buying a gun to make sure I was strapped. The missing serial numbers kept them from identifying the weapon. AND that made it a federal offense. Having a gun with serial numbers filed off was major. It looked like my first charges ever would include federal counts.

They also caught Slick with product on him. They popped all of us for assault on an officer. And, with those joints in my pocket, the federal gun charge made an ugly ass trifecta for me. Man, we were knee-deep in some ugly shit in no time flat. I went from being a drug dealing ninja to sitting in the clutches of the enemy. I was feeling low than a mutha fucka.

We arrived at the precinct and they began to process us. I looked around the whole place and took it all in. Poppy kept talking but I was infuriated with myself. I stayed quiet the whole time they took us through the motions. Poppy wasn't though. He never let any portion of the situation shake him. When we got in the precinct he wasn't as talkative but that was just being smart. They couldn't touch his spirit. I saw that written all over him.

We had very good habits in the field. Everybody that worked on the street had a street name. This isn't unique to the trade but it's an intelligent move for dope dealers. If you remember, none of us had any ID on us. So, the cops had to depend on us for identification. Man, I would have had to be brand new in order to give those assholes my real name.

Amazingly, the cop I faced must have been a newborn.

The cops sat me down and chained me to a desk with an incredibly overweight white male officer. I don't want to feed your likely impression of me being bigoted but this dude was 100% redneck. He had that heavy ass southern accent, smelled like 'chaw' (chewing tobacco) and had a fucking confederate flag tattoo on his bicep. It was the middle of winter and this asshat was wearing short sleeves in the office. Then again, he was 'insulated' so... there's that. His disdain for dealing with me was obvious. It made my necessary disposition much easier.

"Wut's yore damned nayme, boy?" The cop said. He was going full country.

"You're going to need to increase your vocabulary if you want anything out of me." I replied.

"Wut in the Sam Hill d'ya mean?"

"You talking to a grown man. You can call me sir, like a professional, or find a way not to refer to me at all."

"Weyell (well), I'll be dipped in hunny and cawled a bumblebee!"

He turned to talk to an officer at the next desk.

"Hey Smitty, we got us a jin-u-wine grown man ov'hurr. (over here). Foolish me, I thawt he was a full grown nigra boy. Guess he done learnt me sumthin' today."

Punk ass officer 'Smitty' chuckled along with him. There are reasons we despise them mutha fuckas. Lots of reasons.

"So, surr, yes surr, surr! (all sarcasm) Surr, would you please tell me yer'nayme fore the rekkerd (record), surr?"
"Much better. My name is Kevin Lee, Officer Stanley."
"How'd ya know ma... ohp, my damned taig (tag). Welp, one of the awfisurs (officers) heered t'othur (heard the other) negra boy cawl ya' "Booboo". Nao (now), is that shawrt (short) for yore real nayme or is he yer boyfrenn or sumthin'?"

His fat ass started laughing.

"Naw, it's because I'm the shit. Like I said, we're going to work on that vocabulary tonight, Officer Stanley."
"Yer a reguller (regular) smart aisce (ass), orent'ya?
Well, wuts yer nayme agin thurr, smart aisce?" The cop said.
"I'm Kevin Lee."
"Okay thurr, Keaven, what's yer dayte of burth?"

Told you, that mutha fucka's neck was so red it could've been a ketchup waterfall. This is not a figurative description, either. The dude's uniform was so tight he was damned near strangling himself. As big as he was I wasn't certain that couldn't be helped. Anything bigger would have had to be a well-tailored blue sheet. He was an absolute fat ass. The only thing he didn't cram into that uniform was some intelligence. That was fine with me. He took that Kevin Lee shit and I was glad to let him do it.

Well, when 'Officer Jethro' got done he let me have a phone call. I hit up my girl and told her where we were, she said she would handle it. Then 'Officer Bubba' tossed me in the holding cell. Yep, he was every one of those country/redneck stereotypical names. Any one of them would fit.

Poppy and Slick were already processed and chilling in the holding cell when I got there. Poppy was still in high spirits, singing Motown songs and shit when I walked in. If it weren't for the bars, guards, and assortment of hard-legged losers, you might have thought we were in the club or something. He wasn't letting this shit get to him at all.

He greeted me like we were hanging out at the mall. This was my first time in a jail cell ever. I was uptight as shit.

> "Welcome to the party, dawg. Sorry it ain't no music, they done fired the deejay, boah." Poppy said.
>
> "Man, this shit ain't no joke, man! We in jail, Poppy. This shit ain't a game, man." I said.
>
> "C'mon, dawg. You can't let this shit get to you, boah. You can't let these mutha fuckas think they can break you." Poppy responded.
>
> "I ain't broken, I'm mad. This is bullshit. I'm smarter than this. I ain't supposed to be in this mutha fucka, man."

"Gotdammitme, "supposed to" ain't got shit to do with it, Boots. We here, dawg. We gotta face this shit and rise, bruh. We here, we gotta rise!"

"Can't nobody rise in this shit! We in fucking jail, man."

I sat down next to Slick, just to check on him. I was mad as hell and my spirits were shit. Frustration had taken over, I was majorly disappointed with myself. Everything I could think of made it worse. I could've cried right there I was so mad. But we were in jail – there was no fucking chance I would let tears come out of my eyes. Still, I'm gonna be straight up: I was at the end of my rope.

Poppy sat down near us and just started talking to himself. Well, I thought he was talking to himself because he wasn't very loud.

Poppy said:

"When you're up against trouble, meet it squarely, face to face; Lift your chin and set your shoulders, Plant your feet and take a brace. When it's vain to try to dodge it, do the best that you can do; You may fail, but you may conquer, see it through!

Black may be the clouds about you and your future may seem grim, but don't let your nerve desert you; keep yourself in fighting trim. If the worst is bound to happen, spite of all that you can do, running from it will not save you, see it through!

Even hope may seem futile, when with troubles you're beset, but remember you are facing just what other men have met. You may fail but fall still fighting; Don't give up, whate'er you do; Eyes front, head high to the finish, see it through!" (10)

I listened to every word. It was the kind of 'man conversation' I needed at the perfect time. I didn't say shit though, because I was still hostile. My elbows were on my knees and my head was bowed.

Poppy kept going:

> "Out of the night that covers me, black as the pit from pole to pole, I thank whatever gods may be for my unconquerable soul.
> In the fell clutch of circumstance I have not winced nor cried aloud. Under the bludgeoning of chance my head is bloody, but unbowed.
> Beyond this place of wrath and tears looms but the horror of the shade, and yet the menace of the years
> finds and shall find me unafraid.
> It matters not how strait the gate, nor how charged with punishments the scroll, I am the master of my fate,
> I am the captain of my soul." (11)

Poppy didn't say anything else, just that poem. That shit moved me! I sat up straight while nodding my head in agreement,

> "Say that shit again! Say it again!" I said.
> "Which one, boah?" Poppy asked.
> "Both of 'em!"

He kept continued to repeat them. Before long, I stood up with him and recited the parts I learned from him. Particularly, 'I am the master of my fate, I am the captain of my soul' and the last words of the other one, 'See It Through'. There was something in the truth of them that made me get my shit together. We had the entire holding cell amped.

I marveled at Poppy, though. I didn't know if he'd been in jail before but it didn't make a difference to him. He was unbowed and unbroken. He read those poems to make sure I wasn't either. In the darkest hour of my life to that point, Poppy triggered all my man mechanisms to help me stand tall in it. That was invaluable to me.

Not long after, the cops came in to put us in cells. We pleaded with them to put us in the same cell with Slick to make sure he wouldn't sleep. They knew he had suffered head trauma, Slick's head was still wrapped in bandages. So, they obliged. Again, that was a Knoxvillian thing. Any of the major cities would've said tough shit.

Poppy was looking after Slick in the cell, trying to make sure he didn't pass out. It left me in that jail by myself mentally, alone with my thoughts and no room for anything other than the truth. Sitting in that cell was the perfect time to slow down and make an assessment of my life situation. Those dope poems Poppy was dropping had spoken to me. I was in a man moment - I had to see it through! Numerous conclusions smacked me in the face at once.

It makes every bit of sense in the world that you would think I was having regrets about my chosen profession. Most people would probably be rethinking their decisions in that situation. Right? Well, in that regard I was both typical and atypical at the same time. I wasn't upset with myself because what I was doing was wrong. Not at all. My frustration was eating at me because I was doing it wrong.

I was sitting there, in a jail cell, because of sloppiness. I fell asleep on the details and they caught up with me. There is no way we should have been riding around in a 'rolling concert speaker' of a hooptie with guns *and* product. That was asking to get locked up. I was smarter than that. The cops popped my room and got one of my soldiers with product, money and a gun. I was certainly smarter than that. They almost pinched me on the Yard in my own dorm room. Thank God that, somehow, it went differently than that! The way that I was fucking up was crucial and it could have robbed me of my freedom. All of that had to be rectified.

It was clear I had lost my focus on the little things and they were costing me. It was time to revisit planning and organizing so that none of these things would ever be repeats. I was sitting in a fucking cell, for fuck's sake. Me, fucking "Keaven" Lee. In a damned cell. Honestly, I had a good laugh about those mutha fuckas accepting that alias. Even when the shit had bombarded the fan, I loved Knoxville.

My new plan would also include a vision for not letting my written plan get snagged by the cops. Again. That was just fucked up. Really hoped it wouldn't come back to bite me in the ass.

By the time I finished that thought, turnkey was at the cell yelling my name to release me on bail. Skins was on that shit like he said he would be. My girl knew to use Kevin Lee, that was planned in our bailing conversations. It was serendipitous that it worked out. I made a new alias in case it happened again – Michael Jones. That dorm shit spooked me into pre-emptive preparation mode, I tried to universally stay ahead of the game after that.

My girl hollered at Skins and he promptly had someone connect with her to give her money. She got enough for two people. So, she took care of me and I had her bail out Slick before we left. He wasn't doing too hot and I didn't trust the cops. We got him and took him to Fort Sanders hospital. Poppy got sprung not more than an hour later.

We made it back to the block and business proceeded without pause. The difference is, Poppy came out there too. For the first time, he had his own pack and was getting money directly. I was sleeping on him for a bit but we ended that. He proved that he was the vital cog for my operation and I let him know it by making him legit. Poppy became the first officer in my organization. Of course that's an arbitrary title, he never got called such a thing. That was just the respect level I had for him. With Poppy officially on the squad, I knew my empire building had begun.

After less than a week back on the block, we wrapped up one day. We were always out later than the local corner boys. For some reason, they would bail on the streets near midnight or sooner. It was like they were all teenagers living at their parents' houses or something. Anyways, we crossed the street to start the walk back to KC and we heard three distinct distant gunshots.

"Get the fuck outta here, St. Louis mutha fuckas!"

From what we could tell, they weren't shooting at us. They shot in the air to scare us. Punk mutha fuckas. They just wanted to make us run away. We ran, fuh sho. It would be dumb as hell not to take that cue, we got the hell up outta there. But that didn't just piss me off (oh, I was fucking hot) but it woke me up.

Up to that point, I was the only one with a heater. I mean, it had just been me and a bunch of college guys for a while. Once Poppy joined me that changed my options a bit. Clearly we had to get him strapped and we definitely needed to add some goons. We weren't yet ready for war but I could see that peace was about to die an ugly death. It was more than prudent for us to get ready.

Their dumb ass warning shots gave me an epiphany: I hadn't done what Big Lou's brother said. I got so entangled in my adjustments and making things work in front of my face that I lost focus on my vision. It had become clear to me that Skins, while he was no friend of mine, wasn't the guy running the 'Ville street boys. So, even if I took him out it wouldn't improve the situation. My single-minded train of thought never shifted from Skins being the target. Even when I understood that the facts were different than my initial assessment, I didn't recalibrate.

Speaking of Skins, it still surprised me when he sent someone to take care of my bail. I had a stash for my girl to get me out if he didn't deliver but I needed to test him. Turns out he meant it when he said 'never let your people sit in jail'. The way we were tied together he couldn't afford me to be too unhappy. I tried to keep sentimentality to a minimum but it meant something for him to get me out of lockup. It wasn't an emotional something but a business thing. He valued me on high enough of a level to spring me. That did not comport with him trying to take me out by setting me up. Our dynamic, his and mine, hadn't played out like I had foreseen. I decided to take the cue from El-Hajj Malik: process the new truths in order to rethink my initial strategies.

But he went dry again shortly after we got out. I wasn't feeling that dry shit at all. Especially with the timing. Skins had already tried to tell me to stop. He complained about us rolling when the locals weren't... then it hit me. Was this mutha fucka actually trying to regulate me? Was he controlling our output by holding out on the product? Was he intentionally trying to stop our production? Every facet of those ideas was wholly unacceptable. He needed to be replaced and I decided to make that a high priority: find new suppliers. It was an overdue directive.

Beyond that, we were straight arrogant about the locals. In our minds, they were just a bastion of bumpkins trying to live out rap videos. We had both overlooked and underestimated them. The real truth was, they didn't have to be hardened by a big city in order to shoot our asses. History is filled with mighty empires that fell from ignorant arrogance. My empire wasn't even built yet, I definitely wasn't trying to let that happen to me. Those mutha fuckas escalating to the point of firing shots, at all, brought that reality directly to my face in a rude scream. That shit had to be rectified immediately. This specific gravity of the situation made me get a grip and ask the question:

Who was leading the Mechanicsville corner boys?

"POPPY'S TAKE"

We had just pulled up in a new spot to lay our heads. It's the first time Busara and I actually decided to stay in a crib together. Even though we were both from St. Louis, we didn't really meet until we got to Knoxville – almost 500 miles from home. Our high school teams played against each other every year and everything, but I didn't really know him. So, it was crazy as hell when we found out that our moms were homegirls who used to hang out. Small world, right? I'm telling you, dawg, the world is crazy than a mutha fucka.

The apartment had been ours for, like, two days. We had a lease and some keys… that's it. No furniture, no curtains, no food in the fridge – nothing. The crew rolled into the place to have a small meeting, though. We had been in some shit with the locals for a couple weeks and needed to figure out how we were going to handle those mutha fuckas. In fact, the new spot was about rebooting and giving ourselves some room to breathe.

The brothers stayed on the move, we were in new spots all the time. We never posted up in a crib for too long. Every one of us in the crew was like that. Being hard targets kept us from getting got, you know? So, this was my and Busara's new spot for the moment.

It was helping us reset right then, too. Shit was getting a little hot but it wasn't nothing we couldn't deal with. Making small shifts in how we operated was always good for business. It was mandatory to stay unpredictable.

The apartment layout was simple: you walk directly into the living room, it was situated from the entrance of the door and to the left. Our dining room was immediately to the right. Beyond the dining room towards the back of the house was the kitchen. From the front door, the bathroom was just past the living room on the left. The bedrooms occupied the entire rear of the apartment. Busara was in one of those back rooms with Motown. The two of them were planning our next moves in dealing with the Mechanicsville bumpkins. Shit was definitely about to go sideways for the locals. Period!

There were about seven of us in the living room. B-Dub, Jazzy, Keisha, LaTonda, some other girl and Greco. The girls were sitting on the floor, leaning against a wall. B-Dub was rolling some joints on the window sill, making sure we all kept our wigs tight (kept a buzz). Greco and Jazzy were arguing about some shit and I was trying to keep they ass cool.

Greco was madder than a mutha fucka, dawg. I was trying to keep him from blowing up. So, in the middle of them arguing, I tried to stop them from going too far, y'know?

> "C'mon, dawg. Squash this shit, man. Y'all know we just gettin' in this bitch. Y'all gone have the neighbors callin' cops on us and shit. We don't need all that up in hurr."

I was just trying to keep shit from escalating. I mean, I ain't think nothing serious was 'bout to happen but, you know. When you dealing with grown men, though, shit can easily get out of hand, y'nawumsayin' (you know what I'm saying)?

KNOCK! KNOCK! KNOCK!

(What the fuck? Who knocking on our fucking door? Nobody should even know we here!)

"Who the fuck is this?" I said out of reflex.

For real, dawg, I was trippin'. I looked through the peep hole and saw my gal, Rita, standing thurr looking like she got a damned problem or sumthin'.

(What's this shit?)

I was annoyed as hell when I opened the door.

"What's up, girl? What you doin' hurr?" I asked her.
"I'm here to see you, what you think? And to keep you from hanging out with these other bitches." Rita said.

None of the ladies in the room were feeling that shit. I could see them looking at her like she stank. Y'all know that look. But they weren't tripping. They knew we wasn't about all that drama and shit. They still stared at her with a side eye, though.

"Girl... how you even know we here? How you get this address?" I asked.
"I don't know the address. I followed you here." She barked at me.
"You on some old Nancy Drew-ass detective shit. Man, look hurr..."

She had me pissed off with that shit. I wasn't about to handle all that in front of other people, though. You just don't air your laundry like that, dawg.

So, I stopped right thurr and hollered to the fellas.

"...I'll be back."

I walked out the door and closed it behind me. I started walking Rita to her car, ushering her on her way. The only thing on my mind was getting her outta thurr. That's my gal, and all, but I wasn't trying to kick it with her right then. Especially after she 'I spy'-ed her way to my crib. Fuck that, dawg. I wasn't for all that bullshit.

"Wus' goin' on with all the followin' me and shit? When you start doin' that?" I asked.

"When you start getting new places, not telling me and hang-ing out with hoes in yo' house?" She smarmily said.

"See, I'on'kno (I don't know) why you tryin' to do all that. It ain't like that. Do you even know who in thurr?" I asked her.

"Nope. I just know I wasn't." She snapped back.

"Thaswumsayin' (That's what I'm saying), youmev'nkno (you don't even know) wus goin' on. It's three girls in there. You saw Busara's gal, one of them was with Motown and the other was jus' rolling with them. Out of all the dudes up in'urr (in there) *you* think she gotta be with me. C'mon with all that!"

"Well, I didn't see no Busara or Motown." She complained.

"Thaswumsayin'! You don't know what you talkin' 'bout, man. Both of them in the back in thurr, handlin' some bidness. You be trippin'." I returned.

"I wasn't in there taking inventory, Poppy. I just know you didn't ask me to come over. Hell, I wouldn't even know about the place if I didn't follow you." She was not cooling off.

Now, I'm a reasonable cat. I understand it may look like I was trying to bail on her. I get that. But that ain't what's real. I wasn't trying to fade my girl. I just needed some room. It wasn't just the drama goin' on with the business but it seemed like shit was always goin' on with her. Like the conversation we were having right then. I was just getting some air from all that bullshit for a few days. Y'nawumsayin'?

We had stopped walking at her car. I stood close to her while we were talking.

"Lissen, godammitme, I ain't hurr with no gals. We jus' got this spot and I was gone chill hurr a few days, y'nawumsayin'? I was gone bring you...

RATTA TATTA TATTA!!!!

I put my hand on Rita's shoulder and had her squat next to the car with me. I felt my heart thumping fast as fuck! I started thinking about the heater in the house, so I could return fire. We hadn't really moved in but we did have a MAC-10 in there. The situation we were in we had to stay strapped. I looked around the street to see if anybody was shooting at me on a drive-by or something.

It was bad enough my gal had tailed me and found us. We didn't peep that shit, that's not a good look. If those local mutha fuckas followed us and got the drop on us, we were going to need to switch up a lot of shit we were doing. Y'nawumsayin'?

Nobody was on the street, the parking lot…. I didn't see anybody at all. That made me calm down a bit.

As an afterthought, I turned my head to where the sound came from.

(Fuck! That's *in* the house!)

I didn't even realize that I was moving. I had already started running up the stairs into the apartment. I called out to Rita on my way.

"Ay, stay hurr. Better yet, go'on home. I'll come holler at you tonight." I told her.
"Why I gotta leave?" She asked, like I was brushing her off.
"You hurr those gunshots? I'on'kno wus goin' on! I'm trying to keep you safe. Go'on out of hurr! I'll come see you. Now, go'on!"

She beatboxed her way into the car. (She was smacking her lips, sighing and sucking her teeth irreverently). I caught her pulling off as I walked in the apartment.

(Dawg, what the fuck!)

I opened the door and was immediately trippin'. I felt like I was in the middle of a Law & Order episode or some shit.

The girls were all standing, their backs were pressed against the wall as if they were glued to it. B-Dub was kneeling, rubbing out a burn on the carpet: I think he had dropped a joint and was trying to put the fire out.

Jazzy was standing with his eyes wide open. He was a caramel-colored brother but he looked damned near white right then. I saw Busara and Motown standing in the hallway. It looked like they had run up from the back rooms because they were both breathing heavy as hell. I could see in their faces that they didn't know what the fuck was going on, either.

But, dawg, Greco was standing right in front of Jazzy. He was holding the MAC-10 and it was smoking. He had the gun pointed at the floor but he had definitely just let off some. This mutha fucka was crying, literally crying mad. And he was holding the gun! That was some scary shit.

(Dawg, what the fuck is going on?! We shooting at each other and shit! What's wrong with these mutha fuckas? They shot up the apartment and shit. This shit is fucked up.)

Shit was fucked up, y'all! I took a surreal look around the room and got a little more detail. The gunshots were in the dining room, just over Jazzy's head.

(Holy shit, Greco shot at him!)

It was a surprise he wasn't dead and bleeding all over the apartment right then. That ceiling was blown the fuck out! You could see clear through to the apartments over our head. Shit was definitely fucked up.

Greco was crying, Jazzy was white with fear and everybody else was standing there frozen. It was the craziest position I had ever been in. I had one thought on my mind.

(What the fuck happened to us?)

Bibliography

1) Wikipedia on Aberdeen, Mississippi. https://en.wikipedia.org/wiki/
   Aberdeen,_Mississippi

2) National Law Enforcement Museum
   https://lawenforcementmuseum.org/2019/07/10/
   slave-patrols-an-early-form-of-american-policing/

3) Wikipedia on Anwar Sadat
   https://en.wikipedia.org/wiki/Anwar_Sadat

4) Mr. Pest Guy
   Mouse Utopia Experiment | Mr. Pest Guy

5) Pruitt-Igoe historical data
   Pruitt–Igoe - Wikipedia

6) Newton, Huey P. (2009). *Revolutionary Suicide*. Penguin. p. 102.
   ISBN 9781101140475 – via Google Books.

7) Shames, Stephen (2016). *Power to the people : the world of the Black
   Panthers*. New York: Abrams. ISBN 978-1-4197-2240-0. OCLC
   960165174.

8) Black Panther Party - Wikipedia

9) Bassett, Mary T. (2016). *"Beyond Berets: The Black Panthers as
   Health Activists"*. American Journal of Public Health. **106** (10):
   1741–1743. doi:10.2105/ajph.2016.303412. ISSN 0090-0036. PMC
   5024403. PMID 27626339.

10) 'See It Through' – a poem by Edgar Albert Guest

11) 'Invictus' – a poem by William Ernest Henley

12) 'The Replacements' – line performed by Orlando Jones, written by Vince McKewin, produced by Bel Air Entertainment and distributed by Warner Bros. Pictures. Copyright

26042021 0147

17082021 2330